The Empire of Chance

IDEAS IN CONTEXT

Edited by Wolf Lepenies, Richard Rorty, J. B. Schneewind
and Quentin Skinner

The books in this series will discuss the emergence of intellectual traditions and of related new disciplines. The procedures, aims and vocabularies that were generated will be set in the context of the alternatives available within the contemporary frameworks of ideas and institutions. Through detailed studies of the evolution of such traditions, and their modification by different audiences, it is hoped that a new picture will form of the development of ideas in their concrete contexts. By this means, artificial distinctions between the history of philosophy, of the various sciences, of society and politics, and of literature may be seen to dissolve.

Titles published in the series:
Richard Rorty, J. B. Schneewind and Quentin Skinner (eds.), *Philosophy in History*
J. G. A. Pocock, *Virtue, Commerce and History*
M. M. Goldsmith, *Private Vices, Public Benefits: Bernard Mandeville's Social and Political Thought*
A. Pagden, *The Languages of Political Theory in Early-Modern Europe*
D. Summers, *The Judgment of Sense*
L. Dickey, *Hegel: Religion, Economics and the Politics of Spirit, 1770–1807*
Margo Todd, *Christian Humanism and the Puritan Social Order*
Edmund Leites (ed.), *Conscience and Casuistry in Early Modern Europe*
Lynn S. Joy, *Gassendi the Atomist: Advocate of History in an Age of Science*
Terence Ball, James Farr and Russell Hanson (eds.), *Political Innovation and Conceptual Change*
Wolf Lepenies, *Between Literature and Science: The Rise of Sociology*
Peter Novick, *That Noble Dream: The 'Objectivity Question' and the American Historical Profession*

This series is published with the support of the Exxon Education Foundation

The Empire of Chance

How probability changed science and everyday life

GERD GIGERENZER, ZENO SWIJTINK,
THEODORE PORTER, LORRAINE DASTON,
JOHN BEATTY, LORENZ KRÜGER

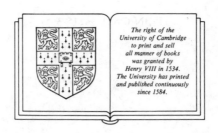

The right of the
University of Cambridge
to print and sell
all manner of books
was granted by
Henry VIII in 1534.
The University has printed
and published continuously
since 1584.

CAMBRIDGE UNIVERSITY PRESS

Cambridge

New York   New Rochelle   Melbourne   Sydney

Published by the Press Syndicate of the University of Cambridge
The Pitt Building, Trumpington Street, Cambridge CB2 1RP
32 East 57th Street, New York, NY 10022, USA
10 Stamford Road, Oakleigh, Melbourne 3166, Australia

First published 1989

Printed in Great Britain at the University Press, Cambridge

British Library cataloguing in publication data

The empire of chance: how probability
changed science and everyday life.-
(Ideas in context).
1. Probabilities – Philosophical
perspectives
I. Gigerenzer, Gerd   II. Series
121'.63

Library of Congress cataloguing in publication data

The Empire of chance : how probability changed science and everyday
life / Gerd Gigerenzer . . . [et al.].
p.   cm. – (Ideas in context)
Bibliography.
Includes index.
ISBN 0-521-33115-3
1. Probabilities. 2. Mathematical statistics. 3. Science –
Philosophy.   I. Gigerenzer, Gerd.   II. Series.
QA273.E57   1989   88-16928 CIP

ISBN 0 521 33115 3

BO

To the memory of Bill Coleman,
who helped sow the seeds for this book

CONTENTS

Acknowledgments

Our first debt is to the Zentrum für interdisziplinäre Forschung (ZiF) of the University of Bielefeld and to the Stiftung Volkswagenwerk for sponsoring in 1982–83 a year of research on the probabilistic revolution, of which this book is one outcome. We are grateful to all our colleagues in the ZiF project for much stimulating conversation and for advice on this project. Our collaboration was enormously assisted by two families who provided accommodations for us to meet to plan and to edit the various chapters in 1986 and 1987. We heartily thank the Wolfs of Freiburg im Breisgau, and the Dastons of Cheverly, Maryland, for their generous hospitality. Much of the typing and word-processor translation was done – with admirable efficiency – by Bonnie Blackwell, Lottie McCauley, Kathleen Miller, Elizabeth Stovall, and Ella Wood of the History Department, University of Virginia.

We have received helpful advice on one or more chapters from Kurt Danziger, Ward Edwards, Klaus Foppa, Heinz Heckhausen, Theo Herrmann, Rolf Oerter, Michael Osborn, Diane Paul, Paolo Palladino, Stephen Stigler and Norton Wise, and bibliographical assistance from Robin Overmier of the Wangensteen Library, University of Minnesota, and Bill Deane of the National Baseball Library, Baseball Hall of Fame. We have numerous foundations and universities to thank for support for travel and leave time: John Beatty the University of Minnesota graduate school; Lorraine Daston the Alexander von Humboldt-Stiftung for support in the summer of 1986; Gerd Gigerenzer the Stiftung Volkswagenwerk for support in the fall of 1987; Theodore Porter the American Council of Learned Societies for travel money, summer 1986, the Earhart Foundation for support, fall 1985, and the University of

Virginia for summer support in 1986. Zeno Swijtink acknowledges with gratitude a grant from the Alexander von Humboldt-Stiftung that permitted him to participate in the ZiF year, and two grants from the Netherlands Foundation for Pure Scientific Research (ZWO) in connection with this project.

Introduction

Fortuna, the fickle, wheel-toting goddess of chance, has never been a favorite of philosophy and the sciences. In that touchstone of medieval learning, Boethius' *Consolations of Philosophy*, sober Dame Philosophy warns that only when Fortuna "shows herself unstable and changeable, is she truthful," and preaches against the very existence of chance, conceived as "an event produced by random motion and without any sequence of causes." Dame Philosophy had illustrious allies. Despite the upheavals in science in the over two millenia separating the Athens of Aristotle from the Paris of Claude Bernard, they shared at least one article of faith: science was about causes, not chance.

Yet even as Bernard sought to banish chance and indeterminism from physiology, Fortuna already ruled a large and growing empire in the sciences. The laws of the realm were probability theory and statistics. By "taming chance," in Ian Hacking's evocative phrase, probability and statistics had reconciled Scientia to her arch-rival Fortuna. From its beginnings in the mid-seventeenth century, probability theory spread in the eighteenth century from gambling problems to jurisprudence, data analysis, inductive inference, and insurance, and from there to sociology, to physics, to biology, and to psychology in the nineteenth, and on to agronomy, polling, medical testing, baseball, and innumerable other practical (and not so practical) matters in the twentieth. But this triumphal march was emphatically not the simple accumulation of applications by a mathematical theory. Perhaps more than any other part of mathematics, probability theory has had a relationship of intimacy bordering upon identity with its applications. Indeed, there was arguably no "pure" theory of mathematical probability until 1933 (see 3.6), and until the early nineteenth century, the failure of an application threatened the theory itself (see 1.5). For much of its history, probability theory *was* its applications. This means that probability theory was as much modified by its conquests as the disciplines it invaded. When, for example, probability became a tool for evaluating compilations of numbers about births, deaths, crimes, barometric fluctuations, dead letters, and other kinds of statistics, the very meaning of probability changed, from a degree of certainty in the mind to a ratio of events counted in the world (see 2.2). When the British polymath Francis Galton invented a way of measuring how much offspring peas deviated from their parent stock, he launched the analysis of correlations (see 2.5; 4.4). Factor analysis has its roots in educational psychology, analysis of variance in eugenics and agronomy, and so on.

It was in fact the rule for probabilistic ideas and techniques to originate in highly specific contexts, and to advance on the strength of vivid analogies. The normal or bell-shaped curve at first represented the probability of observational error in astronomy, then of nature's "errors" from *l'homme moyen* in sociology, then of anarchic individual gas molecules exhibiting orderly collective properties (see 2.5; 5.6). Eventually the normal curve came to represent the distribution of almost everything, from intelligence quotients to agricultural yields, and shed the particular interpretations derived from its early applications (see 8.1). But for almost a century such concrete analogies were the bridges over which it and other probabilistic notions passed from one discipline to another.

This book is about the applications of probability and statistics to science and life, where "application" is understood in this special sense: the mathematical tool shaped, but was also shaped by, its objects. The mathematical development of probability and statistics has been admirably treated in the work of such scholars as Isaac Todhunter, L. A. Maistrov, O. B. Sheynin, Stephen Stigler, and Ivo Schneider. Our primary concern, however, is not theirs. We analyze how probability and statistics transformed our ideas of nature, mind, and society. These transformations have been profound and wide-ranging, changing the structure of power as well as of knowledge. They have shaped modern bureaucracy as well as the modern sciences. The extraordinary range and significance of these transformations has rarely been appreciated, perhaps because the influence of probability on the various sciences has until now been studied only piecemeal. Also, the domain of probability and statistics was less often expanded by decisive conquest and revolution than by infiltration and alliance. In this book, we view these transformations synoptically, as a single historical movement – one whose influence on modern thought and life is second to no other area of scientific endeavor.

These encounters of probability and statistics with science have in no case been neutral – mere translations of extant ideas and methods into the language of mathematical probability. Even when probability has entered at the level of methods rather than of theories, the ultimate impact has transcended technique. When psychologists adopted inference statistics as a tool of the trade, they also came to view the same techniques as models of the mind (see 6.4). When biometricians warred with Mendelians over the proper approach to genetics, the view of biological inheritance implied by Pearsonian statistics was at issue (see 4.4). When physicians opposed the use of randomized clinical trials, they doubted not only the relevance of the results but also the ethics of the therapy (see 2.3; 4.2; 7.3). Whatever they touch, probability and statistics transform, and are themselves often transformed in the process. This book is a study in the interactive effects of quantification.

Not all important notions of chance, however, can be set to numbers – even in the sciences. Some of the most important influences of probabilistic ideas have involved qualitative ideas. Consider, for example, the extent to which discussions of chance permeate philosophy, raising issues of determinism, free will, causality, explanation, evidence, and inference. These strands are braided together with scientific themes in this book. The Belgian statistician Adolphe Quetelet and the British physicist James Clerk Maxwell grappled with the issue of free will in their work (see 2.6; 5.6); the probabilists Jakob Bernoulli and Laplace gave us our most lapidary statements of determinism (see 1.5; 8.3); chance as "absence of design" played a seminal role in evolutionary biology (see 4.3). This book documents how supple the bonds linking philosophical and probabilistic notions could be, depending on the context: statistics in nineteenth-century sociology, for example, was paired with the most inexorable brand of determinism, but in twentieth-century physics it implies the strictest indeterminism.

The empire of chance is too vast for us to map in its entirety in the compass of a single volume. We aim at a comprehensive, but not an exhaustive tour of its domains. We begin with two historical chapters that describe the origins and development of probability and statistics from the mid-seventeenth to the end of the nineteenth century. Here we introduce changing interpretations of the probability calculus, changing attitudes towards determinism, changing conceptions of averages and errors – all, again, in the context of changing applications. In each of the subsequent four chapters, we focus on one area of broad application: experimental methodology, biology, physics, and psychology. Our objective is not simply to list the points at which probability has entered these fields, but to examine the historical circumstances and conceptual consequences attendant to key applications. With chapter 7, we leave the sciences to assess the impact of probability and statistics on daily life, from weather reports to mammography. Again, we lay no claim to an exhaustive study of such applications – to catalogue them alone would require volumes. Rather, we have selected instances that show how deeply, if quietly, these applications have altered our values and assumptions about matters as diverse as legal fairness or human intelligence. Finally, we survey, from something like the victorious general's hilltop, the territory we have covered.

We envision a broad audience comprising both scholars from many fields and interested laymen, and have therefore kept technical material to a minimum. The handful of equations that do appear do not do double duty as explanations.

This is a book by several hands, but it is by no means an anthology. We tell a continuous story, with characters who appear and reappear, episodes that overlap and intersect, and common themes that repeat like a refrain. The plot line zigzags from one discipline to another – Fortuna did not honor these boundaries – and the reader will, for example, meet R. A. Fisher in the chapter on psychology as well as in those on experimental methodology and biology, and encounter debates over the implications of statistics for freedom of the will in physics as well as in sociology. A collaboration was essential because the scope and interdisciplinary nature of the topic required a range of knowledge that exceeds the competence of any single author. Some chapters were drafted by one of us, others by two or even three. But the entire manuscript was planned and then revised in light of criticism and discussion by all members of the group. That its contents reflect a diversity of interests will, we hope, be counted among its strengths rather than its weaknesses. We have not identified chapters by their original authors, but rather present the book as we conceived (and conceive) it: a collaborative work, with a narrative that stretches from beginning to end. Dutiful subjects of the empire of chance, we used a lottery to order our names on the title page.

As all scholars know, such a wholehearted collaboration requires special conditions. All six of us were members of the year-long research project on "The Probabilistic Revolution" at the Center for Interdisciplinary Studies in Bielefeld, Federal Republic of Germany. Essays written by participants in this project now fill two thick volumes (Krüger, Daston, and Heidelberger, eds., 1987; Krüger, Gigerenzer, and Morgan, eds., 1987) that demonstrate the importance of the topic across a wide range of fields, nations, and centuries. Our subset of six hoped to condense and connect the elements contained in these essays into a single narrative, one that viewed the growth of probabilistic and statistical ideas from a unified perspective. We also hoped to perpetuate the intense collegiality of the Bielefeld year with a project that would build upon our preliminary consensus, and one that would demand still greater collaborative efforts. In addition to our many discussions with our Bielefeld colleagues, we have drawn heavily on the collections mentioned above, as well as from recent books by Ian Hacking (1975; forthcoming), Donald MacKenzie (1981), Stephen Stigler (1986), Theodore Porter (1986), Gerd Gigerenzer and David Murray (1987), and Lorraine Daston (1988). We include also the results of much original research on crucial topics not addressed in the existing scholarly literature.

Fortuna's wheel governed not only the fates of men, but also her own. Few biographies contain as many ironic twists, turnabouts, and improbabilities as that of probability itself. Our story confounds expectation at many turns: we find physics borrowing from sociology; words that flip-flop meanings into their opposites; strange pairings of probability with determinism, or mechanism with chance. Philosophy scorned Fortuna as "changeable," and change, both subtle and dramatic, episodic and enduring, is the leitmotif of this study. Yet whereas the vicissitudes of fortune, as Gibbon says, "bury empires and cities in a common grave," we see no sign that Fortuna's empire will suffer a turn of the wheel.

Fortuna (left) and Sapientia (right) are depicted here in traditional opposition. The slow break down of this opposition is the topic of this book. Source: Petrarch, *Remède de l'un et l'autre fortune prospère et adverse* (Paris, 1524); courtesy of the Bibliothèque Nationale, Paris.

God . . . has afforded us only the twilight of probability; suitable, I presume, to that state of mediocrity and probationership he has been pleased to place us in here. . .

John Locke (1690)

1

◁ ══ ▷

Classical probabilities, 1660–1840

1.1 INTRODUCTION

In July of 1654 Blaise Pascal wrote to Pierre Fermat about a gambling problem which came to be known as the Problem of Points: Two players are interrupted in the midst of a game of chance, with the score uneven at that point. How should the stake be divided? The ensuing correspondence between the two French mathematicians counts as the founding document in mathematical probability, even though it was not the first attempt to treat games of chance mathematically (Pascal, [1654] 1970, vol. 1, pp. 33–7; Cardano, [comp. *c.* 1525] 1966). Some years later, Pascal included among his *Pensées* an imaginary wager designed to convert sporting libertines: no matter how small we make the odds of God's existence, the pay-off is infinite; infinite bliss for the saved and infinite misery for the damned. Under such conditions, Pascal argued that rational self-interest dictates that we sacrifice our certain but merely finite worldly pleasures to the uncertain but infinite prospect of salvation (Pascal, [1669] 1962, pp. 187–90).

These two famous Pascal manuscripts, the one mathematical and the other philosophical, reveal the double root of the mathematical theory of probability. It emerged at the crux of two important intellectual movements of the seventeenth century: a new pragmatic rationality that abandoned traditional ideals of certainty; and a sustained and remarkably fruitful attempt to apply mathematics to new domains of experience. Neither would have been sufficient without the other. Philosophical

1

notions about what happens only most of the time, and about the varying degrees of certainty connected with this unreliable experience date from antiquity, as do games of chance. But before *circa* 1650, no one attempted to quantify any of these senses of probability. Nor would the spirit of mathematical enterprise have alone sufficed, for quantification requires a subject matter, an interpretation to flesh out the mathematical formalism. This was particularly true for the calculus of probabilities, which until this century had no mathematical existence independent of its applications.

1.2 THE BEGINNINGS

The prehistory of mathematical probability has attracted considerable scholarly attention, perhaps because it seems so long overdue. Chance is our constant companion, and the mathematics of the earliest formulations of probability theory was elementary. Suggestive fragments of probabilistic thinking do turn up almost everywhere in the classical and medieval learned corpus: Around 85 B.C., Cicero connected that which usually happens with what is ordinarily believed in his rhetorical writings and called both *probabile* (Cicero, 1960, pp. 85–90). In a tenth-century manuscript, a monk enumerated all 36 possibilities for the toss of two dice (Kendall, 1956), and Talmudists reasoned probabilistically about inheritances and paternity (Rabinovitch, 1973). Yet none of these flowered into a mathematics of probability.

Several plausible hypotheses about why mathematical probability came about when it did also dissolve upon inspection. Maritime insurance expanded rapidly in Italy and the Low Countries during the commercial boom of the fifteenth and sixteenth centuries, but insurers did not collect statistics on shipwrecks, much less develop a mathematical basis for pricing premiums. It was the mathematicians who later – much later – influenced the insurers, not vice versa (Maistrov, [1964] 1974; Daston, 1987). Nor did any new recognition of chance inspire the mathematicians; on the contrary, the early probabilists from Pascal through Pierre Simon Laplace were determinists of the strictest persuasion (Kendall, 1956; Hacking, 1975). One might speculate that the mathematics of combinatorics was a precondition for the earliest versions of probability theory, but the two subjects appear to have developed in tandem, with probability theory often stimulating work in combinatorics rather than the reverse (Todhunter, 1865). The Renaissance doctrine of signatures linked the evidence of things with that of words in a way that parallels the objective and subjective senses of mathematical probabilities, but Cicero and the medieval rhetorical tradition that followed him had done so long before

(Hacking, 1975; Garber and Zabell, 1979). Similarly, the passion for gambling was hardly an invention of the seventeenth century, and so could not have been the catalyst that transformed qualitative probabilities into quantitative ones. It is, in short, easier to say where mathematical probability did *not* come from.

The very earliest writings on mathematical probability do supply some clues, however. If we return to the two Pascal musings, we discover that although they are recognizably part of what came to be called the calculus of probabilities, they are not cast in terms of probabilities. The fundamental concept was instead expectation, later defined as the product of the probability of an event *e* and its outcome value *V*:

$$P(e)V = E$$

So, for example, the expectation of someone holding one out of a thousand tickets for a fair lottery with a prize of $10,000 would be $10. As the definition implies, we now derive expectation from the probability, but for the early probabilists expectation was the prior and irreducible notion.

Expectation in turn was understood in terms of a fair exchange or contract. Pascal described his solution to the Problem of Points as rendering to each player what "in justice" belonged to him. In the first published treatise on mathematical probability, *De ratiociniis in ludo aleae* (1657), the Dutch mathematician and physicist Christiaan Huygens made expectation his departure point and defined it in terms of equity: equal expectations obtained in a fair game; that is, one that "worked to no one's disadvantage" (Huygens, [1657] 1920, p. 60). Since later probabilists would *define* a fair game as one in which the players possessed equal expectations, this definition of equal expectations in terms of a fair game strikes the modern reader as circular. But for the first generation of probabilists, notions of equity were intuitively clear enough to serve as the stuff of definitions and postulates.

These intuitions drew upon a category of legal agreement that had become increasingly important in sixteenth- and seventeenth-century commercial law, the aleatory contract. Jurists defined such agreements as the exchange of a present and certain value for a future, uncertain one – staking a gamble, purchasing an annuity, taking out an insurance policy, bidding on next year's wheat crop, or buying the next cast of a fisherman's net. Pascal's wager hinged upon a similar trade of the certain enjoyment of present vices for the uncertain joy of salvation. Aleatory contracts acquired prominence and a certain notoriety as the preferred way of exonerating merchants who made loans with interest from charges of usury

(Coumet, 1970). The element of risk, argued the canon lawyers, was the moral equivalent of labor, and therefore earned the merchant his interest as honestly as the sweat of his brow would have. Thus Jesuits successfully petitioned the Sacred Congregation for Propaganda in 1645 for a special dispensation for their Chinese converts, who were charging 30% interest on loans, on the condition "there is considered the equality and probability of the danger, and provided that there is kept a proportion between danger and what is received" (Noonan, 1957, p. 289).

It was this "proportion between danger and what is received," the element of equity fundamental to all contracts, that the mathematicians attempted to quantify in almost all of the early applications of probability theory. Both the problems they addressed – gambling stakes, annuity prices, future inheritances – and the terms in which they did so – using the concept of equal expectations – bear witness to the seminal influence of the law of aleatory contracts.

Pascal's wager is an example of how reasoning by expectations had become almost synonymous with a new brand of rationality by the mid-seventeenth century. His libertine interlocutor must be led back into the Christian fold by uncertain wagers rather than theological certainties. In the sixteenth century, Reformation controversies between Protestants and Catholics on the one hand, and the revival of the sceptical philosophy of Sextus Empiricus and his school on the other combined to undermine the ideal of certain knowledge that had guided intellectual inquiry since Aristotle. In its place gradually emerged a more modest doctrine that accepted the inevitability of less than certain knowledge, but maintained nonetheless that it was still sufficient to guide the reasonable man in precept and in practice. Aristotle's dictum from the *Nicomachean Ethics* (1094b 24–25) was much quoted: "it is the mark of an educated man to look for precision in each class of things just so far as the nature of the subject admits: it is evidently equally foolish to accept probable reasoning from a mathematician and to demand from a rhetorician demonstrative proofs."

The ultimate result of the Reformation and Counter-Reformation clashes over the fundamental principles of faith and their justification, and of the radical scepticism of Michel de Montaigne and other sixteenth-century thinkers was vastly to erode the domain of the demonstrative proof and to expand that of probable reasoning. Their immediate impact was more devastating, challenging all claims to any kind of knowledge whatsoever. Religious apologists who sought to undercut the other side's claims to legitimacy on the basis of either (ambiguous) revelation or (dubious) authority soon discovered that their destructive arguments were a double-edged sword. The revived pyrrhonism of the "libertins érudits" denied the reliability of even sense impressions and mathematical demonstrations; Descartes' *Meditations* began with a sceptical reverie of this extreme variety. Thus all of the traditional sources of certainty, religious and philosophical, came simultaneously under attack. Confronted with a choice between fideist dogmatism on the one hand and the most corrosive scepticism on the other, an increasing number of seventeenth-century writers attempted to carve out an intermediate position that abandoned all hope of certainty except in mathematics and perhaps metaphysics, and yet still insisted that men could attain probable knowledge. Or rather, they insisted that probable knowledge was indeed knowledge (Popkin, 1964; Shapiro, 1983).

In order to make their case for the respectability of the merely probable, these "mitigated sceptics" turned from rarified philosophical discourse to the conduct of daily life. The new criterion for rational belief was no longer a watertight demonstration, but rather that degree of conviction sufficient to impel a prudent man of affairs to action. For reasonable men that conviction in turn rested upon a combined reckoning of hazard and prospect of gain, i.e. upon expectation. Pascal's wager is about neither the bare probability of God's existence, nor the infinite bliss or misery that awaits saint or sinner, respectively. Rather, it is about the product of the two, significantly conceived in terms of a gamble, and the relationship between certain stake and uncertain pay-off, and thus a sterling example of the new rationality. Pascal's Port Royal colleagues Antoine Arnauld and Pierre Nicole made such mixed reasoning the *sine qua non* of rational judgment in their influential *Logique*, cautioning their readers that it is not enough to consider how good or bad an outcome is in itself, but also the likelihood that it will come to pass (Arnauld and Nicole, [1662] 1965, pp. 352–3). English and Dutch spokesmen for the new rationality of expectation preferred commercial analogies, but the idea was the same. John Wilkins, Anglican bishop and founding member of the Royal Society of London, argued in his *Of the Principles and Duties of Natural Religion* (1675) that just as merchants were willing to risk the perils of a long voyage in the name of profit, so "he that would act rationally, according to such Rules and Principles as all mankind do observe in the government of their Actions, must be persuaded to do the like" in matters of science and religion (Wilkins, [1675] 1699, p. 16). The emphasis upon action as the basis of belief, rather than the reverse, was key to the defense against scepticism, for as these writers were wont acidly to observe, even the most confirmed sceptic took his meals just as if the external world existed.

Expectation was thus central to the new rationality or "reasonableness," as it was sometimes called. The mitigated sceptics were less interested in equity than in rational belief, but they drew heavily upon the doctrine of aleatory contracts for examples to show that it was accepted practice and therefore reasonable to exchange a present, certain good – be it money to invest, a long-accepted scientific theory, or the indulgence of our lusts and passions – for a future, uncertain one – more money, a better theory, salvation. Mathematicians seeking to quantify the legal sense of expectations inevitably became involved in quantifying the new rationality as well. So began an alliance between mathematical probability theory and standards of rationality that stamped the classical interpretation as a "reasonable calculus"; as a mathematical codification of the intuitive principles underlying the belief and practice of reasonable men. The identification of classical probability theory with reasonableness was so strong that when the results of the one clashed with the other, it was the mathematicians who anxiously amended definitions and postulates to restore harmony, as we shall see below.

1.3   THE CLASSICAL INTERPRETATION

Thus the calculus of chance was in the first instance a calculus of expectations, and thereby an attempt to quantify the new, more modest doctrine of rationality that surfaces almost everywhere in seventeenth-century learned discourse. The first published works on the subject, from Huygens' little treatise of 1657 to Jakob Bernoulli's definitive *Ars conjectandi* of 1713, covered a range of topics that cohere only against this background. Aleatory contracts like gambling (Huygens, Pierre de Montmort, Jakob Bernoulli) and annuities (Johann De Witt, Halley, Nicholas Bernoulli), and later evidentiary problems like the evaluation of historical or courtroom testimony (John Craig, George Hooper, Nicholas and Jakob Bernoulli) constituted the domain of applications for the new theory. By the end of this period, probability had emerged as a distinct and primitive concept, although most of the applications continued to revolve around questions of expectation for some time thereafter.

Just what these probabilities measured was ambiguous from the outset, and remains a matter of controversy to this day. Originally the word "probability" had meant an opinion warranted by authority (Byrne, 1968); hence the Jesuit doctrine of probabilism, which casuists wielded to absolve almost every transgression on the grounds that one theologian or another had taken a mild view of the matter (Demain, 1935). However, the mitigated scepticism of the early seventeenth century modified even this qualitative sense of probability. The proponents of reasonableness spoke not of certainty but of certainties, ranging from the highest grade of "mathematical" certainty attained by demonstration, through the "physical" certainty of sensory evidence, down to the "moral" certainty based on testimony and conjecture. The precise descriptions of these levels varied slightly from author to author, but the notion of such an ordered scale, and the emphasis that most things admit only of moral certainty, remained a staple of the literature from Hugo Grotius' *De veritate religionis christianae* (1624) to John Locke's *Essay Concerning Human Understanding* (1690) and thereafter. When Bishop Joseph Butler claimed in 1736 that "probabilities are the very guide of life," he was by then repeating a cliché (Butler, 1736, p. iii).

In the context of these discussions, the very meaning of the word "probability" changed from its medieval sense of any opinion warranted by authority to a degree of assent proportioned to the evidence at hand, both of things and of testimony (Locke, [1690] 1959, IV. xv–xvi). These probabilities were qualitatively conceived, and owed much to the language and practice of legal evidence, as the numerous courtroom examples and analogies make clear (Daston, 1988, chapter 2). However, mathematicians like Gottfried Wilhelm Leibniz and Jakob Bernoulli seized upon the new "analysis of hazards" as a means of quantifying these degrees of certainty, and in so doing, converting the three ordered points into a full continuum, ranging from total disbelief or doubt to greatest certainty (J. Bernoulli, 1713, IV.i). Indeed, Leibniz described the fledgling calculus of probabilities as a mathematical translation of the legal reasoning that carefully proportioned degrees of assurance on the part of the judge to the kinds of evidence submitted (Leibniz, [comp. *c.* 1705] 1962, pp. 460–5). The fact that these legal probabilities were sometimes expressed in terms of fractions to create a kind of "arithmetic of proof" (for example, the testimony of a relative of the accused might count only ⅓ as much as that of an unimpeachable witness) may have made them seem mathematically tractable.

The mathematicians who set about trying to measure these probabilities in some non-arbitrary fashion came up with at least three methods: equal possibilities based on physical symmetry; observed frequencies of events; and degrees of subjective certainty or belief. (Other seventeenth-century meanings of "probability," such as the appearance of truth or the strength of analogy, were not successfully quantified.) The first was well suited to gambling devices like coins or dice but little else; the second depended on the collection of statistics and assumptions of long-term stability; and the third echoed the legal practice of proportioning degrees of certainty to evidence.

The various senses emerged from different contexts, and suggested different applications for the mathematical theory. Sets of equiprobable outcomes based on physical symmetry derived from gambling and were applied to gambling – very few other situations satisfy these conditions in an obvious way. Statistical frequencies originally came from mortality and natality data gathered by parishes and cities from the sixteenth century onwards. In 1662 the English tradesman John Graunt used the London bills of mortality to approximate a mortality table by assuming that roughly the same fraction of the population died each decade after the age of six (Graunt, [1662] 1975, pp. 29–30). (Since the bills of mortality registered only cause, not age at death, Graunt's table was based on informed guesswork about what diseases killed whom at what age, and the faith that mortality was regular.) Eighteenth-century authors collected more detailed demographic data and enlisted probability theory in order to compute the price of annuities, and later life insurance, and to argue for divine providence in human affairs. The epistemic sense of belief proportioned to evidence arose from legal theories about just how much and what kind of evidence was required to produce what degree of conviction in the mind of the judge, and inspired applications to the probabilities of testimony, both courtroom and historical, and of judgment.

Latter-day probabilists view these three answers to the question, "What do probabilities measure?" as quite distinct, and much ink has been spilt arguing their relative merits and compatibility (Nagel, 1955). In particular, a bold line is now drawn between the first two "objective" meanings of probability, which correspond to states of the world, and the third "subjective" sense, which corresponds to states of mind. Yet classical probabilists used "probability" to mean all three senses, shifting from one to another with an insouciance that bewilders their more nice-minded successors.

Why were classical probabilists able to conflate these different notions of probability so easily, and often very fruitfully? In part, because the objective and subjective senses were not then separated by the chasm that yawns between them in current philosophy. Legal theorists of the sixteenth and seventeenth centuries found it plausible to assume that conviction formed in the mind of the judge in proportion to the weight of the evidence presented, and Locke repeated the assumption in a more general context, invoking the qualitative probabilities of evidence: the rational mind assents to a claim "proportionably to the preponderancy of the greater grounds of probability on one side or the other" (Locke, [1690] 1959, vol. II, p. 366). At least two further elements were required to connect the objective and subjective senses of qualitative probabilities. First, precept had to be guaranteed in practice. It was not enough that the mind *should* apportion assent in strict relation to the evidence; it had to be shown that it actually did so. Second, the evidence had to be quantified.

The empiricist philosophy-*cum*-psychology of the late seventeenth and eighteenth centuries satisfied both desiderata. John Locke, David Hartley, and David Hume created and refined a theory of the association of ideas that made the mind a kind of counting machine that automatically tallied frequencies of past events and scaled degrees of belief in their recurrence accordingly. Hartley went so far as to provide a physiological mechanism for this mental record-keeping: each repeated sensation set up a cerebral vibration that etched an ever deeper groove in the brain, corresponding to an ever stronger belief that things would be as they had been. Hume notoriously rejected the rationality of such inferences to the future based on past experience, *pace* Locke and Hartley, but he retained the psychology that made them inevitable. Images of past experiences conjoin to heighten the vivacity of a mental impression, each repetition being "as a new stroke of the pencil, which bestows an additional vivacity on the colours." (Hume, [1739] 1975, p. 135). Since the mind irresistibly conferred belief in proportion to the vivacity of an idea, the more frequent the conjunction of events in past experience, the firmer the conviction that they would occur again. Locke and Hartley contended that this matching of belief to frequencies was rational (Hartley appealing explicitly to the calculus of probabilities; Locke, [1690] 1959, IV.xv; Hartley, 1749, vol. I, pp. 336–9). Hume replied that it was merely habitual, although his "Essay on Miracles" elevated belief based on unexceptioned past experience to at least a kind of reasonableness (Hume, [1758] 1955, chapter 10). All however concurred that the normal mind, when uncorrupted by upbringing or prejudice, irresistibly linked the subjective probabilities of belief with the objective probabilities of frequencies.

They also showed an increasing tendency to reduce all forms of evidence whatsoever to frequencies, in contrast to the legal doctrines that had originally been the prototype of degrees of belief proportioned to evidence. For the judge, the probative weight of eye-witness testimony that the accused had been seen fleeing the scene of the murder with unsheathed bloody sword derived from the quality of the evidence, not its quantity. It mattered not how many times in the past similar evidence had led to successful convictions. Locke remained very close to this legal tradition in his discussion of the kinds of evidence that create probabilities: number of witnesses, their skill and integrity, contradictory testimony, internal consistency, etc. He told the cautionary tale of the King of Siam, who dismissed the Dutch ambassador as a liar because his tales of ice-skating on frozen canals ran counter to the accumulated experience of generations of Siamese that water was always fluid. The King erred in trusting the mere quantity of his experience, without evaluating its breadth and variety. Yet Locke also made a place for "the frequency and constancy of experience" and for the number, as well as the credibility of testimonies (Locke, [1690] 1959, IV.xv). Later philosophical writings on probabilities narrowed the sense of evidence to the countable still further. Hume represents the endpoint of this evolution, in which evidence has become the sum of repeated, identical events. According to Hume, the mind not only counted; it was exquisitely sensitive to small differences in the totals: "When the chances or experiments on one side amount to ten thousand, and on the other to ten thousand and one, the judgment gives the preference to the latter, upon account of that superiority" (Hume, [1739] 1975, p. 141).

The guarantee that subjective belief was willy-nilly proportioned to objective frequencies and also, according to some authors, to physical symmetries allowed classical probabilists to slide from one sense of probability to another with little or no explicit justification. Only when associationist psychology shifted its emphasis to the illusion and distortions that prejudice and passion introduced into this mental reckoning of probabilities did the gap between subjective and objective probabilities become clear enough to demand a choice between the two. It was not so much the development and triumph of a thoroughgoing frequentist version of probability theory that marked the end of the classical interpretation, as the realization that a choice must be made between (at least) two distinct senses of probability. The range of problems to which the classical probabilists applied their theory shows that their understanding of probability embraced objective as well as subjective elements: statistical actuarial probabilities happily co-existed with epistemic probabilities of testimony in the work of Jakob Bernoulli or Laplace.

1.4 DETERMINISM

But the writings of these two towering figures in the history of mathematical probability also contained the manifestoes that, rightly or wrongly, led to the standard view of the classical interpretation as incorrigibly subjective. Both maintained that probabilities measure human ignorance, not genuine chance; that God (or Laplace's secularized super-intelligence) had no need of probabilities; that necessary causes, however hidden, governed all events. Therefore probabilities had to be states of mind rather than states of the world, the makeshift tools of intellects too feeble to penetrate immediately to the real nature of things. Theirs was an epistemological determinism that maintained that all events were in principle predictable, and that probabilities were therefore relative to our knowledge. Bernoulli remarked that backward peoples still gambled on eclipses that European astronomers could now predict; some day gambling on coins and dice would seem equally primitive when the science of mechanics was perfected (J. Bernoulli, 1713, IV.i).

The very mathematicians who had carved out a place for chance in the natural and moral sciences insisted to a man that chance, in Abraham De Moivre's words, "can neither be defined nor understood" (De Moivre, [1718] 1756, p. 253). They did concede that certain statistical rates varied from year to year and from place to place, but they were confident enough in the underlying regularity of phenomena like mortality to simplify and adjust the unruly data accordingly (Pearson, 1978, pp. 319–29). Variability, they believed, would prove just as illusory as chance when fully investigated.

In order to unknot the apparent paradox of the ardent determinism of the classical probabilists, we must look beyond probability theory to the panmathematical spirit of the period in which it emerged. Classical probability arose and flourished during a time of spectacular successes in fitting mathematics to whole new domains of experience, from rainbows to vibrating strings. Natural philosophers like Galileo assumed that if nature spoke the language of mathematics, this was because nature was fully determined, at least from God's viewpoint: the glue that connected causes and effects must be as strong as that which connected premises and conclusions in a mathematical argument. Determinism thus became a precondition for the mathematical description of nature.

At first glance, chance events therefore seemed the least likely candidates for mathematical treatment; even Pascal admitted that there was something paradoxical about a "géométrie du hasard" (Pascal, [1654]

1970, vol. I, part 2, p. 1034). The very earliest mathematical attempts to analyze gambling problems stumbled over just this problem. In his manuscript on the subject (composed *c.* 1525), the Italian physician, mathematician, and inveterate gambler Girolamo Cardano felt mathematically obliged to assert that each face of a die occurred once in every six rolls, although this flew in the face of his own experience at the gaming tables. He resolved the conflict with an appeal to the intervention of luck (he was a great believer in his own), which disrupted the necessary connection between the underlying probabilities and the actual events in favor of particular players (Cardano, [comp. *c.* 1525] 1966, pp. 264–5). He thus relinquished his claim to founding the mathematical theory of probability. Classical probability theory arrived when luck was banished; it required a climate of determinism so thorough as to embrace even variable events as expressions of stable underlying probabilities, at least in the long run. Determinism made a "geometry of chance" conceivable by anchoring variable events to constant probabilities, so that even fortuitous events met what were then the standards for applying mathematics to experience. Those standards were not compatible with older notions of chance as real, or with what we might call genuine randomness in the world.

"Chance" and "fortune" had been part of the philosophical vocabulary since Aristotle, meaning variously coincidence (meeting someone who owes you money on the way to the market), absence of purpose (often identified with necessity, as in the "blind necessity" of Epicurean atoms), or an ample endowment of the "external" goods of good health, wealth, beauty, and children (Sorabji, 1980). All of these meanings survived in ordinary usage, but only one played an important role in classical probability theory. This was the opposition of chance and purpose, particularly divine purpose, of which natural theologians and their probabilist allies like De Moivre made much. John Arbuthnot remarked upon the tiny probability that, year after year, male should exceed female births in a disproportion neatly arranged (or so Arbuthnot argued) to guarantee the future of the institution of monogamous marriage (Arbuthnot, 1710); Daniel Bernoulli pointed to the close alignment of the planets in the plane of the ecliptic as evidence for a single cause of the solar system (D. Bernoulli, 1752). Almost any symmetry or stability unlikely to have come about by "mere chance" – the intricate construction of the human eye; the regular mortality rate – became an argument "from design" for the existence of an intelligent and beneficent deity. The mathematical versions of the argument from design like Arbuthnot's were criticized by contemporaries like Nicholas Bernoulli and d'Alembert, who noted that all other irregular arrangements of planets or birth ratios were just as improbable. However, the natural theologians persisted until Darwin in seeing chance refuted everywhere by the traces of divine handiwork (see chapter 4). Indeed, such beliefs inspired many of the eighteenth-century statistical demographers, who, like the German pastor Johann Süssmilch, saw in rates of natality, marriage, and mortality, "a constant, general, complete, and beautiful order." (Süssmilch, [1741] 1775, vol. 1, p. 49). Only in the mid-nineteenth century, when the alleged statistical regularities were examined against the background of very different aims and controversies, was variability given its due and chance a new lease on life. But for the classical probabilists "chance" and "luck" that stood outside the causal order were superstitions. If we could see the world as it really was, penetrating to the "hidden springs and principles" of things, we would discover only necessary causes. Probabilities were merely provisional, a figment of human ignorance and therefore subjective.

The classical interpretation of mathematical probability was thus characterized in precept by determinism and therefore by a subjective slant, and in practice by a fluid sense of probability that conflated subjective belief and objective frequencies with the help of associationist psychology. It is however somewhat misleading to call this an "interpretation" of the mathematical theory, for to the classical probabilists the interpretation *was* the theory. The "doctrine of chances," or "art of conjecture," as probability theory was variously called in the eighteenth century, was a part of "mixed mathematics," a term deriving from Aristotle's explanation of how harmonics or optics mixed the forms of mathematics with the matter of sound and light (*Physics*, 193b22–194a15). In contrast to the more modern applied mathematics, mixed mathematics did not necessarily presuppose a prior and independent mathematical theory to be applied to various subject matters. Classical probability theory had no existence independent of its subject matter, *viz.* the beliefs and conduct of reasonable men. As Laplace put it in a famous passage, mathematical probability was in essence "only good sense reduced to a calculus" (Laplace, [1814] 1951, p. 6). Its status was less that of a mathematical theory with applications than that of a mathematical model of a certain set of phenomena, like the part of celestial mechanics that described lunar motion. As such, it was held up to empirical test. If astronomical theory failed to predict lunar perturbations, so much the worse for the theory. When the results of classical probability theory did not square with the intuitions of reasonable men, it was the mathematicians who returned to the drawing board.

1.5   REASONABLENESS

The protracted controversy over the St. Petersburg problem was just such a clash between reasonableness and the dictates of probability theory, and illustrates how seriously mathematicians took their task of modeling "good sense." The problem was first proposed by Nicholas Bernoulli in a letter to Pierre de Montmort, and published in the second edition of the latter's *Essai d'analyse sur les jeux de hasard* (1713). Pierre and Paul play a coin toss game with a fair coin. If the coin comes up heads on the first toss, Pierre agrees to pay Paul $1; if heads does not turn up until the second toss, Paul receives $2; if not until the third toss, $4, and so on. Reckoned according to the standard method, Paul's expectation (and therefore the fair price of playing the game) would be:

$$E = (\tfrac{1}{2} \times \$1) + (\tfrac{1}{4} \times \$2) + (\tfrac{1}{8} \times \$4) + \ldots + [(\tfrac{1}{2})^n \times \$2^{n-1})] + \ldots$$

Since there is a small but finite chance that even a fair coin will produce an unbroken run of tails, and since the pay-offs increase in proportion to the decreasing probabilities of such an event, the expectation is infinite. However, as Nicholas Bernoulli and all subsequent commentators were quick to observe, no reasonable man would pay even a small sum to play the game. Although the mathematicians labeled this a paradox, it contained no contradiction between results derived from assumptions of equal validity. The calculation of expectation is straightforward, and there is nothing in the mathematical definition of expectation that precludes an infinite answer. Rather, it struck them as paradoxical that the results of the mathematical theory could be so at odds with the manifest dictates of good sense. Applied mathematicians in the modern sense might simply have questioned the suitability of the mathematical theory for this class of problems, but that route was not open to the mixed mathematicians of the eighteenth century. In their eyes the clash between mathematical results and good sense threatened the very validity of mathematical probability.

This is why the St. Petersburg problem, trivial in itself, became a *cause célèbre* among classical probabilists. In 1738 Nicholas' cousin Daniel Bernoulli published a resolution of the paradox in the annals of the Academy of St. Petersburg, the first of many such attempts. Daniel's memoir not only named the problem after the Academy; it also raised the fundamental issues of the definition of probabilistic expectation and its relationship to reasonableness that animated the subsequent controversy. In essence, he proposed a new notion of reasonableness, and a redefinition of expectation to match. Observing that the standard definition of expectation was like an impartial judge who ignores the individual characteristics of the risk-takers, Bernoulli argued that in situations like the St. Petersburg problem more than equity was at stake. Here the players acted more out of prudence than of fairness, and the definition of expectation had to be modified accordingly. In contrast to the "mathematical" expectation of equity Bernoulli proposed the "moral" expectation of prudence, defined as the product of the probability of the outcome and what later became known as its utility. That is, Bernoulli substituted values relative to individual preference for monetary values, with the understanding that the richer you are, the more it takes to make you happy. By making utility a logarithmic function of monetary wealth, he was able to derive reassuringly small expectations, depending on one's fortune, for the St. Petersburg game. He was also able to show that moral expectation harmonized with other widely accepted practices and beliefs: for example, sober men of affairs knew to avoid the gaming tables and to distribute their cargo among several ships, and moral (but not mathematical) expectation gave results that confirmed their wisdom (D. Bernoulli, [1738] 1954).

Significantly, Daniel Bernoulli's examples were drawn from the world of trade and commerce, in contrast to the legal examples that had dominated the earlier discussions of expectation. Nicholas Bernoulli, who was professor of both Roman and canon law at the University of Basel as well as an accomplished mathematician, objected that moral expectation failed "to evaluate the prospects of every participant in accord with equity and justice." His cousin Daniel replied that his new definition of expectation "harmonize[d] perfectly with experience." What was at issue between the Bernoulli cousins was not whether probabilistic expectation should model reasonableness, but rather wherein such reasonableness consisted. Nicholas sided with the older sense of equity derived from aleatory contracts; Daniel with the increasingly important sense of economic prudence, derived from commerce. The prototypical reasonable man was no longer an impartial judge but rather a canny merchant, and the mathematical theory of probability reflected that shift.

Daniel Bernoulli's solution to the St. Petersburg problem was by no means universally accepted by other classical probabilists. Some, like Jean d'Alembert, thought the problem lay not with the monetary values but with the probabilities – was it really physically possible for a fair coin to continuously turn up tails? (see Swijtink, 1986). Others, like Siméon-Denis Poisson, pointed out that the length of the game was limited by the wealth of the two players. Still others, like M. J. A. N. Condorcet, argued that mathematical expectation was indeed correct, but only when applied as an average to many repetitions of the game (Daston, 1980; Jorland, 1987). However, all agreed that the paradox was a real one, and struck at the very foundations of the mathematical theory. The fact that classical probabilists were willing to tinker with definitions and postulates as fundamental as expectation in order to realign their calculus with good sense attests to their commitment to the mixed mathematical goal of quantifying the reasonable.

Given this goal, the classical probabilists always ran the risk of superfluity. If their calculus yielded results that echoed what the enlightened had known all along – as preface after mathematical preface emphasized was the case – then all the elaborate machinery of equations and calculations did seem a belaboring of the obvious. The probabilists replied that, in Voltaire's words, common sense was not that common. Only a small elite of *hommes éclairés* could reason accurately enough by unaided intuition; the calculus of probabilities sought to codify these intuitions (which the probabilists believed to be actually subconscious calculations) for use by *hoi polloi* not so well endowed by nature. This mathematical model of good sense could be compared to spectacles. By applying the same optical principles responsible for normal eyesight it was possible to extend vision artificially; similarly, the calculus of probabilities formalized the good sense that came naturally to the fortunate few to help out the befuddled many. And several probabilists suggested that even *hommes éclairés* could sometimes benefit from mechanized reasoning when the issue at hand was extremely complicated or obscured by sophistry.

The ideal of a calculus of reasoning, a set of formal rules independent of content, exerted a certain fatal attraction for many seventeenth- and eighteenth-century thinkers. The probabilists' hope of turning the "art of conjecture" into such a calculus echoes the seventeenth-century fascination with method taken to an extreme. In the end, the methods of Bacon, Descartes, and a host of lesser lights always relied to some extent on judgment, and therefore were of limited use in truly perplexing situations. As Leibniz quipped apropros of Descartes' famous rules of method, one takes what one needs and does what one ought. Leibniz also best captured the allure of a formal calculus that eliminated personal discretion, and with it, strife. Observing that among the learned only mathematicians ever resolved their problems to everyone's satisfaction, he envisioned a kind of "universal characteristic" that would somehow assign numbers to fundamental ideas and invent arithmetic-like operations to combine them. Henceforth, whenever a controversy arose a call to pen and paper would replace a call to arms: "Let us calculate, Sir; and thus by taking to pen and ink, we should soon settle the question" (Leibniz, [1677] 1951, p. 15). Classical probabilists from Jakob Bernoulli through Siméon-Denis Poisson wielded their calculus as an instrument of consensus in uncertain matters, attempting to make the new-style reasonableness as coercive as the old-style demonstration.

Classical probability theory was thus at once a description of and prescription for reasonableness. Mathematicians checked their results against the intuitions of the elite of reasonable men, and when the two did not jibe, it was the mathematicians who amended their theory, as in the case of the St. Petersburg "paradox." The theory was so far descriptive. But the probabilists also aimed to instruct the great majority in rational decision under uncertainty, be it about whether to accept a theory about the formation of the solar system, purchase an annuity, or believe the testimony of a witness. Here the theory was prescriptive, and sometimes presumptuously so, as when Condorcet sent Frederick II of Prussia a weighty tome of calculations on how to improve the judicial system (Condorcet, 1785).

Two ambiguities, neither ever clearly recognized, confused and ultimately undermined the classical program to render reasonableness mathematical. The first surfaced early on in the debate over expectation sparked by the St. Petersburg problem: there were several distinct brands of reasonableness, and they sometimes led to very different solutions of the same problem. The fair judge and the shrewd merchant did not agree on the proper definition of expectation, but both belonged to the select company of *hommes éclairés*. However, the probabilists persisted in believing that reasonableness was monolithic, despite endless debate over just how to define it. It took an upheaval of the magnitude of the French Revolution to shatter their faith in the natural consensus of the enlightened few. No doubt their dream of a calculus that would widen that consensus contributed to their tenacity in the face of clear evidence that reasonableness was of several sorts.

The second ambiguity concerned just where to draw the line between description and prescription. The debate between Daniel Bernoulli and d'Alembert over smallpox inoculation dramatized the difficulty. During the middle decades of the eighteenth century smallpox ravaged Europe, carrying off as much as one-seventh of the populations of Paris and London. The reports of Lady Wortley Montagu in England and Voltaire in France on the technique of inoculation against the disease, long practiced in Turkey, fanned popular and medical hopes that the scourge might be curbed. However, inoculation itself was not without its dangers, and there was a small (about one in two hundred) chance that recipients would die from the treatment in the space of a month or so. In 1760 Daniel Bernoulli submitted a memoir to the Paris Academy of Sciences that used what data could be had on smallpox mortality and probability theory to calculate the average gain in life expectancy from inoculation for any given age. Bernoulli's statistics were scanty and his simplifying assumptions dubious, but these were not the principal reasons why d'Alembert, himself a proponent of inoculation, opposed Bernoulli's favorable conclusions. Rather, d'Alembert claimed that Bernoulli's conventional probabilistic treatment of the problem ignored the actual psychology of risk-raking: confronted with a choice of a small short-term risk (inoculation) and a large long-term risk (smallpox), many reasonable people prefer in effect to bet on the long-term. D'Alembert did not altogether condone this preference, which he called the "common logic . . . half good, half bad." But he held probability theory to its task of describing the conduct of people otherwise acknowledged to be reasonable, whereas Bernoulli saw this as an opportunity for mathematicians to reveal to the benighted public where its own self-interest lay (Daston, 1979). Over the course of its long career, the emphasis within classical probability theory slowly shifted in Bernoulli's direction, from the descriptive to the prescriptive, as a result both of disillusionment with the ideal of reasonableness and of the widening gap between objective and subjective probabilities. By the time Laplace published his *Essai philosophique sur les probabilités* in 1814, probability theory had become a tool rather than a model of enlightenment.

These, then, were the hallmarks of the classical interpretation of mathematical probability: a fruitful conflation of subjective and objective senses of probability; a thoroughgoing determinism that firmly denied the existence of real chance and that highlighted the subjective sense of probability in programmatic statements; a commitment to the mixed mathematical goal of modeling phenomena; and above all an identification of the theory with that form of practical rationality that came to be known as reasonableness. To those schooled in twentieth-century distinctions, the mathematical theory is independent of both its innumerable possible interpretations and its applications, but for classical probabilists they were all of a piece. They believed that their calculus succeeded or failed on the strength of its applications, and the applications they attempted reflected their vision of the theory and its proper subject matter.

1.6 RISK IN GAMBLING AND INSURANCE

Gambling was the paradigmatic aleatory contract, and the very first problems solved by the mathematicians were of this sort. Pascal and Fermat's correspondence and Huygens' treatise were exclusively devoted to gambling problems, which continue to be the staple of elementary probability texts to this day. Between Huygens' *De ratiociniis in ludo aleae* (1657) and the first edition of De Moivre's *Doctrine of Chances* (1718), the complexity of the problems and the sophistication of the mathematical methods had advanced from simple computations of expectation using a bit of algebra to involved computations of duration of play using what were then the most advanced techniques of analysis (Schneider, 1968). Interestingly enough, these early writers on the mathematics of gambling made no hard-and-fast distinction between games of pure chance and those of mixed chance and skill, albeit with a rather arbitrary assignment of probabilities for the latter. Jakob Bernoulli, for example, undertook a long analysis of the probabilities of a game of tennis, and several eighteenth-century manuals on cock-fighting appended calculations of betting odds assuming equal chances, contradicting the message of the text that factors like breeding, size, and past performance gave some cocks a definite edge over the others.

Despite rapid progress, most probabilists were ill at ease with their stock-in-trade gambling problems and their disreputable associations. Some crusading spirits, Daniel Defoe among them, hoped that mathematicians might cure the reckless of their passion for cards and dice with a strong dose of calculation (Defoe, 1719). The mathematicians preached the folly of such pursuits along with the moralists, but apparently most gamblers had little appetite for either sort of edification. Those few who did turn to the probability texts for guidance were likely to be cruelly disappointed, like the hero of Thomas Smollett's *The Adventures of Ferdinand Count Fathom* (1753). Fathom learned to "calculate all the chances with the utmost exactness and certainty," only to be fleeced by a team of sharpsters. The eighteenth-century lottery craze that began in England and the Netherlands and swept Europe provided the mathematicians with problems but very little employment. Neither the designers nor the patrons of the several national lotteries in Britain, France, Italy, and the German states consulted the probabilists for an expert opinion. (Frederick II was a notable exception: he wrote Euler several anxious letters about the Genoan-style lottery proposed to raise money to pay Prussia's war debts.) Indeed, there was little reason on either side to do so. The traditional nonprobabilistic pay-off schemes gave governments a sizable profit margin, and the majority of those who bought lottery tickets pitted the improbability of winning against the still greater improbability that they could alter their situation in any other way. Talleyrand may have been correct in criticizing the French national lottery as a tax upon the poor, who favored the ruinous high risk/big win combinations (Talleyrand, 1789, p. 6). But given the rigidity of the social order, it is at least arguable that this was a rational if desperate strategy for the ambitious. A few lessons in probability theory were therefore unlikely to influence either the buying or the selling end of the lottery business (Daston, 1988, chapter 3).

Feeling themselves thus at once neglected and despised for their interest in the mathematics of gambling, classical probabilists eagerly turned their attention to other, more respectable types of aleatory contracts. The writings of Jakob Bernoulli and his nephew Nicholas abound with such applications: wine futures, annuities, maritime insurance, the expectation of an inheritance, dowry funds, and usufructs were all grist for their mill. However, the Bernoullis recognized that probability values were not easily derived for these more interesting examples of aleatory contracts, in contrast to games of pure chance.

This was not an insuperable obstacle for the Dutch statesman and mathematician Johann De Witt, who in 1671 presented the Estates General of Holland and West Friesland with the first mathematically based annuity scheme (never implemented) to raise money for the war with England. De Witt applied Huygens' new calculus of expectations to the pricing of annuities, simply assuming that the chances of dying in any six-month period between ages 3 and 53 were equal, and that they decreased in a regular fashion for subsequent intervals until age 80. He did nonetheless avail himself of the opportunity to check his assumptions against the data on mortality on purchasers of Amsterdam annuities with the help of mayor and fellow mathematician Johannes Hudde, although he did not revise his original price estimates in the direction suggested by these records (De Witt, 1671). In general, mathematicians all over Europe were quick to recognize the relevance of mortality tables like John Graunt's to extensions of probability theory beyond gambling, and in 1693 Edmund Halley published the first truly empirical mortality table, compiled from the data gathered by the Protestant pastor of Breslau at Leibniz' instance (Halley, 1693).

Statistics during this period took the form of demographic data on births, marriages, and deaths because this was information that governments had been requiring parishes to register since the first half of the sixteenth century, for reasons having nothing to do with probability theory. English and French parishes were ordered to record christenings, weddings, and burials to provide official proof of age and status before the law; and as early as 1562 the city of London published bills of mortality to keep track of plague deaths as a warning of a major outbreak. These bills listed only place and cause of death, and only after 1625 any cause of death other than plague. The London bills were not kept continuously until 1603, and ages at death were first recorded in 1728. This is why Graunt had to resort to shrewd guesswork and regularizing hypotheses to construct his mortality table from the London bills, and why a number of readers, including Huygens and Hudde, were wary of his figures. Governments differed greatly in the alacrity and thoroughness with which they assembled such data: Sweden led the way, with France close behind, but several central European nations did not register birth and death until well into the nineteenth century (Meuvret, 1971).

Mathematicians unhesitatingly read these statistical frequencies as probabilities, and saw in them the means of advancing from gambling to more reputable kinds of aleatory contracts. Halley immediately put his mortality table to use calculating the price of annuities, claiming that traditional methods inequitably ignored different life expectancies. Other mathematicians like Nicholas Bernoulli and De Moivre also emphasized that equity in such matters was best served by the new probabilistic techniques, an indication that they still viewed annuities within the context of contract law. By the mid-eighteenth century, there existed a sizable mathematical literature on the subject in English, Dutch, French, German, and Latin. De Moivre's *Treatise of Annuities* (1725) was perhaps the most mathematically distinguished of these works, although his methods and assumptions were sometimes contested by other probabilists. Two conceptual issues in particular exercised the probabilists, in addition to the empirical dilemma of which mortality statistics to trust: the definition of life expectancy, and the shape of the mortality curve.

Life expectancy entered mathematical probability on direct analogy to expectation. Christiaan Huygens' brother Lodewijk was among the first to grasp the significance of Graunt's table for the fledgling calculus of chance, and in 1699 he wrote to Christiaan posing the problem of how to compute "the expectation of life" using Graunt's table. (Graunt himself had no mathematics beyond his "shoppe Arithmetique," and apparently knew nothing of Huygens' 1657 treatise: for over a century, the borrowing between mathematical probability and statistics was almost all in one direction.) Lodewijk's own solution was closely patterned on Christiaan's definition of probabilistic expectation in *De ratiociniis in ludo aleae*: multiply the number of people in each of Graunt's age brackets by the average number of years they survive, and divide by the total number of people, giving 18 years, 2 months. Christiaan however proposed a different method, based on a graph he had drawn from Graunt's figures: use the graph to find the age by which half of the original cohort has died – about 11 years. Drawing a distinction that roughly paralleled that between mathematical and moral expectation, Christiaan recommended Lodewijk's method for annuities, where equity prevailed, and his own for wagers, where profit was all that counted (Société Générale Néerlandaise, 1898, pp. 57–69). His successors found it more difficult to decide which method applied when, and wrangled over the issue throughout the eighteenth century. Nicholas Bernoulli for example preferred Lodewijk's method, while De Moivre sided with Christiaan.

When the mortality curve had a certain shape – when death carried off an equal proportion of the population in equal time intervals – these two methods gave the same answer for annuities on single lives, though not on joint lives. Halley, De Moivre, and others assumed that mortality did indeed follow an arithmetic progression, although their initial grounds for doing so had more to do with ease of calculation and a faith in nature's proclivity for simple curves than with the data itself. Graunt's lack of data forced such sweeping assumptions on him, while Halley blithely proclaimed that had data on Breslau mortality been collected for twenty years rather than five, it would surely have approximated such a regular curve more closely. Thus encouraged, De Moivre took Halley's Breslau table as empirical confirmation for his assumption of an arithmetic progression. Not all probabilists were so sanguine – the Dutch mathematician Nicholas Struyck for example warned that "nature doesn't listen to our suppositions" (Société Générale Néerlandaise, 1898, p. 89). But the great majority of those who wrote on the mathematics of mortality believed implicitly in its regularity. Indeed, that belief was almost a precondition for collecting such statistics and *a fortiori* for subjecting them to mathematical analysis.

Why mortality should have been assumed regular and not other phenomena of equal practical importance like the incidence of fires or shipwrecks is somewhat mysterious. It was an age in which all were subject to wild fluctuations due to plague, huge conflagrations like the Great Fire of London, or war on the high seas. Yet only mortality was singled out for study, a fact that greatly influenced the applications of probability theory during the eightenth century. It was not the case that the available data revealed the regularities; on the contrary, the data was collected only once such regularities were posited, and it was often adjusted to fit the hypothetical regularities more closely. Natural theologians like William Derham in England and Johann Süssmilch in Germany who argued from design to God's providence eagerly seized upon alleged regularities in the rates of birth and death, but natural theology does not seem to have been the original source for belief in such regularities. Although it is a recurring theme in De Moivre's work on probability, there is no trace of natural theology in the pioneering works of Graunt and Halley. The vogue for demographic theology began later, with John Arbuthnot's 1710 memoir "An Argument for Divine Providence Taken from the Constant Regularity Observed in the Birth of Both Sexes," and received its most extreme and expansive expression in Süssmilch's compendium of demographic proofs for God's handiwork in human natality and mortality rates. Seeing God's hand in the mortality curve was the result of rather than the reason for asserting simple regularities.

Two aspects of mortality may have made it a more promising candidate for regularity seekers than fires or other catastrophes: its inevitability, and its ancient connection with the continuous numerical variable of age at time of death. With luck one might escape fire or shipwreck, but death comes to all. Therefore a complete enumeration of the population was in principle possible, and long custom made age the obvious choice for the independent variable: even the Bible duly records the age to which Adam survived. Independent variables were not so easy to come by for other events. Was it building material or trade that mattered most in susceptibility to fires? Was it the experience of the captain and the crew, the seaworthiness of the vessel, or the route and season that weighed heaviest in a safe passage? And how were any of these factors to be quantified? Of course, age was not the only possible choice for mortality; state of health was also a candidate, but one not so easily numbered. Neither the inevitability nor the age-linked character of death were sufficient conditions for believing mortality to be regular. Centuries of observers had recognized both without drawing that conclusion. However, in an age that sought regularities everywhere, particularly quantitative ones, these features may have been suggestive.

By 1750 the mathematics of mortality, particularly as applied to annuities and other reversionary payments, was the cutting edge of research in probability theory. Beginners still learned their probability from gambling problems, but the best minds were more interested in the latest mortality table than in what went on in London clubs like White's or in the Paris "académies de jeu." Annuities were simply the obverse of life insurance – the annuitant pays a lump sum in return for regular payments so long as he (or some designated person) lives; the policy holder makes regular payments in return for a lump sum paid to his beneficiaries upon his death. Hence some mathematicians like James Dodson also turned their attention to the mathematics of this second variety of aleatory contract that made use of mortality tables. Armed with statistics and the most refined analytic techniques, the probabilists set about rationalizing the business of risk taking. And it was big business: in 1753 Dodson observed that "of much the greatest part of the real estates" of Great Britain depended on "the value of lives" (Dodson, 1775, vol. II, pp. vii–viii). The mathematicians wrote handbooks for men of affairs as well as treatises for their colleagues. They pitched their manuals to the barely numerate clerks with only arithmetic, translating the equations into words and appending tables to spare the reader onerous calculations. Although the lack of statistics prevented them from mathematizing other aleatory contracts like maritime insurance, the probabilists hoped to make themselves useful and perhaps prosperous by reforming the bustling trade in "values of lives."

That hope was seldom realized. By and large, eighteenth-century buyers and sellers of annuities and life insurance were no more interested in probability theory than the gamblers. Their indifference seems at first glance inexplicable, particularly in the percolating London and Amsterdam markets where purveyors of annuities and a motley assortment of insurance schemes scrambled for competitive advantage. Yet the first mathematically based enterprise of this sort, the Equitable Society for the Assurance of Lives, was established only in 1762, and then by the mathematician Dodson rather than by an insurer (Ogborn, 1962, pp. 24ff). Indeed, the project met with almost universal scepticism from the London insurance community, and went another twenty years without imitators. Most annuity and life insurance plans instead charged flat rates, regardless of age, and those few that did take some account of age did so apparently without consulting the available mortality statistics and mathematical manuals on the subject. Far from profiting from the law of large numbers, these societies strictly limited the size of their membership. The influence of the mathematical theory of risk on the practice of risk was thus effectively nil for most of the eighteenth century.

Why were dealers in annuities and insurance, not to mention gamblers, so reluctant to avail themselves of a technology custom-made (and often custom-written) for them? Their failure to do so seems a *prima facie* case of irrationality: mindless conservatism blinded them to the manifest superiority of the new mathematical methods. It is however difficult to recognize in this description the booming, innovative business centers of eighteenth-century London and Amsterdam, which were also the centers for probabilistic research in these applications. Daniel Defoe called his "the Projecting Age" and his own *Essay on Projects* (1697) testifies to the efflorescence of schemes to make money and/or improve life by hook or crook, by "Banks, Stocks, Stock-jobbing, Assurances, Friendly Societies, Lotteries, and the Like" (Defoe, 1697, pp. 8–9). The London merchants who invented insurance against fire, cuckoldry, and even losing at the lottery may be accused of many things, but inertia was not one of them.

The context in which annuities and life insurance was sold goes a bit further towards explaining the general neglect of probabilistic techniques. Annuities were an ancient form of investment, but they acquired a new function in eighteenth-century London after loans at more than 5% interest were declared usurious. Many of the annuities taken out thereafter were essentially loans at a much higher rate of interest, made legal by the aleatory nature of the contract: annuities were sold very cheaply (mostly at six years' purchase) on the life of the *seller*, in need of quick cash even on very unfavorable terms (Campbell, 1928). These financial arrangements clearly subverted the original purpose of the annuity as a kind of pension for the lifetime of the buyer, and mortality statistics were therefore not so relevant. Life insurance at this time was also dedicated to very different ends. Since the sixteenth century, and possibly earlier, a life insurance policy was almost always a wager on the life of a third person, often a celebrity not personally acquainted with the buyer – for example, a cardinal or a sovereign. As such, it was summarily banned in almost all European countries except England, where it continued to flourish in this form throughout most of the eighteenth century. London life insurance offices made book on everything from the life of Sir Robert Walpole to the succession of Louis XV's mistresses. Those who took out such betting policies were usually as little interested in probability theory as the purchasers of lottery tickets.

There were other, still deeper reasons why the practitioners of risk resisted the mathematical theory of risk. Long before the advent of mathematical probability and statistics, parties to aleatory contracts like gambling, annuities, and maritime insurance had agreed upon the price of a future contingency on the basis of intuitions that ran directly counter to those of the probabilists. Whereas the dealers in risk acted as if the world were a mosaic of individual cases, each to be appraised according to particular circumstances by an old hand in the business, the mathematicians proposed a world of simple, stable regularities that anyone equipped with the right data and formulae could exploit.

For the practitioners of risk, accepting the mathematical theory of risk required profound change in beliefs, and in the case of life insurance, also of values. They had to replace individual cases with rules that held only *en masse*, and to replace seasoned judgment with reckoning. What the mathematicians dismissed as local perturbations that would cancel one another out in the long run, the practitioners viewed as the very stuff of their trade – the spry sixty-year-old who outlived the ailing thirty-year-old; the ship waylaid by pirates on the way to the Levant; the unusually cold winter that ruined that year's vintage. Although the sixteenth-century manuals on maritime insurance were full of detailed advice on every other particular, they were mute on the subject of premiums, except to urge the insurer to take full account of the season, the route, the cargo, the condition of the ship, rumors of pirates, etc. Only good judgment and a thorough versing in these minutiae could price the risk in question. Writers on annuities gave analogous advice. The practice of risk was not simply astatistical; it was positively antistatistical in its focus on the individual case to the neglect of large numbers and the long term. The practitioners equated time with uncertainty, for time brought unforeseen changes in these crucial conditions; the probabilists equated time with certainty, the large numbers that revealed the regularities underlying the apparent flux. For the practitioners of risk to accept the mathematical theory of risk required a new conception of the world, and it is therefore perhaps not so surprising that they accepted the new techniques and the beliefs they implied slowly, if at all (Daston, 1987).

1.7   EVIDENCE AND CAUSES

Aleatory contracts were not the only area of application that the classical probabilists took over from the jurists. They also turned their attention early on to problems of evidence, particularly those of witness testimony. Although their inspirations owed much to the courtroom, however, their most spectacular example was historical rather than legal: the Judeo-Christian lore of miracles. Several streams fed the current of Enlightenment interest in the subject. In the late sixteenth century, Protestant and Catholic apologists had clashed over the relative weight carried by scripture and tradition in matters of faith, the Protestants insisting that scripture alone carried the divine imprimatur, and the Catholics retaliating with a sophisticated comparison of various biblical texts that threw doubt on the existence of some pristine original. During the seventeenth century the critical hermeneutics that emerged from this debate and from the sceptical challenge of the new pyrrhonists changed the attitude of historians to their sources, and the trustworthiness of witnesses became a major methodological problem. New conceptions of God and of nature, as well as a heightened sense of the gap between learned opinion and popular errors, made accounts of marvels and miracles particularly suspect. Jean Calvin declared that the age of miracles was past; Francis Bacon warned against the promiscuous mix of fact and fable in natural history; Pierre Bayle ridiculed the idea that God would resort to singular events like comets to announce his intentions; John Toland attempted natural explanations of biblical miracles. A chasm yawns between the arguments and motives of Calvin and the Deist Toland, but they both helped forge a new vision of a God more revered for rules than for exceptions. David Hume's famous "Essay on Miracles" was simply one of many contributions to the large Enlightenment literature on this topic (Burns, 1981).

Both the philosophical and mathematical treatments of the problem took their cue from the venerable legal distinction between intrinsic and extrinsic evidence. Intrinsic evidence derives from the nature of things; extrinsic evidence from testimony. Plausibility and internal consistency bore on the one; number, integrity, and competence of witnesses on the other. Combinations of the two, duly sifted and weighted by a sagacious judge, created rational belief in varying degrees. For the probabilists, the trick was to find measures of both sorts of evidence and some function for converting them into probabilities. At first they floundered. John Craig attempted an elaborate Newtonian model of "motive forces" of argument that impelled the "velocity of suspicion" through a "space" representing "degrees of assent" in his *Theologiae christianae principia mathematica* (1699). In the same year the Royal Society of London published an anonymous article (probably by George Hooper) that analyzed the problem in terms of Huygenian expectation (Hooper, 1699). Jakob Bernoulli began part IV of the *Ars conjectandi* (1713) with a tangled exposition of "pure" and "mixed" forms of both sorts of evidence (J. Bernoulli, 1713, IV. ii–iii). Nicholas Bernoulli's *De usu artis conjectandi in jure* assumed a "true proportion" of veracity for each individual witness, to be computed from past performance (N. Bernoulli, 1709, chapter 9). No wonder the French probabilist Pierre de Montmort in 1713 wrote off the whole enterprise as doomed by an "infinity of obscurities" and arbitrary assumptions (Montmort, 1713, Préface).

Not only did the mathematicians face the problems of quantifying the probative force of evidence; they also had to incorporate a number of widely held assumptions about how such evidence was to be weighted and combined into their model. For example, jurists and historians agreed that written records were more reliable than oral tradition – but by how much? Everyone knew that eye-witness testimony of two independent witnesses counted for more than that of two who had conversed before-hand – but how to capture this in calculation? It is proof of the strong and lingering influence of the old legal "probabilities" upon the new mathematical probabilities that the classical probabilists were undaunted by these formidable difficulties. Almost every probabilist from Jakob Bernoulli through Poisson tried his hand at the probability of testimony, and Montmort was exceptional in asking whether such matters were really legitimate applications of the mathematical theory.

The question of miracles had the great advantage of drastically simpli-fying these vexed considerations almost beyond the need for calculation. Hume's formulation was probably the clearest: miracles are by definition violations of the laws of nature, and therefore their intrinsic probability is zero. No amount of extrinsic probability would thus suffice to make reports of miracles credible; no witness was so sincere, so reliable, as to counterbalance the overwhelming improbability of such an event. Poisson later went so far as to recommend rejecting one's own perception of a miracle as a hallucination on these probabilistic grounds (Poisson, 1837, pp. 98–9). Hume also had recourse to a guilt-by-association argument – the more ignorant and barbarous the people, the keener their appetite for marvels – but the crux of his essay was the annihilation of extrinsic by intrinsic evidence. His more astute critics, like the English probabilist and Unitarian divine Richard Price, recognized this, and tried to boost the intrinsic probability above the zero point, and to buttress the extrinsic probability by appeal to everyday intuitions and practices (Price, [1767] 1811, pp. 226–7). But even defenders of miracles like Price accepted the underlying assumption that intrinsic and extrinsic probabilities multiplied to produce degrees of rational belief.

Hume's argument that extrinsic probability derived from past experi-ence, conceived as the repetition of identical events, stemmed from another important branch of classical probability, the probability of causes. Here the probabilists broke new ground in natural philosophy with a novel model of causation. In the late seventeenth century it was a commonplace that nature admitted of two sorts of investigation: from causes to effects and from effects to causes. The former method of "syn-thesis" deduced phenomena from underlying causes, as the mathematician deduced theorems from axioms and postulates. This was the royal road to natural philosophy, the one which would at once secure both clear understanding and rigor. Alas, the dimness of the human senses, the fallibility of human reason, and the intricacy of nature hid the causes of all but a very few phenomena, forcing natural philosophers back upon the complementary method of "analysis." Since the same effects could be deduced from various hypothetical causes – the phases of Venus from both the Copernican and Tychonic systems, to take a seventeenth-century example – success was no guarantee of certainty.

Beginning with Jakob Bernoulli's celebrated theorem, the probabilists addressed the problem of how much success generated what degree of certainty. This meant recasting ideas of cause and effect in terms tractable to probability theory, i.e. relating them to the ubiquitous urn model that became the hallmark of the classical interpretation. Imagine an urn filled with colored balls in some fixed proportion, from which repeated drawings with replacement are made. Bernoulli's theorem states that in the limit, as the number of drawings N approaches infinity, the probability P that the observed proportion of colored balls m/N corresponds to the actual proportion p within the urn approaches certainty.

$$\lim_{N \to \infty} P(\,|\,p - m/N\,| < \varepsilon\,) = 1, \quad \text{for any } \varepsilon$$

Here, the fixed but unknown proportion of balls in the urn corresponds to the hidden causes, and the results of the repeated drawings to the observed effects. Bernoulli's theorem amounted to a guarantee that in the long run observed frequencies would stabilize around the "true" underlying value, that regularity would ultimately triumph over variability, cause over chance (J. Bernoulli, 1713, IV.v).

This result was a curious mixture of the banal and the revolutionary. Banal, because as Bernoulli himself admitted in a letter to Leibniz, "even the stupidest man knows by some instinct of nature *per se* and by no previous instruction" (Leibniz, [1703] 1962, vol. III, part 1, pp. 77–8) that the greater the number of confirming observations, the surer the conjecture; revolutionary, because it linked the probabilities of degrees of certainty to the probabilities of frequencies, and because it created a model of causation that was essentially devoid of causes. Heretofore causes had been understood as essences, or as microscopic mechanisms. In either case, they produced their effects necessarily, if obscurely. Causes were more loosely connected to effects in Bernoulli's model of *a posteriori* reasoning, just as the results of individual drawings were only loosely connected to the actual proportion of balls. Necessity obtained only in the infinitely long run. Moreover, the new model abandoned all search for mechanisms, for the hidden springs and principles that ran the clockwork of the world. In Bernoulli's urn model, numbers generated numbers; the physical processes by which they did so were wholly inscrutable.

Bernoulli had intended his "golden theorem" to be of use in practical matters; a way of investigating human mortality, the weather, and other variable but vitally important phenomena. The common sense of the "stupidest men," though recognizing that more observations meant more reliability, did not suffice to show how *many* observations warranted what *degree* of certainty – hence the great utility of his theorem. But Bernoulli's own way of performing these computations was so conservative that even he seems to have been daunted by the enormous number of trials required for a reasonable degree of cerainty. If one was drawing (with replacement) from an urn with 30 white balls and 20 red balls, and wished to know the true ratio to within $\frac{1}{50}$ with a probability of at least $\frac{1000}{1001}$, his methods required 25,550 trials. It took Abraham De Moivre's more refined methods of approximating the sums of the terms of a binomial to bring the number of trials down to a more practicable number (Stigler, 1986, pp. 72–85).

But the greatest obstacle to the use of Bernoulli's theorem for the purposes he had intended it, to plumb "the work of nature or the judgment of men," was more fundamental. The theorem was the cornerstone of the probability of causes, and yet it did not really provide a way of reasoning from known effects to unknown causes even in the restricted sense of frequencies and probabilities, although Bernoulli sometimes wrote as if it did. For one was not justified in simply reading off the underlying probability from the observed frequency in any finite number of trials: without some additional simplifying assumption, the frequencies never converge unambiguously to a single value. *Given* the probability, Bernoulli's theorem revealed how likely it was that observed frequencies would approximate that probability to any desired degree of precision. What was required was the inverse: Given the observed frequency, how likely is it to approximate the unknown probability? Or, as the problem was more often posed, given that an event has occurred so many times before, what is the probability that it will occur again on the next trial? In short, what is the probability that the future will be like the past?

These so-called inverse probabilities became the core of the probability of causes. Thomas Bayes and Pierre Simon Laplace independently proved versions of the inverse of Bernoulli's theorem (Bayes, 1763; Laplace, 1774), whose applications remain controversial to this day (see 3.4). In modern notation, the theorem is usually stated as:

$$P(C \mid E) = P(C \cap E)/P(E)$$

or equivalently:

$$P(C \mid E) = P(C) \, P(E \mid C)/P(E)$$

In words: the probability of a cause C given an observed effect E (or of a hypothesis given certain data) equals the combined probability of C *and* E divided by the probability of E. In fact, the original statement of the original theorem was somewhat more complicated, because it involved a set of causes, $C_1, C_2, \ldots, C_i$. In order to apply the theorem, both Bayes and Laplace made the problematical assumption that in the absence of any information to the contrary, we may assume all competing causes C_i to be *a priori* equally likely, a so-called uniform prior probability distribution. Bayes appears to have been troubled by the assumption, perhaps even to the point of not publishing his results (it was his literary executor Richard Price who submitted Bayes' essay to the Royal Society of London), and he resorted to an elaborate physical analogy of a ball tossed at hazard onto a flat table top to justify his calculations. Just as the ball seemed equally likely to land anywhere on the table, so "in the case of an event concerning the probability of which we absolutely know nothing antecedently to making any trials concerning it, I have no reason to think that, in a certain number of trials, it should rather happen any one possible number of times than another" (Bayes, 1763, p. 143).

Laplace was more nonchalant in making the same assumption that ignorance could be converted into a uniform distribution of prior probabilities, offering no justification whatsoever (Stigler, 1986, p. 103). His notorious law of succession then follows from the inverse theorem, leading to calculations that the probability that an event once observed – Adam's first sunrise in the garden of Eden was a favorite example – would happen the next time was two-thirds. In the hands of Laplace and his followers, Bernoulli's theorem was a mathematical model of causation, particularly useful for detecting the existence of "weak" causes like animal magnetism, while the inverse theorem was a mathematical model of the scientific method itself, of evaluating the status of hypotheses like the preponderance of male to female births in light of new data. As ever in the classical interpretation, the beliefs of the reasonable man, in this case those reasonable men known as natural scientists, were the compass by which the probabilists steered. As late as 1837 Poisson was adjusting the probability of causes to take account of the fact that only one well-performed experiment suffices to convince scientists that phenomena like the polarization of light were real (Poisson, 1837, p. 165). Even in its applications to the natural sciences classical probability theory was meant to capture, not correct, these reasonable intuitions.

1.8 THE MORAL SCIENCES

However, it was in the moral sciences of the Enlightenment that the reasonable man of classical probability theory was most in evidence. For this reason the probabilists tried long and hard to make theirs the calculus of the moral sciences, a "social mathematics," in Condorcet's phrase (Baker, 1975). Jakob Bernoulli pioneered this vision in part IV of his *Ars conjectandi*, meant to set forth the application of the mathematical art of conjecture to "civil life," including the probability of evidence and his theorem linking statistical frequencies to degrees of certainty. The fact that part IV was never completed stands as a symbol of the unfulfilled ambitions of the classical probabilists in this domain. Their nineteenth-century successors ridiculed the program as an amalgam of the impracticable and the presumptuous, a slur upon the good name of mathematics. But to the classical probabilists nothing seemed more obvious than that their calculus should be applied to jurisprudence, political economy, and other parts of the moral sciences.

In order to understand their confidence, we must first understand the assumptions and aims of the Enlightenment moral sciences, and how these harmonized with those of classical probability theory. In contrast to the social sciences of the nineteenth century, the students of the moral sciences took the individual rather than society as their unit of analysis. Insofar as they dealt with society at large, they conceived of it as an aggregate of such individuals. Moreover, the regularities that the moral sciences sought to uncover were the result of rational decisions made by these individuals rather than of the overarching structures of culture and society. Reasoning individuals were in this sense the cause of social regularities; social order flowed from orderly individuals. Although the moral scientists greatly admired the successes of Newtonian mechanics, and aped its language of natural laws, they constantly harangued their fellow citizens to obey these laws. No physicist wasted his breath trying to persuade people to obey the law of gravitation; this was a matter of physical necessity, not free choice. But the moral sciences were well named, for here the necessity was indeed moral. Self-interest might make following the laws of the moral realm rational, yet human beings were free, if only to err. Arguments in the moral sciences often resembled those in classical probability theory: both were at bottom attempts to convince the recalcitrant – gamblers, judges, insurers, monarchs – that it was in their own best interest to mend their ways. Like classical probability theory, the moral sciences were both descriptive and prescriptive. On the one hand, they claimed to reveal the immutable order of human thought and action; on the other, they urged changes in existing social arrangements to better approximate this order.

The kind of reason postulated by the moral sciences also meshed well with classical probability theory, for it was reason conceived as implicit calculation and even as the capacity to combine and permute ideas. These mental operations were for the most part too swift and subtle to be conscious, and they were occasionally overtaxed by the complexity of the problem at hand. Hence the need for the moral sciences, with the aid of probability theory, to render them explicit. If sound reason were simply implicit reckoning, then it was not absurd to try to model it mathematically. Here the moral scientists gave the classical probabilists a free hand, all the more so because they depended mainly on persuasion rather than discovery to realize the "laws" of the moral realm. These laws exacted obedience in the sense that mathematical demonstration coerced assent, through an appeal to reason, and the authority of mathematics was a most welcome support to the arguments of the moral sciences.

The probabilists entered the moral sciences through jurisprudence, for reasons having to do with the history of the calculus itself and with the political climate of the time. Judicial reform was a campaign of the French philosophers, fueled by Voltaire's denunciations of the infamous trials of Jean Calas and the Chevalier de Barre, and by Cesare Beccaria's influential *Dei delitti e delle penne* (1765). It became an urgent political reality in the succession of French regimes between the outbreak of the Revolution in 1789 and the July Monarchy of 1830. The probability of judgments, invented by Condorcet in his *Essai sur l'application de l'analyse à la probabilité des décisions rendues à la pluralité des voix* (1785), was a mathematical attempt to redesign judicial tribunals, and conceptually much indebted to Beccaria's idea of summed fractions of individual liberty balanced against societal authority. Condorcet equated this fraction with the maximum risk an individual citizen might run of being wrongly convicted of a crime, and set it equal to a risk that anyone would take without a second thought – say, a ride on the Calais/Dover packet boat, the eighteenth-century equivalent of the New York/Washington shuttle. The *Essai* purported to quantify this maximum acceptable error in judicial proceedings, and to calculate the number of judges, their individual degree of "enlightenment" (*lumières*), and the minimum plurality required to guarantee that probability of safety (Condorcet, 1785, pp. lxxvii–ix).

As in the case of the probability of causes, far-reaching assumptions about the subject matter had to be made in order to launch the probability of judgments. Condorcet supposed that the individual probabilities of each judge were equal, and that their decisions were independent of one another. All subsequent contributions to the subject made similar assumptions to the effect that a verdict rendered by a tribunal composed of a given number of judges was mathematically equivalent to the same number of drawings from an urn containing a given proportion of balls marked "right" and "wrong." This made it possible to apply Bernoulli's and Bayes' theorems to the analysis, assimilating the probability of judgments to the probability of causes. However, other assumptions were more specific to the political predilections of the mathematicians. In Condorcet's hands the probability of judgments was a broadside for liberal reforms, including the abolition of the death penalty and the protection of individual liberties. Laplace took a more conservative view, emphasizing societal security over individual rights: each judge must assess not only the probability that the accused was guilty or innocent, but also the probability that the verdict served the interests of society. Poisson pushed the probability of judgments still further right, assuming an *a priori* probability of guilt of at least one-half. Indeed, he argued that the judges should contemplate whether public safety was better secured by a verdict of guilty or innocent rather than whether the accused was actually guilty or innocent. In the service of the moral sciences, mathematics itself took on a moral tinge (Daston, 1981).

1.9   CONCLUSION

By the time Poisson claimed to have demonstrated his conclusions with all the rigor of mathematics in 1837, the classical interpretation of probability was under attack on several fronts. Poisson's own results stirred up a storm of controversy among his colleagues, who sharply criticized the probability of judgments as "the real opprobrium of mathematics," as John Stuart Mill put it a few years later (Mill, [1843] 1881, p. 382). These critics also heaped scorn on the probabilities of testimony and of causes;

the one for attempting to quantify imponderables like veracity, and the other for substituting armchair algebra for honest empirical investigation. By 1840, the theory that had been touted as good sense reduced to a calculus struck many mathematicians and philosophers as an "aberration of the intellect." For the first time, mathematicians began to distinguish the theory of probability from its suspect applications.

The intellectual and social context which had made the classical interpretation and its characteristic applications conceivable dissolved in the early decades of the nineteenth century. The French Revolution and the social tensions that followed it shook the confidence of the probabilists in the existence of a single, shared standard of reasonableness in a way that decades of controversy over the proper definition of expectation had not. The reasonable man fragmented and then disappeared altogether, along with the consensus of the intellectual and political elites he was supposed to embody. In the first flush of romanticism, reason itself ceased to be a matter of implicit calculation, and was instead identified with unanalyzable intuitions and sensibility. The classical interpretation had lost its subject matter.

It had also lost its justification for amalgamating objective and subjective probabilities. In the late eighteenth century the associationist psychology that had initially joined the two sides of probability, frequencies and degrees of certainty, shifted its emphasis from accurate tallies to distortions and illusions. Hume's associationism had apportioned belief to experience on a probabilistic scale, but Condillac's enslaved belief to fantasy and desire (Condillac, [1754] 1798, vol. 3, p. 95n). Subjective belief and objective frequencies began as equivalents and ended as diametric opposites. When Laplace discussed how the association of ideas influenced the estimation of probabilities in his *Essai philosophique sur les probabilités* (1814), it was under the heading of "illusions" (Laplace, 1951, ch. 16). Once the psychological bonds dissolved between objective and subjective probabilties, and between the calculus of probabilities and good sense, the classical interpretation came to seem both dangerously subjective and distinctly unreasonable.

Poisson was the first to distinguish clearly between subjective and objective senses of probability in print, in 1837 (Poisson, 1837, p. 3), and in the next decade probabilists on both sides of the Channel forged a new interpretation of probabilities as observed frequencies. The statistics amassed in government offices all over Europe during this period provided a prominent model for the new interpretation. In the mouths of the frequentists "subjective" became an epithet, and they were unrelenting in their criticisms of applications that equated "equally undecided" with "equally possible," as in many classical applications of Bayes' theorem. The applications that survived this transition were those compatible with a purely objective interpretation of probability: gambling and actuarial problems, and the method of least squares (Stigler, 1986; see 3.3). In contrast, the probabilities of evidence, judgment, and causes were discredited for what now looked like bizarre assumptions and oversimplifications of their subject matter. The rise and fall of the classical interpretation of probability shows that quantification is not irreversible, and that mathematical theories can lose as well as gain domains of application.

A handful of prominent mathematicians, most notably Augustus De Morgan and W. S. Jevons in England, upheld one or another variant of the classical interpretation of probability during the middle decades of the nineteenth century, but they were an embattled minority. By then much of the classical program was the object of ridicule among philosophers and mathematicians, including John Stuart Mill, George Boole, and Joseph Bertrand. The background of assumptions about the world and the mind that had made sense of the program had eroded, taking the reasonable man of classical probability theory and most of what he represented with them. Probabilists turned from the rationality of the few to the irrationality of the many.

But the age of chivalry is gone – That of sophisters, economists, and calculators, has succeeded; and the glory of Europe is extinguished for ever.

Edmund Burke (1790)

2

◁ ═══════════════════════════════════════ ▷

Statistical probabilities, 1820–1900

2.1 INTRODUCTION

By about 1830, *l'homme éclairé* had given way to *l'homme moyen*. The same awareness of a dynamic and perhaps unstable mass society that super-annuated the reasonable man as the most characteristic object of probability theory simultaneously brought into existence a new one. There was, to be sure, some continuity. The application of probability to error theory, in-surance, and gambling problems survived unscathed. More abstractly, what could be subjected to mathematics was yet assumed to have a certain latent rationality, notwithstanding the dispiriting unruliness of manifest events. The allure of aggregate figures for many social thinkers lay pre-cisely in their insensitivity to political and economic crises. The reason-able man might still exist, but he did not and could not control public life. Statistics was valued as a way of searching for the larger order that, it was hoped, would prevail nonetheless. Statisticians exulted in their ability to find such an order, for chance disappeared in large numbers, and with it the discontinuities of revolution – "always the most precarious of all games of chance," in Gustav Schmoller's words (quoted in Semmel, 1968, p. 197). The main object of probabilistic analysis became mean values. Its most important and conspicuous field of application was now statistics.

Social numbers, of course, were not invented in the nineteenth century, and the application of probability to them was almost as old as mathematical probability itself. Ironically, the great improvement in accuracy of demographic, economic, anthropometric, and social records early in the

37

nineteenth century reduced dependence on probability. The difference between statistics and political arithmetic, according to a common nineteenth-century view, was precisely that the former had been freed from reliance on estimates and conjectures, and could aspire to near-perfect accuracy. "Statistics," first used in the eighteenth century as a descriptive and nonhistorical science of states, became in the early nineteenth century increasingly identified with numbers, until by the 1830s it was perceived almost unanimously in Britain and France as the numerical science of society. Only at the end of the century was there a reasonable basis for defining it as a mathematical field concerned with manipulating and, more particularly, with inferring conclusions from numerical data. In its capacity as a social science, statistics presupposed the availability of census records and other tabulations that only began to be systematically collected and published by the governments of western Europe and the United States around 1800.

2.2 STATISTICAL REGULARITY AND *L'HOMME MOYEN*

Statistics was quintessentially an objective science, which is to say that "statists" were loath to go beyond the facts. The statistical societies that sprang up beginning in the 1830s in France, Germany, the United States, and most abundantly in Great Britain, the International Statistical Congresses that Adolphe Quetelet organized and that met regularly after 1853, and even the official statistical offices that proliferated after 1790, were devoted to the acquisition of neutral knowledge, and that ideal required a routine, mechanical, and thorough process of collection and presentation. This outlook reached its zenith in the decision of the London Statistical Society to take as its motto *Aliis exterendum* – to be threshed out by others. Statistics, according to the council of that great scientific organization, was not concerned with causes or effects; indeed, its "first and most essential rule" was "to exclude all opinions" (quoted in Cullen, 1975, p. 85; see also Hilts, 1978). And, William Farr added: "The dryer the better. Statistics should be the dryest of all reading" (quoted in Diamond and Stone, 1981, p. 70). To carve out a domain for science within the contentious field of society and politics required great personal restraint – at least in principle – on the part of practitioners of this new form of investigation.

For most statisticians, mathematical probability was too arbitrary, too much like speculation, to be admitted into this sober, solid science. Probabilistic inference from samples to a population was almost unknown in nineteenth-century social statistics. Statisticians were mainly concerned – when they went beyond the numbers at all – with inference from numerical appearances to the underlying causes. It was occasionally recognized that there was randomness, at least from the standpoint of the statistician, in the events themselves, and not only in the choice of individuals to observe. But nobody maintained that human or other actions were due to chance alone – to believe so was, as was commonly argued, to confuse a mere word with a cause. Most statisticians did not concern themselves with chance at all, but were content to let "the facts" speak for themselves. Still, if the use of mathematical probability to study statistical findings was extremely rare, it was the essence of the statistical approach to assume that social knowledge was more efficiently promoted by ignoring the sources of individual actions, and seeking instead causes whose effects could be discerned in large numbers. Thus statistics took individuals to be, if not random, at least too variable and inconsistent to serve as the basis of the moral sciences. Statisticians looked away from the individual to "society."

The idea of society as a dynamic entity, somehow more fundamental than the state, and requiring a "social science" to comprehend it, was largely a product of the early nineteenth century. Condorcet, or at least one of his correspondents, first spoke of a social science around 1792 (see Baker, 1975). Claude Henri St. Simon and Auguste Comte gave it an anti-individualistic tone that would survive to Emile Durkheim and beyond. Statistics was a powerful rival for the title of science of society. It was far less illiberal than Comte's sociology, for it made society a sum of individuals. But it still assigned primacy to society. Balzac captured this paradox nicely in *Le curé de village* (1841): "Society isolates everyone, the better to dominate them, divides everything up to weaken it. It reigns over the units, over numerical figures agglomerated like grains of wheat in a cup." Quetelet similarly made society practically determinative of the psychology and behavior of individuals. Statistical results even contributed to the definition of society as an object of scientific study. That each nation can be characterized by unique but relatively stable rates of crime, suicide, and marriage was cited as evidence of the reality of society even at the end of the nineteenth century by pioneer sociologists such as Spencer and Durkheim (see Porter, 1986, pp. 68–9).

The customary mathematical justification of this statistical doctrine, when probability was invoked at all, was the rule known in the nineteenth century as the law of large numbers. Technically, this was Poisson's version of Jakob Bernoulli's law, a purported mathematical demonstration that the indefinite repetition of events must lead to stable mean values even if the underlying probabilities are allowed to fluctuate. Poisson intended his law as a more realistic basis than Bernoulli's for applying probability to society, and he was himself author of a notable study of the probabilities of testimonies and judicial decisions. Nineteenth-century statisticians used the phrase routinely, but they meant by it something much looser. The law of large numbers referred simply to the tendency for events frequently repeated and not too closely dependent on one another – that is to say, virtually everything counted by government statistical agencies – to occur in approximately constant numbers from year to year. Some such assumption is implicit whenever statisticians suppose that a major shift in the returns for trade or suicides or marriage calls for an explanation, and the number of them who invoked this law, while considerable, is only a fraction of those who may be said to have used it. By this standard, we should perhaps say that statistical thinking has been widespread at least since the time of John Graunt, and that what Ian Hacking calls the "avalanche of numbers," beginning in 1820 or 1830, corresponded merely to a vast increase in its prominence.

The change in the quantitative consciousness around 1830, however, was more than a matter of numbers. Although Bernoulli and others had long before explained regularities in births and deaths as natural consequences of the laws of probability, these uniformities were customarily understood even by mathematicians as pertaining to the natural history of man, and often as reflections of the divine plan for the preservation and multiplication of the species. Characteristic, if a bit extreme, is Arbuthnot's observation, repeated by William Derham and J. P. Süssmilch, that the stable ratio of male to female births (around 21:20), taken in conjunction with the stable death ratios (childhood mortality for boys being higher than for girls), was perfectly designed to bring the sexes into harmony at the age of marriage and thus facilitate God's plan for maximal population increase (see 1.6). Although Arbuthnot had found the birth ratio surprising in 1710, by the late eighteenth century it seemed perfectly reasonable that natural phenomena should exhibit natural regularities.

That regularity should emerge from disorder and irrationality was, in contrast, astonishing. Laplace's announcement of a uniformity in the number of dead letters in the Paris postal system was cited as remarkable throughout the nineteenth century. The main event in this development, however, was the publication in 1827 of the first volume of French judicial statistics, which led both Adolphe Quetelet and A.-M. Guerry to express their amazement at the regularities that prevailed even in crimes and suicides. Who could have anticipated that such acts, transgressions of morality and of law, should yet have an order of their own? Their regularity, it appeared, was evidence of a mysterious fatality, a force unknown to consciousness driving disparate individuals to fulfill the budget of immorality. Or so it seemed at first. But social statisticians, and Quetelet in particular, soon learned to cherish these regularities. Poisson argued that regularities of all sorts are natural, and that if anything exceptions from this uniform order would require divine intervention. According to Quetelet, statistical laws showed that order was universal, that irrationality had its reasons, that even crime was subject to law. The findings of statistics implied that antisocial acts were products of the social condition, and that these social maladies could be cured, or at least alleviated, by the scientific reformer. These figures might justify the intrusion of expertise into statecraft. They also provided a certain metaphysical comfort to the troubled liberal in a time of revolution. Just as numbers implied certainty to many of the classical probabilists, scientific order seemed to Quetelet to connote some deep social order, perhaps hidden from view, but discoverable using the broad perspective of the statistician. Quetelet himself was profoundly affected by the Belgian revolution of 1830, after which he made statistical regularity the central element in his social vision.

The stability of statistical aggregates, and hence of mean values, was the foundation of the science of social physics that Quetelet announced in 1831. Its key concept was *l'homme moyen*, the average man. This being was, he realized, a mere abstraction. But abstraction was essential to social science. Real individuals were too numerous and diverse for psychological study to contribute much to an understanding of the social condition. Besides, real individuals are much more complicated than the average man. Who can comprehend the forces that drive a person to commit an act so contradictory and irrational as suicide? What deprivations of education, sanitation, morality, or sustenance lie behind a particular murder or theft? These questions are rarely answerable. But the average man can be understood. In the average, everything particular or exceptional balances out, and we are left with a certain penchant for crime characteristic of a given community, and dependent on circumstances which, it is hoped, can be isolated, measured, and then rectified. "If one seeks to establish . . . the basis of a social physics, it is he whom one should consider, without disturbing oneself with particular cases or anomalies, and without studying whether some given individual can undergo a greater or lesser development in one of his faculties" (Quetelet, 1835, vol. 1, pp. 21–2).

The average man was invented as a tool of social physics, and was designed to facilitate the recognition of laws analogous to those of celestial mechanics in the domain of society. In retrospect, however, Quetelet's statistical ambitions seem noteworthy rather as a departure from than an extension of the methods of astronomy and mechanics (see 5.1). Scientific investigation according to Newton begins with a complete analysis, yielding general laws that govern the most elementary objects or phenomena. Statistics begins by conceding that individual humans are too complex and diverse to serve as the basis of science, and has recourse instead to numerical frequencies as its elemental data. Quetelet and his successors believed that large-scale regularities were quite reliable enough to serve as the basis of science. Skilled statisticians would naturally continue to make use of analysis, to find how crime or fertility or mortality varied with wealth, occupation, age, marital status, and the like. But even these figures would be averages, whose reliability would not grow but decline when the numbers became too small. Quetelet's statistical approach was the purest form of positivism, requiring no knowledge of actual causes, but only the identification of regularities and, if possible, their antecedents. Such causation was much like the imaginary urn drawings posited by Jakob Bernoulli to model contingent events of all sorts. Statistics was indeed too positivistic – too detached from knowledge of causes – for the founder of positivism himself, Auguste Comte.

In his programmatic writings on social physics, Quetelet renounced analysis almost entirely – though his programmatics were belied by his actual practice. Social physics would not subdivide and compare, but use records of height, weight, education, mortality, marriage, suicide, and so on to calculate an average man, endowing him with probabilistic "penchants" to take account of discrete acts like marriage and crime. These figures could be expected to change slowly, so that study of the average man would enable the social physicist to calculate a trajectory over time which, Quetelet anticipated, would reveal simple laws of motion and permit prediction of the future. The forecast was subject to some alteration by legislative action, and in fact guidance of legislation was its ultimate purpose.

This willingness to rely on statistical regularities may seem a radical departure from the ideal of celestial mechanics, but Quetelet had a way of evading this charge. He simply invoked the concept of society. The regularities of statistics were not merely summaries of a clutter of discrete acts, but signs of a deeper social reality. They did not pertain to a miscellaneous assortment of individuals, but to the particular, if fictitious, individual, the average man, representative of the "social body." Thus was the elite "reasonable man" of classical probability supplanted by that embodiment of mass society, if not of mediocrity, *l'homme moyen*, and the search for mechanical rules of rational belief and action by the identification of laws of society. According to Quetelet, actions like crime should not be attributed to the will of individuals, but to "the customs of that concrete being that we call the people, and that we regard as endowed with its own will and customs, from which it is difficult to make it depart" (Quetelet, 1847, p. 142). This fictitious average had, in Quetelet's theory, more reality than the miscellaneous assortment of actual individuals who populate a town or state. Quetelet even made *l'homme moyen* into the "type" of a nation. There are, to be sure, some difficulties in attaching the term "essentialist" to Quetelet. An individual in Quetelet's world does not belong uniquely to one type, but to an array of types nested within one another, of which none has a privileged status. There is a true type of the Belgian, from which real individuals deviate accidentally, but there is also a true mean, and an error curve, associated with narrower categories – inhabitants of Brussels – and with broader categories – Caucasians, or simply humans. Still, Quetelet's interpretation of statistics certainly does not amount to "population thinking" in the sense defined by Ernst Mayr.

Quetelet's exposition had significant political and moral implications. Of this he was quite aware; indeed, it is clear that a political vision underlay his social philosophy. Basically, he was a liberal, a believer in the spontaneous forces of history, and he argued forthrightly that any attempt to turn back the historical development of society would be futile. Or rather, it would be worse than futile, for repression could only block the continuous expression of social forces and lead to their accumulation. Eventually they would escape in a revolution. But Quetelet was more of a bureaucratic liberal than a *laissez-faire* one, and he had high hopes for statistics as a source of expertise. The legislator must not seek to block the historical path of the social body, but he can hope to avoid the perturbations to which it is subject. It is the task of social physics to identify each force of perturbation, so that it can be nullified with an equal and opposite force (Quetelet, 1848a, p. 289). That is, the social physicist can learn how to avoid disorder and social turmoil, which Quetelet assumed to be inessential or perturbational. He also found congenial the consequence of his model that crime was a social responsibility, subject to social amelioration, and that the criminal was more a victim than an agent. After all, "every social condition presupposes a certain number and a certain arrangement of offenses as a necessary condition of its organization." The budget of crime is exacted each year without mercy

– "a tribute that man acquits with greater regularity than he owes to nature or the state treasury" (Quetelet, 1835, vol. 1, pp. 8–11). Quetelet was not determinist enough to deny the individual any freedom at all, and he took considerable pains to define the small domain of free will that surrounded each individual (Quetelet, 1848b). But he stipulated that this could never exert more than an infinitesimal influence on society as a whole.

Quetelet evaded more problems than he solved, but the details of his argument are not too important, since his ablest successors thought little of this attempt to make social statistics into a variety of mechanics. They were, however, impressed by the production of large-scale regularities from chaotic individual events. Quetelet's effusions on this point were already well known in the 1840s, and after Henry Thomas Buckle had incorporated the same examples into his then notorious *History of Civilization* as compelling counterevidence to the doctrine of free will (Buckle, 1857, pp. 15–25), they became common currency. Buckle's aim was to establish, at last, a scientific history by moving beyond anecdotal incidents to the wide laws that, he thought, governed history in its broadest contours. He saw statistics as a model for this kind of endeavor, which presupposes the effacement in the long run of the particular by the general. The regularities of statistics also provided the most compelling evidence available that history is indeed subject to deterministic causality, that the regular, lawlike course of social affairs is not interrupted by the intervention of God or unexplained free acts of the human will. He, even more than Quetelet, presented these regularities in a way that would suggest they might be peculiar to society; one of his main points was that society had become too powerful to be constrained any longer by the feeble efforts of government. But others interpreted them as applicable by analogy to a variety of problems, and social statistics became a model for certain areas of physics, biology, economics, and philosophy.

The fields whose theories became statistical in the nineteenth century were, not surprisingly, ones that dealt with individual entities or phenomena too numerous or too remote to be understood separately. But the example of social statistics helped greatly in recognizing that a model of numerous autonomous individuals could be helpful, and that regularities characterizing the collective could suffice to explain macroscopic laws such as the second law of thermodynamics. This was no trivial contribution. It is hard to see that Francis Galton could have recognized the statistical possibilities of Darwin's hypothesis of Pangenesis (see 2.5) without the benefit of a social analogy. In gas physics, positivists and without the benefit of a social analogy. In gas physics, positivists and energeticists quite plausibly wondered whether anything was gained by reducing deterministic, macroscopic laws of thermodynamics to statistical uniformities in the motions of as-yet hypothetical molecules. It took great confidence in the regularities of large numbers for James Clerk Maxwell and Ludwig Boltzmann to believe that statistical laws were reliable enough to serve as the foundation of this branch of physics. To the untutored intellect, nothing could seem more chaotic than the motions and collisions of billions of molecules. Maxwell and Boltzmann (see 5.6) independently invoked the well-known regularities shown by Buckle and Quetelet to justify their statistical interpretation of the gas laws. Both Galton and the gas theorists also derived their use of the astronomer's error law, or normal curve, indirectly from Quetelet. This is a striking instance of the importance of social science for the natural sciences.

Probability theory itself also felt the influence of the nineteenth-century statistical movement. Now that the ideal of the reasonable man was becoming increasingly implausible as the referent of probability theory, the reliability of averages provided a convenient and promising substitute. The frequency interpretation of probability was initially worked out during the late 1830s and early 1840s, and around 1843 reasonably full and coherent versions of it were proposed simultaneously by four authors in three countries. Not all were equally critical of the old interpretation in terms of partial belief, but they were agreed that the regularities of social statistics and insurance provided a fine model for an alternative view. J. S. Mill, R. L. Ellis, A. A. Cournot, and J. F. Fries held, against the eighteenth-century tradition, that statements of probability are properly understood as being about the frequency of like events in the long run, and not as measures of expectation concerning the outcome of some particular uncertain event. This was worked out in considerable detail by John Venn two decades later. It is no accident that during the 1830s and 1840s social statistics and insurance were coming to be seen as the most useful and important applications for a field of mathematics that for more than a century had been trying to escape its association with frivolous games of chance. The frequency interpretation originated as a statistical interpretation of probability (Porter, 1986, chapter 3).

2.3 OPPOSITION TO STATISTICS

While statistics was influential, it was also controversial. Criticism of its aims and procedures was sometimes dismissive, but it also led to a reinterpretation of statistical knowledge that had important implications both for statistical methods and for the deterministic world view. Among the earliest and most important attacks on statistics was that of the French social economist J. B. Say, who argued that statistics was merely descriptive, and could offer little to the savant who sought to identify underlying laws. Political economy did not stand above facts, of course, but the facts it needed were ones carefully chosen to reveal the essential condition of things uncorrupted by accidental causes and fortuitous circumstances. The nature of statistics was to lump disparate factors together, yielding a confused aggregate that applied to nothing in particular. Every actuary knows, or must quickly learn, that tables of mortality apply neither to the indigent nor to the leisured classes (Say, 1803, disc. prélim.; 1827; Ménard, 1978, pp. 187–91; 1980).

Auguste Comte, though no admirer of political economy, made a similar point. Society is in transition, and contains a confused mix of the theological, metaphysical, and positive stages. Statistics smears together what a historically conscious social science keeps separate. Comte was particularly annoyed because that "mere" statistician Quetelet had appropriated his "social physics" and obliged him to coin a new term, sociology, but his opposition to statistics, and to social quantification in general, long preceded Quetelet's theft (Comte, 1830–42, vol. 2, p. 371; vol. 4, pp. 513–15).

Although the "numerical method" of P. C. A. Louis was among the most influential early uses of statistics, doctors had particularly good reason to oppose it. Medicine, after all, is founded on the judgment of the physician dealing with an individual patient in all his or her complexity. Comte considered the numerical method a profound degeneration of the medical art. Risueño d'Amador argued before the Royal Academy of Medicine in Paris that the use of probability in medicine was anti-scientific – that it presupposed a level of homogeneity among patients which might be appropriate for physics, but is utterly unrealistic in medicine. It was also anti-medical, for it aimed "not to cure this or that disease, but to cure the most possible out of a certain number" (Risueño d'Amador, 1836, pp. 634–5). The aim of medicine is to treat sick persons; it may be left to nature to preserve the species. Since there will always be refractory individuals, the physician must ignore the law of the majority in certain cases or condemn these patients to death. He must rely on induction and intuition, not the mechanical reasoning of statistics.

John Warner's (1986) study of nineteenth-century American medicine shows with particular clarity how alien the numerical method was to the prevailing therapeutic ethos. American medical practice took as a premise that disease was specific to the constitution of the individual, and hence that crucial and ineffable variation characterized distinct times, places, races, and occupations. Disease was defined as a departure from the "natural," to be distinguished from the customary state of health of the *individual affected*. It was not generally recognizable through objective measures except perhaps after death, but rather by interpreting sympathetically the patient's own assessment of his or her condition. The acceptance of medical quantification generally, and of averages taken over individuals in particular, accompanied the redefinition of health as the "normal" rather than the "natural" state, with normality characterized in terms of objective measures, valid for all persons. That is, the rise of statistics in therapeutics was part of the process of objectivization through which science entered medicine in a big way and diagnosis became increasingly independent of the patient's own judgment.

Scientific medicine presupposed that different instances of the same disease were in some formal way comparable, but many versions of it were no more receptive to statistics than traditional practice. Claude Bernard, who vehemently opposed all willingness to rest content with "medical tact," also rejected statistics decisively, and for much the same reason as Say, Comte, and Risueño d'Amador (see 4.2). To be content with an average is to fail to deal with the variation that is of supreme importance when curing patients is at stake. There is, he insisted, no average pulse, but only a pulse when resting, working, or eating. There is no average disease, and no average urine. Bernard championed a program of physiological medicine which he thought far superior to therapeutic innovation rooted in statistics. Through careful experiment, science can teach the physician to control every detail, so that averages and medical tact alike will be rendered otiose (Bernard, [1865] 1957, pp. 134–40).

Moral statistics, too, evoked serious doubts concerning homogeneity. Quetelet had used the regularity of crime to argue that it was a property of the community, not of the malevolence of certain individuals. His assignment of penchants for crime to the average man implied that every individual had some such penchant, if only latently. Quetelet was here making a moral point rather than a prediction, but there were some, like Moritz Wilhelm Drobisch and Harald Westergaard, who argued from the evidence for recidivism that crime was mainly committed by a certain subpopulation, and that no uniform "penchant for crime" could justifiably be assigned to the average man in a society. The communitarian theologian Alexander von Oettingen called Drobisch a "proud pharisee" for this, and while the imputation of self-righteousness may not have been justified, he was correct to observe that Drobisch sought to return responsibility to the individual in place of society (Porter, 1987).

2.4 STATISTICS AND VARIATION

It is, in fact, impossible to separate nineteenth-century discussion of the nature of statistical knowledge from the particular context of the social science that bore the name statistics. In England the issue of free will preoccupied most writers. Several reviewers of Buckle, most notably Fitzjames Stephen in the *Edinburgh Review*, argued that statistical regularity provided an insufficient basis for any conclusions about the determination of individual behavior. Robert Campbell, an old friend of Maxwell's and brother of his biographer, published in 1859 a pioneering study of statistical dispersion to show that Buckle's regularities were in fact less stable than those produced by pure chance, and hence a poor basis for any deterministic arguments. John Venn (1866) argued forcefully for the importance of individual variability. That variability, in fact, provided a key reason why probability statements should be interpreted as predictions of long-run frequencies rather than as the quantification of uncertainty in a particular case. In any event, he too insisted that probability presupposes nothing about individual cases. W. S. Jevons, although he advocated a subjective interpretation of probability, agreed with Venn on statistics and free will. "Number is but another name for diversity," he wrote (Jevons, [1874] 1877, p. 156). We are willing to make use of statistical regularities precisely because the laws of individuals are not accessible to us. Hence statistics is irrelevant to personal freedom, and in fact the absence of known laws of individuals rules out the discovery of determinate social laws as well.

In France, the statistical argument against free will seems not to have made much of an impression. Perhaps the issue was disposed of earlier; the correspondence between the Belgian Quetelet and the Parisian Louis-René Villermé includes complaints that they were being accused of fatalism. Probably they were, but evidently not in publications of enduring influence, since nobody has located any such material. It is worth noting that the leading opponents of statistics were French, and that even Darwinism made limited headway in France for some time because evolution by natural selection seemed so adventitious to French biologists. Social and administrative statistics were strong in France, but it appears the countrymen of Descartes could not take statistical determinism seriously. The relation of statistics to free will generated the most heat, and perhaps also light, in Germany. There the aspirations, or pretensions, of statistics were even greater than elsewhere. *Statistik* had been a university discipline, albeit one whose definition was painfully nebulous, from the mid-eighteenth century. In the 1830s and 1840s it was near extinction, but then it was revived in a new form – as a numerical social science rather than a descriptive political one – in response to the social dislocations of early industrialization, and following the Anglo-French model. The revolutions of 1848 gave a big push to official statistics, and thus indirectly to the academic field, much as the "condition of England" question had done in Britain fifteen years earlier. The revised discipline of statistics was still located at the universities, however, and its practitioners felt obliged to make the foundations of their field clear. At this they never succeeded, partly because agreement could not be reached as to whether statistics was properly a science defined by its subject matter (mass phenomena in society) or by a method of mass observation applicable to a range of sciences. In the end they failed even to sustain their discipline. But their inquiry into the foundations of statistics was not all a sterile debate about words, and the understanding of statistical reasoning reached by Drobisch, Gustav Rümelin, G. F. Knapp, and Wilhelm Lexis was both important and influential.

Buckle's history was as controversial in Germany as in England. He was supported, in a way, by the economist Adolph Wagner, who was equally impressed by the regularity of crime and suicide. Wagner told a parable of a ruler whose power was so great that he could decree at the beginning of each year how many of his subjects would get married, or commit murder or suicide – and indeed by what method, whether by hanging or poison or drowning, with a gun or a knife. No real ruler could ever exert such power, he observed, yet all this is quite within the competence of society, against which the will of individuals is powerless (Wagner, 1864, p. 46). The state, too, could do little to oppose social tendencies; Wagner, like Buckle, was a strong *laissez-faire* liberal, until his "Damascus experience" about 1870, when he renounced liberalism for state socialism.

Although Wagner did not quite deny the existence of free will, his work, with Buckle's, provoked a spirited defense of it by a variety of writers, some, like Drobisch, of real ability and accomplishment. It quickly was made clear in Germany, as in England, that laws of mass phenomena provided a poor basis for inference about the individual will. But the implications of statistics for free will were even more confused in Germany than in England, for German philosophy tended to view lawlike order as a sign of wills that were doing their job, following self-imposed rules, rather than as evidence of external constraint. The German critique of statistics, in fact, addressed a somewhat broader issue, the standing of society in relation to the individuals who made it up. Statistics, though it had contributed to the very concept of society, threatened to reduce society to a mere sum of individuals. Quetelet never conceived this as a problem, but to virtually all German academic statisticians it was ideologically unacceptable.

Academic statistics in Germany was closely bound to historical economics, and to the *Verein für Sozialpolitik*. The social policy pursued by these "academic socialists" presupposed a considerable responsibility of the community, and more particularly of the state, in looking out for peasants and workers. To hold that the members of society were autonomous atoms who had entered into a social contract for their own personal convenience was to undermine the whole endeavor. French "social physics" (Quetelet's ideas were almost always treated by these Germans as characteristically French) and English *Manchestertum* seemed in different ways to embody this spirit of selfish individualism, and while the historical-school picture of English and French thought must be recognized as a caricature, their search for an alternative conception was authentic. In general, German statisticians tried to substitute an organic, holistic interpretation of their discipline for what they took to be the reductionistic mechanism of the French (Wise, 1983).

In this vein, German statisticians emphasized the importance of variation. The idea that society could be typified by an average man simply reflected an impoverished conception of the human community. Individuals have a measure of autonomy, and act in part according to self-interest, but they also form part of a higher entity, a social organism. An organism by its very nature is differentiated; otherwise it would be a mere aggregation. If statistics is to be the science of society, it must take account of the diversity that is intrinsic to society.

Gustav Rümelin provided the standard apology for statistics as a holistic social science. Variability, he asserted, is a characteristic of higher life forms: the educated are more variable than the unlettered, men than women, Caucasians than Negroes, moderns than ancients, and in particular, people are far more diverse than any species of animal. Far from providing grounds for positing an average man as the embodiment of a culture, he argued in 1863, statistics would be superfluous if such homogeneity prevailed. It is precisely because diversity is so great among humans that a special method of investigation is needed by which "the inadequacy of the isolated experience of each of us can be alleviated, and our experience grasped as a whole" (Rümelin, [1863] 1875, pp. 218–19). Statistics achieves this by collecting together numerous individuals, so that accidental causes disappear. But it does not average out all variability; it is not content with a comprehensive mean taken over a large population. Instead, the statistician must break a population up into its various parts, or compare the changes in various figures over time, in order to learn something about causes. Still, statistics could not attain laws, since these must apply to every individual. By adopting a method of mass observation, the statistician had given up the search for natural laws. This was no accident of statistical method, but the only appropriate way of dealing with an object so diverse as a modern society (Rümelin, 1881, p. 139).

Rümelin's proposition that statisticians should break numbers down and look for causes, rather than settling for wide averages, was novel only in its justification. Others, including Wagner, had expressed the same dictum, and virtually every able statistical researcher proceeded in this way. Quetelet's faith in social physics and the average man was hardly visible in his actual work. His book *On Man* makes frequent use of decomposition and analysis, designed to shed light on the factors that increase marriage, or crime, or suicide. Rümelin's abstract appreciation of diversity was in sharper contrast to Quetelet than was his actual statistical practice.

The most important innovations in statistical mathematics to emerge from the German social-statistical tradition were made by Wilhelm Lexis, who studied the dispersion of statistical series. Like Robert Campbell's paper on the same subject, Lexis's work was inspired in part by the debates over free will ensuing from Buckle's and Wagner's books. Some such ideological context seems to have been essential for these ideas to be developed. A stream of writers beginning with Jakob Bernoulli had shown that regularities in the human domain are no greater than would be predicted by probability, but not until the late nineteenth century did the interest of statisticians shift from demonstrating stability to investigating variability. Lexis was an ally of the historical school, a *Sozialpolitiker*, and an opponent of excessive reliance on deduction in economics. His scepticism of "natural laws" of society was grounded in a holistic perspective like that of Rümelin, but this viewpoint in turn was closely connected with his politics. The existence of social laws seemed to historical economists to rule out the possibility of meaningful reform. Thus Gustav Schmoller, leader of the historical school, argued against

Ricardo's "iron law" that wages could never rise above subsistence by pointing to historical evidence of an actual increase in wages in recent years, and G. F. Knapp rejected the related "wages fund" doctrine on similar grounds. Lexis had begun his carrer in social science with a study of French labor unions, in which he concluded that organized workers could compel their employers to raise wages, notwithstanding the "so-called economic 'natural laws' " maintained by allies of Manchester (Lexis, 1879, p. 7).

Hence the statistical laws of Quetelet and Buckle were objectionable for a variety of reasons. The idea of an average man seemed at worst reductionistic, and at best insufficiently appreciative of the importance of organic diversity. Lexis and his contemporaries were provoked by Quetelet's preoccupation with mechanical analogies into seeing his statistical laws as "natural laws" of society. But society was separate from nature – the domain of history, not of mechanics – and to speak of laws of society seemed to the Germans inconsistent with the possibility of social change, whether spontaneously historical or state-directed. Finally, these laws of society implied that the individual had little or no autonomy, and hence no moral responsibility, but was a victim of social forces. Much of what they attributed to Quetelet, particularly on the impossibility of reform and of change, was thoroughly inconsistent with his intentions, but the historical economists were naturally more concerned with what they saw as the implications of his thought than with his own, sometimes contradictory, utterances.

Lexis thus proposed that the proper aim of statistics was not simply to calculate mean values, but to characterize the probability schemes (*Chancensysteme*) that underlay society. To do this required that a society be broken up into as many groups as possible, and that an attempt be made to characterize the changes in the behavior of each group over time. Then in 1876 he had another idea for the mathematical study of social diversity. That was to measure the dispersion of a statistical series, or its fluctuations from year to year, and compare the result with what one would expect from a series composed of sets of independent chance events. If the fluctuations were less than those predicted according to the theory of probability, it might make sense to talk of the power of social laws somehow overwhelming the paltry will of individuals. But this he never found, and he was in fact enough of a methodological individualist to deny that it was possible. If the dispersion of a statistical series equalled that of a probabilistic one, then one could speak of a stable average, perhaps even an average man, from which all deviations were accidental.

Lexis found one series that conformed reasonably well to probability, the ratio of male to female births. That is, sex determination is an independent random event, like the toss of a (slightly unbalanced) coin. But the sex ratio is part of the natural history of man, and this result was in good accord with the German statistical ideology. When Lexis applied the same analysis to moral statistics, he found virtually without fail that the dispersions were much wider than those predicted by chance. That is, suicides, crimes, marriages, and also deaths and births, fluctuated much more sharply from year to year than could be reconciled with chance. The amazing regularities held up by Quetelet and Buckle were not amazing at all. Careful statistical analysis showed the importance of variation and of history in human society, and undermined all talk of statistical laws (Lexis, 1877, and Lexis, 1903, chs. 7–8).

2.5 THE ERROR LAW AND CORRELATION

An appreciation of the importance of variation was also crucial to the development of mathematical statistics in Britain, which is where the modern field of statistics was founded. As Donald MacKenzie has shown, the founders of modern statistics were deeply committed to eugenic control of human evolution. Insofar as this was a movement with positive ambitions, and not merely one to stop what was taken to be the rapid degradation of the Anglo-Saxon race, it depended on the preservation and reproduction of exceptional individuals. Francis Galton frequently expressed his disdain for the crowd of mediocrities that made up the middle and lower ranks of society. Accordingly, he never paid any attention to Quetelet's exaltation of the average man, but insisted always on the need for statistics to study the sources of variation.

Ironically, it was Quetelet who provided Galton with the principal tools for this investigation, by showing how the error curve – later dubbed the normal law, and now known to everyone as the bell-shaped curve – could be used to study variation. The conceptual importance of this shift is discussed in chapter 4. That discovery was the culmination of Quetelet's social physics, of the desire that had obsessed him ever since 1823 when he traveled to Paris to become an astronomer and returned a statistical enthusiast. This formula

$$(1/\sqrt{2\pi}) \, \exp \, (-x^2/2)$$

had been invented by De Moivre and applied by Laplace to statistical matters, but was best known after Gauss as the law governing the distri-

bution of errors from true values in astronomical and geodetic observations (see 3.3). Social physics had not accomplished very much, and
application of the astronomer's error law to human variation might vin-
dicate the project. Moreover, Quetelet had always idealized the mean as
the point of virtue lying between vicious extremes, and the embodiment
of moderation in a world forever threatened by revolution. Already in
the early 1830s he had discussed the average man as the type of a nation,
in comparison to whom all real individuals are flawed. His determination
in 1844 that human variation was governed by the error law confirmed
this analysis. It showed that the average man really was the type of nature,
just as the mean of astronomical observations really is (approximately)
the true position of the star. Quetelet had already been inclined to reify
the statistical concept of the average man. With this ostensible mathematical demonstration that deviations from the average are indistinguishable from error, he thought, the reality of the average man as a
social type could no longer be doubted. Actual individuals are mere imperfect copies of the virtuous golden mean.

The most extravagant formulation of this conception, though one
consistent with everything Quetelet wrote on the average man and the
error law, appeared in his *Letters on Probability* of 1846. Suppose, he instructed the monarch to whom these letters were formally addressed, that
one wished to make a thousand copies of a statue, say the Gladiator. Like
astronomical observations of a single object, these copies would be subject to a variety of errors – in measuring the various dimensions, in
workmanship, and so on. The independent errors are like terms of a
binomial, and combine in a characteristic fashion. Hence the variation
among the copies would be governed by a profound regularity, the error
law, or normal curve, with the dimensions of the original Gladiator at the
mean. But this is an impossible experiment: how did Quetelet know what
the result would be? "I shall perhaps astonish you very much by stating
that the experiment has been already made. Yes, surely, more than a
thousand copies have been measured of a statue, which I do not assert to
be that of the Gladiator, but which in all cases differs little from it. These
copies were even living ones. . ." (1846, p. 136). They were in fact
measurements of the chests of some Scottish soldiers, governed
almost perfectly, Quetelet thought, by the normal curve. Later he un-
covered some minor but systematic fraud in the induction of French
soldiers by showing that there was a considerable departure from normality
in the distribution of heights just at the point where young men are ex-
empted from conscription because of their shortness. He believed, in any

event, that each individual is an imperfect replica of a prototype, which is *l'homme moyen*.

For Quetelet, the error law proved that variation was mere perturbation. Galton, though his reasons were opposite to Quetelet's, was no less impressed by it. Already in 1869 he applied it to numerous human traits that could not be measured directly, such as ability in music or mathematics, and achievement as a wrestler, jurist, or divine. In *Natural Inheritance* he called the error curve "the supreme law of Unreason," proposing that it "would have been personified by the Greeks and deified, if they had known of it" (1889, p. 66). Galton used the error law to give an economical expression of the variability in a population. For him, it provided a way to get beyond mean values, not to exalt them. Those who stop their inquiries at averages have souls "as dull to the charm of variety as that of a native of one of our flat English counties, whose retrospect of Switzerland was that, if its mountains could be thrown into its lakes, two nuisances would be got rid of at once" (1889, p. 62). Galton wished particularly to understand the hereditary sources of genius, of great achievement in mathematics, science, statesmanship, law, and religion. Having shown in *Hereditary Genius* that these things tend to run in families, he began in the early 1870s to seek the actual laws by which variation was transmitted from parents to offspring.

He made use of the astronomer's error curve from the beginning. He learned of it from a friend in geography, William Spottiswoode, who had sought to apply Quetelet's analysis as a criterion of unity of type in a series of mountain ranges (1861). Galton invoked it in *Hereditary Genius* to illustrate that "the rarity of commanding ability, and the vast abundance of mediocrity, is no accident, but follows of necessity, from the very nature of these things" (1869, p. 35). But he was there able to do scarcely more than assert its sovereignty over mental as well as physical traits; he did not use it to learn anything new. The key insight that enabled him to employ the mathematics of probability in studying hereditary transmission came from his cousin, Charles Darwin. Eugenics, of course, was dependent on Darwinism, even if some analogy between selective agricultural breeding and the results of human mating had long been recognized. It was, however, Darwin's "provisional hypothesis of Pangenesis," first published in 1868, that provided Galton with an appropriate statistical model (Darwin, 1868, chapter 27).

Galton's reliance on analogies was extreme, but is exemplary rather than uncharacteristic of the diffusion of statistical ideas in the nineteenth century. Apart from error theory, the most important uses of statistics in this period were to model phenomena, and not just to draw inferences about them. The prototype of statistical reasoning from Quetelet's time to that of Maxwell and Galton was social statistics, and the recognition of analogies between some given field and social science was enormously helpful, if not indispensable, to the application of statistical models. Maxwell, Galton, and Francis Edgeworth all displayed remarkable analogical imaginations, and in Galton's case analogy often served as a substitute for explanation. Although this may seem a defect of Galton's approach, these similes were intrinsic to his creativity, which was considerable, and to his notable achievements in the domain of statistical mathematics.

In Darwin's version of Pangenesis, the ultimate constituents of reproduction were gemmules, tiny particles produced by budding from every part of the body, and transmitted to offspring in equal parts by each parent. Many would remain there latent, but some would form themselves into an embryo by a process of "elective attractions." Galton dismissed the budding of gemmules from somatic tissues, and the inheritance of acquired characteristics that it would imply, but he was much impressed by the idea of an embryo forming spontaneously from a host of autonomous gemmules. This was just like the formation of towns or the election of delegates to a parliamentary body. In an appendix to *Hereditary Genius*, clearly inspired by Darwin's publication of a year earlier, Galton provided an elaborate simile, explaining how each of the main phenomena of biological heredity could be identified with some electoral or social process (Galton, 1869, appendix). The gemmules transmitted from parents to offspring provided a statistically accurate representation of those possessed by the parents. The biological type of any given individual would generally be determined by a plurality of gemmules, as in a British parliamentary election. The process by which gemmules formed into an embryo was like the growth of towns of distinct types, due entirely to the elective affinities of the individuals who choose to settle there. But the transmission of gemmules from parents to offspring and, with some qualifications, the selection of those to form the embryo, was like a series of urn drawings, the classic model for probability calculations.

These similes, Galton stressed, were not mere literary extravagances, but precise and accurate analogies. As such, they could facilitate the application of the characteristic form of social mathematics – statistics – to the study of heredity, and though Pangenesis was stillborn so far as most biologists were concerned, the statisticians Galton and Pearson continued to invoke it through the end of the century. The relation of Pangenesis to statistics, to be sure, was not unproblematical; the simplest probabilistic mathematics presupposed statistical independence, and there was good reason to suppose some "correlations" in the placement of gemmules. That is, an individual might have her father's nose, or be of the "Irish type," suggesting that gemmules tended to some extent to be inherited in clusters. This was one reason the statistical problem of heredity was not an easy one. Conversely, it is the reason Galton's results were not just of biological interest, but had also great importance for statistical mathematics. Old methods applied to new problems often yield new results, and this was the principal mechanism by which statistics progressed in the nineteenth century. To a considerable extent, it is true also of the twentieth.

Galton's method of correlation made its initial appearance in 1877 as a law of reversion, the result of some experiments on inheritance of size in peas. He had initially supposed that the mean of offspring would equal that of their parents, though once experience proved otherwise he quickly realized this would be incompatible with a stable size distribution, since variability within each family tended always to broaden the distribution. Evidently the latent gemmules transmitted from more remote progenitors tended to move the offspring back towards the population mean. Galton invented the elementary mathematics of correlation as the statistical law governing what he called "reversion" to ancestral forms. It involved a law of the form $y = rx$, where y is the average divergence of offspring from the mean for the population, x the divergence of the parents, and r a constant, between zero and one. The variation exhibited by a generation of offspring could be divided into two parts: some was due to the (partial) perpetuation of the variation present in the parental generation, and there was also some variation that would appear among the offspring even if the parents were all identical. This subdivision of biological variation was governed by mathematical relationships that Galton initially envisioned as laws of heredity, expressing the tendency for offspring to revert back towards ancestral forms. Galton's statistical mathematics was, in this sense, like the "mixed mathematics" of the classical probabilists (see 1.3).

By the mid-1880s Galton had decided that this convergence to the mean reflected something more fundamental than reversion. Evolution, he now believed, is discontinuous, because the affinities among gemmules render each organic type stable. Unless a new point of stability is approached, the force of biological correlations will tend always to replace exceptional gemmules with those more characteristic of the type. The mathematical sign of organic stability was the error law, and Galton, notwithstanding his disdain for mediocrity, gave in to Quetelet's interpretation: the average really is the type of a race (see 4.4). Convergence to it is better called regression, which here implied no more than convergence to the mean, rather than reversion, which in the contemporary biological vocabulary denoted a return to more remote ancestors.

Social statistics intruded once again to provide Galton with a viable formulation of the problem of biological correlation, the tendency, made famous by Cuvier, for certain traits to appear together in an individual or species. The French criminologist Alphonse Bertillon had recently taken up classifying criminals according to four measurements: height, and length of finger, arm, and foot. Galton, who had spent much of the 1880s collecting anthropometric data, knew that these measurements would be "entangled" (in the language of error theory), that long arms would tend to accompany exceptional stature, and so on. When he began plotting height against left cubit, in order to determine the nature of this entanglement, he realized that the mathematics of the relationship was the same as that of regression. Here was a mathematical solution to the problem of biological correlation (Galton, 1890, p. 421).

But it was more than that. Galton was already convinced that his statistical methods had applications far more extensive than the problems for which they had been designed. The statistical part of *Natural Inheritance*, he wrote, "may be said to run along a road on a high level, that affords wide views in unexpected directions, and from which easy descents may be made to totally different goals to those we have now to reach. I have a great subject to write upon" (1889, p. 3). Correlation, he realized, was not just a biological principle, but a method of assessing the interrelations between any variables at all. And he was not alone in thinking this. By 1889, users of statistics in a great variety of fields had become discontent with the mere presentation of numerical facts, and were looking for more refined methods of analysis. Galton's method of correlation was quickly taken up in anthropometry, in sociology, in economics, in psychology, and in studies of education. It, and more generally the methods in *Natural Inheritance*, provided also the inspiration for the founding of a mathematical statistics, closely related to biometry but standing above any particular application.

Population biology continued to provide the most important field within which statistical methods were developed in the early twentieth century. Karl Pearson, like Galton, was deeply committed to attaining the knowledge of human genetics and evolution necessary for a scientifically informed eugenics. R. A. Fisher, too, took up statistics because of an early concern with eugenics, and the conceptual gap between eugenics and agriculture, where he did his most important statistical work, was easily crossed. But Pearson had already taken up Galton's challenge, to develop a mathematical statistics that stood above any particular application. Not that Pearson sought a pure mathematics of statistics. The virtue of formulating the truths of statistics more abstractly and mathematically was not that it provided access to a higher realm of pure number, but that it gave one's methods the generality and power to confront a wide range of scientific and practical problems.

This constant attention to applications accounts in part for Pearson's success, where Francis Edgeworth never won much of a statistical following. Edgeworth, though an economist, kept his economics and his statistics mostly separate. But Pearson, even when he wrote on abstract topics such as probability distributions or methods of separating compounded curves (see Pearson, 1948), included concrete examples, often many of them, applying these new methods or assumptions to problems in psychology, education, meteorology, insurance, and anthropometry, as well as biometry. Moreover, he set up a laboratory, to which he attracted students from a variety of disciplines and industrial applications and from all over the world (see 3.7). Pearson himself was devoted not just to eugenics, but to a vast augmentation of the public role of scientific experts, and the principal tool of these heroes of Pearson's version of scientific socialism were to be the statisticians (see MacKenzie, 1981). The wide influence that suddenly came to be exerted by mathematical statistics in the early decades of the twentieth century reflected the vast energy and ability Pearson devoted to precisely this goal.

2.6 THE STATISTICAL CRITIQUE OF DETERMINISM

The willingness of biologists and social scientists to make increasing use of statistical ideas and methods would appear to be among the most reliable indicators of an emerging indeterminism in science, and there is some truth in these appearances. Karl Pearson, who for institutional as well as intellectual reasons should be seen as the founder of mathematical statistics, argued that statistical knowledge is the best that is accessible to us, and that to believe in complete causality is no better than an act of faith (Pearson, 1911, p. 173). But Pearson's statement is more nearly one of positivism than of indeterminism, and probability has continued to be interpreted by many social and biological scientists in classical terms, as a consequence of the imperfection of knowledge. Even in quantum physics, where chance applies to the most elementary reactions and particles known, some scientists have avoided indeterminism by invoking causation at a still lower level. Whether biologists or psychologists choose to endorse indeterminism is probably less important than their frequent willingness to rest content with probabilistic explanations rather than seeking to pursue causality in the details.

The reason for this is reasonably clear. Science is the business of producing knowledge. It is well enough to admit that our knowledge is and will always be imperfect, but to attribute some particular phenomenon to pure chance comes close to denying that anything useful will ever be known about its causes. This is not the kind of proposition that researchers find attractive. In most fields they have learned to value statistical knowledge, but they value it as knowledge, not as evidence of its limitations, and it is usually possible to believe that further research will more narrowly circumscribe the domain of ignorance. In fields such as particle physics where chance is generally seen as fundamental, it appears in the form of well-defined, stable probabilities, that can be used to predict the results of other interactions. Of evolutionary biology, where chance figures on a slightly less fundamental level, the same may be said. "The effects of chance," wrote R. A. Fisher, "are the most accurately calculable, and therefore the least doubtful, of all the factors in an evolutionary situation" (Fisher, 1953, p. 515). Even random genetic drift, whose importance Fisher denied, is a concept used to explain certain aspects of evolutionary change, and not to deny the possibility of explanation (see 4.5).

In short, the recognition within science of a role for chance in the world was a byproduct of what Ian Hacking refers to as its taming (Hacking, forthcoming). The meaning and associations of chance had in fact changed dramatically during the nineteenth century, largely as a result of the apparent success of social statistics, complemented by new developments in other sciences concerned with life and mind. Chance had traditionally been associated with fate, as in the casting of lots, but by the eighteenth century was more often identified with an absence (always disproven) of divine planning or control. Thus Arbuthnot viewed his demonstration that the excess of male over female births was real as a vindication of providence over blind chance. William Paley, conversely, allowed in his natural theology that, notwithstanding the compelling evidence in nature of design, minor irregularities such as warts might be due to mere chance (see 4.3). This did not mean they had no cause at all, but only that they were not the direct expression of providential intent. As late as the 1830s, Augustus De Morgan felt obliged to refute the claim that probability was inconsistent with providence by explaining how the rules of probability presupposed a certain stability and order in the world. Were the world really governed by chance, past experience would furnish no basis for assessing future probabilities (De Morgan, 1832). For De Morgan, as for Laplace, chance was an epiphenomenon of human limitations, a reflection of imperfect knowledge. It was not counterposed to determinism.

Until the mid-nineteenth century, determinism had been debated mainly as a theory of the will, the denial of metaphysical freedom, and rarely in connection with the theories of natural science (Hacking, 1983). Determinism in nature was rarely at issue, aside from the analogous problem of God's ability to intervene in the world. As we note in section 4.2, determinism was challenged by a few vitalists in the early nineteenth century, but natural philosophers from Newton to Laplace and later generally took it for granted. Developments in scientific thinking during the nineteenth century broadened the meaning of determinism, and increased the urgency of the issue. The heart of the problem was the new proficiency and aggressiveness of studies of life, mind, and society. The crux of determinism in the late nineteenth century was still the denial of freedom of the will, but whereas the determinist of 1800 would usually emphasize psychological forces – the strength of passions and habits – the determinist of 1860 or 1870 had a new repertoire of arguments to supplement, or replace, these. Phrenology had emphasized the connection between mind and matter, as did studies of nerves and brain physiology by the likes of Emil Du Bois-Reymond and Henry Maudsley. Darwinian evolution reaffirmed the connection between thought and brain, as it established conclusively the tie between man and animals. Helmholtz's principle of energy conservation, inspired in part by opposition to vitalism, became part of every argument against free will. Finally, the possible inconsistency of statistics with free will was widely bruited for two decades following Buckle's grandiloquent presentation of the regularities of crime and suicide in 1857.

The new determinism was mainly a doctrine about the material universe, which was held to embrace mind as well as body. That situation evoked a new indeterminism, in which the complete determination of events by physical laws was challenged. Religious physicists and philosophers were pioneers in this – Joseph Boussinesq and others in France,

James Clerk Maxwell in Britain (Nye, 1976). Maxwell in particular emphasized that since the physical world is made up of molecules, our knowledge of it is statistical in character (see 5.6). It is noteworthy that he conceived the kinetic gas theory in terms of an analogy with social statistics, and even compared the laws of gases and of the diffusion of heat with the uniformities of crime and suicide. "The modern atomists," he wrote, have "adopted a method which is, I believe, new in the department of mathematical physics, though it has long been in use in the section of Statistics. . . The data of the statistical method as applied to molecular science are the sums of large numbers of molecular quantities. In studying the relations between quantities of this kind, we meet with a new kind of regularity, the regularity of averages. . ." (1873b, pp. 373–4). Ludwig Boltzmann made the same point: "As is well-known, Buckle demonstrated statistically that if only a sufficient number of people is taken into account, then not only is the number of natural events like death, illness, etc. perfectly constant, but also the number of so-called voluntary actions – marriages at a given age, crimes, and suicides. It occurs no differently among molecules" ([1886] 1905, p. 34).

The style of reasoning that we call statistical, involving collective regularities and frequencies rather than close attention to the causes of individual events, derived mainly from social science, and this influence is evident even in physics. The social statisticians had provided the kinetic gas theory with its most important mathematical tool, the error curve, which of course had been worked out in the context of gambling problems and error theory, but was first conceived as applicable to real variation by Quetelet. Charles Gillispie and others have now made it clear that Maxwell's derivation of the error curve in 1860 was based on an important long review of Quetelet's *Letters on Probabilty* by John Herschel (Gillispie, 1963; Brush, 1976; Porter, 1981). The appreciation of statistical uncertainty within physics also owed clearly to work in the tradition of social numbers. Maxwell's letters in the late 1850s, and his published writings beginning a decade later on problems such as the relation of science to free will, indicate a serious concern with Buckle's statistical arguments against free will. With the incentive of this offense to his ideas about morality and personal responsibility, he began to argue that most of our knowledge of actual occurrences in the world, even physical ones, is statistical in character. To him this meant, although statisticians had generally evaded the point, that knowledge is imperfect and hence that declarations against free will cannot be justified on the basis of physics (1873a).

This was a remarkable shift of perspective, since statistics had almost always been identified, at least by its supporters, with scientific certainty. But social statistics could by this time provide models of fluctuations and uncertainty as well. Joseph Thirion, who, with Joseph Delsaulx, first connected Brownian motion with the kinetic gas theory, argued in an 1880 article on the subject: "It is thus that statistics reveals more and more the inconstancy and the irregularity of much of social phenomena, when in lieu of applying it to a great nation altogether, one descends to a province, a town, a village. It should then be sufficient to isolate portions of smaller and smaller surfaces of evaporation or of pressure, in order to arrive finally at dimensions incapable of assuring compensations of irregularities. . ." (quoted in Nye, 1972, p. 25). Maxwell and Thirion were among the first physicists to recognize the limitations of statistical knowledge. They, along with contemporary social thinkers, provided the concepts that by the end of the century had made it routine to identify statistical neglect of detail with an incompleteness of explanation, within which factors quite unknown might operate. To defend free will was not, of course, to insist on the operation of pure chance. Most thinkers still saw objective chance as virtually unthinkable, and few were prepared to identify the rational will with it. But at least the connotations of chance had changed. Previously it had seemed impious to allow chance a role in the world, as if God did not attend to every sparrow. Now chance stood for the incompleteness of mechanical law, for the possibility of non-material causation.

Maxwell's interest in indeterminism grew out of concerns about free will, the old meaning of indeterminism. He argued that we cannot know the causes of molecular motions in much detail. This space of ignorance he used to provide room for an active will. Where mechanical causality is incomplete, as it can be in cases of physical instability, the mind can enter as a cause and determine which possible course will be the actual one. The determination of the mind is not itself uncaused, but only free from complete mechanical causation. Maxwell never said there is chance in the operation of mind, nor did he assign any importance to pure chance in sciences such as thermodynamics. Still, his rejection of complete mechanical causality in physics was a radical probabilistic move. The indeterminism in mechanics that he proposed to provide space within which the will could act implied a possibility of real indeterminism whenever a mechanical system reaches a point of instability. It was thus quite general in its implications.

A related and no less important issue for discussion of determinism was the relation between mechanics and history. That was one of the main concerns of Maxwell's most illustrious fellow kinetic theorist, Ludwig Boltzmann, who devoted his career to the reduction of thermodynamics to mechanics, and struggled for decades to reconcile the directionality of time, implicit in the second law of thermodynamics, with the time-reversibility of classical mechanics (see 5.7). Essentially the same issue was being discussed at the same time in social science and philosophy. Gustav Rümelin, in a late essay on laws of history (1881), reflected that two decades of intensive research had yielded nothing that could properly be called a social law. This, he decided, was in retrospect unsurprising, for psychical phenomena are wholly unlike physical, and there is no reason to think the same concept of law applies to each. The difference is that the mind is free. Wilhelm Wundt, similarly, emphasized the relation between intentionality and directionality in arguing for a category of psychical causality that is nondeterministic (see Wise, 1987). Rümelin and Wundt were not so much breaking with tradition as working out the implications of what by then was almost a commonplace in Germany, that nature was the realm of causal law, and history the domain of freedom.

Charles Bernard Renouvier, who defended human freedom (or "indeterminism") in France, was similarly convinced that history is the result of free individual decisions, and not of great historical laws. This was a natural response to St. Simonian and Comtean arguments, and not particularly original in the 1850s, when Renouvier began arguing this way. What was original was his enlistment of probability in the defense of freedom. His willingness to associate freedom with chance was itself surprising, particularly for an admirer of Kant, though he made clear that the two differed, since freedom required moral deliberation as well as the absence of law. His identification of probability with absence of causation is yet more remarkable, and is presented so guilelessly that one wonders how aware he was of the contemporary understanding of probability. Even in the age of statistical frequencies, probability was associated with imperfect knowledge rather than pure chance, and Laplace's idea that perfect knowledge would permit perfect prediction remained influential throughout the century. But Renouvier did, in a sense, have a predecessor – Auguste Comte, who argued that mathematical probability is incoherent, since it presupposes that some events occur for no reason. Renouvier, who fell under the influence of Comte while at the Ecole Polytechnique, viewed this proposition from the other side: since the events of moral statistics conform well to the rules of probability, there is good reason to think they are genuinely indeterministic. The law of large numbers is a splendid exemplar of the compatibility between individual freedom and social order (Renouvier, 1854–64, vol. 1, p. 329; vol. 2, pp. 146, 341). History was even more central to the defense of liberty published in 1882 by Joseph Delboeuf. Determinism rests on an equality between cause and effect, he maintained, but even thermodynamics shows that nature moves in a preferred direction, since heat never flows from cold to warm bodies. The whole of biology attests to the same principle; growth and development occur always in the same direction, and one never sees oak trees shrink down to acorns, then leap up to a neighboring branch. Human freedom is possible too. It can act by choosing the right moment at which to transform the potential energy accumulated in an organism into work (Delboeuf, 1882, p. 156). Ludwig Boltzmann, as we show in chapter 5, also struggled with the relationship between history and mechanics, though his aim was always to expand the domain of mechanical explanation, not to show its limitations. But there was no way to get directional change in time from the reversible laws of mechanics, and Boltzmann was compelled in the end to admit that there must have been something special in the initial conditions of the world to permit the regular and lawlike diffusion of energy embodied in the second law of thermodynamics.

Charles Sanders Peirce, the most systematic proponent of indeterminism in the nineteenth century, based his first argument against mechanical determinism, in 1887, on this same principle, the directionality of time. But his perspective was much wider than those of Delboeuf, Renouvier, and Rümelin. A product of Cambridge, Massachusetts, and its distinctive traditions, his introduction to probability came in the form of the method of least squares, to which his father, the noted astronomer, had contributed. He was well informed about the French writings just mentioned, which were also admired by his friend William James. Peirce's interest in physics extended to thermodynamics, and he frequently invoked Clausius and Maxwell – though not Boltzmann – to illustrate the role of chance in the physical world.

It was, however, biological evolution, and its Spencerian extensions, that were most central to Peirce's probabilistic viewpoint. By the end of the nineteenth century, Darwinism had become highly prominent as a model for other sciences. In some ways it can be seen as a rival and alternative to physics, and historians have often treated it as such. There are particularly good reasons to assign Darwin an important role in the probabilistic revolution. Not just Peirce, but also Galton, used biological evolution as the basis for an important advance in statistical thinking. The crucial idea that both derived from Darwin was the importance of variation. That was no hidden presupposition of evolution by natural selection, but a critical element in Darwin's theory, and clearly recognized as such. Perhaps Darwin himself should be seen as the pathbreaker in the development of modern statistical thought, and Galton, Pearson, and Peirce merely disciples, working out the implications of his ideas.

But it would be misleading to argue this way. These "implications" of Darwin's approach were not initially perceived, and their eventual recognition was dependent on new problems and new intellectual contexts as well as the Darwinian model itself. This is not to deny that Darwin was a "population thinker." A species for him was no type, no timeless metaphysical form. His theory implied that differences between species are continuous with varieties, and with individual variation. He even performed a numerical analysis of the frequencies of varieties in an effort to establish that varieties are incipient species (see Parshall, 1982; also Browne, 1983, chapter 8). Probability rarely entered his analysis, and then always in the classical sense, as a property of our imperfect knowledge, and not as a characteristic of the workings of nature. Indeed, Darwin scarcely even made use of what we may call statistical reasoning. In the theory of natural selection, nondirectional variation leads to progressive evolution as a result of the struggle for existence, but Darwin treated the process of natural selection as practically analogous to artificial selection, where the best individuals are always chosen – except that it is yet more subtle and refined. Darwin could hardly have been unaware that extraneous circumstances will sometimes lead to the death of an ostensibly fit individual, but there is nothing about this in the *Origin*. A statistical thinker might have said that these peculiarities will average out over a large population, or in the long run, but the only effect of large numbers in Darwin's theory is to increase the rate of production of favorable (as well as unfavorable) variations. Both the general theory of evolution by natural selection and the hypothesis of Pangenesis provided excellent frameworks for statistical investigation, but Darwin himself made use of statistical thought only occasionally. He never took advantage of the statisticians' view that what appears as chance in the individual can be dissolved into the large regularities governing the collective.

Darwin's neglect of statistics is the more surprising in that the nineteenth-century faith in statistical regularity could have supported an argument that was important to him – that evolution is not fortuitous after all, that the role of chance in it is at most vanishingly small. Chance was one of Darwin's greatest problems. Almost from the time he conceived his theory, he was troubled by his inability to explain the variation that provided the essential material upon which selection acted. He always insisted that variation was not really the product of chance, except in the biological sense discussed in chapter 4: that its direction was quite independent of adaptation – of what contemporaries misunderstood as teleological purpose. He regretted that the causes of variation were imperfectly understood, and offered a number of mechanisms in the *Origin* that might account for it. But the problem did not go away, and the next year he wrote to Asa Gray that "small trifling peculiarities of structure often make me very uncomfortable. The sight of a feather in a peacock's tail, whenever I gaze at it, makes me sick" (quoted in Young, 1985, p. 116). John Herschel was said to have called his theory "the law of higgledy-piggledy" (see Hull, 1973, p. 61), and in 1861 Huxley lamented to Joseph Hooker that because "no law has yet been made out, Darwin is obliged to speak of variation as if it were spontaneous or a matter of chance" (L. Huxley, 1901, vol. 1, p. 245).

We cannot say, as we did of statistics, that the probabilistic implications of Darwinism were at first unperceived. But they were denied, and the imputation that the theory of evolution depended on chance was seen as a criticism of it. The American pragmatists, and Peirce in particular, treated this connection quite differently. Peirce, it should be said, was no fan of Darwin's. Like Marx, he saw the theory of natural selection as the ideal of greedy capitalism written into nature, and he preferred a more Lamarckian kind of evolution. Still, Peirce's Lamarckism, unlike Lamarck's, depended on random variation of a Darwinian sort. And while Darwin sought always to explain it away, Peirce and James applauded chance as evidence that there was a degree of decentralized spontaneity in the universe. The existence of chance, along with a mechanism for its fixation, provided also for progress in the world – unlike mechanics, which was static and timeless. Peirce made this same process responsible for cosmic evolution, for biological evolution, and for the development and refinement of consciousness.

Once convinced of the reality and importance of chance in the world, Peirce had no trouble showing that the available arguments for determinism were hollow (Peirce, 1892). In particular, there was no reason the scientist must be a determinist. Even the most exact of the sciences, astronomy, had found that its measurements were subject to a certain degree of random variation. It was quite possible to produce excellent scientific results even where chance relationships obtain. The kinetic gas theory, which Peirce also frequently invoked, shows this no less clearly. Chance was no enemy of science, but its tool. The methods of probability are associated in practice more closely with an increase in knowledge than with its limitations.

2.7 CONCLUSION

Both the indeterminism of Peirce and the new methods of Lexis and Galton reflected the importance of the study of variation for the development of statistical thinking. It was characteristic of the last two-thirds of the nineteenth century that the most important contributions to statistical theory came from fields in which statistics was used to model variation, not just to estimate or reduce error. The quantitative study of diversity presented problems of a quite different character from what science had done before. The partial but significant success that was achieved in dealing with them had important implications for a wide range of studies. The new mathematical field of statistics that arose as the culmination of these efforts has proven enormously fruitful for inferential purposes as well as for statistical modeling.

From one standpoint, some appreciation of diversity was essential if science was not to find whole areas of experience almost entirely closed to it. But this experience, and the desire to understand it, had cultural roots as well. Recognition of the importance of variation was inseparable from a heightened individualism, which by 1830 reflected both liberal and romantic sources. Liberal faith in progress gave reason to tolerate and even to applaud the exceptional, though this was tempered by a certain fear of instability. Concern about the stifling effects of mass society, expressed most memorably by Tocqueville, Mill, and Burckhardt, reinforced this consciousness of the worth of individuality. Classical political economy and Darwinian evolution both reflected and contributed to it.

Statistics, as a numerical science of society, was from the beginning a part of ninetenth-century liberalism. But liberalism was no monolithic entity. To count each individual for one had hardly been possible in old-regime societies of estates and orders. But centralizing monarchs, assisted by bureaucracies, pursued precisely this flattening of the social landscape that straightforward enumeration implied, even if they were inclined to view the information obtained as a state secret. This bureaucratic impulse was still strong in nineteenth-century statistics, and indeed remains so. It was perhaps most perfectly exemplified by Quetelet's idealization of the average, implying a lack of interest in individuality and an antagonism to diversity. The more individualistic strands of liberalism were somewhat harder to reconcile with a statistical outlook, though they did contribute to an appreciation of the importance of diversity for historical progress. This esteem for variation, however, was developed most fully within a scheme that combined faith in progress with a conservative-tending organicism, or perhaps a hierarchical socialism.

The development of statistical thinking in the nineteenth century thus reflected a mix of social and political views. Its interpretations capture much of the ambiguity of "liberalism" in this dynamic century. Even in 1900, after the successful application of statistical reasoning to physics and biology, and the beginnings of a mathematical field of statistics, the term still referred first of all to social numbers, and only by analogy to this branch of applied mathematics. To use statistical techniques in the nineteenth century was still to benefit from an analogy between the explicit object of study and the problems of social science. But after 1900 the status of statistics changed radically, perhaps even more radically than did its mathematics. With Karl Pearson, and then R. A. Fisher, statistics became a branch of applied mathematics, viewed by them and by a rapidly increasing number of people in science, business, and government as a tool created by mathematicians for providing quantitative solutions to scientific and practical problems. Although the diffusion of statistics to new fields is as important a theme in the twentieth century as in the nineteenth, the haphazard character of the influences surveyed in this chapter gave way to a firm structure of authority, as users of statistics increasingly looked to mathematicians for ways to collect observations or set up experiments and to analyze the resulting data. In consequence, the mathematical statistician has become a universal expert, whose specialty is not so much a subject matter as a method of inference applicable to all subject matters.

This . . . overflow of statistical techniques from the quiet backwaters of theoretical methodology . . . into the working parts of going concerns of the largest size, suggests that hidden causes have been at work . . . , preparing men's minds, and shaping the institutions through which they work . . .

Ronald A. Fisher (1953)

3

◁ ═══ ▷

The inference experts

3.1 IN WANT OF A "SYSTEM OF MEAN RESULTS"

The British agriculturist James F. W. Johnston wrote in 1849: "As yet we do not possess any . . . system of mean results, though few things would at present do more to clear up our ideas as to the precise influence of this or that substance on the growth of plants" (Johnston, 1849, p. 59). Johnston came from a long tradition of writers who had discussed and developed ideas on how experiments in agriculture should be performed and their results interpreted (Cochran, 1976). The experiments addressed practical questions. Which of these fertilizers is better? What crop rotation system works best for this region? What strain of potatoes gives the highest dry yield? These could be matters of great economic importance for the individual farmer, or the landed gentry, or the prosperity of the whole nation. They were too serious to be left to the haphazard initiative of private individuals, and conclusive findings were only to be expected when the experiences of many were combined and compared. The agricultural societies that began to be founded in the eighteenth century sometimes gave prizes for the best conducted and best reported agricultural experiments. Johnston was a chemist to one such society, reflecting a trend towards rationalizing agriculture beginning in the late eighteenth century (Krohn and Schäfer, 1976).

Science, however, did not provide him with the tools he needed to solve his problem. In the physical sciences, until recently, the opinion

70

reigned that a well designed and performed experiment is one whose data do not need interpretation and statistical analysis. An experiment should be a well posed question by which nature is forced to yield an unambiguous answer, one that is obvious upon cursory inspection of the data. But the experience of practical men like Johnston showed that a glance at the results would not suffice to interpret experiments with naturally occurring objects and processes, as in medicine, biology, meteorology, and agriculture. In physics, one could experiment on purified substances and with practically complete control of all conditions that theory had deemed causally relevant. The nature of the subject matter defeated similar strategies in the sciences of life. No effort sufficed to bring all sources of variation under control; data always showed differences arising from causes in which the experimenter was not interested (see also 4.2). Such variation could mask the effects of the agencies under investigation. And even if completely controlled experiments could be performed, it might not be possible to apply the causal knowledge thus obtained to the buzzing variation in naturally occurring populations. The sciences that concern themselves with the natural world are stuck with its variability.

How, then, should one set up an experiment? Johnston made insightful remarks about the case of agriculture, but he did not have a theory of experimental design and, as the introductory quotation shows, he was at a loss as to what to make of the experimental outcomes. Since his questions were comparative ones (sometimes just whether applying this substance as a fertilizer makes a difference) Johnston realized that all experiments should be comparative:

If the effect of a certain influence . . . is to be ascertained, that effect must be compared with what is seen upon another spot to which this manure has not been applied. But to ascertain the precise effects of this one influence, every other influence likely to modify it must be excluded. This is a requirement of vital importance – one exceedingly difficult to be attained; which requires attention to many circumstances, which has been frequently neglected and which has not only led to very discordant results in different places, but has greatly lessened the value of nearly all the field experiments that have hitherto been published (Johnston, 1849, pp. 45–6).

It turned out to be impossible to exclude all the other influences, and plots treated alike showed considerable variation. But if this is so, "in what ways are the results of the two or more experiments we may make to be regarded? Are we to take the mean or average result of the whole, and to consider this as an expression of the absolute natural productiveness of the land where nothing is applied to it, or of the absolute effect of this or that substance which we have laid on? Or are the results of the several experiments of each kind to be compared each with each, and the absolute effects to be deduced according to some other method?" (Johnston, 1849, p. 52). For instance, in an experiment on the effect of a fertilizer, three plots without it gave yields of 18, 21 and 24 bushels of grain (average 21), while a fertilized plot yielded 24 bushels. How are we to compare these results? Nothing could be made of them, he believed.

Johnston apparently realized that the variability of plots treated alike, and the overlap of yields from plots treated differently, should affect the confidence with which one can draw a conclusion. For instance, having noticed that turnips naturally show up to 25% variation from plot to plot, he argued that if a proposed fertilizer gives only 10% more turnips, this is not indicative of a real improvement because it could as well be due to natural variation. However, Johnston did not realize that the 25% variability from plot to plot becomes less and less important as the number of plots on which an average is based increases. This lack of understanding of "sample size" – the number of plots in a fertilizer trial, the number of patients treated to a possibly healthy stay at a sea resort, etc. – was quite common among those in the nineteenth century who only compared mean values to make judgments about the effectiveness of treatments. Similarly, his phrase, a "method of means," reflects the early nineteenth-century concentration on averages, with a neglect of the variation of a series of results. In this respect he is similar to Quetelet with his *l'homme moyen* (see 2.2).

Several themes are intertwined in Johnston's problem: causality, public demonstration, and action. Is a certain manure causally effective in increasing the yield of a particular crop? Under what conditions – that is, with respect to what "population" of circumstances? To what extent? What system of mean results can publicly and objectively show that it is so, removing the answer from mere opinion? Or, short of this, what objective measures can be developed to measure how concordant or discordant data are with particular hypotheses about a treatment's effectiveness? When can we act and advise our farmers to use the fertilizer? These themes, plus the methods that have been proposed to answer them, recur in one form or another throughout this chapter.

3.2 ANALYSIS OF VARIANCE

By the 1930s, one solution to Johnston's problem had been formulated. The main architect of the new theory of experimental design and analysis was the Englishman Ronald A. Fisher (1890–1962), who was then chief statistician at the agricultural experimental station in Rothamsted. Fisher's solution is called the "analysis of variance," a name that stresses the need to partition the variation into different components, ascribable to different groups of causes (one of them called "error"), to ascertain whether a difference in means between treated population and controls indicates the causal efficacy of the treatment. Fisher, to be sure, stood on the shoulders of many predecessors. In fact, the simple experimental design and analysis we will be discussing in this section was known before Fisher, to W. S. Gosset of the Guinness brewery in Dublin, who used the name "Student" in his publications on the analysis of experimental data. Fisher's analysis of variance is part of an experimental methodology that tries to answer two sorts of questions in regard to problems like Johnston's: first, is the manure effective? and also (a more complicated question) to what extent is it effective? The second question includes the first and is obviously, to a farmer, the critical one; if the manure only slightly improves the crop, it may not be worth the expense. The central statistical tools for answering the first question are so-called *tests of significance*; and for the second, *interval estimation methods* (which, from a purely mathematical point of view, are closely related to tests of significance). In this chapter we will concentrate on tests of significance, since this simpler technique has been used more extensively. How would a problem like Johnston's be solved along Fisherian lines?

Johnston thought that he could not derive any reliable conclusions from the experiment in which three plots without manure gave yields of 18, 21, and 24 bushels of grain (average 21), while the manured plot yielded 24 bushels. Fisher would have agreed. The experiment performed was simply not sensitive enough and the data were too meager. Let us imagine a similar experiment, but taking a larger area to experiment on. The field available happens to be a relatively narrow piece of land that runs down a hill. From previous experience, we know that the field has a fertility gradient: the lower area always produces a higher yield than the upper area. This is probably caused by better irrigation in the lower parts, and by the fact that more of the fertile topsoil has been washed off from the higher parts. We want to study the effects of fertilizing with bone meal on grain yields. A reasonable design under these circumstances would be to divide the long strip into two even narrower strips, and then to divide these strips into, say, ten equal portions. We thus get ten pairs of plots (*replication*), where the members of each pair lay equally high on the hill; this means, we believe, that the two members of each pair have comparable fertility. We will only directly compare members of the same pair. This is what Fisher called *blocking*. We will fertilize one member of each pair, to be decided by a flip of a coin that gives an equal chance to each of the two (*randomization*).

To randomize in comparative experiments is to determine, not just arbitrarily, but by use of a "physical experimental process," such as coin tossing, the treatment allocation – that is, which plots within a block will receive which treatment (Fisher, 1935, §22). The protocol of experimental randomization was almost entirely worked out by Fisher, although there were isolated cases of the use of random devices in parapsychological experiments, which may have been known to him (Hacking, in press; Fisher, 1929). For Fisher, physical randomization was necessary to ensure that the estimates of error and tests of significance "should be fully valid" (Fisher, 1935, §26). By this he meant that "the very same causes that produce our real error shall also contribute the materials for computing an estimate of it" (§20). The estimate of error, or the probability of making a set of observations as discordant from a "null hypothesis" as the actually observed data, is, as we will see, based on some "modeling assumptions." Randomization introduces a "causal matrix" that may be different from the causal matrix where an experimenter chooses the treatment allocation haphazardly or arbitrarily. That is, random choices will on average be different from choices made by an experimenter, who might subconsciously let his opinions and preferences influence his choices. Non-random allocation requires different models. Randomization was hailed by Jerzy Neyman, who in matters of the logic of statistical inference was Fisher's most vehement opponent, as "the most basic of Fisher's numerous ideas" (Neyman, 1976a, p. 163), and by working scientists as "perhaps Fisher's most fundamental contribution" (Campbell and Stanley, 1966, p. 2) and "the central component of his contribution to the practice of scientific experiment" (Finney, 1964, p. 327). It was, nonetheless, probably Fisher's most controversial contribution to the methodology of comparative experiments. Randomization has been opposed even by some of those who followed him most closely in the analysis of experimental data. Gosset, for instance, argued that by judicious choice of treatment allocation, an experimenter could often obtain results with a smaller real error than was possible with randomized allocation ("Student," 1937). For Fisher, who tried always to make statistics more objective, validity of estimates remained the more important aim. However, since randomization makes at least some reference to what happens "in the long run," it has been tied up with the larger controversy between frequentists and Bayesians about the meaning of probability statements (Barnard and Cox, 1962).

Replication, blocking, and randomization are all part of the *design* of the experiment. Before we actually perform the experiment – apply the manure, sow the grain, take equally good care of all the plots, harvest the plots individually, and weigh carefully their yield – we must also make up our minds how to analyze the data we will obtain, although unexpected events may later make us modify the analysis. This is to ensure that an experiment with this particular design is sensitive enough, in the sense that it can actually provide us with information that can form the basis for an inference.

Our experiment will give us ten pairs of data (x_i, y_i), where the first number is the yield of the fertilized plot and the second that of the neighboring, untreated plot. Johnston's question was whether these data indicate that bone meal is beneficial or ineffective with respect to yield. Perhaps he also wanted to get an estimate of how beneficial it is. Because of the fertility gradient in the field, we decided that we should only compare plots in the same pair. Since we believe that, if the fertilizer has any effect at all, it will be an "additive" one (and not, say, a multiplicative effect), we can concentrate on the differences $(x_i - y_i)$ in each pair. It is these differences that can tell us whether there is an additive effect. Call these differences z_i. Additivity is the first of a series of *modeling assumptions*. We have to construct a *model* in order to see what the data say about the question of interest. Without a model, however rudimentary, the data are mute. Another component of the model is the hypothesis to be tested. In significance testing one tries to reject the hypothesis that the fertilizer has no effect. To do this, we must formulate the hypothesis in probabilistic terms, in a so-called "null hypothesis."

There are various ways of doing this. Which one is most appropriate depends on our past experience with this type of experiment. A commonly used statistical hypothesis would posit that our ten numbers are independent random observations from a normal distribution with mean zero and unknown variance (i.e. the variance has to be estimated from the data). What does this mean in agricultural terms? On the basis of previous experience, we have supposed the members of each pair of plots are comparable, which means that we find no reason to expect a higher yield from one of them over the other. But our experience has shown that plots we consider comparable will actually show great variation in yield, and that this variation, if represented graphically, looks very much like the bell-shaped curve of a normal distribution. Similarly, when we compared in the past the width of the bells of different groups of comparable plots in situations like ours, we found these to be more or less the same. Hence we can assume a uniform variance for all of our plots. We also take the differences to be independent – for example, we do not expect the manure to be more effective on the poor soil higher up than on the richer soil near the bottom.

Note that such modeling assumptions are motivated by past experience, and past experience, if we have it, makes up a part of the relevant evidence we use to interpret our results. Similarly, to make sure that the modeling assumptions are not partly determined by the data we will collect in this experiment (this is called *data snooping* and offers the temptation to select the model with an eye on the particular conclusion we would like to draw), we should formulate the model before the data are obtained. There is also a strong link between the design and the analysis. Our knowledge of the fertility gradient leads us to divide the field into blocks, and to compare only the yields within a block, which means here that we are only looking at the differences z_i. The physical act of randomization also justifies one of the modeling assumptions: it is needed to prevent subliminal experimenter bias from vitiating our assumption that the yields of the treated and untreated plots are from the same distribution. Finally, the number of plots used in an experiment is determined by what size effect one expects or wishes to detect. The more plots, the more sensitive the experiment – that is, the smaller the minimum size effect a comparative experiment is able to detect.

The data we have in this experiment are now reduced to the differences z_i. How discordant are these data z_i with our hypothesis that they are a random sample from a normal distribution with zero mean and unknown variance? It is common to evaluate the fit between the data and the null hypothesis in terms of the so-called "*t*-statistic," which here would be a function of the differences z_i and the number of differences measured:

$$t(\text{data}) = \frac{\bar{z}}{s/\sqrt{n}}$$

where $\bar{z}$ is the mean of the z_i, n is the number of data points (here 10), and s is the standard deviation around the mean:

$$s = \sqrt{\left(\frac{\Sigma_i \, (z_i - \bar{z})^2}{n-1} \right)}$$

The higher the absolute value of t, the less consistent are the observed data with the nullhypothesis. This use of the t-statistic reflects several intuitions about discordancy. If the distance between the x_i and the y_i becomes larger, there is more evidence that the treatment has an effect (positive or negative). Similarly, if the spread of the z_i becomes greater while their sum remains the same, the evidence of discordancy becomes weaker.

To understand that an experiment as small as Johnston's is not sensitive enough and could not have given us enough information, it is instructive to imagine that we have only data on two pairs of plots – call them z_1 and z_2. If we cannot assume anything about the variation in the data, the probability of the most discrepant data, where z_1 and z_2 are both positive or both negative, is still 50% under the null hypothesis. Such an experiment could never have provided evidence that is strongly discordant with the null hypothesis, since even the most discrepant data are not strongly so. The performance of such an experiment is a meaningless exercise.

Suppose now we actually perform our experiment and obtain the following data:

$$(5.2,\ 4.5)$$
$$(4.8,\ 4.9)$$
$$(4.7,\ 4.6)$$
$$(5.0,\ 4.6)$$
$$(5.1,\ 5.3)$$
$$(\text{missing, missing})$$
$$(5.6,\ 5.0)$$
$$(5.3,\ 4.9)$$
$$(6.0,\ 5.5)$$
$$(5.5,\ 5.5)$$

where the first number gives the yield in bushels of the fertilized plot and the second that of the untreated plot. Notice that data on the sixth pair are missing. Here a gopher dug up large portions of the plots, something we could not possibly have anticipated when building our model. According to the Fisherian program, we should ask whether the damage done by the gopher tells us anything about the difference $(x_6 - y_6)$. In the present case, this seems unlikely, and so we proceed conditionally, as if we had done the experiment from the beginning with only nine pairs (Barnard, 1947). In other cases the fact that data are missing may in itself be relevant information. For example, in a medical experiment with outpatients, the blood-pressure data of some patients may be missing, since they were unable to come in on the day the blood pressure was measured. But it could be that patients with high blood pressure tend to be less mobile, so that the fact that a data point is missing may suggest that it would have been higher than average had it actually been available. This is one of the many points in which statistical thinking has sharpened our intuitions about evidence.

The t-statistic for our agricultural data has a value of approximately 2.5. The next step is to calculate how probable such a value or an even more discordant value of the t-statistic is under the assumption that our null hypothesis is true. That is, we have to determine $p(|t| > 2.5 ; H_0)$. In most statistical textbooks nowadays, one can find a table where the probabilities that $|t|$ (the absolute value of t) will exceed various values have been calculated as a function of the number of "degrees of freedom," or number of independent comparisons, in this case 8. We find there that this probability is about 0.02. This is called the *estimate of error* or the *significance level* of the data. The smaller the level of significance the more discordant the data are with the null hypothesis. Our data are thus quite discordant with the null.

The exact significance level of the data is now published, to be communicated to our "fellow research workers." At what level of significance of the data a null hypothesis will be rejected – that is, what counts as a "significant" experimental result – is not part of the logic of testing, but of its pragmatics. In some fields there is a strong tradition of rejecting the null hypothesis as soon as the data are at least significant at a particular level, such as 5% or 1%. Sometimes this has even been made a condition for publication of experimental findings. Fisher's early writings encouraged this as a "convenient convention," though the criticism of Neyman and Egon Pearson drove him to a more nuanced view. This later view was that "no scientific worker has a fixed level of significance at which from year to year, and in all circumstances he rejects hypotheses; he rather gives his mind to each particular case in the light of his evidence and his ideas" (Fisher, 1956, p. 42). This fits Fisher's general emphasis on scientific communication, already apparent in his 1922 statement that statistics aims to provide a "summary of data without apparent loss of information." The restatement of his position in 1955 even had overtones of the cold war: "We have the duty of formulating, or summarizing, and of communicating our conclusions, in intelligible form, in recognition of the right of *other* free minds to utilize them in making their own decisions" (Fisher, 1955).

Fisher's achievement was to develop a powerful, new, and coherent conception of experimental research, one that transformed the very idea of what an experiment is. We can begin to see this by looking separately at the two main components of Fisher's synthesis: significance testing, and ideas about experimental design for complex subjects such as agriculture. Both of these had roots stretching back to the nineteenth or even the eighteenth century, though they were almost never brought together until about 1900. In the section that follows, we offer a few illustrations of significance testing applied to observational data, and of comparative experimentation without much statistical analysis. Their import is not to deny Fisher's originality, but to show how greatly he changed the character of statistics and of experimental methodology.

3.3 FISHER'S ANTECEDENTS: EARLY SIGNIFICANCE TESTS AND COMPARATIVE EXPERIMENTATION

The use of probability to determine whether an effect could be due to chance has a history almost as long as the mathematics of chance itself. Arbuthnot's primitive test to decide whether chance or divine planning was responsible for the slight excess of male over female births every year is perhaps the earliest example (see 1.4). The calculation given by Daniel Bernoulli and then Laplace concerning the orientation and orbital plane of the planets is another example in this genre. Probabilistic tests, however, never became routine operations in any discipline until the beginning of the twentieth century, and hence there was no sustained effort to develop and improve a methodology of significance testing. The only standardized form of such tests was Laplace's "probability of causes," which depended on Bayes' rule and thus was thoroughly suspect among the frequentists of the nineteenth century.

Some evidence of a revival of significance testing can be seen in the work of the economic and social statisticians Wilhelm Lexis and Francis Edgeworth. But the beginning of a full-fledged research program aiming to develop and apply new methods of significance testing, like much of mathematical statistics, was the work of Karl Pearson and the biometric school. It can conveniently be dated to 1900, when Pearson published his chi-square test of "goodness of fit" of a set of data to a curve to which they are supposed to conform. (He developed this test to prove the inadequacy of the normal curve and the superiority of his own generalized family of distributions; see Pearson, 1948.) In 1908, Gosset published his epochal papers on the sampling distributions of a mean and of a correlation coefficient, based on training received and work begun in

Pearson's laboratory, but adapted for the need to have tests involving small samples if statistics was to be of any use to brewers (Student, 1908). The first of these papers (see Student, 1958) made possible the t-test that we applied to the agricultural data above (3.2). Before Gosset, the available tests had to assume either that the population variance was known, or that the sample was "sufficiently large" so that the estimate of the population variance based on it could be taken as the true population variance. Student's t-distribution was the first exact distribution, and the first to avoid reliance on questionable approximations. Gosset later turned to agricultural experiments, where he collaborated with E. S. Beaven, and his work was in many ways the intermediary between Karl Pearson's statistics of large samples drawn from observation and R. A. Fisher's methods based on experiments and small samples. He was well acquainted with both men and, remarkably, even remained on good terms with them.

The approaches developed by Pearson, Gosset, and Fisher share at least the goal of Arbuthnot's 1710 paper: to evaluate hypotheses based on data. The twentieth-century founders of mathematical statistics, however, owed much more to error theory and the method of least squares than to Arbuthnot. Error theory made use of significance tests with a subtly different purpose – not to reject hypotheses based on data, but to reject discrepant data (outliers) based on hypotheses about their distribution. The theory of errors, unlike the "probability of causes," was in the nineteenth century a well-developed area of research, firmly allied to the most sophisticated of the observational sciences, astronomy. Many of the more technical results of statistical inference were in fact developed in the context of the problem of measuring and minimizing errors of observation.

Significance testing in the rejection of outliers

That measurements always have an error becomes clear as soon as one tries to measure repeatedly a stable system, like the position of a comet or the time it takes for a pendulum to make a complete swing. The measured positions of the comet do not follow a smooth line, nor does the measured functional relation between the length and the period of the pendulum follow a continuous curve. Long before the development of error theory, scientists sometimes selected certain measurements and rejected others, in order to get rid of inconsistencies. But the criteria for selection were subjective. A good example is the first astronomer royal and head of the Greenwich observatory, John Flamsteed (1646–1719). He spent his whole life at a telescope collecting astronomical data for his new 3,000-star catalog. Flamsteed gave meticulous attention to accuracy in the most minute details, and showed a rare concern for the reduction and manipulation of his data. He was extremely close to his data; he knew them in their most circumstantial details from having collected them with his very own eyes and hands. He would rely mainly on those he regarded as of superlative quality, and disregard others he judged questionable. Whole series of observations never had any consequence for the star positions published in his catalog (Baily, 1835).

Around 1600, practical guidelines emerged for scientists to combine such "inconsistent" observations (Eisenhart, 1971). In the case of repeated measurements of a single quantity, some would take the median – the value such that there are the same number of observations above as below it – and others the arithmetic mean of the observations. The cogency of these practices was much debated. Simpson's contribution of 1755 still stands out in this regard, for previously scientists had conceived error only in terms of inaccuracies in the individual observations (about which very little could be said). Simpson redefined the problem as the extent to which a *method* of measurement would lead to errors of a certain size – that is, about the error distribution connnected with a measuring procedure (Eisenhart, 1964).

In 1805, Legendre published his new method of combining observations, the method of least squares. This generalized the procedure of taking the arithmetic mean to the case of repeated measurements of more than one single quantity. The method quickly became the dominant one, in part because Gauss later announced he had already discovered it in 1795, and had used it in 1801 to re-identify a new heavenly body, discovered by the Italian astronomer Giuseppe Piazzi (1746–1826) on the first day of the year 1801, but lost sight of soon afterwards. (This was the first known asteroid or minor planet, to which Piazzi gave the name of Ceres.) Gauss added greatly to the method of least squares. He developed the "mechanics" of it, and showed by what series of simple calculations a least squares solution could be found. These tools were taken up by astronomers as well as observers of geomagnetic and meteorological phenomena all over the world.

But more importantly for statistical inference and for the measurement of uncertainty, Gauss developed two, quite different, justifications of the method of least squares. The first one is Bayesian in tone and assumptions, while the second one can now be labeled decision theoretic.

It is in Gauss' first justification of 1798, not published until 1809, that the famous normal (or Gaussian) distribution was made prominent. Suppose, Gauss began, that the mean is in general the most probable value (in the Bayesian sense of posterior probability), while all values are *a priori* equally probable. Then, he showed, measurement error should follow a bell-shaped distribution, quickly falling off to zero at both sides when errors become larger (although never reaching zero, clearly an unrealistic assumption made for mathematical convenience). Taking least squares in the general case is then justified, since it finds the combination of estimates that is the most probable – that is, has the highest *a posteriori* probability.

Besides the true value of the measured quantity, which determines the center of the distribution of measurements, one more feature of a measuring procedure must be known to single out a particular bell-shaped curve. This is the precision of the procedure, its tendency to be close to the mark, and corresponds to the width of the bell. Gauss showed how to estimate the precision (i.e. of a single measurement) from the data themselves. Since the width of the distribution of an average decreases according to the square root of the number of observations taken, it followed that by taking, say, four times as many observations one could approximately double the reliability of the average as an estimate of the true value. (Similar calculations are nowadays used to determine how many people should be interviewed to get a reliable estimate of so-called public opinion.) It is this estimate of probable error that makes Gauss' method statistical in the modern sense, since it gives a measure of the uncertainty remaining, and of the trust one can have in the average calculated (Stigler, 1986).

It is important, however, to realize that the customary interpretation of the notion of probable error and of the notation $x \pm a$ ["on the basis of the observations cited alone, it is an even chance that the true value of the quantity measured lies in the interval $(x - a, x + a)$"] assumes, as Gauss always did, that the measurement procedure has no constant or systematic error that attaches to all measurements similarly. This has proved to be false in every interesting case of scientific measurement. W. J. Youden of the U.S. National Bureau of Standards, for instance, listed fifteen determinations of the Astronomical Unit (the average distance of the Earth to the Sun) made between 1895 and 1961, and observed that each new determination lay outside the limits of probable error reported for the previous determination. Each new determination was based on new techniques and made by different observers, and so was subject to a different systematic error (Youden, 1972). Obviously, the smallness of the probable error indicates only the statistical control the scientist was able to obtain in the particular experimental technique used, and even then is often exaggerated by not securing independence of the raw data.

By 1820, it thus seemed that subjective elements in the treatment of measuring error had been completely eradicated (Harter, 1974–76). The ghost of Flamsteed had been laid to rest, or so it appeared. However, in empirical studies of *residuals* (the differences between the measurements made and the estimates) it became clear that often one or two of the residuals were unusually large compared with the others. Was this not because these measurements had incurred an unusual error that was not noticed when they were made, and was it not better to discard completely those rogues and recalculate the least square solution afresh? The problem speaks most vividly from the pages of some letters exchanged by Gauss and the astronomer Olbers. Explaining the problem of unusually large deviations, Olbers asked Gauss: "What should count as an unusual or too large a deviation? I would like to receive more precise directions" (Olbers, 1827). Gauss, however, was disinclined to give any more directions, and in his answer he compared the situation to everyday life, where one often has to make intuitive judgments outside the reign of formal and explicit rules (Gauss, 1827).

The need for subjectivity in such matters (expressed by Gauss himself only in private letters and never in print) was gradually eliminated, as a division of scientific labor necessitated by group projects led to differentiation of the jobs of experimenter/observer and of calculator. New habits were formed for the purpose of mechanically rejecting, or modifying, measurements in cases in which the residual differed too much from that of the bulk of the data. In this context, the first elaborate and probabilistically motivated rule for the rejection of outliers was developed by Benjamin Peirce, father of the American philosopher Charles S. Peirce (Peirce, 1852; Rider, 1933).

Peirce's rule, and others developed in that period, were tests of significance. They were designed to test whether one or more measurements were taken from the same (normal) distribution as the remaining ones. The rules were understood to be yes/no rules and gave a strict criterion. This is another dimension in the development of significance tests: they may be used to make objective, rule-driven, or mechanized decisions to accept or reject a hypothesis, or provide a simple means, as in Fisher's significance tests, to measure and communicate the discrepancy between the data and a hypothesis. It is also one source of the custom of using the whole tail area beyond the observation as a measure of discrepancy. If a measurement is rejected as a rogue, an even more outlying one has to go too.

Thus the search for formal mechanical rules, so characteristic of statistics in the twentieth century, also derives from a well-developed tradition in error theory. Indeed, the objectification of subjectivity, as we may call this development, is central to the history of statistical testing (Swijtink, 1987). It is the socialization of the individual through the standardization of experimental procedures and methods of data analysis. Wilhelm Jordan, author of an important nineteenth-century handbook on geodesy, understood this well when he emphasized the moral aspects of using standardized methods in his profession. "The advantages to our discipline of using the Method of Least Squares have been, to a large extent, of a *moral* nature: one has become more honest in making measurements and doing the calculations. . . [D]ishonest suppression of measurements and the like undoubtedly happens less often since the method was introduced" (Jordan, 1895).

Comparative experiments: some historical examples

The other main component of Fisher's statistical synthesis, experimental design, was also embodied in a longstanding tradition, whose strongest disciplinary attachments were to agronomy, physiology, and medicine. But, just as significance testing had rarely been applied to experiments before Gosset and Fisher, experimental design was only beginning to be related to probability and statistics when Fisher commenced his original research on statistics around 1910. Their traditional separation is illustrated by Johnston's desire to draw inferences from a comparison of a sample of one plot with a control of three plots.

By Johnston's time, the comparative experiment was already recognized as an invaluable tool for testing general causal hypotheses. The logic of that experimental methodology is closely tied to the operational aspects of the meaning of causal statements. To be a cause generally means to make a difference: in the hypothetical situation where the cause is absent, the effect would not have occurred. But one cannot do experiments with hypothetical situations. In comparative experiments, actual situations take the place of hypothetical situations. To do so they have to be copies of them, at least in all causally relevant aspects. The art of experimental design consists in getting as close as possible to this ideal situation. The experimental requirements in comparative trials can all be understood as increasing the degree of similarity.

Especially in the German-speaking countries, there existed in the nineteenth century a rich tradition of agricultural experimental research and a slowly emerging body of statistical techniques that, towards the close of the century, even began to obtain a probabilistic interpretation. The controversial significance test for the difference of means when the variance of the two samples may be different, proposed independently of Fisher by the German agricultural chemist W. U. Behrens (1929), was thus no fluke, but part of a long tradition. This history is almost forgotten now, ousted by the more successful and prestigious developments originating in Ireland and England. Fisher must have known of this German material, since the library at Rothamsted was well stocked with German literature, although to what extent remains unclear (Fisher, 1931). Certainly that literature had parallels in early twentieth-century England. F. J. M. Stratton, Fisher's tutor at Cambridge, had written about the application of error theory to agriculture, and there was a considerable body of formal and tacit knowledge at institutions like Rothamsted that any agricultural experimenter would have to learn. We find already in the German agricultural literature expressions of themes we now associate with the tradition of which Fisher was a part, including an emphasis on experimental design, replication, and investigator blindness. On the other hand, nothing like a comprehensive statistical formulation of these problems was worked out in the German tradition – no statistical models, no partitioning of variance, no correlations or factor analyses, no use of randomization or blocking. Experimental design had become quite sophisticated in these pre-biometric agricultural studies, but probability had little role.

The German agricultural literature reveals the beginnings of a sense of the intimate connection between the design of an experiment and the proper method of analyzing the data it provides. A data analyst can only perform a statistical analysis on a set of data if he knows by what procedures these data were obtained. Moreover, to perform an experiment before deciding how to analyze the data is to risk being unable to draw reliable conclusions about the question studied. This insight is most often attributed to R. A. Fisher, who insisted that statisticians must be involved already in the design of experiments. After all, "[s]tatistical procedure and experimental design are only two different aspects of the same whole, and that whole comprises all the logical requirements of the complete process of adding to natural knowledge by experimentation" (Fisher, 1935, p. 3). But the German experimenter H. Rodewald had already formulated this insight in 1909:

During the last decades, field trials to compare varieties and kinds of fertilizer have played an important role in agriculture. The question arises how one should conduct such trials and how one can derive from the results of the trials generally valid and therefore scientific conclusions. *The last question has to be answered first, since from its answer one can see how the trials have to be conducted* (Rodewald, 1909, p. 12).

Some sense of the need for replication is already to be found around 1800 in the work of the enlightened German physician turned agricultural experimenter Albert Thaer. Thaer studied, in a true Baconian spirit, the comparative fertilizing effects of animal dung, horn-shavings, hair and wool, human excrement, rotten fish, ground bones, etc. He remarked that "to be complete these trials . . . have to be repeated under a variety of circumstances that are not under our control, in different climates, under different weather conditions and on different kinds of soil" (Thaer, 1809–12, § 24). Thaer's was not the modern idea of replication – applying the same treatment to different plots on an experimental field. But his attention to natural diversity did lead toward appreciation of the need for replication during the nineteenth century. Johnston, recognizing that one trial was not enough, repeated his measurements on three different plots. But notice that Johnston only replicated the "control plot" (to which no treatment was applied). His motivation was to get an indication of "the natural variability of the soil." Unfortunately, in this case it overlapped the experimental result, which he did not replicate, and so he complained that no firm conclusion was possible. Still, Johnston's purpose was conceptually close to Fisher's main reason for replication, to estimate the error (Fisher, 1935, §26). That a large number of replications also serves to diminish the error was not well understood by agriculturalists like Johnston, given the confusion about sample size referred to in section 3.1. A similar lack of understanding was often evident in contemporary medical experiments (see 4.2).

Although the concept of subject and experimenter blindness was not considered in Fisher's recommendations, this may only be because he was not himself involved in psychological or medical experiments. The need for it is strongly connected with the reasons for randomization. It is now part of the preferred methodology in those fields, and its origin lies also in the nineteenth century. Subject blindness is of course limited to experiments in such fields as medicine and psychology; an experiment is subject blind if the subjects do not know what treatments they are receiving. It is useful because having a certain attitude about the received treatment may partially determine its causal effects. Similarly, an experiment is experimenter blind if the experimenter does not know what treatment the individual subjects have received. Its need is illustrated by an example from the German agricultural literature. Paul Wagner wrote in 1880, in a methodological paper on improvements in fertilizer trials:

Given the fact that knowing what fertilizer was used on each plot may influence a judge's opinion, and given the fact that seeing someone else forming a some-what different judgment can easily influence a judge's opinion, we proceeded as follows. The signs with the names of the fertilizer used on a plot were removed. The writer [Wagner] then walked several times over the experimental field to get a general impression of the limits of variation. He then made his judgment and put it aside without looking at it any further. Dr. Rohn also then made these judgments and his numbers also were put aside without comparing them with the fertilizers that were applied and without any of us seeing the numbers the other had obtained. The next day, but now in the afternoon – we chose for the second examination another time of the day since different light can easily change the appearance of the plants – the experiment was repeated and the num-bers were then finally combined (Wagner and Rohn, 1880, p. 47).

The need for experimenter blindness was also discussed in nineteenth-century psychology. In place of the general sceptical attitude towards the reliability of human perception, Fechner and others made the human observer a subject of serious psychological attention. This was expressed as an interest in explaining and managing differences in perceptual acuity among individuals. Astronomers determined that human observers react with different but characteristic response times to simultaneous events, and methods based on the so-called "personal equation" were developed to take this variation between human observers into account (Bessel, 1823; Radau, 1866). Investigation of these phenomena, especially after the importance of subliminal stimuli was recognized (Pfungst, 1907), required new experimental techniques. An especially important source for emphasis on experimenter blindness was parapsychology, where it de-fined the difference between experimental tests of clairvoyance and of telepathy (Hacking, in press).

The infusion of the methodology of comparative experimentation into statistics was of crucial importance to both. It provided a coherent frame-work for the further refinement of comparative experimentation. And for statistics it provided a rich field of new problems for which it could be of day-to-day relevance. Earlier applications of statistical reasoning to experimental data had often been little more than window-dressing, a pre-liminary step to explanation on the basis of physical principles. This can be illustrated with two examples of the statistical analysis of experimental data that were not the product of a Fisherian experimental design, and thus were subject to the same ambiguity as much statistical inference from observational data. Our first example is a study by Gustav Kirchhoff of the spectrum of dark and bright lines given off by the sun. Joseph Fraunhofer, who first described these lines in detail, had already observed that the dark lines in part of the solar spectrum corresponded to those given off by sodium flames. In 1862, Kirchhoff sought to justify such identifications with a probabilistic argument, preliminary to a physical explanation of the phenomenon.

He applied what we would call a test of significance to show that the coincidence between the bright lines of, say, the spectrum characteristic of iron and a series of dark lines in the solar spectrum could not be just a contingent fact due to chance. He posed the question: what is the probability that sixty randomly chosen lines of the iron spectrum more or less coincide with sixty dark lines in the solar spectrum? The distribution he used in the calculation of this probability was the uniform distribution, according to which the probability that a line falls in a certain interval is proportional to the length of that interval. But his aim was not to test whether the spacing in the iron lines was really uniform. His concern was coincidence. His data were sixty locations for the dark lines in the solar spectrum and sixty locations for the bright lines in the spectrum one obtains by heating iron filings in a Bunsen burner. If a line of the iron spectrum fell within ½ millimeter of a line in the solar spectrum, Kirchhoff considered it a match. Given that the distance between lines in the solar spectrum is on average 2 millimeters, Kirchhoff concluded that the probability that any line of the iron spectrum would match (fall within ½ millimeter to the right or left of) any line of the iron spectrum, simply as a matter of chance, was 0.5. That sixty lines from a spectrum produced by heating iron filings in a Bunsen burner should, by chance, match sixty lines of the solar spectrum would be highly unlikely; he calculated (not quite correctly) the probability as $(0.5)^{60}$, which is smaller than 10^{-17}. But the sixty pairs did match, something that would be highly improbable if the null hypothesis were true (Kirchhoff, 1862, pp. 78–9).

Reconstructed in modern terminology, his null hypothesis was that the one hundred and twenty data were independent observations from a uniform distribution. The test he used was a conditional one: given that the dark lines have the location they have, what is the probability that the bright lines coincide with them within the margins of perceptual and instrumental error? Why this test? Obviously since the observations deviate from the null hypothesis in this direction: the data suggest this correlation. Thus, Kirchhoff rejected the null on the basis of highly significant findings, by using a test that was suggested by the observations themselves. Little is known about the origin of Kirchhoff's reasoning, but similar arguments concerning coincidences had been given before. For instance, before William Herschel gave observational proof, in 1803, of the existence of binary stars, the English astronomer John Michell had argued in a paper published in 1767 that the high frequency of small angular separation of close pairs of stars could not be due to chance. "The natural conclusion from hence is, that it is highly probable, and next to certainty in general, that such double stars as appear to consist of two or more stars placed very near together, do really consist of stars placed nearly together, and under the influence of some general law . . . to whatever cause this may be owing, whether to their mutual gravitation, or to some other law or appointment of the Creator" (Michell, 1767).

Both arguments invite certain objections. In particular, both the hypothesis and the test were chosen after the data had been studied – a problem that most often arises in observational sciences. Edward Forbes raised just this objection to the Michell calculation when John Herschel repeated it in the 1840s (see Gower, 1982). Similarly, we can imagine that Kirchhoff may have searched through files and files of spectra until he found one that closely matched part of the dark lines of the solar spectrum. This would be to commit the same fallacy as throwing millions of coins sixty times and calling biased all those that gave a huge preponderance of heads or of tails. All in all, that Kirchhoff was able to explain the coincidences on the basis of experimental fact gave much more credence to the assertion that the coincidence is not a fluke than any calculation of the tiny probability the phenomenon would have if it were not due to a cause.

In these examples statistical reasoning provided little more than window-dressing, and the real inferential burden was carried by physical explanation or direct observational evidence. Investigation into the causal powers of drugs or fertilizers is different. There the only evidence we have is often provided by comparative experiments, while detailed explanation of how the causes operate is not available. Fisher's program of comparative experimentation made it possible to deal with such problems. It separated statistics from the extreme positivism of Karl Pearson, who simply denied the meaningfulness of causal claims. It made a systematic discussion of general causal claims possible.

But Fisher provided no panacea. Especially in the social sciences, the unification of experiment and statistical analysis that he inspired has been highly troubling to some thoughtful observers. In psychology, for example, the idea of what an experiment is was strikingly narrowed to fit the Procrustean Bed of Fisherian statistics. Alternatives, such as the Gestalt psychologists' endeavor to use experiment simply to *demonstrate* a universal effect, have virtually been ruled out of the field (see chapter 6). The experimental psychology that relies on Fisherian experimental design is often associated with an abandonment of the search for universal psychological phenomena that apply equally to all people. It concentrates on establishing general causal statements, with their implicit reference to a population, that require only an increase in the incidence of the effect when the cause is present. Since these claims do not necessarily apply to the individual, they are of foremost interest to the state and its administrators (Danziger, 1987a). Within statistics, Fisher's views on experimental design were largely accepted, but there his analysis of statistical inference was sharply criticized by advocates of alternative programs. His controversy with Jerzy Neyman and Egon Pearson, the son of Karl Pearson, is discussed in the following section.

3.4   THE CONTROVERSY: FISHER VS. NEYMAN AND PEARSON

Since the beginning of the twentieth century, several distinct views have emerged about how to draw conclusions from statistical data. The very different approaches of R. A. Fisher, of Jerzy Neyman and Egon Pearson, and of the Bayesians, all involve a considerable advance over earlier views: they are more systematic and each can account for a wider range of practices. They are the successful outcome of a tremendous intellectual effort. In that sense one can speak of a breakthrough, although there has been no declared winner. The issues that distinguish the several schools go deep into the foundations and practice of statistical inference. The different schools often disagree fiercely about basic issues, and value-laden words from ordinary speech such as "efficient," "unbiased," and "coherent," have been enlisted as names of central concepts in the various theories. By implication, rival approaches are charged with inefficiency, bias, and incoherence.

In statistical reasoning it has not (yet) proven possible to come to an all-encompassing theory, of which the current positions are special cases, appropriate if certain conditions are satisfied (but see Barnard, 1980). In fact, some working statisticians advocate an ecumenism in which one should apply different approaches to the same set of data (G. E. P. Box,

1986). In other areas there has been some convergence between different schools. For instance, Bayesians were for a long time opposed to experimental randomization, but now recognize the importance of paying attention to the procedures by which observations are collected (Rubin, 1978; Swijtink, 1982). Similarly, statisticians within the Neyman–Pearson school have recognized the importance of conditional inference (Lehmann, 1986, chapter 10).

There is a remarkable line of cleavage between the fields of applications conquered by the various schools. Methods and concepts of the two "frequency" schools, Fisher and Neyman–Pearson, have penetrated the experimental sciences, whereas Bayesians, usually designated the "subjective" school, have not. But Bayesians have made inroads in economics and have recovered traditional eighteenth-century applications of probability such as legal judgment and human rationality. We will discuss some of the recent applications of Bayes' theorem when we turn to the experimental study of thinking in chapter 6 and to applications in everyday life in chapter 7. There we will see that modern Bayesians often have fewer reservations about the range of applicability of Bayes' theorem than Bayes himself seems to have had.

In the following we will emphasize the conflicting views of the school founded by R. A. Fisher and of the Neyman–Pearson school. We will concentrate on the analysis of significance testing. Bayesian thinking will be discussed only insofar as it is relevant to understanding the conflicting viewpoints. These two are the dominant points of view, at least in the sciences discussed in this book. The form of statistical inference used in the social sciences mixes elements from these two views.

Sir Ronald A. Fisher

At Cambridge University, Fisher studied physics, mathematics, and biology. With this background, he became a leader in the inference revolution and one of the great geneticists of his time. He helped reconcile the Mendelian and the biometric approaches to the study of evolution and inheritance, not least because of his abilities as a statistician (see chapter 4). Eugenics was indeed Fisher's driving motivation, and he judged social measures according to the effects they had on the biological inheritance of man. As an undergraduate he explained the rise and fall of societies in terms of the birth rate among those whose hereditary superiority enabled them to accumulate wealth. Before he embarked on an academic career, he tried subsistence farming, since farming was, in his view, a eugenic way of life, in which not money, but personal qualities were the dominant factor (J. F. Box, 1978). It was his investigations of inheritance that led Fisher to the concept of variance, and to the technique of the analysis of variance components to separate the contributions of different causal factors to observed correlations (J. F. Box, 1980; Fisher, 1918; see also 4.4).

In 1919, Fisher accepted the newly created post of statistician at Rothamsted Experimental Station, refusing an offer to become the chief statistician under Karl Pearson at the Galton Laboratory. Rothamsted was established in the late 1830s to investigate the effects on the soil of different combinations of bone meal, burnt bones, and various types of mineral phosphate with sulphate or muriate of ammonia. Continuous field experiments, begun in 1843, provided a wealth of agricultural field data, still largely unanalyzed when Fisher joined the station. Indeed, when one looks through the second edition of *The Book of the Rothamsted Experiments*, published in 1917, it is striking how little had been done with the data of over sixty years of experimentation (Hall, 1917). For the most part, only average yield per annum was tabulated, and inferences were based on a judgmental comparison of means. Rothamsted presented Fisher with just the right challenge. It provided daily confrontations with inferential problems that arose in the work of the station itself, and in that of visitors attracted there by Fisher's rapidly growing fame. Fisher's first book on statistical methodology, *Statistical Methods for Research Workers* (1925), was successful in introducing biologists and agriculturalists to the new techniques of statistical analysis, with nearly 20,000 copies sold during the first 25 years of the book's existence, to an increasingly international audience (Yates, 1951). His third book, *The Design of Experiments* (1935), provided a systematic account of the principles of comparative experimentation: replication, blocking, randomization, the factorial design, and confounding. It was similarly successful, and had reached a seventh edition by the time of Fisher's death in 1962.

Fisher's basic belief was that we learn from experience, although our knowledge must always remain provisional. His efforts in statistical inference were directed toward developing concepts of statistical evidence – ways to measure and express the uncertainty of hypotheses in the light of data. Fisher was not, however, satisfied with the approach based on Bayes' theorem, in which the uncertainty of a hypothesis in the light of data is expressed by a posterior probability. The use of Bayes' theorem presupposes the availability of a prior probability distribution over the possible hypotheses. Since Fisher was a frequentist, he insisted that every probability judgment must theoretically be verifiable to any chosen degree of approximation by sampling its reference set (Fisher, 1962). Bayes' theorem can, according to Fisher, only be used in those cases where there is *a priori* distributional information about the population being sampled, that is, the cases where we know that the population from which the observations are drawn has itself been drawn at random from a super-population of known specification. These cases are obviously very uncommon. Fisher also held that Bayes' theorem cannot be consistently applied to other cases. For where we are ignorant and have no *a priori* distributional information, there will exist more than one way to express that ignorance probabilistically. To allow different researchers mutually inconsistent prior probabilities to express the very same state of ignorance, would lead to an unacceptable subjectivism, where strength of evidence is just a matter of taste.

Fisher's research program in statistical inference should thus be understood in the light of his highly nuanced objections to the use of Bayes' rule. The Bayesians, he thought, are wrong to assume that all uncertainties can be expressed in terms of probabilities. There are, in fact, different ways to represent uncertainty that are appropriate in different situations. In comparative experiments, when one does not have a good idea about what is going on, one can make a significance test. A significance test is a weak argument and can only suggest that a hypothetical model (the null hypothesis) is implausible in the light of the data, assuming that the experiment was performed properly. A significance test does not permit one to assign any specific degree of probability to the hypothesis. When past experience and theoretical considerations make one confident in accepting a "full parametric model," Fisher proposed other methods to calculate and represent uncertainty, such as a likelihood function of the parameters in the model given the data. Only in certain special situations, where his so-called fiducial argument applies, the uncertainty of hypotheses, Fisher believed, can be expressed in terms of probability. It is especially here that many have questioned the consistency of Fisher's adherence to frequentism, since it is not clear with respect to what reference class a particular hypothesis has a frequency of being correct.

We will deal here only with significance testing. This does not mean that the other tools caused less controversy. For instance, Richard von Mises, himself a major proponent of the frequentist point of view, agreed with Fisher's analysis of a frequentist use of Bayes' theorem. But he believed that the route taken by Bayes was the only way to express uncertainty of hypotheses in the light of data. To draw meaningful conclusions from a small number of observations without using Bayes' theorem, as

Fisher wanted, meant getting too much from nothing, and he proclaimed in 1951 that "the heyday of small sample theory . . . is already past" (von Mises, [1928] 1957, p. 159). Only large samples, he believed, could form the basis of objective inference, since here the influence of prior probability assumptions on the posterior distribution vanishes. He confessed not to understand "the many beautiful words used by Fisher and his followers in support of the likelihood theory" (von Mises, [1928] 1957, p. 158). Jerzy Neyman, still less cautiously, held: "the theory of fiducial inference is simply non-existent in the same way as, for example, a theory of numbers defined by mutually contradictory definitions" (Neyman, 1941, p. 149).

For the purposes of this exposition, the essential features of a test of significance can be summarized as follows. In a test of significance, such as the one given in section 3.2, one confronts a null hypothesis with observations to see whether the observations deviate enough from the hypothesis that one can conclude the hypothesis is implausible. There are thus three concepts here: the null hypothesis, an ordering of the possible observations as to their deviation from the null hypothesis, and a measure of how far a particular observation deviates from the null hypothesis. We will take up these three concepts in that order.

(1) The null hypothesis must allow the specification of a unique distribution function for the test statistic. For instance, in the agricultural example of section 3.2, the null hypothesis stated that each member of a pair was a random observation from the same population, in which the characteristic observed (yield of grain in bushels) has a normal distribution with unknown mean particular to the pair, and unknown variance the same for all pairs. The differences z_i are then random observations from a normal distribution with mean zero and unknown variance. The t-statistic will have a known distribution, independent of the unknown variance. It has to be emphasized here that, although one speaks here of "random observations from the same populaton," the population is not a real one that could in principle be sampled repeatedly. For instance, if we were to repeat the experiment on the same field, using the same design, a lack of rain might lead to a quite unrelated body of data that could not be considered as taken from the same population as the first body of data. Fisher called the population hypothetical, both since it concerns the possibly hypothetical situation that the treatment is ineffective, and since it refers to a hypothetical series of repetitions in which the same "causal matrix" is operative. We will return to the importance of this point later.

(2) The ordering of the possible observations should reflect their relative degree of deviation from the null hypothesis. But the observations

can deviate in different respects from a null hypothesis. It may be necessary to consider different orderings, reflecting different kinds of deviation, and thus different tests. For instance, if the null hypothesis is that a process behaves like independent coin-tossing, and one wants to test for independence, one may choose a test based on the number of runs, or a test based on the length of the longest run (Bradley, 1968). The choice of the test statistic, and of null hypotheses worth testing, remains, for Fisher, an art, and cannot be reduced to a mechanical process:

It is, I believe, nothing but an illusion to think that this process can ever be reduced to a self-contained mathematical theory of tests of significance. Constructive imagination, together with much knowledge based on experience of data of the same kind, must be exercised before deciding on what hypotheses are worth testing, and in what respects. Only when this fundamental thinking has been accomplished can the problem be given a mathematical form (Fisher, 1939, p. 6).

(3) As a measure of how much a particular observation deviates from the null hypothesis, Fisher used the probability under the null hypothesis of the tail area of the test statistic s beyond its observed value s_{obs}, $p(s \geqslant s_{obs}; H_0)$. We noted earlier that this custom derived from the use of significance tests in the rejection of outliers. The original explanation Fisher gave of this was not very satisfactory, since it called something obvious that needed more motivation (Fisher, 1935, §7). Why should the discrepancy between an observation and a hypothesis depend on outcomes not actually observed? In his later book of 1956, *Statistical Methods and Scientific Inference*, Fisher conceded that this was a questionable feature of significance testing, "not very defensible save as an approximation" (Fisher, 1956, p. 66), and, indeed, it is at odds with his likelihood theory. All in all, the question remains whether the Fisherian significance level is a useful measure of the discrepancy of the data with respect to a hypothesized model. A lower significance level in the *same experiment* and with respect to the *same test statistic* will indeed indicate a greater discrepancy. So, if we had obtained, in the comparative experiment of section 3.2, observations with a significance level of, say, 1%, these observations would be more discordant with the hypothesis than the observations actually made. *Across experiments* or with *different test statistics* the situation is less clear. The question whether a significance level is a meaningful measure for discrepancy, or whether any other meaningful measure can be developed, remains unsettled (Martin-Löf, 1974; Seidenfeld, 1979; Berger and Sellke, 1987).

It should be recognized that, according to Fisher, rejecting the null hypothesis is not equivalent to accepting the efficacy of the cause in question. The latter cannot be established on the basis of one single experiment, but requires obtaining more significant results when the experiment, or an improvement of it, is repeated at other laboratories or under other conditions. Therefore, not only significant, but also non-significant results should be published in order to let the literature correctly reflect the frequency with which a certain type of experiment has led to significant results. Already in his book *The Design of Experiments* of 1935 he wrote: "no isolated experiment, however significant in itself, can suffice for the experimental demonstration of any natural phenomenon. . . In relation to the test of significance, we may say that a phenomenon is experimentally demonstrable when we know how to conduct an experiment which will rarely fail to give us a statistically significant result" (Fisher, 1935, §7). In this passage, Fisher distinguished *significance testing* from *the demonstration of a natural phenomenon*. Careless writing on Fisher's part, combined with selective reading of his early writings has led to the identification of the two, and has encouraged the practice of demonstrating a phenomenon on the basis of a single statistically significant result. As we will show in section 3.5, this practice is part of what we will call the *hybrid theory* of statistical inference that mixes elements of Fisherian significance testing with ideas from the so-called Neyman–Pearson–Wald school of hypothesis testing.

Both in this and in his insistence that a null hypothesis can only be shown implausible, and can never be shown plausible, Fisher's *Design of Experiments* has the same message as another remarkable book published in the very same year, 1935: Karl Popper's *Logic of Scientific Discovery*. Popper gave the same characterization of the demonstration of a natural phenomenon: "[T]he scientifically significant *physical effect* may be defined as that which can be regularly reproduced by anyone who carries out the appropriate experiment in the way prescribed" (Popper, [1935] 1968, p. 45). And just as Fisher wrote: "Every experiment may be said to exist only in order to give the facts a chance of disproving the null hypothesis" (Fisher, 1935, p. 16), meaning that performing an experiment that cannot possibly disprove the null hypothesis is futile, Popper used falsifiability as a criterion of demarcation between science and non-science: "it must be possible for an empirical scientific system to be refuted by experience," for "theories are . . . *never* empirically verifiable" (Popper, [1935] 1968, pp. 40–1). Indeed, just as Popper needed a notion of "degree of corroboration" to express the degree to which unfalsified hypotheses had stood up to tests and "proved their mettle" (Popper, [1935] 1968, pp. 40–1),

Fisher also vacillated, and gave non-refutation some credit: "it is a fallacy, so well known as to be a standard example, to conclude from a test of significance that the null hypothesis is thereby established; at most it maybe said to be confirmed or strengthened" (Fisher, 1955, p. 73). Fisher never elaborated upon this remark.

The above is one reading of Fisher (Cox, 1977). But his writings are diverse, and not always transparent to even the most hermeneutic reader. For instance, Fisher sometimes formulated the null hypothesis as: "the treatment has no effect, period." One can call this the *substantive* null hypothesis. If "rejecting" this hyothesis is the same as "adopting the belief that it is false," one does indeed accept that the treatment has an effect. But, in actual fact, the hypothesis that is rejected is the *statistical* null hypothesis – that the two samples are drawn from the same distribution. The statistical null hypothesis is not equivalent to the substantive null hypothesis. For one thing, there may be systematic errors in the execution of the design that make the statistical null hypothesis false even if the treatment has no effect, or true while the treatment is effective. Efforts to replicate the result may thus still be required. Furthermore, Fisher did not mean by "rejecting or disproving a null hypothesis" a categorical adoption of the belief that it is false. As he added to the seventh edition of *The Design of Experiments*, "in learning by experience, . . . conclusions are always provisional and in the nature of progress reports, interpreting and embodying the evidence so far accrued" (Fisher, [1935] 1960, §12.1). In other words, inductive conclusions cannot be detached from their evidential basis.

These nuances, however, were often not picked up by Fisher's readers. They found, both in his earlier book of 1925, *Statistical Methods for Research Workers*, and in *The Design of Experiments* a great emphasis on tests of significance, which were relatively simple in comparison with fiducial intervals. Partly in consequence, social scientists adopted a statistical practice that did not call for assessing the size of the effects they studied, but merely claimed to have established their existence by means of a single significant experimental result (Yates, 1951).

Fisher's contributions to statistics remain controversial. A. W. F. Edwards, who has done much to develop further Fisher's likelihood theory, hailed him as "an inventive genius of the highest order," but also wrote that "the significance tests he promoted I now think ill-founded, though they work most of the time, and have contributed greatly to scientific advance" (Edwards, 1972, p. 212).

J. Neyman and Egon S. Pearson

Egon S. Pearson was the son of Karl Pearson, and worked at his father's Galton Laboratory at University College, London. Father and son disagreed actively, however, about some of the most fundamental issues in statistics. In 1925, Jerzy Neyman, a young lecturer at the University of Warsaw and at the Central College of Agriculture in the same city, arrived at the Galton Laboratory in London. Over the next couple of years, Neyman and Egon Pearson formed a personal and intellectual friendship that led to a whole new school of inferential statistics. Both agreed with Fisher's criticism of the use of Bayes' theorem. Both were also dissatisfied with Karl Pearson's work, in part because it sometimes involved Bayesian assumptions, and in part because it seemed to them too eclectic. They were impressed by Fisher's new ideas, especially by his theory of estimation and his concept of a statistical model (Fisher, 1922b). But especially Neyman, who had a continental European attitude towards mathematical rigor (he used to say, "I am a student of Lebesque"), felt that Fisher lacked a unified point of view that was strictly deduced from first principles. He and E. S. Pearson tried to provide this in what later became known as the Neyman–Pearson theory of "statistical inference as inductive behavior."

Fisher never perceived the emerging Neyman–Pearson theory as correcting and improving his own work on tests of significance. Right up to his death in 1962 he rejected the key concepts of the Neyman–Pearson theory, such as "errors of the second kind," "repeated sampling from the same population," and "inductive behavior." His recurring reproach was that Neyman and Pearson were mere mathematicians without experience in the natural sciences, and that their work reflected this insulation from all living contact with real scientific problems. Fierce disagreement was not new to statistics. For many years, Karl Pearson had declined to publish Fisher's work in *Biometrika*, which he edited, possibly since Fisher had pointed out errors in Pearson's work. Fisher never forgave Pearson this slight; he held that: "the terrible weakness of his mathematical and scientific work flowed from his incapacity in self-criticism, and unwillingness to admit the possibility that he had anything to learn from others, even in biology, of which he knew very little" (Fisher, 1956, p. 3; see also 4.4). Neyman (1967) reported that he and E. S. Pearson tried to avoid getting involved in this feud, but they could not long stay above the fray, and their debate with Fisher was marked throughout by a bitter personal tone.

Already in the late 1920s, Neyman and Pearson began to argue that Fisher had no logical basis for his choice of test statistics (such as the t-statistic discussed in 3.2), or for choosing the tail area beyond the observed value of the test statistic as the significance level of the observations. But while Fisher became more and more dissatisfied with the latter feature of significance testing, Neyman and Pearson proposed to supply this logical basis by replacing Fisher's single null hypothesis with a set of rival hypotheses. They conceived of a statistical test as providing a means to choose among such alternatives. A mechanism of choice, they held, would be reasonable if it rarely led to an error. As they understood him, Fisher had defined only one kind of statistical error: rejecting the null hypothesis when it is in fact true. This they called an "error of the first kind." Their theory implied that one should also consider another kind of error, the "error of the second kind" – that is, accepting a hypothesis when it is false. In the simplest example of Neyman–Pearson hypothesis testing, two hypotheses are given, and it is assumed that one of these is true. The purpose of making an observation is to distribute, on the basis of observation, praise and blame over these two hypotheses, viz. to reject one and accept the other. If the two hypotheses are called H_1 and H_2, a test of H_1 against H_2 is defined by a set of observations, the so-called rejection region, say R. If one makes an observation in R, one rejects H_1 and accepts H_2, and if one makes an observation outside R, one accepts H_1 and rejects H_2. The probabilities $p(R; H_1)$ and $p(R; H_2)$ are called, respectively, the size and the power of the test, that is, of the rejection region R. These are conventionally indicated by α and $1-\beta$. α and β are thus, respectively, the probability of making an error of the first kind, or type-I error, and of making an error of the second kind, or type-II error. Given this specification of statistical acceptance/rejection strategies, a rational procedure could be defined. First, identify the more important of the two hypotheses, that is, that one for which one wants to keep the error of the first kind small. Next, search for a rejection region R of the desired small size that is most powerful. In the simple case considered here – of two so-called simple hypotheses that specify probability distributions for sets of observations – a fundamental lemma by Neyman and Pearson shows that such an R always exists. (If one of the hypotheses is composite, things become more complicated.)

Neyman and Pearson were able to explain both the traditional choices of test statistics and the use of the tail area to measure significance using their idea of a rejection region of a certain size and maximum power. For it turned out that both methods were mathematically equivalent. The tail area is, for the usual choices of alternative hypotheses, nothing more than the projection of a rejection region on the real line, and can be justified on the grounds of avoiding an error of the first kind. Furthermore, it turns out that many Fisherian choices of a test statistic are equivalent to a choice of an alternative hypothesis.

But let us now examine some of the major differences between Fisher's significance test and the Neyman–Pearson theory of testing statistical hypotheses using a typical application of the latter theory, quality control in industrial manufacturing. Imagine a manufacturer who produces metal plates that are used in medical instruments. It is important that the diameter of these plates should not exceed an optimal value, say 8 millimeters, by too much, since this would cause unreliability in the medical instruments. The manufacturer considers a certain diameter, say 10 millimeters, as definitely unacceptable. Every day she takes a random sample of n plates from production in order to decide between the two hypotheses that interest her, i.e., whether the diameter is 8 millimeters (H_1) or 10 millimeters (H_2). From past experience she knows that the random fluctuation of diameters is approximately normally distributed; furthermore she knows the standard deviation of these fluctuations, which is not dependent on the mean. This allows her to determine the sampling distributions of a sample statistic, such as the mean diameter for each of the two hypotheses. Based on this statistical model and the actual mean found in the sample, the manufacturer wants to make one of two decisions (with important practical consequences): either to accept H_1 and reject H_2, i.e. to place the whole production lot on the market; or to reject H_1 and accept H_2, i.e. to stop the production and look for the cause of the apparent malfunctioning.

Each of the two decisions involves a possible error, with very different consequences. If she accepts H_2 while H_1 is true, this will cause unnecessary delays in the production process. If she accepts H_1 although H_2 is true, the defective instruments may cause harm to some patients, and the firm's reputation may suffer. Since the latter seems to her the greater danger, she decides to make this the error of the first kind, and to set its probability α at 0.1%. An error of the first kind would thus be made if she accepted that the production run was faultless (H_1), when the run was in fact flawed with the plates having a diameter of about 10 millimeters (H_2). Now she has to choose a rejection region that minimizes the error of the second kind, false alarms. Since by varying the sample size, she has control over the error of the second kind, she decides to set β at 10%, and makes the calculations of the required sample size that will give her a test of this size and power. The actual sample is taken after this initial phase of combined personal judgment (about the validity of the statistical model and about the respective costs of the possible errors) and mathematical calculation. From here on, the procedure is quite mechanical. If the sample falls into the rejection region, H_2 is rejected and the whole production lot is placed on the market; otherwise H_2 is accepted and the production is stopped.

As Neyman emphasized, to accept a hypothesis is not to regard it as true, or to believe it. At most it means to act as if it were true. Because the manufacturer has set $\beta = 10\%$, for example, she must expect in one out of ten days to produce a false alarm – to stop the production even though it is satisfactory. She will not necessarily believe that H_1 is false, but only proceed as if it were.

In this example, it makes sense to give a behavioral interpretation to acceptance and rejection, and the relative severity of making the two kinds of error can be evaluated in terms of costs, thus providing a basis for choosing size and power. But these very features indicate that the Neyman–Pearson theory may be less suitable for scientific inference. To see this, we will return to the example of section 3.2. There we wondered, with the agricultural chemist Johnston, whether a certain proposed fertilizer would be causally effective in increasing grain yield. Here we take as one hypothesis, H_1, the null hypothesis of the Fisherian treatment. H_1 states that the treatment is ineffective, or, in statistical terms, that the z_i's are independent observations from a normal distribution with mean $\mu = 0$. To give a Neyman–Pearson treatment of that example, we need explicit introduction of at least one other hypothesis. For this we take the hypothesis that our treatment has an (average) positive effect of 0.3 bushels of grain per treatment plot. Statistically the hypothesis H_2 states that the z_i's are independent observations from a normal distribution with positive mean $\mu = 0.3$. We want to act conservatively, and to keep the probability of rejection H_1, when it is true, small. As α we take 0.05. Our task is now to define a rejection region R such that $p(R; H_1) = \alpha$, with maximum power of all possible rejection regions of that size. That is, $p(R; H_2) = 1-\beta$ should be made as large as possible. The fundamental lemma of Neyman and Pearson implies that such an R exists in this simple situation. Since we have nine independent observations, the rejection region is a region in a nine-dimensional space, which is hard to visualize. However, in this situation, the t-statistic projects this space on the real line in such a way that one-sided tail areas correspond to a Neyman–Pearson most powerful rejection region. If we choose R to be the set of observations with a t-value larger than 1.86, we will have a region of approximately the right size. To calculate the power of this rejection region is complicated; it involves the so-called non-central t-distribution (Resnikoff and Lieberman, 1957). If the alternative hypothesis is that $\mu = 0.21$, the power of the test is about 0.90; if the alternative is $\mu = 0.33$, the power becomes about 0.99. If we want to opt for a smaller α, say $\alpha = 0.01$, the power of the test, when $\mu = 0.3$, becomes dangerously low: about 0.6. There would be a chance of one in three that we will fail to reject the null hypothesis, if it is in fact false – that is, if μ is about 0.3. We could alleviate this by increasing the number of plots in the experiment. Considerations of power are, thus, quite useful in the design of an experiment, and in a sense they make explicit what in Fisher's approach is called the sensitivity of an experimental design (Cox, 1958; Cohen, 1977).

However, in a scientific application we rarely want to assert the disjunction "$\mu = 0$ or $\mu = 0.21$," and the interpretation of the errors of the first and second kind loses its cogency when we cannot do that. Although this is partly a consequence of our simplistic treatment of the example as a disjunction, it remains true that in science we will often have used the wrong hypothesis, and thus need a way to measure the discordance between data and hypothesis. Similarly, it is not clear how a scientific context can provide the utility considerations that go into the choice of the size and power of a test. In the mixed case of an applied science, such as agriculture, the alternative may be defined by a break-even point, where the present costs of applying the fertilizer are just offset by the present market price of the increase in yield. But this may not be too helpful, since these are subject to sharp fluctuations. Thus even in a semi-utilitarian science such as agronomy, we need conclusions that are independent of the present market prices of fertilizers and bushels of grain.

There are three ways in which Neyman and Pearson believed they had made Fisher's theory of significance testing more complete and consistent. First is the introduction of a rival hypothesis, which allows one to look at testing as a choice between hypotheses. It has already been accepted that one of the hypotheses must be true, a procedure that traditionally has been called "induction by elimination." This makes it possible to talk about the power of a test, and to calculate the required sample size for the desired power, where Fisher had only informally talked about the sensitivity of an experimental design. The Neyman–Pearson theory thus gives a more complete framework for planning an experiment.

Second, the frequencies of the errors of the first and second kind are calculated on the basis of repeated sampling of the distributions in the original mathematical specification of the problem, and the probabilities have therefore a direct frequency interpretation (although, perhaps, still a hypothetical one: the manufacturer will never commit an error of the first kind if her production process always runs faultlessly). Recall Fisher's belief that, in scientific applications, the population of the appropriate statistical model for the analysis of experimental data cannot in any realistic sense be sampled repeatedly, and has "no objective reality, being exclusively the product of the statistician's imagination." Therefore, after the sample is in, certain features of the sample (ancillary statistics) may be used to discern a subpopulation with respect to which the more relevant probabilities can be calculated (i.e., a conditional analysis). This led Fisher to say that "the infrequency with which in particular circumstances, decisive evidence is obtained, should not be confused with the force, or cogency, of such evidence" (Fisher, 1956, p. 92), a remark that Oskar Kempthorne has called a frontal attack on the repeated sampling principle (Kempthorne, 1976).

Third, in place of what Neyman and Pearson saw as Fisher's quasi-Bayesian view that the exact level of significance somehow measures the discordancy of the data with the null hypothesis, their interpretation of statistical inference was a purely behavioristic one that refrained from any epistemic interpretation. The concepts of size and power apply to a test, whereas Fisher's significance level is a property of the sample. If "inductive inference" is inferring an evidential relation between a sample and a hypothesis that determines a certain mental attitude towards the hypothesis, as Fisher wanted to have it, inductive inference, according to Neyman, cannot exist and, therefore, science cannot depend on it. What had been thought to be inductive reasoning or inference, Neyman argued, is really better called *inductive behavior*. To accept or reject a hypothesis is "an act of will or a decision to take a particular action, perhaps to assume a particular attitude towards the various sets of hypotheses" (Neyman, 1957). Whether one calls this inference or behavior may be a matter of taste. Indeed, if inference is the assertion of sentences on the basis of assumptions, the Neyman–Pearson theory may well be looked at as a theory of inference (Hacking, 1980). Valid deductive inference is strictly truth-preserving: if the premises on which the inference is based are true, its conclusion is bound to be true. Inductive inference cannot guarantee that much. But the Neyman–Pearson theory can promise high frequency of getting it right. Suppose the decision one makes is to assert one of the possible conclusions, here "H_1" or "H_2." If the assumption of "H_1 or H_2" is true, one will assert the true hypothesis with probability of at least the minimum of $1-\alpha$ and $1-\beta$. If both α is chosen small and β is made small, through experimental design and choice of rejection region, an inference rule with high frequency of asserting a true statement results, assuming the premises to be true. The latter qualification is important, and shows that, even if one accepts the Neyman–Pearson theory of hypothesis testing as a theory of inductive inference, significance testing still may have a role to play. For statistics may still need tests that are able to call into question the whole assumed model, the whole disjunction. If one makes an observation that is discordant with both H_1 and H_2, the Neyman–Pearson test will accept the hypothesis the data are least discordant with. In practice, we would reject the disjunction "H_1 or H_2," for it is also important to avoid an error of the third kind: giving the right answer to the wrong question, asked by the wrong model (Kimball, 1957). Its probability, however, is not well-defined.

In various publications (e.g. 1955, 1956), Fisher rejected each of these three "corrections" and "improvements." He believed Neyman had mistakenly reinterpreted his tests of significance in terms of acceptance procedures, an ideological point of view that valued expediency over truth. Indeed, Fisher likened Neyman to

Russians [who] are made familiar with the ideal that research in pure science can and should be geared to technological performance, in the comprehensive organized effort of a five-year plan for the nation. . . [While] in the U.S. also the great importance of organized technology has I think made it easy to confuse the process appropriate for drawing correct conclusions, with those aimed rather at, let us say, speeding production, or saving money (Fisher, 1955, p. 70).

Neyman, for his part, said that some of Fisher's tests "are in a mathematically specifiable sense 'worse than useless,' " since their power is less than their size (see Hacking, 1965, p. 99). Although acceptance procedures and quality control require utility considerations such as costs of possible errors, Fisher argued, these play no role in and must not be confused with inductive inference in the sciences, which is what tests of significance are about. Fisher drew a bold line between his significance tests and the hypothesis tests of Neyman and Pearson, and ridiculed the latter as having only a very limited field of application because derived from "the phantasy of circles [i.e. mathematicians] rather remote from scientific research" (1956, p. 100). Proponents of the other camp, however, argued that there was no difference in fields of application, because they had simply made Fisher's theory more consistent. For instance, in a paper presented to a conference on the question "For what use are tests of hypotheses and tests of significance?" Neyman wrote: "The title of the present session involves an element that appears mysterious to me. This element is the apparent distinction between tests of statistical hypotheses, on the one hand, and tests of significance, on the other. If this is not a lapse of someone's pen, then I hope to learn the conceptual distinction" (Neyman, 1976b).

Because of Fisher's remarkable talent for polemic, the debate never lacked for overblown rhetoric. He branded Neyman's position as "childish" and "horrifying [for] intellectual freedom in the west." Both parties called up the heroes of the past, such as Laplace and Gauss, to be their witnesses. The authority of W. S. Gosset was claimed by both camps. Fisher described him as a man "actively concerned with research in the natural sciences" (Gosset worked for Guinness, the brewers), and claimed that Gosset used his test in the same spirit as had Fisher. In answer, Pearson published a letter from Gosset stating that a test "doesn't itself necessarily prove that the sample is not drawn randomly from the population even if the chance is very small, say .00001: what it does is to show that if there is any alternative hypothesis which will explain the occurrence of the sample with a reasonable probability, say .05, . . . you will be very much more inclined to consider that the original hypothesis is not true" (E. S. Pearson, 1938, p. 243). Here Gosset made a strong point for rival hypotheses, although not for cost-benefit considerations. As Hacking (1965, p. 83) put it, the man who first conceived one of the great tests was now urging "that it is not merely low likelihood which matters, but rather the ratio of the likelihoods."

These, then, were vigorous controversies, and they have not ended. Disputes no less heated have characterized the relationship between Bayesians and frequentists. So it is especially remarkable that all of these unresolved controversial issues, conceptual ambiguities, and personal insults have been more or less completely suppressed from the textbooks that have taught significance testing to the customer – the experimenter in the sciences. The need for personal judgment – for Fisher in the choice of model and test statistic; for Neyman and Pearson in the choice of a class of hypotheses and a rejection region; for the Bayesians in the choice of a prior probability – as well as the existence of alternative statistical conceptions, were ignored by most textbooks. As a consequence, scientific researchers in many fields learned to apply statistical tests in a quasi-mechanical way, without giving adequate attention to what questions these numerical procedures really answer.

3.5   HYBRIDIZATION: THE SILENT SOLUTION

The intellectual effort of statisticians to provide a mathematical foundation for hypothesis testing has had a tremendous impact on the sciences, especially on biology and the social sciences. In sociology and psychology, significance testing has become practically the only statistical tool, and other developments such as confidence intervals, the likelihood function, or Bayesian inference have been for the most part ignored by experimenters. In part, this is probably due to the stress Fisher put on significance testing in the first edition of his 1925 book, and to the theory of experimental design he provided, together with significance testing, in his 1935 *Design of Experiments*. Although the debate continues among statisticians, it was silently resolved in the "cookbooks" written in the 1940s to the 1960s, largely by non-statisticians, to teach students in the social sciences the "rules of statistics." Fisher's theory of significance testing, which was historically first, was merged with concepts from the Neyman–Pearson theory and taught as "statistics" *per se*. We call this compromise the "hybrid theory" of statistical inference, and it goes without saying that neither Fisher nor Neyman and Pearson would have looked with favor on this offspring of their forced marriage.

The creation of the hybrid can be understood on three levels – mathematical statisticians, textbook writers, and experimenters. On the first level, there was a tendency to resolve the controversial issues separating the three major schools by distinguishing between theory and application, and by saying that practical-minded people need not be bothered by these mainly theoretical issues (noted in Hogben, 1957). To users of statistics, this seemed perfectly acceptable, since often the same formulae were used and the same numerical results obtained. The great differences in conceptual interpretation were overlooked in the plug-in-and-crank-through use of statistical rules.

But, on the second level, writers of textbooks for education, psychology, sociology, and so on, commenced peace negotiatons and created a hybrid theory, to which shelves and shelves in research libraries now pay tribute. The hybrid theory combines concepts from the Fisherian and the Neyman–Pearson framework. It is presented anonymously as statistical method, while unresolved controversial issues and alternative approaches to scientific inference are completely ignored. Key concepts from the Neyman–Pearson theory such as power are introduced along with Fisher's significance testing, without mentioning that both parties viewed these ideas as irreconcilable. For instance, checking (without random sampling) thirty books on statistics for psychology, education, and sociology that were readily available, we found that the names of Neyman and E. S. Pearson were not even mentioned in twenty-five of them, although some of their ideas were presented. None even hinted at the existence of controversy, much less spelled out the issues in dispute. The crucial concepts were not identified with their creators – which is very unusual in fields like psychology, where textbooks list competing theories and the researchers who proposed them for almost every phenomenon discussed. Statistics is treated as abstract truth, the monolithic logic of inductive inference.

The hybrid theory comes with a list of prescriptions that are held to constitute what is "scientific" and "objective." The researcher must specify the level of significance before conducting the experiment (following Neyman and Pearson rather than Fisher); he must not draw conclusions from a non-significant result (following Fisher's writings, but not Neyman–Pearson); and so on. Neyman's behavioristic interpretation did not become part of the hybrid, and the type-I and type-II errors are given an epistemic interpretation. This has led to an enormous confusion about the meaning of a significance level. For instance, in practice (contrary to prescript), experimenters often will note, when inspecting the data, at what most stringent conventional level the data are significant with respect to the null hypothesis. They then report that the null hypothesis is, say, "rejected at the 0.01 level," an expression that occurs neither in Fisher nor in the writings of Neyman and Pearson.

The hybrid theory was institutionalized by editors of major journals and in the university curricula, in what has been called the "inference revolution" (Gigerenzer and Murray, 1987). By the mid-1950s, the use of significance tests and of conventional rejection levels was well established in sociological research, and researchers not using significance tests felt the pressure to explain and defend their deviant behavior (Morrison and Henkel, 1970). In the hands of the experimenters and editors, the hybrid theory often degenerated into a mechanical ritual, although Fisher, Gosset, Neyman, and Pearson had all warned against drawing inferences from tests without judgment. In some fields, a strikingly narrow understanding of statistical significance made a significant result seem to be the ultimate purpose of research, and non-significance the sign of a badly conducted experiment – hence with almost no chance of publication (see 6.3). This practice of neglecting non-significant results may have been derived directly from an ill-considered passage in Fisher's *The Design of Experiments*: "It is usual and convenient for experimenters to take the 5 per cent. as a standard level of significance, in the sense that they are prepared to ignore all results which fail to reach this standard, and, by this means, to eliminate from further discussion the greater part of the fluctuations which chance causes have thrown into their experimental results" (1935, §7). Here Fisher seems clearly to sanction the practice of taking no notice of statistically insignificant results. But this reading is in direct contradiction to his analysis of the relation between significance testing and the demonstration of a natural phenomenon, presented in the very same section. Since he thought that experimental demonstration of, say, an interesting psychological phenomenon required confirmation by similar experiments in other laboratories, it would follow that non-significant results should also be published, so that the literature will correctly reflect the frequency with which a type of experiment has led to significant results. This implication of Fisher's writings was not heeded in the social sciences. Negative results submitted for publication are often rejected with a facile declaration that "the sensitivity of the experiment [is] substandard for the type of investigation in question" (Melton, 1962, p. 554).

As an apparently non-controversial body of statistical knowledge, the hybrid theory has survived all attacks since its inception in the 1940s. If only for practical reasons, it has easily defeated ecumenism (Box, 1986), in which one applies the different approaches to the same data, acknowledging that the different approaches are conceptually unlike. It has survived attacks from proponents of the Neyman–Pearson school, and the Bayesians (Edwards, Lindman, and Savage, 1963), and Popperians (Meehl, 1978). Its dominance permits the suppression of the hard questions. What, if any, is the relation between statistical significance and substantial importance within the scientific discipline? To what aspects of the scientific enterprise do the ideas of Fisher, and of Neyman and Pearson, appeal, and how can these be combined? Are the experimental designs developed by statisticians in agriculture and biology really a good model for all experimentation in the social sciences?

What is most remarkable is the confidence within each social-science discipline that the standards of scientific demonstration have now been objectively and universally defined. In fact, the standardization of statistical methods becomes much less complete if one looks across disciplines. In econometrics, to take the most striking contrast, experiment is comparatively rare, and the standard statistical tool is regression analysis. It has often been applied by economists with a lack of imagination that matches the psychologists' use of hypothesis testing (McCloskey, 1985). Graduate students within the social and biological sciences have routinely been taught to view their statistical tools as canonical, given by logic and mathematics. The methods of statistical inference could be seen by practitioners uncomfortable with higher mathematics as someone else's concern, the province of statistical specialists.

3.6 THE STATISTICAL PROFESSION: INTELLECTUAL AUTONOMY

Statistical inference, and the accompanying mathematics, have become the basis for an expertise that extends to an enormous range of disciplines and practical problems and that supports a whole profession of statisticians. The abstracting journal *Statistical Theory and Method Abstracts*, a publication of the International Statistical Institute (ISI), lists over 130 journals mainly devoted to statistics, from the Indian *Aligarh Journal of Statistics* to the West-German *Zeitschrift für Wahrscheinlichkeitstheorie und verwandte Gebiete*. Beside the ISI (founded 1885), there are now many other international statistical organizations, such as the Bernoulli Society for Mathematical Statistics and Probability. Many industrialized countries have their own organization for theoretical statistics, one of the oldest being the Royal Statistical Society, founded in 1834 as the Statistical Society of London. Universities now often have a separate department for statistics, or even for biostatistics. Inferential statisticians work in many other departments, such as psychology, economics, and archeology. Statisticians are consultants in science, industry, and government. More and more we find statisticians acting as expert witnesses in the courts, and it is debated whether the way evidence should be combined in the courts can be modeled using ideas from probability theory (see 7.4; also Eggleston, 1978; DeGroot *et al.*, 1986).

This professionalization of statistics and of statisticians has several aspects. Two of them we call autonomy and influence. In this section we ask how statistics became a discipline *per se*, where it earlier had been an appendage of other disciplines like sociology, or biology. That is, how did statistics become autonomous? In section 3.7, we consider the institutions of statistics, and ask how statisticians were able to reach out to, and affect, so many other disciplines and other social institutions.

Whence this tremendous influence? What were its channels and what needs did it satisfy? How did it change the disciplines involved and how was it changed itself in the process? Without trying to answer these questions in depth, we will indicate some of what we think are the key issues.

Specialized knowledge

A scientific discipline is characterized by a body of specialized knowledge and skills, and by a complex of institutions, formal and informal, that guide its development and workings. The specialized knowledge of statisticians consists in methods to determine how data should be gathered, to analyze and summarize data, to make inferences on the basis of data, and to propose decisions on the basis of theories, data, and goals. Their skills include the tacit knowledge needed in the application of this knowledge, since it often involves a degree of subjective judgment. Those skills are developed by working as a consultant for fellow scientists and for clients outside the academic environment, in government, industry, and the like.

The methods the statistician uses are mathematical and abstract. They do not result from one single idea, but form a network of interrelated ideas. Most, but not all, use the concept of *probability*. Many, but not even most, use the concept of a *statistical model*. Still, these two concepts, probability and model, are central to the network of knowledge of the statistician, since even the methods that do not use them, such as exploratory data analysis (Tukey, 1977a) or distribution-free statistical tests (Bradley, 1968), are often partly characterized by the very fact that they do not use them! The two concepts are highly abstract, and because they are so abstract they can be applied to, and recognized in, many different situations. The historical events through which these two abstract concepts were defined were seminal for the development of statistics as a scientific discipline.

The concept of probability was defined in the early 1930s by the Soviet mathematician A. N. Kolmogorov, who further developed an axiomatization of comparative probability due to S. N. Bernstein by incorporating ideas from set theory and the theory of functions (Maistrov, [1964] 1974). Of course, long before Kolmogorov, people had referred to and used the concept of probability. This whole book is a testimony to that. But their use was often tied to what in hindsight appears to be only a limited application. And their calculations sometimes seem incoherent to us when they implicitly assume probability to have properties we do not attribute to it (Shafer, 1978). In his 1933 paper 'Grundbegriffe der

Wahrscheinlichkeitsrechnung," Kolmogorov laid down axiomatically what properties the concept of probability should have. Probability is defined as a set-function. It assigns to each set in a "field of sets" its "probability," a real number between zero and one. If two sets have no elements in common, the probability of their union is equal to the sum of their probabilities. The probability of a certain basic set, the set E of all elementary events, is equal to one. All other sets in the field are subsets of E. The notion of a random variable is defined as a function from the set E into the real numbers; prior to Kolmogorov this was taken to be a primitive notion, not defined in terms of other more basic notions. With these definitions, Kolmogorov showed that there are striking analogies between the notion of the measure of a set and the probability of an event, between the integral and mathematical expectation, and between orthogonality of functions and the independence of random variables. In this way he was able to systematize on the basis of first principles many results on the law of large numbers obtained by Khinchin, Borel, Cantelli, and Hausdorff. The work of the Russian school of probabilists, including Chebyshev, Markov, Lyapunov, Bernstein, Khinchin, and Kolmogorov, reestablished probabilty theory as a serious mathematical discipline, which it had not been since new standards of rigor in mathematics were introduced early in the nineteenth century by Cauchy and others (see Schneider, 1987). Its influence reached far beyond the borders of the Soviet Union: first over Central Europe and then, through the diaspora of the 1930s, all over the world. Many of the now retired probabilists in the United States have their roots in this Central European tradition (Gani, 1982).

The concept of a statistical model was introduced by Ronald A. Fisher in 1922, in his fundamental paper "On the Mathematical Foundations of Theoretical Statistics." Fisher did not formally define the concept; he was not interested in abstract mathematics, but used an intuitive, conceptual approach. In fact, it was a citizen of one of the smaller European countries, the Swede Harald Cramér, who, between 1930 and 1950, mediated between the British and American science of statistics – which was based mainly in the empirical and experimental tradition – and the mathematical rigor of the Continental European work in probability theory. He tried to unify the two traditions in his 1946 book *Mathematical Methods of Statistics*. This unification has never been complete, and one still finds probability theory typically worked on in departments of mathematics, while statisticians, who apply results in probability theory to statistical inference, have their own organizational units. Characteristic of this is the split, in 1973, of the *Annals in Mathematical Statistics*, into the *Annals of Statistics* and the *Annals of Probability Theory*.

Still, since Fisher consciously pursued conceptual clarifications in his 1922 paper, we can look at it as introducing the abstract concept of a statistical model. In his paper, Fisher emphasized the distinction between a sample and the population from which the sample is drawn. The population may be an actually existing one, as in a survey of the farming community of a country, but more generally it may be a hypothetical and even infinite population, as in the set of all possible coin tosses with a certain coin (where it is assumed that the same type of toss is being performed and that the coin does not wear out), or the set of all possible repetitions of a comparative agricultural experiment (where it is assumed that the same experimental procedure is followed and that the soil does not become impoverished). The tosses actually performed and the trials actually made are then considered as a random sample from this conceptual population. The distinction between population and sample had not been sufficiently heeded by his predecessors, Fisher felt. For instance, they often talked about a *mean* indiscriminately, as the average of a sample or as the average of the population from which the sample is drawn. Fisher used small Greek letters, like σ, for the characteristics of the population, called parameters, and small Roman letters like s for characteristics of the sample $(x_1, \ldots, x_n)$. These characteristics he then called *statistics*. The parameters may be partially unknown and the sample can give information about these unknown parameters. It is the task of statistical inference, Fisher stated, to find summaries of the data, that is to obtain statistics of the data, that contain as much as possible of the relevant information the data provide about the population and its parameter values. A statistic that contains the same information as the full data about the population Fisher called a *sufficient statistic*.

In abstract terms, a *parametric statistical model* M consists of a specification of an observable variable X, a parameter Θ, and for each value of Θ a probability function $p(x; \theta)$, that gives the probability of making the observation $X = x$ when $\Theta = \theta$ (Dawid, 1983). Fisher's idea is that an observation x is informative about Θ when $p(x; \theta)$ is not the same for all values θ of Θ. Suppose it is observed that $X = x$ and that $p(x; \theta_1)$ is larger than $p(x; \theta_2)$; then it is said that the likelihood of θ_1 is larger than the likelihood of θ_2, and that, on the basis of the observation that $X = x$ alone, θ_1 is more likely than θ_2.

A statistical model is a very abstract and flexible concept of wide applicability. For instance, the nineteenth-century problem of measurement and measuring error can be conceptualized in terms of a statistical model. A measurement procedure and the object to be measured determine a possible measurement result x. Assuming there is no constant error in the measurements, the precision σ of the procedure determines how close the measurements are grouped around the true value μ to be measured. Assuming that there is a lot of experience with the procedure, σ may be known (say 1), and the only unknown parameter is μ. In the traditional error theory $p(x; \mu)$ is then often taken to be a normal distribution with variance 1 and mean μ. If we take twenty measurements, X is the vector $(X_1, \ldots, X_{20})$ and $p(x; \mu)$ is the product $p(x_1; \mu) \ldots p(x_{20}; \mu)$, since in error theory repeated measurements are considered to be independent, and, ideally, experimental safeguards are used to guarantee this. The average of the sample $\bar{x} = \Sigma\, x_i\, /n$ is a sufficient statistic, in the sense that $p(x \mid \bar{x}; \mu) = p(x \mid \mu)/p(\bar{x}; \mu)$ is the same for different values of μ, and thus contains no information about μ. That is, given we know the value of the average of the measurements, to know more about the individual measurements will not give more information about μ. A scientist is therefore justified, assuming that the precision of his procedures is known, in communicating to his colleagues only the average value of his measurements plus the number of individual measurements taken (the size of the sample). The average is at the same time the maximum likelihood estimate of μ: if we set μ_0 equal to x then $p(x; \mu_0)$ is maximized; assuming any other value for μ will assign a smaller probability to the observation x actually made. It is assumed throughout that M is a "correct" statistical model, in the sense that it contains the true probability distribution for the observed quantities X.

Karl Pearson had sought to move statistics away from the tendency to assume that data are distributed according to the normal curve, and to this end he defined a whole family of curves, of which the normal was only a special case. He generally fit these curves to observational, not experimental data. In determining their "frequency constants," or "quaesita," as the parameters were often called before Fisher, he did not aim to identify entities with causal powers, but merely to summarize the observations. The biometricians, therefore, provided a biological theory without causes, completely in line with Pearson's *Grammar of Science*. Fisher's parametric statistical models, in contrast, were closely tied to experiment. His parameters gave estimates of the causal power of a fertilizer or drug under test. The parametric families of distributions Fisher used in his statistical models were usually simpler than Pearson's, and one may argue that the success of Fisher's new concepts, like sufficient statistics, was bought by limiting himself to these more restricted families of distributions (Stigler, 1976). Ironically, Fisher's work was in this respect a return to nineteenth-century ideas, since he often assumed that the observations, or some known function of the observations, were normally distributed, thus contributing to the "myth of normality." Recently, concern about how good statistical methods are under mild deviations from normality or other classical distribution functions has led to a study of the "robustness" of these methods (Huber, 1981). Similar concerns have fueled interest in so-called distribution-free tests (Bradley, 1968).

Still, Fisher's idea of a parametric statistical model is a powerful and unifying concept, and is not restricted to the special kind of models he studied himself and for which his concepts of statistical inference, such as the sufficient statistic, seem so appropriate. In fact one may say that the load carried in the Bayesian approach by the prior probability distribution, is borne by the model in this part of Fisher's analysis of statistical inference (Hotelling, 1951).

A particularly important kind of statistical model is a so-called stochastic process, which describes a system that changes over time according to probabilistic laws. The error-theory models of the nineteenth century assumed independence of the successive measurements (Lancaster, 1972), and even the correlational studies, in which measurements like the height of fathers and the height of sons were obviously not independent, did not have the dynamic character that one now associates with time series and stochastic processes. Interestingly, the probabilistic theory of stochastic processes is not an outgrowth of the empirical study of random phenomena, but of the Russian theoretical studies in mathematical probability theory that culminated in Kolmogorov's axiomatization (see, however, the discussion of stochasticity in physics in 5.7).

According to Bernoulli's theorem (see 1.7), frequencies of independent chance events must converge to the underlying probabilities. When, near the end of the nineteenth century, an explicit interest in the notion of dependent trials arose, it was still thought by many that this so-called "law of large numbers" – the term is Poisson's – is only true for independent trials. In the context of a general investigation by the Russian school of necessary and sufficient conditions for laws of large numbers, A. A. Markov showed in 1906 that the convergence holds even under conditions of weak dependency (Markov, 1906). What is now called a Markov chain is a mathematical model of a process without after-effects, which describes a physical system in which the probability of transition to another state depends only on the state of the system at the given time and not on the previous history of the process. Questions about dependence and the importance of the work of Lexis and Karl Pearson were further raised in a correspondence between the probabilist Markov and the statistician Chuprov, which became a starting point of a general theory of stochastic processes (Ondar, 1981). The Swedes, especially Harald Cramér and Herman Wold, were again central in combining the mathematical work of the Russians with the more observational approach of Karl Pearson and G. Udny Yule (Bartlett, 1959).

Stochastic processes are now a modeling tool for a wide variety of scientific disciplines: econometrics, meteorology, oceanography, sociology, epidemiology, plant and animal ecology, chemistry, physics, architecture, and cosmology, to mention just a few (Gani, 1986). For the social sciences they deliver, in part, what Adolphe Quetelet expected from "social physics" (Quetelet, 1869; see also 2.2), by making it possible to explain social trends and to make short-range predictions (Bartholomew, 1967). In the physical sciences they provide a way to show the lawlikeness of some natural phenomena that elude the more classical approaches, such as the regular shape of ripples on a beach (Barndorff-Nielsen, 1985).

3.7 THE STATISTICAL PROFESSION: INSTITUTIONS AND INFLUENCE

The discipline of inferential statistics is characterized not only by a coherent network of specialized knowledge, but also by a complex of institutions, formal and informal, that guide its development and workings. These include international and national professional organizations and the sections of universities where statisticians work.

The central international organization is the International Statistical Institute, which celebrated its centenary jubilee in 1985 (Atkinson and Fienberg, 1985). It is instructive to compare the ISI when it was founded in 1885 with what it is today. At its foundation the ISI was intended to be a continuation of the International Statistical Congresses, the first of which was organized, under the leadership of Quetelet, by the Central Statistical Commission of Belgium, and held in Brussels in 1853 (Neumann-Spallart, 1885). These congresses aimed to formulate uniform methods of classification and collection to promote international comparability of statistical data. Their members were mostly directors of official statistical bureaus. Some of the scientific members hoped, with Quetelet, that the amassing of careful and comparable statistical data would bring into the open statistical laws and regularities for a future "social physics." Thus the congresses had also given attention to methods of statistical data analysis and data representation. However, the congresses slowly lost their initial zeal and became a victim of their double goal: to be a meeting place for government officials with the power of binding resolutions (which also exposed them to political turmoil, as in the Franco-Prussian war), and to provide an opportunity for private individuals to exchange ideas and arguments of a moral or scientific nature. The ISI was therefore proposed as a purely free association analogous to the *Institut de France*, where members were selected on the basis of their personal qualifications, but with the same goal as the congresses: to introduce uniformity in the compilation of statistical data and to promote and foster the knowledge of statistical science.

The proceedings of the ISI provide interesting source material for a comprehensive history of statistics, since on its pages we see the clash in styles and interest of statisticians from many different local traditions. One such debate concerned the very possibility of using samples to get knowledge about a population, such as the farming community in Bulgaria. In the nineteenth century, statisticians who collected data had relied more and more on what Georg von Mayr called the "erschöpfende Beobachtung der primären sozialen Masse," that is, on complete investigation of the population under study (Mayr, 1895). "Partial investigations" were considered imprecise and unscientific. It was again a statistician from one of the smaller European countries, Anders Kiaer, director of the Central Bureau of Statistics of Norway, who pressed for using samples, or what he called "the representative method" (Kiaer, 1898). One of his arguments was that the quality of the data in a sample would often be much better than if the whole population had been investigated, since more care by better trained interviewers could be exerted. Kiaer's "representative method" did not, however, make use of random sampling; it was a systematic search for a sample that agreed in important characteristics with the population at large. These characteristics had to be learned from a complete investigation, a census. Random sampling was only understood in the beginning of this century (Jensen, 1926). An early paper by Jerzy Neyman still battled against Kiaer's version of sampling and was important in getting the general idea of randomness in sampling accepted (Neyman, 1934).

In the interwar period, organizations appeared that competed with the ISI, either in its aim to collect statistics and to set standards for data gathering or in its scientific goals. Among them were the League of

Nations, the International Labor Organization, the International Institute of Agriculture, the Econometric Society, and the International Union for the Scientific Investigation of Population Problems (Zahn, 1934). But it was the Second World War that marked a sharp break in the history of the ISI, and led to fundamental changes in the organization, constitution, and aims of the Institute (Nixon, 1960). Numerous international agencies in the context of the United Nations took over the administrative functions of the ISI. The ISI was more narrowly defined as an "international statistical academy" – a voluntary and scientific rather than an official organization; a community of statistical experts who were to be judged exclusively on their professional merit, and not on what country or organization they represented (Rice, 1947). Its activity shifted towards theory and methodology. It thus became the international agency of professionalized mathematical statistics, and shed all association with semi-governmental activities. Its active members are now mostly university professors. Of the forty-one contributors to the *Centenary Volume* (Atkinson and Fienberg, 1985), thirty-three hold university positions. The ISI recently approved a "Declaration of Professional Ethics" (International Statistical Institute, 1986).

Departments of statistics as we now know them are successors to the so-called "statistical laboratory." The earliest of these influential laboratories was the Galton Laboratory, endowed by Francis Galton in 1904, whose first director was Karl Pearson. This laboratory took in advanced students from science and industry to learn statistical methods that could be applied to the problems of their own field. A few of these students, such as W. S. Gosset, a chemist by training, became important pioneers in the mathematics of statistics. Most of them contributed mainly by mastering existing techniques and applying them to new problems. Some of their work was published in *Biometrika*, the journal founded by Francis Galton, Karl Pearson, and the zoologist W. F. R. Weldon in 1901 to collect biological data of a statistical kind and to spread the statistical methods and perspective that would promote a biology based on the study of variation, as opposed to morphological understanding in terms of ideal types. Pearson's laboratory institutionalized the new intellectual structure of statistics, in which statistics was first of all a body of mathematical tools and formulations which could be applied to an almost unlimited domain of topics. The laboratory slowly began to attract an international group of postgraduates. In 1925, when Neyman came from Warsaw to study with Karl Pearson, only one of the eight students was an

Englishman. The others were all from the U.S., with the exception of a Japanese. The next year brought students from Spain, Canada, China, India, and Yugoslavia. By that time Pearson had managed to incorporate the laboratory into a Department of Applied Statistics.

Fisher's presence in Rothamsted, and then University College, London, played a similar fertilizing role. Harold Hotelling, who exerted a great impact on statistics and the way it was taught in the USA before the Second World War, was a volunteer on the farm during the academic year 1929–30 (Hotelling, 1940). In the period 1934–44, when Fisher was Galton Professor of Eugenics at University College in London (having succeeded Karl Pearson) more than fifty people from all over the world, and from a variety of experimental disciplines – chemistry, biology, medicine, agriculture, and social science – came to work with him (Youden, 1951).

The influence of Fisher's first book, *Statistical Methods for Research Workers*, was tremendous (Yates, 1951). It went through eleven editions in the first twenty-five years of its existence, with nearly 20,000 copies sold, and was translated into French, Italian, Spanish, German, and Japanese. In that period, analysis of variance found applications in agricultural trials, biological assays, industrial experimentation, quality control, and many experimental scientific fields.

One of the broadest channels for the flow of information from Europe to the United States was the Statistics Laboratory of Iowa State College, the first of the great academic statistical centers in the United States. George W. Snedecor, the Director of the Laboratory, arranged for Fisher to lecture at two summer sessions in 1931 and 1936. Snedecor himself, in his teaching and in his well-known book *Statistical Methods*, made Fisher's methods available to a host of workers in agronomy and animal husbandry (Youden, 1951). Other centers for the new enthusiasm in statistics were the University of North Carolina at Chapel Hill, the University of Michigan at Ann Arbor, and Columbia University in New York.

Perhaps the most direct influence from Europe on the development of statistics in the United States was Neyman's acceptance, in 1938, of a faculty position at the University of California at Berkeley, where he remained the rest of his life. First within the Department of Mathematics, and later in a separate Department of Statistics, Neyman copied Pearson's statistical laboratory as he had seen it in London. From this base, Neyman collaborated fruitfully with a wide variety of scientists, including astronomers, biologists, and meteorologists.

Statistics goes to war

Neyman's arrival in the United States was, by chance, well timed. His philosophy of statistical inference, brought forward with particular explicitness in the expression he coined in 1938, "inductive behavior" (in contrast to "find reductions of data to communicate to fellow research workers," as statistical inference was understood by Fisher), fit well the mood of the time and the requirements dictated by the approaching war. "The only useful function of a statistician is to make predictions, and thus to provide a basis for action," wrote W. E. Deming of the War Department in 1942 (Wallis, 1980). And earlier the War Preparedness Committee of the Institute of Mathematical Statistics, an offspring of the less mathematical American Statistical Association, had stressed that statisticians were not just good in calculating averages and index numbers, but could also contribute to the National Defense Program in such areas as quality control, sample surveys, experimentation, personnel selection, gunnery and bombing, and weather forecasting (Eisenhart *et al.*, 1940).

In fact it was through their activities in the Second World War that statisticians were able to influence so many other disciplines and social institutions. Both the positive reception of statistics – by engineering and the social sciences, by industry and the military – and its departmental autonomy were furthered by the war effort (Fienberg, 1985; Barnard and Plackett, 1985). It led to new developments along the lines of Neyman's doctrine of inductive behavior, which was made more prudent in the theory of sequential analysis and more mathematical in the theory of statistical decision functions, both developed by Abraham Wald and published after the war (Wald, 1947, 1950). The theory of statistical decision functions was given a subjective twist in the personalistic or Bayesian decision theory of L. J. Savage (Savage, 1954).

In the United States during the Second World War, there were several major groups of statisticians working under contract of one of the branches of the armed forces, notably at Columbia (the Statistical Research Group, or S.R.G., under W. A. Wallis), at Princeton (under S. S. Wilks), and at Berkeley (under Neyman). Sequential analysis originated in the S.R.G. at Columbia through a suggestion of a Navy officer, an ordnance expert at the U.S. Naval Proving Ground in Dahlgren, Virginia. He argued that one could see after the first so many rounds that the experiment need not be completed, either because the new method was obviously superior or obviously inferior. This idea was picked up by Wallis and the economist Milton Friedman and transformed by Abraham

Wald into a full-blooded modification of the Neyman–Pearson theory, the theory of sequential analysis. Wald was a Romanian Jew who had worked for a short time at the Austrian Institute for Business Cycle Research, where Oskar Morgenstern was then director. He had been able to flee Austria after the *Anschluss* with Germany in 1938, and found refuge in the United States with the financial support of the Carnegie Foundation. Sequential analysis is the theory of sequences of Neyman–Pearson decisions in which, instead of choosing between two decisions (reject or accept), the statistician also has the option of deciding to make more observations. This means that the sample size is not fixed in advance. It turns out that sequential testing can lead to more powerful tests of the same size, in the Neyman–Pearson sense. Wald's theory of statistical decision functions interprets statistical problems as decision problems in a "game against nature." Using the theory of games and its formal utility theory developed by John von Neumann and Oskar Morgenstern, Wald was able to take into account the losses that one would incur when making a wrong decision as an error of the first kind.

It is clear that the Second World War influenced the specifics of statistical research. A large number of applied research projects that fit into the war effort got funded. After the war the same military funding sources, such as the Office of Navy Research, kept financing the basic research of the scientists and their students whom they had funded during the war (Old, 1961). Our claim here, however, is that it also strengthened the decision theoretic approach to statistical problems, and accustomed people to the idea that reasonable decisions can be made on the basis of formal, mechanized reasoning combined with measurements. A prime example of this is the role of statistics in psychology. Before 1940, psychologists used largely informal and unstandardized methods to assess their experimental and observational results (Gigerenzer and Murray, 1987). Through the impact of such war studies as Stouffer *et al.* (1949, 1950) on the social psychology of American soldiers during the Second World War, statistical techniques of the accept/reject variety strengthened their hold on the psychologists, a trend that was reinforced by the needs of educational administrators for an "objective" technique to guide them in their bureaucratic decisions on curriculum innovation (Danziger, 1987a).

3.8   CONCLUSION

The agricultural chemist Johnston found himself confronted with a problem concerning experimental design and the inference from observational data to causal hypotheses. These problems were not pursued by trying to analyze the laws that govern the subject matter under investigation – in Johnston's case, the physiology and chemistry of plants. Because of the variation displayed by natural objects in their natural environment, questions like this one have come to be studied in a quite different way. In fact, this agricultural example is typical of problems in a variety of disciplines that scientists are now accustomed to investigating according to a canon of research defined by the new abstract discipline of scientific inference, mathematical statistics. Bits and pieces of this discipline emerged here and there; they have accompanied the entire history of probability. Yet this combination into a single unified conceptual structure and methodological doctrine came late and is far from being completed. Alternative schools of inferential statistics compete, and doubtful compromises dominate in the practice of social scientists (see chapter 6). Nevertheless, impressive conceptual and institutional achievements, together with economic needs and political interests, have shaped a new profession of inference experts.

In the upbeat tone of his 1953 presidential address to the Royal Statistical Society, which provided the epigraph to this chapter, R. A. Fisher speculated that "hidden causes have been at work for much longer than the period of manifest efflorescence, preparing men's minds, and shaping the institutions through which they work, so that, quite suddenly when the academic tools had become sufficiently sharp and accurate, or perhaps, equally important, sufficiently realistic, there was no end to the number of applications impatiently awaiting methods which could, really, deliver the goods" (Fisher, 1953). The philosopher and the historian have to be more fastidious, and recognize that applications are equally often created because the tools are there to address them, and that existing problems come to be redefined in terms of the new concepts that accompany these tools. We have seen in this chapter some striking instances of this, such as the change in the ideal of a scientific experiment and in the meaning of causality. This is perhaps most clearly exemplified in psychology, which was transformed by statistics from a science asking for general psychological laws to a discipline dedicated to searching for causal factors that operate on the average in a population. We will return to this in chapter 6.

The changes brought by the new methods of statistical inference are ubiquitous and profound. In early modern science, knowledge had to be publicly demonstrated, and it was customary to have witnesses sign a document that the events reported had actually happened. But these witnesses were not required to be able to replicate the demonstrations, whose proper execution still depended on the high priests of science. In modern bureaucratic and utilitarian societies, such reliance on private knowledge to reach conclusions important for social life has become ideologically unacceptable. In less democratic times and places, the judgment of a political and social elite had no need to be clothed in facts and figures. Scientists, having little public accountability, could be satisfied with eye-balling data and relying on intuition, shared by the members of their group. But experts in modern democracies, as we argue in chapter 7, must be armed with "objective" inferential tools and mechanized experimental setups. Numbers and the methods of manipulating them are crucial to their authority. Those methods are sanctioned by a new kind of professional, the statistical specialist.

Perhaps these developments, most decisively of all those described in this book, epitomize the deep transformation of our view of the world and our methods of dealing with it that was brought about by the advance of probability. And yet, as is characteristic of this story, the progress of ideas about statistical inference was closely tied to the development of methods in particular studies. During the last century, two such fields have played an especially important role. One of these, agriculture, has been given considerable attention in this chapter. The other, genetics, is treated in the next chapter.

What does chance ever do for us?
William Paley (1802)

4

◁ ══════════════════════════════════ ▷

Chance and life: controversies in modern biology

4.1 INTRODUCTION

Developments in probability theory and statistics have certainly had a great impact on biology. But the rise and role of probabilistic and statistical thinking in biology is no mere reflection of those developments. In the first place, as was discussed in chapter 2, biology itself has had a significant influence on statistical thought. In the second place, there are episodes having to do with the rise and role of probabilistic thinking in biology that are neither greatly illuminated by, nor shed much light on, the development of what we have come to call "probability theory" and "statistics" proper. These latter developments mainly have to do with problems internal to biology.

In continuing the discussion begun in previous chapters about attitudes of biologists toward chance, let us now shift our perspective and look at the topic from the point of view of biologists *qua* biologists with their specifically biological concerns in mind. A number of the episodes to be discussed involve the most recalcitrant biological controversies of modern times: controversies concerning vitalism, mechanism, teleology, essentialism, and levels of organization and explanation. The special senses of "chance" invoked in each of these controversies, and the various motivations for or against taking chance seriously in each case are bound up with the terms of the dispute in question. The senses of chance to be discussed here are thus quite varied, and do not all (though some do) fit neatly into conceptual frameworks designed to accommodate notions of chance in other areas of science.

4.2   SPONTANEITY AND CONTROL: CHANCE IN PHYSIOLOGY

Laplacian-style determinism – the tradition of explaining away un-predictability in terms of ignorance of relevant conditions – was already under fire by 1800, if not in the physical sciences, at least in the biological. Laplace himself had played a role in promoting this sort of determinism in biology, mainly through his collaboration with the French chemist, Antoine Lavoisier. In 1780, Lavoisier and Laplace had taken what seemed to be a giant step in the direction of reducing physiology to chemistry and physics. They had determined through experiments with an "ice cal-orimeter" that animal respiration was equivalent to the combustion of charcoal. In both cases, the subject takes up oxygen from the atmosphere and releases carbon dioxide. What they had actually shown was that the ratio of heat to carbon dioxide given off by burning charcoal was equal to the ratio of heat to carbon dioxide given off by a respiring guinea pig (Lavoisier and Laplace, 1780; see also Holmes, 1985, pp. 151–98).

In fact, there was some discrepancy in the figures: the guinea pig gave off more heat per unit volume of carbon dioxide than did the charcoal. Moreover, the figures varied from experiment to experiment. But, Lavoisier and Laplace concluded, given the "errors" involved in such complicated experiments, the results were as close as could be expected (1780, p. 405; Holmes, 1985, pp. 190–1). The discrepancies could be eliminated if only the experimental conditions could be completely con-trolled, but that would be a very difficult task. It was a task taken up by a number of investigators in the early 1800s. The discrepancies did not completely disappear, but neither did the faith in their in-principle eliminability (Holmes, 1964, pp. xxxvii–xxxix).

Some, however, found the exercise misguided. And no one scorned it more than the French physiologist and vitalist, Xavier Bichat. Referring to the study of respiration, he complained that certain "chemists and natural philosophers accustomed to studying the phenomena over which the physical forces preside" had unfortunately carried their "spirit of cal-culation" to organic phenomena (Bichat, [1801] 1822, vol. 2, p. 54). But they would be forever frustrated in this effort, for the vital forces governing organic phenomena resist precise quantitative analysis ([1801] 1822, vol. 2, pp. 54–5).

Bichat did not mean thereby to deny the possibility of a science of life. Indeed, he felt every bit as justified in attributing specific vital forces to organic matter as were Newtonians in attributing specific forces of attraction and repulsion to inorganic matter. In both cases, it proved possible to explain a wide variety of phenomena in terms of a much smaller number of causes ([1801] 1822, vol. 1, pp. 9ff.). And yet, according to Bichat, there was a great difference between the inorganic and organic worlds, as a result of the different sorts of properties that inhabit the latter realm. For instance, while gravitational forces vary in intensity in a generalizable manner, the vital forces do not. Their changes in intensity are spontaneous and unpredictable. "They defy every sort of calculation, for it would be necessary to have as many rules as there are different cases" ([1801] 1822, vol. 1, p. 23; [1809] 1829, pp. 66–9; see also Albury, 1977).

That the organic world was so absolutely unpredictable was no mere article of faith. It was indeed difficult (and biology laboratory students will surely be sympathetic) to obtain constant outcomes in experiments on respiration, metabolism, etc. For example, one would only rarely be able to record the same degree of acidity, or total volume, of urine from two animals on the same diet, or even from the same animal on a fixed diet on two consecutive days. Consider, for instance, the way in which Bichat reported the results of one of his own investigations on respiration. His purpose was to lend support to the view that oxygen enters the blood through the lungs. To that end, he inserted stopcocks in a dog's trachea and in one of its major arteries in order simultaneously to control air intake through the lungs and blood flow. He was thus able to affirm that the amount of air intake through the trachea was inversely correlated with the time that it took for the color of the blood to change from dark to bright red. Such a change in coloration was in turn known to be associated with the blood's combination with oxygen. Reporting the results, Bichat claimed some success, but also admitted that there was no precise uniformity in the time required for the change in color to take place, nor did he suppose that stricter controls would help in this regard: "In general it is, as I have said, to know little of the animal functions to wish to submit them to the least calculation, because their instability is extreme. The phenomena remain always the same, and that is what matters to us, but their variations in degree are innumerable" ([1809] 1829, p. 211; quoted and discussed in Albury, 1975, pp. 49–50, 61–5).

From the point of view of members of the Montpellier School of Medicine, which had a considerable influence on Bichat, to succeed in obtaining numerically precise, constant outcomes from an experiment would actually be to fail completely in an investigation of natural organic phenomena. For one could control experimental organisms so rigidly as to obtain precisely constant outcomes only by "denaturing" the objects under investigation, so natural in other words was the supposed indeterminate variability of life processes (Albury, 1975, pp. 59–61). Thus, for instance, Bichat warned those who sought precise analyses of the chemistry of body fluids not to confound their style of "cadaveric anatomy of the fluids" with physiological chemistry proper ([1809] 1829, p. 67).

The Laplacian archdeterminist, Claude Bernard, opposed the line of reasoning of the vitalist-indeterminists on several counts. In the first place, he found variability in the outcomes of physiological experiments a poor excuse for the invocation of specifically vital properties (see Schiller, 1973). He found misleading the manner of speaking of those physicians who said things like "ordinarily, more often, generally, or else express themselves numerically by saying, for instance: nine times out of ten, things happen in this way" (Bernard, [1865] 1957, p. 70). Insofar as these physicians were just expressing their ignorance about the conditions of the phenomena in question, their manner of expression was not so pernicious.

But certain physicians seem to reason as if exceptions were necessary; they seem to believe that a vital force exists which can arbitrarily prevent things from always happening alike; so that exceptions would result directly from the action of mysterious vital forces. Now this cannot be the case; what we now call an exception is a phenomenon, one or more of whose conditions are unknown; if the conditions of the phenomena of which we speak were known and determined, there would be no further exceptions, medicine would be as free from them as is any other science ([1865] 1957, p. 70).

Previous investigators had rested their case for the absolute indeterminacy of physiological processes on attempts to control only those variables "external" to the organism (e.g. room temperature, dietary intake, etc.). In the meantime they had, Bernard argued, overlooked crucial variables "internal" to the organism, metabolic states. If they would only control the "internal milieu" as well, they would achieve constant outcomes and would have no further need for invoking indeterministic vital properties ([1865] 1957, pp. 74–80). So, for instance, when, in the course of his own experiments on the glycogenic (sugar-producing) function of the liver, Bernard found different amounts of sugar in the livers of two animals controlled for dietary intake, he came to suspect a difference between them with respect to their internal environmental conditions. What he finally found was that in the animal that lay dead longer (while he was analyzing the first), the glycogenic process had continued ([1865] 1957, pp. 164–7).

Actually, Bernard was not in principle opposed to the invocation of specifically vital properties. He did not rule out the possibility that the phenomena might demand them. But, he insisted, vital properties, if ever discovered, would be completely deterministic in their effects ([1865] 1957, p. 69).

Bernard saw no sense in the contention that the employment of strict controls "denatures" life, and hence provides no insight into the real nature of life. Every physician who ever administered a therapeutic (and he must have intended to include the Montpellier physicians in this regard) had interfered with the course of nature, and, unless they pretended to learn nothing from it, had interfered in an experimental sort of way ([1865] 1957, pp. 196–200). What grounds could they have to contend that interference can be illuminating, but that interference to the point of ensuring precisely constant experimental results is not?

From Bernard's point of view, spontaneous physiological phenomena were only apparently so, the causes actually determining them being hidden from view within the organism. By the turn of the century, "spontaneous" physiological activities had come to *mean* activities that are internally caused, and hence less subject (in practice if not in principle) to prediction and control than those activities externally caused (e.g. Loeb, [1899] 1964, p. 70). Thus, experimental physiologists like the German-American Jacques Loeb, and his rival, the American Herbert Spencer Jennings (brother of Charles Darwin Jennings!), could argue at length about the occurrence of spontaneous movements in lower organisms without ever raising questions about vitalistic (or any other brand of) indeterminism (Pauly, 1981, 1987). The Loeb-Jennings dispute merits a bit more attention, not only because the issues of spontaneity and "randomness" raised in that context are extensions of similar issues raised by Bichat and Bernard, but also because the issues involved in this episode in the history of physiology parallel issues in natural history that will be discussed later.

Loeb extended to the animal kingdom the concept of "tropism" applied so widely in the plant kingdom by his teacher at Würzburg, Julius Sachs. Sachs had explained many directed movements of plants primarily as responses to external stimuli, as when plants orient themselves toward the position of the sun in the sky, a phenomenon known as "heliotropism" (Sachs, [1882] 1887, pp. 587–602, 677–97). Loeb argued the same for various invertebrates; he found evidence not only of heliotropisms, but geotropisms (where gravity is responsible for the direction of motion), chemotropisms, galvanotropisms, and others (e.g. [1909a]

1964, [1909b] 1964). Loeb's ability to manipulate the movements of the animals he studied in this way was part and parcel of his deterministic view that the aim of any scientific undertaking is complete control over the behavior of the objects under investigation (Pauly, 1987).

Loeb acknowledged that these tropistic movements were often "adaptive." For instance, a newly emerged caterpillar moves up the closest plant stalk toward the light, and thus to the top of the plant, where it can then feed upon young tender leaves. But for Loeb, the adaptiveness of such motions was entirely coincidental to their occurrence; their adaptiveness did not in the least increase the probability of their occurrence (e.g. Loeb, 1906, p. 160).

Jennings was part of a rather different tradition, according to which adaptive movements of many animals were explained in terms of trial-and-error processes in which the animals were engaged. The basic idea is that external stimuli trigger "random" changes of orientation on the part of the animal, changes partly also due to internal causes. One of these movements is "selected" (i.e. settled upon) by the organism, that movement being the one that has the most "adaptively" favorable consequences for the organism (Jennings, [1906] 1962, pp. 300–13, 338–50). Jennings saw this as analogous to Darwinian evolution.

Despite his occasional references to the "random" movements from which the most adaptive response is selected, Jennings was by no means an indeterminist. As he explained his use of the term: "The word 'random,' of course, implies only that these movements are not defined by the position of the stimulus; it does not signify that the movements are undetermined. The principle of cause and effect applies to these movements as well as to others. But the causes lie partly within the animal . . ." ([1906] 1962, p. 251).

This idea of random motions has a couple of interesting features. In the first place, it is reminiscent of Bernard's idea that apparently random activities of organisms have their causes partly hidden within the organisms. Were all the causes of those phenomena external to the organisms, they would be more easily discovered and the phenomena would be easier to predict and control. But the notion of randomness invoked here is richer than this Laplacian interpretation implies. By saying that the motions triggered by external stimuli are random, Jennings means in addition that the external causes of motion do not selectively favor the occurrences of motions that are adaptively advantageous. It is entirely coincidental that an organism that "needs" to respond in a particular way should indeed have that response among various responses it generates.

In contrast, and especially in contrast to Loeb's tropistic theory, it is not a coincidence that the organism should *continue* to pursue an adaptive response after its initial occurrence. The random (in this sense) generation of motions is followed, in other words, by a non-random selection of more appropriate motions. As we shall see, this notion of randomness is analogous to the notion of random variations in Darwinian evolutionary thought.

Before we leave the area of physiology, though, let us return to another set of issues concerning the handling of variability. For all his concern to rule out indeterministic, vitalistic variability, Bernard was, in another sense, a true believer in variability. He was opposed to the vitalistic indeterminists for making variability inexplicable. But he was equally opposed to others for reducing variations to averages. As noted in section 2.3, the rising popularity in public health of the "numerical method," championed by Louis-René Villermé and P. C. A. Louis, was worrisome to Bernard because it suggested to him the reification of unreal, average physiological conditions.

If we collect a man's urine during twenty-four hours and mix all this urine to analyze the average, we get an analysis of a urine which simply does not exist; for urine, when fasting, is different from urine during digestion. A startling instance of this kind was invented by a physiologist who took urine from a railroad station urinal where people of all nations passed, and who believed he could thus present an analysis of *average* European urine! ([1865] 1957, pp. 134–5).

Averages were, for Bernard, no substitute – or at best just a provisional substitute – for a complete investigation of the differences in the internal and external conditions that give rise to the variability (Coleman, 1983; Porter, 1986, pp. 160–3). A true determinist would settle for nothing less. Or rather, a community of determinists would settle for nothing less, the physiologists of that community doing their part and the physicians doing theirs. The physiologists would work mainly to discover general laws, on the basis of which variations in physiological outcomes could be predicted given information about internal and external conditions. The physicians would work mainly on discovering the internal and external conditions peculiar to each and every case. How could a physician interested in curing each patient, and not just some proportion, rest content with averages?

I will cite still another example borrowed from surgery. A great surgeon performs operations for stone by a single method; later he makes a statistical summary of deaths and recoveries, and he concludes from these statistics that the mortality law for this operation is two out of five. Well, I say that this ratio means literally nothing scientifically and gives us no certainty in performing the next operation; for we do not know whether the next case will be among the recoveries or the deaths. What really should be done, instead of gathering facts empirically, is to study them more accurately, each in its special determinism. . . In the patient who succumbed, the cause of death was evidently something which was not found in the patient who recovered; this something we must determine, and then we can act on the phenomena or recognize and forsee them accurately ([1865] 1957, pp. 137–8).

But Bernard's deterministic enthusiasm did little to solve the problems that had inspired researchers like Louis to count and average. It is one thing to believe that causes of variability in physiological experiments can in principle be found and controlled such that the variability disappears. It is another thing altogether to know how to proceed in the search for general principles of physiology given the variability that we cannot yet control. The various subjects of a clinical or physiological experiment are perhaps no more different, but certainly every bit as different, as "the leaves on the same tree" (Louis, [1835] 1836, p. 57). For this reason, inferences to general principles on the basis of individual cases are misguided. One is much better advised to compare the average outcomes in cases where the supposed cause is operative with the average outcome in cases where the supposed cause is not operative ([1835] 1836, pp. 59–60). Of course, when taking an average, one must consider a number of cases, so that "the errors (which are inevitable) . . . mutually compensate each other" ([1835] 1836, p. 60). Granted Louis' talk of "errors" here (reminiscent of Quetelet; see 2.2) has the effect of reifying averages, but how can one proceed in the search for general principles of physiology without, at some point, comparing means ([1835] 1836, p. 57)?

The place of averages and other statistical concepts in deterministic physiology received thoughtful consideration by the German physicist, mathematician, and would-be advisor to physiologists, Gustav Radicke (Radicke, [1858] 1861; see Coleman 1987). Radicke was concerned about the all too prevalent practice of comparing the means of test and control groups to determine the effect of some controlled variable. He was concerned that differences in means were not always telling. The problem had to do with the variability surrounding each mean: such variability, Radicke supposed, reflected the influences of uncontrolled variables, and was in that sense just a matter of chance. But if the variability around each mean was a matter of chance, then perhaps a difference between the means of test and control groups could also be just a matter of chance –

i.e. merely the result of uncontrolled variables. Radicke devised a set of rules for deciding when the difference between two means was big enough not to be due to chance, big enough to reflect the effectiveness of the controlled variable. The rules took into account the extent to which the recorded values of each group differed from the mean of that group. (Radicke's rules reflect considerable appreciation of the difficulties of testing causal hypotheses on variable populations; but they also reflect some of the same lack of appreciation of sample size as the agriculturist Johnston whom we met in chapter 3.) Radicke used his rules to assess previously performed tests on, for instance, the diuretic properties of sarsaparilla, the effects of sugar intake on the amount of phosphates in urine, and the chemical effects of sea air and sea bathing on urinary excretion (related to the therapeutic value of seaside spas).

Radicke's critics (including, unsurprisingly, those whose tests he had criticized) admitted much of worth in his proposals, but argued that they could not rest satisfied with the uncertainties involved in his statistical approach (Vierordt, [1858] 1861; Benecke, [1858] 1861). The calculation and comparison of means was for them just the first step in investigating hypotheses about physiological causation. To reduce the uncertainty left by such statistical reasoning, they brought to bear something that could not be so formally or mathematically expressed, namely, their medical or physiological "tact," their past personal experiences with organisms subjected to a variety of circumstances. Ultimately, it was a form of reasoning upon these individual case experiences, a kind of inference that they referred to (without apology) as the "logic of facts," that made them certain about even a small difference in means, or made them reject as physiologically impossible even a large difference in means: "The numbers in which the results of our researches are expressed . . . carry with them intrinsically more or less confidence in proportion as they agree or disagree with general physiological or medical experience" (Benecke, [1858] 1861, p. 267). There was always the hope that the variations to one or the other side of the mean would, upon reflection and comparison with past experience, be ultimately understood in terms of special prevailing circumstances. So like the insurance agents that preferred tactful analysis of individual cases to statistical tables (see 1.6 and 7.3), deterministic physiologists also remained suspicious of the uncertainty of statistical reasoning. Radicke's efforts to develop a statistical approach to hypothesis testing were forgotten shortly after they were aired. In contrast to his more famous twentieth-century counterparts like Karl Pearson, W. S. Gosset, R. A. Fisher, Jerzy Neyman, and Egon Pearson (all of whom are discussed in chapter 3), Radicke did not place much emphasis on "sample sizes" when deciding how large a difference in means would be telling, and perhaps for this reason more than any other he was not remembered by the later workers.

4.3   COINCIDENCE AND DESIGN: CHANCE IN NATURAL HISTORY

In the context of the issues just discussed, mechanistically (as opposed to vitalistically) minded biologists were the ones most opposed to chance. They sought to root it out by identifying it with mere ignorance of prevailing conditions. Yet, in the context of another set of issues, mechanists could happily admit the importance of chance. To emphasize chance in this context was to deny the intervention in nature of any non-mechanical sort of purpose. Here, it was the teleologists who deprecated chance. As the German biologist Ernst Haeckel described the issues dividing mechanists from teleologists:

One group of philosophers affirms, in accordance with its teleological conceptions that the whole cosmos is an orderly system, in which every phenomenon has its aim and purpose; there is no such thing as chance. The other group, holding a mechanical theory, expresses itself thus: The development of the universe is a monistic process, in which we discover no aim or purpose whatever; what we call design in the organic world is a special result of biological agencies; neither in the evolution of the heavenly bodies nor in that of the crust of our earth do we find any trace of a controlling purpose – all is the result of chance. Each party is right – according to its definition of chance (Haeckel, [1899] 1900, pp. 273–4).

Teleologists invoked causes above and beyond the strictly mechanical in order to account for the apparent "purposefulness" of nature, and especially to account for the purposefulness of the organic world. The parts and processes occurring in every organism of every type seemed to be integrated in such a way as to promote certain purposes having to do with devleopment, survival, and reproduction. That the organic world should display such appropriateness in its constitution could not, teleologists urged, be explained solely in terms of blind, mechanical causes. The purposefulness of nature could not, in this sense, be a coincidence, solely a matter of chance.

As, for instance, the German embryologist Karl Ernst von Baer understood chance: "When natural processes coincide, but without being connected by any common purpose, or in any other way, then their coincident relationship can only be termed accidental" (von Baer, 1876, pp.

173–4). Von Baer was, as an embryologist, most impressed with the purposeful, non-accidental character of development; developmental timing was everything to him. Chicks still in the egg develop two hard spikes on the tips of their beaks at just the time when their backbones are well enough developed for them to move and stretch their necks (1876, pp. 198–9). By these movements, and with these two spikes, they break their eggs and emerge. Is the coincident timing of these phenomena an accident? Surely the breaking of the egg and the emergence of the chick is the purpose of the appearance of the spikes. Sarcastically, von Baer formulated the alternative, mechanistic perspective of the phenomenon: instead of saying that the chick developed the spikes for the purpose of breaking the egg, the mechanist would say, "Because the hard spikes are there, it is possible for the egg to be broken from within" (1876, p. 199). But then why do the spikes fall off just after the chick emerges, when they serve no further purpose?

Von Baer invoked vital, species-specific "essences" to explain what physics and chemistry alone could not explain about the development and functioning of organisms, namely, the appropriate integration of the various physical and chemical processes that occurred (von Baer 1828–37, 1876; see Blyakher, [1955] 1982, pp. 339–64, 489–512; Lenoir 1982, pp. 72–95, 246–75). Essence-guided development was not strictly mechanical: the principles of physics and chemistry were controlled, if not violated, in the process. The materials and principles of physics and chemistry were, in this sense, means to an end; there had to be some way of guiding physical and chemical processes to an appropriately adaptive result. For just as a productive laboratory needs a chemist, and not just chemicals and chemical principles, so too adaptively organized organisms must have some way of integrating their own various chemical processes (von Baer, 1876, p. 188). The chance concatenation of organic processes would never result in life, but only the breakdown of life (1876, p. 229).

Even Bernard was sympathetic to this line of reasoning in favor of the invocation of vital forces and properties:

In every living germ is a creative idea which develops and exhibits itself through organization. . . . [E]verything is derived from the idea which alone creates and guides; physico-chemical means of expression are common to all natural phenomena and remain mingled, pell-mell, like the letters of an alphabet in a box, till a force goes to fetch them, to express the most varied thoughts and mechanisms ([1865] 1957, pp. 93–4).

Other teleologists opposed the invocation of vital directing agents to explain the purposefulness of the organic world, but they were no less vigorous in their opposition to the notion that nature is the product of only coincidentally adaptive, strictly mechanical causes. For instance, Theodor Schwann, who was so well known for his strictly mechanical account of cell development – which he conceived as analogous to crystal growth – strongly opposed the vitalist conceptions of development of his countryman von Baer. But Schwann did not deny that his own brand of mechanism was insufficient to explain the apparent purposefulness of nature. He preferred, however, to see purpose *throughout* the world, i.e. not just in the vital world. He attributed this cosmic purposefulness to the utilitarian intentions of the Creator (Schwann, [1838] 1842, pp. 186–215; see Mendelsohn, 1963).

Of course, the attempt to understand the purposefulness of nature in terms of God's own purposes was pursued most relentlessly not in Germany, but in England. The Reverend William Paley put the argument forcefully at the very beginning of the nineteenth century (Paley, 1802). His line of reasoning is still familiar. On what grounds do we infer that a watch, or a telescope, or any other obvious object of contrivance was indeed so contrived? Surely we infer a maker for such an object on the grounds that its parts are so constructed and arranged as to suit their purposes relative to the overall purpose of the object. In the case of a watch, the spring is so neatly designed and placed as to move the gears, the gears are so neatly designed and placed as to move the hands, and the hands are so neatly designed and placed on the face as to tell the time. There must have been a watchmaker whose purpose was to construct an object to tell time. The existence of a telescope would be similarly explained. Why not then an eye? Like a telescope, the eye has a lens for the refraction of light rays to an area where the image is registered. And like a telescope, whose lens positions can be manipulated to focus on objects near and far, the lens of the eye also changes shape to focus on objects at different distances. Better even than a telescope, the eye has an automatic protective cover, and an automatic cleaning system, as well as a mechanism for directing it to objects of interest. The eye is manifestly an object of contrivance, its purposefulness clearly a reflection of the purposeful intentions of its Maker.

To understand nature strictly in terms of the interplay of mechanical forces, without acknowledging the purposes of its Architect, would be to construe the wonderful adaptations of nature as mere coincidences – the results of chance alone. But, as Paley reasoned,

What does chance ever do for us? In the human body, for instance, chance, i.e., the operation of causes without design, may produce a wen, a wart, a mole, a pimple, but never an eye. Amongst inanimate substances, a clod, a pebble, a liquid drip, might be; but never was a watch, a telescope, an organized body of any kind, answering a valuable purpose by a complicated mechanism, the effect of chance. In no assignable instance hath such a thing existed without intention somewhere (1802, p. 46).

Paley's argument was extended to various biological topics, as well as to topics in astronomy, physics, and chemistry, by many of the most influential English scientists of the nineteenth century. The nine *Bridgewater Treatises* represent the epitome of this particular anti-chance view of nature.

The natural theological notion of chance as the "operation of causes without design" is not, in and of itself, terribly sophisticated from a probabilistic or statistical point of view. But it could certainly be supplemented in this respect. Recall Arbuthnot's proof of the existence of God on the basis of the balanced sex ratio of humans (Arbuthnot, 1710; see 1.6 and 3.3). The slight predominance of male births seemed to be just enough to make up for relatively greater male mortality, so that there would be one male for every female to marry. The probability of such a slight male predominance occurring generation after generation as a result of chance alone was calculated by Arbuthnot to be so infinitesimally small that it must be due instead to a wise and benevolent God. But Arbuthnot's quantitative detail is the exception in this sort of literature. The theological, teleological opposition to chance was rarely explicitly probabilistic; "chance" represented for most of these natural historians no more and no less than absence of design.

Von Baer actually blamed this sort of theological teleology for the "teleophobia" of his time (1876, p. 73). The theological brand of teleology had proven not only misleading, but positively silly, as was illustrated by the tale of the schoolmaster who explained the location of the world's major rivers by arguing that God had put them there to supply water to the world's major cities (1876, pp. 61–2). Von Baer scorned this geography-theology no more and no less than the "insect-theology" and "fish-theology" that had too long substituted for good entomology and icthyology (1876, p. 63).

Among those more positively influenced by Paley's argument was the young Charles Darwin, who is supposed to have gotten himself at least a middling grade on his B.A. exams at Cambridge by excelling on the Paley part of the test (Darwin, [1876] 1969, p. 59). Having pursued that line of reasoning for some time, even in his early evolutionary speculations (Ospovat, 1981, pp. 6–86), he was then considered by many to have demolished it, the greatest blow coming with the publication in 1859 of his *On the Origin of Species*. A great mechanist in his own right, Ludwig Boltzmann, celebrated Darwin's work as constituting the century's major achievement in the development of mechanistic thinking: "If you ask me about my innermost conviction whether our century will be called the century of iron or the century of steam or electricity, I answer without hesitation: it will be called the century of the mechanical view of Nature, the century of Darwin" ([1886] 1974, p. 15).

In his strictly mechanical account of the forms and patterns of nature, Darwin invoked "chance" occurrences in much the same sense as teleologists prior to him had understood, if not accepted, them: that is, as happening independently of adaptive benefit. Darwin did not, however, construe the forms and patterns of nature as *merely* the result of chance, as teleologists had supposed mechanists *must* construe the world.

Darwin usually invoked "chance" or "accident" in the context of discussions about how new variations arise from time to time among the organisms of a species. His notion of chance variation was especially important for distinguishing his own theory of evolution from the older, so-called "use-and-disuse" theory (Hodge and Kohn, 1986, pp. 197 ff.), which had been defended in one form or another by his grandfather Erasmus and by Jean-Baptiste Lamarck (Lamarck, [1809] 1914, pp. 106–27). A brief discussion of the differences between those two theories might thus be useful. The paradigm application of the theory of use-and-disuse is the evolution of longer-necked giraffes from shorter-necked ones (Lamarck, [1809] 1914, p. 122). As the account goes, the shorter-necked giraffes found themselves in an environment in which they had little upon which to graze, other than leaves of trees. They stretched their necks to reach more and more leaves, and were physically modified in the process. Their offspring inherited the modification – i.e. had longer necks as juveniles than their parents had as juveniles. The offspring also stretched to reach more and more leaves, lengthening their necks even beyond the length inherited. The third generation inherited the further modification. And so on, until all the decendants of the original group were quite long-necked. The important point here concerns how the variations that aid the survival of their possessors first arose – namely, in response to the survival needs of their possessors. That is, such variations were occasioned by their very adaptive significance. Their occurrence was by no means a matter of "chance," as teleologists construed that concept.

On the Darwinian account, we are asked to consider what would have happened if, among the shorter-necked giraffes, some slightly longer-necked offspring happened "by chance" to be born. Those who had the slightly longer necks would be able to reach slightly more food, and hence would slightly out survive and outreproduce the others. Assuming that neck length was inheritable, a slightly greater proportion of the next generation than of the previous generation would be longer-necked. This process alone would result in an ever-increasing frequency of the slightly longer-necked individuals. But now consider what would happen if, among those slightly longer-necked organisms, some offspring with still longer necks happened by chance to be born. These in turn would slightly out survive and out reproduce the others. Thus, the proportions of longer- and longer-necked individuals would increase from generation to generation, until the present proportions were reached.

The important point for now concerns how, according to the Darwinian account, the variations that aid the survival and reproduction of their possessors arise. In contrast to the use-and-disuse account, the probability of a particular variation occurring in an individual is not increased by the fact that that variation would promote the survival and reproduction of that organism – no vital or divine agency summons it up to that end. In that sense, it is a matter of "chance" that an organism would be born with a variation that promotes its survival and repro-duction. On the other hand, whether or not a variation further increases in frequency does depend on whether it serves survival and reproductive needs. As Darwin thus distinguished his account from the use-and-disuse account, the latter explains the evolution of adaptation in a way "anal-ogous to a blacksmith having children with strong arms," while the for-mer relies on "the other principle of those children which *chance* pro-duced with strong arms, outliving the weaker ones" (Darwin, 1859, p. 78). As he elsewhere more eloquently explained the notion of chance variation,

[Evolution by natural selection] absolutely depends on what we in our ignorance call spontaneous or accidental variability. Let an architect be compelled to build an edifice with uncut stones, fallen from a precipice.The shape of each fragment may be called accidental. Yet the shape of each has been determined . . . by events and circumstances, all of which depend on natural laws; but there is no relation between these laws and the purpose for which each fragment is used by the builder. In the same manner the variations of each creature are determined by fixed and immutable laws; but these bear no relation to the living structure which is slowly built up through the power of selection . . . (Darwin, 1887, vol. 2, p. 236).

At the risk of confusing matters, it is important to acknowledge that Darwin's views on chance variation were not entirely uniform. By "chance" variation, he sometimes also meant to emphasize that the cause of variation was unknown, suggesting to some that his notion of chance was primarily Laplacian (Darwin, 1859, p.131; Schweber, 1982; Sheynin, 1980). To be sure, the causes of variation were unknown to Darwin, but by referring to them as matters of chance, he meant something more specific. He may not have known how variations were actually occasioned, but he knew how they were *not* occasioned – they were not occasioned by their potential adaptiveness. His notion of chance variation was thus complementary to, but richer than, a merely Laplacian interpretation.

There are other complications. To suggest that Darwin provided a mechanical substitute for teleological reasoning is to give just one of the interpretations offered by Darwin's contemporaries. For instance, he was criticized by the German anatomist A. Kölliker for having championed teleological thinking (Kölliker, 1864). Kölliker was, however, trounced by "Darwin's Bulldog," T. H. Huxley, and by Darwin's schnauzer, Haeckel, both of whom praised Darwin for having so soundly discredited teleology (Huxley, [1864] 1888; Haeckel, 1866, pp. 94–105).

Darwin was praised by the American botanist Asa Gray for having placed teleology – theological teleology at that – on a sounder foundation. Gray liked to imagine that God directed the course of variation, always providing adaptively appropriate variations for natural selection to act upon (e.g. Gray, [1860] 1963, pp. 121–2). As Darwin objected, to reason thus was to miss the whole point about variation being a matter of chance (1887, vol. 2, pp. 427–8). Darwin did not have to point out the random aspects of evolution by natural selection to others like von Baer, who criticized him for completely ignoring teleology and abandoning the organic world to chance. With all its emphasis on chance variation, Darwin's account of evolution was patently absurd to von Baer.

That evolution by the natural selection of random variations would ever lead to well-adapted forms of life seemed to von Baer no more likely than that the residents of the isle of Laputa would ever succeed in developing knowledge in the manner reported by Gulliver. At the Academy of Lagado, in Laputa, a thoroughly mechanical approach to knowledge acquisition was supposedly being tried. The members of the Academy had inscribed words in all their grammatical forms on the sides of wooden dice. They had then connected the dice in such a way that the dice could be spun independently, and such that strings of words could be read off.

After each spin of the dice, the strings of words were reviewed and those that formed sensible phrases were recorded. The dice were then spun again, with the hope that additional phrases would appear that could be conjoined with the former, and thus knowledge would be obtained. "The elimination of those that did not go together was . . . completely mechanical, and was completed much more rapidly than occurs in the 'struggle for existence' " (von Baer, [1873] 1973, p.419). Unfortunately, no one had taken Gulliver's account seriously, or they might have been in a better mind-set to appreciate Darwin's theory.

For a long time the author of these reports was taken to be joking, because it is self-evident that nothing useful and significant could ever result from chance events. On the contrary, order must emerge as a complete whole at the outset, even though there might well be room for considerable improvement. Now we must acknowledge this philosopher as a deep thinker since he foresaw the present triumphs of science! (von Baer, [1873] 1973, p. 419).

Just as it was incomprehensible to von Baer that knowledge could be generated in any other way than by choosing one's words carefully, so too it was incomprehensible to him that adaptation could be generated by chance.

Of course, the Laputans did not rely entirely on chance, and neither did evolution by natural selection. It was not *just* a matter of chance that truths (vs. falsehoods and senseless phrases) would fill the pages of the books of the Academy of Lagado. The Laputans employed a selection mechanism in additon to their spins of the dice. Nor was it *just* a matter of chance that evolution by natural selection would produce adapted life forms. But in the same sense in which it was a matter of chance *which* truths should find their way into the Academy, it was also a matter of chance *which* adapted forms of life would populate the earth. Von Baer found it incomprehensible that the forms of life on earth could be as much a matter of contingency as Darwinism dictated. Just as it was unthinkable to him that it might be a matter of chance which adult form would develop from a particular embryo, so too it was unthinkable that it might be a matter of chance which higher forms of life would develop from any given lower forms (von Baer, [1873] 1973, p. 420).

As a teleologist, von Baer was committed to understanding the various life forms as adaptations to their various circumstances. For instance, in connection with speculations about life on other planets, he reasoned that there would appear differences between life forms here and life forms there, to the extent, that is, that circumstances on the other planets differed (1876, pp. 229–30). Von Baer had no reason to believe that worlds with circumstances identical to ours might be inhabited by different forms of life.

Indeed, teleologists had had problems explaining why such similar environments as one finds on our own planet, for instance in Africa and South America, should be inhabited by such different forms of life (Agassiz, [1857] 1962, pp. 13–18; Ospovat 1981). Theologically inspired teleologists could, and did, argue that this variety was an indication of God's immense creativity. As one *Bridgewater Treatise* author, Peter Mark Roget, expressed this line of reasoning, "even when the purpose to be answered is identical, the means that are employed are infinitely diversified in different instances, as if a design had existed of displaying to the astonished eyes of mortals the unbounded resources of creative power" (Roget, 1834, vol. 1, p. 9; see Yeo, 1986).

Darwin found this account of variety in similar circumstances a thoughtless one: "Some authors maintain that organic beings have been formed in many ways for the sake of mere variety, almost like toys in a shop, but such a view of nature is incredible" (Darwin, 1872, vol. 1, pp. 240–1). How different was Darwin's own perspective! In a taxon containing many species, presumably all with a common ancestor, Darwin could see evolution occurring over and over, often in the same environmental circumstances, but with very different results. The orchids especially fascinated him in this regard (e.g. Darwin, 1872, vol. 1, pp. 241–4). So many different means of fertilization had been evolved in virtually the same circumstances – i.e. given certain kinds of insects and a certain degree of wind to distribute pollen, etc. Sometimes this part of the flower would be modified to entice or trap insects, sometimes another part is modified to do the job. Even the same parts can be modified in very different ways. Among the various orchid species, presumably derived from one, we can see the evolution of reproductive mechanisms occurring over and over again with no generally determined outcome. And this is to be expected on the basis of the natural selection of random variations. Selection acts on the opportunities that present themselves – sometimes a useful modification to this part of the flower, sometimes to that part of the flower – with never the same order of useful modifications presenting themselves. Darwin's book *On the Various Contrivances by which British and Foreign Orchids are Fertilized by Insects* (1862) has justly been called a "metaphysical satire" on the works of previous teleologists (Ghiselin, 1969, pp. 131–59).

Before turning to another set of issues, there is one loose end to tie up.

Arbuthnot's argument for the existence of God on the basis of the happy, but otherwise extremely improbable ratio of males to females is such a cherished episode in the history of probabilistic thought (see, e.g., Stigler 1986, pp. 225–6) that it is worth considering briefly the Darwinian account of sex ratios that superseded it (Darwin, [1871] 1981, pp. 315–20, suggested this response, but it was only spelled out in detail by Fisher in 1930). Suppose that a considerable predominance of females should exist. Under these conditions, males would on average have more success finding mates than would females, and organisms that tended (for whatever reasons) to have more male offspring would probably have more descendants in the generations to follow as a result of their sons' success at finding mates. Organisms that tended to have more female offspring, or even equal proportions of male and female offspring, would have fewer descendants in the following generations as a result of their daughters' failure to find mates. Assuming that the trait that conferred the tendency to leave more male offspring was inheritable, then that trait would increase in frequency over the generations, until the proportion of males equalled or surpassed the proportion of females. Should the proportion of males considerably surpass that of females, then females would have more success finding mates than males, and as a result, organisms that tended to have more female offspring would have more descendants. Whatever trait conferred the tendency to leave more female offspring would thus increase in frequency until the proportion of females equalled or surpassed that of males. From the Darwinian evolutionary perspective, a 50:50 sex ratio is an equilibrium ratio. Taking into account a slightly greater male mortality level, a sex ratio at which males were slightly predominant would be the equilibrium frequency instead.

4.4 CORRELATIONS AND CAUSES: CHANCE IN GENETICS

Darwin's notion of "chance" variation was very little influenced by more formal developments in probability theory and statistics. By the turn of the century, however, two approaches to the study of variation within species had emerged, the "biometrical" and the "Mendelian" schools, both of which brought developments in probability theory and statistics to bear on the subject. Notwithstanding this broad similarity between the two approaches, the two schools found probability and statistics useful in very different degrees, in very different respects, and for very different ends. Of special interest in this section is the biometricians' scorn for the statistical immaturity of the Mendelians, and the Mendelians' resentment of the purely statistical, non-biological approach of the biometricians (Provine, 1971; Norton, 1973).

The biometrical school and its founder Francis Galton were introduced in chapter 2. The influence of Quetelet on Galton was also discussed there. It will be helpful, though, to review here just a couple of points previously raised. Around the time that Darwin was developing his ideas about the extent and causes of species variability, Quetelet was expounding his. For Quetelet this involved, first, showing how variation conforms to the law of errors, described by the familiar bell-shaped curve (Quetelet, [1835] 1842; see Porter, 1986, pp. 41–54; Stigler, 1986, pp. 161–220). The law of errors had originally been used to describe such things as the distribution of repeated measurements of a particular object or event. In applying the law of errors to human variation, Quetelet understood variation within species as something very akin to measurement error, or rather, replication error. What was being replicated in the case of humans was the "average man," the essence of humankind (or, alternatively, the essence of a particular race). Variations from the average man were accidental – matters of chance – in the same sense that measurement errors were. To use a better analogy, variations from the average man were accidental in the same sense that errors in the replication of a statue – say, the Gladiator – by a variety of sculptors would be (Quetelet, [1846] 1849, pp. 90–3; see also 2.5).

Quetelet's conception of variation could not be more different from Darwin's. While Quetelet saw through variation to the species or racial prototype, Darwin focused on the variation itself. This is what the evolutionary biologist, historian, and philosopher of biology, Ernst Mayr, means when he says that the Darwinian revolution occasioned a change from "essentialistic" to "population" thinking, the latter perspective being one in which variation has great biological significance (Mayr, 1982, pp. 45–7 *et passim*; Sober, 1980). For Darwin, variations from the mean were the crucial materials of evolution by natural selection.

The degree to which variation blurred racial and species boundaries was also very important to Darwin. Rather than trying to see through the variation to distinct racial and species essences, he preferred to focus on the range and overlap of variation as evidence that new forms *gradually* descend from old forms by the cumulative selection of slight variations, species thus merging into one another. It was in part in this sense, and for this reason, that he often denied the reality of species (Beatty, 1986, pp. 275–7).

Although Darwin himself never considered the applicability (or inapplicability) of the law of errors to variation, his cousin Galton did. In fact, Galton made considerable use of the law of errors in describing variation within species. But variations governed by the normal curve were not considered by Galton to be in any sense misrepresentations of the species or racial mean as they were by Quetelet (see 2.4; Hilts, 1973; Porter, 1986, pp. 128–46; Stigler, 1986, pp. 265–99). They were not, in this sense, "errors." "It has already been said that mathematicians laboured at the law of Error for one set of purposes, and we are entering into the fruits of their labours for another. Hence there is no ground for surprise that their Nomenclature is often cumbrous and out of place, when applied to problems in heredity" (Galton, 1889, p. 57).

Rather than accounting for the divergence of offspring from the species or racial mean in terms of larger or smaller errors in representing that mean, Galton proposed to explain the degree of divergence of offspring in terms of their ancestors' various degrees of divergence. He formulated two "laws" of inheritance along these lines, both of which are representative of the approach to variation taken by the biometric school. On the "law of regression," the average deviation of offspring from the mean was equal to one-third of the average deviation of the parents from the mean (with corrections for male–female differences included – Galton, 1889, pp. 95–100). Galton supposedly induced this law from actual data on parent–offspring correlations. The "law of ancestral inheritance" (which Galton supposed himself to have derived from the law of regression) took into account the influences of ancestors beyond the parents. By this law, the average degree of deviation of offspring is equal to one-half of the deviation of the parents, plus one-quarter of the deviation of the grandparents, plus one-eighth of the deviation of the great-grandparents, etc. (Galton, 1889, pp. 134–7; 1897, p. 402).

For all his concern to interpret variation as more than just error in representing the mean, however, Galton still construed means as having special biological significance (see 2.5). By the 1880s, Galton believed in distinct and "constant racial types," represented by distinct and constant racial means, and kept distinct and constant by the law of regression (1889, pp. 15–24). Selection for variation in either direction away from a racial mean, as long as that variation lay within the normal distribution around that mean, would not result in any shifting of the mean. One race could be descended from another only through the occurrence of larger, more distinct variations ("sports") lying beyond the ancestral racial distribution, followed by selection in favor of those new variations and against those centered around the ancestral mean. Galton's views on evolution were at odds with Darwin's in this respect.

Karl Pearson, the leader if not the founder of the biometric school, criticized Galton for having suggested that regression keeps racial means constant even in the face of selection. Regression, Pearson argued, is always to the mean of the parents, not to the mean of all members of the parents' generation. Raise or lower the mean of the parents, by selection (natural or artificial – see further), and you raise or lower the mean to which the offspring will regress (Pearson, 1900, pp. 481–6; 1914–30, vol. 3, p. 86). In that way, you can get gradual shifts in a mean from generation to generation via selection for slight variations away from that mean. Pearson's talk about gradually changing means (e.g. 1900, pp. 405–11) left it unclear what if anything a species or racial essence would amount to.

Evidence for the effectiveness of selection in bringing about gradual changes was forthcoming in studies such as those of the biometrician W. F. R. Weldon on crabs (Weldon, 1895). Weldon invoked selection to explain a very gradual three-year shift in the distribution of "frontal breadths" of carapaces of crabs in Plymouth Sound. Recent changes in the Sound, he argued, had increased the siltiness of the water. The silt in turn posed a new danger for the crabs, in that it tended to interfere with their respiration. In such circumstances, crabs with smaller frontal breadths faced less danger of being suffocated. Slight differences in this regard resulted in slight differences in survival and reproductive ability, and thus the mean frontal breadth had been continually, gradually, on the decline.

Thus, in spite of the fact that the biometricians claimed Galton as their founder, identifying themselves with a strictly statistical approach to variation and evolution, they allied themselves against the notion, defended by Galton, that selection for greatly discontinuous variations is the only effective sort. They allied themselves firmly with the Darwinian position that evolution occurs gradually by the selection of slight, continuous variations. Their dual statistical and Darwinian agendas are well expressed in Weldon's description of the direction of their research: "The questions raised by the Darwinian hypothesis are purely statistical, and the statistical method is the only one at present obvious by which that hypothesis can be experimentally checked" (1895, p. 381).

In contrast, the Mendelian approach to the study of variation originally took on a decidedly anti-Darwinian flavor. And although the approach relied heavily on probabilistic (at least combinatorial) reasoning, it further distanced itself from the biometrical approach on the grounds that the latter was an overly statistical enterprise. According to the Mendelians, the biometricians, with their distributions of variation, had restricted the study of variation to *mere correlations* between *groups*, when what was needed was a truly *causal* understanding based on what happens at the *individual* level.

The problem addressed by the Czech monk, Gregor Mendel, in the mid-nineteenth century, was the nature of variability in hybrid crosses, the larger issue having to do with the possibility of establishing more or less constant hybrid plant breeds of economic and/or ornamental importance (Olby, 1966; Orel, 1985). The problem had been well posed by the German botanist and breeder Carl Gaertner, who noted what had long been acknowledged, namely, that hybrids often show an unequal mixing of their parents' characters, one of the parents' characters tending to predominate over the other. "So the question arises: which laws govern these modifications in the construction of hybrids? For these types are not vague or the result of chance, on the contrary, they always arise in the same manner and are of the same sorts" (Gaertner, 1849, p. 251; quoted in Olby, 1966, pp. 159–60). Not the result of chance? Well, according to Mendel, yes and no. As Mendel came to believe, hybrid variability is governed by statistical laws (Meijer, 1984).

It is important to note that Mendel, and "Mendelians" during the first decades of the twentieth century, did not study the sorts of variations that could be described by the normal curve, i.e. the slight, continuous variations that were, according to Darwin and the biometricians, the material of evolution by natural selection. Rather, they studied discontinuously varying traits – for example, texture of peas, where the textures are smooth and wrinkled with no variation between. With respect to any such pair of alternative, discontinuous traits, Mendel argued, organisms come in three types (Mendel, [1865] 1966): (1) the organisms result from the union of maternal and paternal gametes that are identical with respect to one of the traits (e.g. smooth), the organisms manifest that trait, and, in turn, they contribute only one sort of gamete (the kind associated with smooth) to their own offspring; or (2) the organisms result from the union of maternal and paternal gametes that are identical with respect to the other trait (wrinkled), they manifest that trait, and, in turn, they contribute only that sort of trait to their own offspring; or (3) the organisms result from the union of gametes that differ with respect to the two traits (one is associated with smooth, the other with wrinkled), and, although these organisms manifest only the dominant trait (say, smooth), they can nonetheless contribute either sort of gamete to their offspring. Mendel referred to the pure types and the hybrid type discussed above as *A*, *a*, and *Aa* respectively. *A* organisms contribute only *A* gametes to their offspring, while *a* organisms contribute only *a* gametes. What about *Aa* organisms? It is "entirely a matter of chance" which kind of gamete they contribute to any one of their offspring (Mendel, [1865] 1966, p. 30). Thus, among very large numbers of hybrid crosses, one would expect to find offspring in the ratio *A* : 2*Aa* : *a* – which, considering that *Aa* organisms manifest only the dominant trait associated with *A*, yields the familiar 3 : 1 ratio.

This represents the *average* course of self-fertilization of hybrids when two different traits are associated in them. In individual flowers and individual plants however, the ratio in which the members of the series are formed may be subject to not insignificant deviations. Aside from the fact that the numbers in which both kinds of germinal cells occur in the ovary can be considered equal only in the average, it remains *purely a matter of chance* which of the two kinds of pollen fertilizes each individual germinal cell (Mendel, [1865] 1966, p. 31).

By the first decade of the twentieth century, the *A*'s and *a*'s were hereditary "factors"; soon thereafter they were "genes," specifically localized along the chromosomes. The three types of organisms described above became more appropriately represented as *AA*, *Aa*, and *aa*. The cross described above became represented in the now familiar way:

Parental cross: *Aa* × *Aa*
Offspring ratio: *AA* : 2*Aa* : *aa*

Early twentieth-century Mendelians believed that their approach to the study of inheritance, as opposed to the approach of the biometricians, would be most useful for evolutionary purposes. Among the various reasons offered in this regard was the fact that selection was known to be absolutely ineffective in changing the means of some of the continuously distributed characteristics studied by the biometricians. As the Mendelians ultimately understood, however (certainly by the second decade of the century), some continuous character distributions reflect only different environmental influences on organisms that actually have the same hereditary constitution. That selection is ineffective in these cases does not mean that it is ineffective in all cases of continuous variation (Johannsen, 1909; Provine, 1971, pp. 91–108; Carlson, 1966, pp. 17–38).

Another reason why the Mendelians at first thought their approach was most suitable for evolutionary purposes was that in the case of so many other continuously distributed traits, like height, the characteristics of the parents were blended to some degree in the offspring. And traits that blend cannot, *a priori*, be accumulated by natural selection. The reason (and it was already a concern in Darwin's time – Jenkin, 1867) is that the initially rare variant is most likely to mate with a more normal organism, leaving offspring with diluted versions of the rare variant's degree of deviation. Even if these diluted types were still better off than the more normal type, they would nonetheless most likely mate with the still much more numerous normal type, leaving third-generation variants that were even more diluted in their degree of deviation. Thus, the effects of selection for deviations in any particular direction would constantly be opposed by blending.

As the Mendelians ultimately understood (again certainly by the second decade of the century – e.g. East, 1910), traits governed by many gene pairs do often blend in the offspring, but as long as the genes underlying those traits do not blend, selection can still modify species considerably with respect to those traits (Provine, 1971, pp. 108–21; Carlson, 1966, pp. 22–38). Prior to recognizing this fact, though, the Mendelians had insisted that discontinuously varying traits were the only sorts of traits that could be accumulated by natural selection. Their very discontinuity was evidence that they did not blend.

The early Mendelians not only stressed empirical problems with the biometricians' approach, but also voiced methodological objections. What especially concerned them was the attitude of the biometricians, as expressed for instance by Pearson, that the problems of genetics and evolution were "in the first place statistical, in the second place statistical, and only in the third place biological" (Pearson to Galton, February 12, 1897, in Pearson, 1914–30, vol. 3, p. 128). As long as the biometricians restricted their analyses of heredity to mere correlations between generations, and ignored the physiological mechanisms underlying inheritance, they were, according to the Mendelians, not doing good biology, if biology at all. Good biology was, for many Mendelians, the up-and-coming "mechanistic" physiology advocated by Jacques Loeb and the German embryologist Wilhelm Roux (Roux, 1895; Loeb, [1912] 1964; Allen, 1975, pp. 21–111; Allen, 1978, pp. 51–153.).

Mendelism may not look any more mechanistic than biometry, if one attends only to the Mendelians' interest in comparing ratios of traits in parents and offspring. But those ratios were, for many if not most Mendelians, not only explanations but also themselves phenomena to be explained. And early in the second decade of the century there was a well-accepted causal account of those ratios. The work of the American geneticists, T. H. Morgan, H. J. Muller, Calvin Bridges, and Alfred

Sturtevant, is central in this regard. Morgan and his collaborators localized gene pairs along chromosome pairs, the latter of which could be observed microscopically at various stages throughout the process of gamete formation (meiosis). The distribution of chromosomes among newly formed gametes was seen to occur in a manner generally appropriate to explain Mendelian ratios. By hypothesizing the existence of appropriate numbers of gene pairs at appropriate locations along the chromosomes, Morgan and his collaborators were able to explain a variety of hereditary phenomena (Morgan *et al.*, 1915).

Weldon's wayward (i.e. Mendelian) student William Bateson was sure that we, the historians of his future, would find the biometric approach "unsound in construction," and would wonder how it possibly could have been regarded as scientific, when it was actually a "merely formal" exercise. "That such work may ultimately contribute to the development of statistical theory cannot be denied, but as applied to the problems of heredity the effort has resulted only in the concealment of that order which it was ostensibly undertaken to reveal" (Bateson, 1913, p. 7). "We are biologists, not applied statisticians," echoed Charles Davenport, in claiming biological status for the Mendelian camp and denying it to the biometricians (Davenport, 1914, p. 7).

As already explained, the controversy between the biometricians and the Mendelians was in large part about which approach to inheritance was the most appropriate basis for evolutionary discussions. But why should evolutionary issues have been the major points of controversy among students of inheritance? Of course, coherence with other disciplines is a virtue, and a theory of inheritance that proved to be of no use to evolutionary biologists would, other things being equal, be less desirable than a theory of inheritance that evolutionary biologists could make use of. It is also worth considering in this regard the extent to which the biometricians and Mendelians were involved in eugenic research and eugenic propagandizing. Indeed, the biometric and Mendelian schools were the academic/intellectual foci of eugenical discussions during the last part of the nineteenth century and the first part of this century (MacKenzie, 1981; Kevles, 1985). Eugenics is, of course, an evolutionary issue, an issue concerning the future direction of the evolution of the human species. From the points of view of many biologists during the first part of the century, a good theory of inheritance was one upon which governments could act to better the evolutionary outcomes of nations and races. To act on the wrong theory could impede or delay eugenic improvement. Another fear was that the whole eugenic movement might be sabotaged by being associated with a misguided or unsophisticated genetics program. Thus it was that some of the most vitriolic disputes between Mendelians and biometricians came to be recorded in the context of eugenical issues and even in the pages of eugenics journals.

In a publication of the Galton Eugenics Laboratory, David Heron presented a scathing attack on the Mendelians' approach to the problem of "feeble-mindedness." The Mendelians' work was not only dangerous to social welfare, but constituted "a serious offense against the infant science of Eugenics" (Heron, 1913, pp. 61–2). Of course, bickering among the intellectuals involved in the eugenics movement could undermine the cause of eugenic legislation. Referring to one piece of legislation in particular, though, Heron argued, "only recently we were told that to attack the application of Mendelian laws to the phenomena of feeble-mindedness was to wreck the passage of the Mental Deficiency Bill. [But] if any argument for that Bill be based on such slender considerations as the truth of Dr. Davenport's hypotheses, then the sooner the movement for the segregation of the feeble-minded is freed from such top-hamper, the less danger will there be of shipwreck" (1913, p. 10). In a response published in the Mendelians' eugenics journal, the *Eugenics Record Office Bulletin*, Davenport lashed back at the biometricians. He recalled Galton's wish that the study of inheritance be carried out by a team managed by a statistician *and* a biologist. But then Galton would surely be disappointed by his legacy for, as Davenport reported, "the biologist [Weldon] is dead and the young man he was training as his successor [Bateson] has gone over to the Mendelians and now biological problems are treated only statistically in the home of Biometrika" (Davenport, 1914, p. 24).

By the 1920s the biometric and Mendelian approaches had been reconciled, thanks in large part to the work of the statistically sophisticated Mendelian, R. A. Fisher (e.g. Fisher, 1918; Provine, 1971, pp. 130–78). To this day, the two approaches (with modifications) exist side by side. Some biologists study the inheritance and evolution of traits that clearly abide by the 3 : 1 Mendelian ratios, or by some combinatorial variants thereof (depending on how many gene pairs underlie the traits in question, and depending on the degree of dominance that obtains with respect to the genes of each pair). Other biologists (so-called "quantitative geneticists") study continuously distributed traits whose patterns of inheritance can perhaps in principle, but not so easily in practice, be resolved into combinatorial variants of the 3 : 1 ratios.

With the reconciliation of the theoretical ideas of Mendelism and the statistical techniques of biometry came greater statistical sophistication in the testing of Mendelian hypotheses. Fisher's role in this process was crucial. For instance, in his influential, multi-edition textbook *Statistical Methods for Research Workers* (1st ed., 1925), he discussed, for the first time in detail, what is now the standard way of measuring the fit between particular Mendelian hypotheses and the evidence of breeding experiments. The problem with evaluating particular Mendelian hypotheses is that the evidence derived from breeding experiments involving limited numbers of offspring (or limited numbers of matings) never exactly corresponds to expected Mendelian ratios. Only among very large numbers of offspring (or matings) are anything like exact Mendelian ratios observed. Among small numbers, there may be chance deviations – the smaller the number considered, the larger the chance deviations. For example, it is unlikely that the group of four offspring born to two Aa parents will consist of exactly $1AA : 2Aa : 1aa$. Only as the number of offspring increases to infinity do we expect the ratios to approach the $1 : 2 : 1$ pattern (or $3 : 1$ of traits, given dominance).

Mendel was certainly aware of this problem. Although he had obtained $3 : 1$ ratios among the sum total of offspring from presumed $Aa \times Aa$ matings, he had also obtained quite wide deviations in individual cases. One such mating resulted in 43 offspring manifesting the dominant trait and only 2 manifesting the recessive; another such mating yielded 14 offspring manifesting the dominant trait and 15 the recessive (Mendel, [1865] 1966, p. 12). As he acknowledged, "isolated values must necessarily be subject to fluctuations and even extreme cases are possible . . . The true ratios can be given only by the mean calculated from the sum of as many separate values as possible; the larger their number the more likely it is that mere chance effects will be eliminated" ([1865] 1966, p. 31).

The chi-square test invented by Pearson in 1900 was shown by Fisher to provide a neat way of deciding when deviations from expected Mendelian ratios were significant enough to reject the particular Mendelian hypothesis under test (Fisher, 1925). The chi-square test had in fact already been applied to the testing of Mendelian hypotheses in 1912 by the American biometrician J. A. Harris. As he noted at the time, Mendelians had been "satisfied" to judge the fit of actual to expected ratios "by inspection merely" (Harris, 1912, p. 741). He offered a formula for calculating chi-square, and showed how it could be used to substantiate some, and undermine other, purportedly good tests of Mendelian hypotheses. His message was that "the Mendelian has only the simple task of calculating chi-square and looking up the value of P in Elderton's tables" (1912, p. 743), implicitly suggesting that this was a task that even the most statistically illiterate Mendelian could perform. Mendelian applications of this statistical test during the next two decades were, however, very few and far between. This must be attributed in part to the fact that Harris provided no rationale – only a recipe – for the test. But the lingering dispute between the more biologically minded Mendelians and the more statistically minded biometricians must also have had something to do with this. Fisher's later, much more detailed investigation of the same issue relegated Harris's test to history. But even Fisher's treatment of the issue did not immediately transform the statistical (anti-statistical) habits of Mendelians. They continued to eyeball discrepancies between actual and expected ratios for some time (see, for example, the *Journal of Genetics* throughout the 1920s and into the 1930s).

Nevertheless, in large part because of Fisher's clear illustrations of such "significance" testing techniques in genetics, many biologists ultimately adopted them (the development of significance testing in general is discussed in detail in chapter 3). By the mid to late 1930s significance testing was in wide use in genetics, and was even receiving increased use in evolutionary biology, for example, by the Russian-American evolutionary biologist Theodosius Dobzhansky, in his "Genetics of Natural Populations" series (Lewontin *et al.*, 1981). It is also fair to say that Fisher's genetics illustrations aided the adoption of significance testing techniques not only in biology, but in general. Tests of Mendelian hypotheses manifest so distinctly the general difficulties of testing statistical hypotheses, that Mendelian illustrations became stock examples in general statistics texts (e.g. Snedecor, 1946; Neyman, 1950). Many pure statisticians and non-biological experimentalists come to know at least the rudiments of Mendelian genetics through these illustrations.

Perhaps Fisher's most notorious use of significance testing was his 1936 evaluation of Mendel's own data. Mendel's tally for round and wrinkled peas was 5,474 round : 1,850 wrinkled, surprisingly good evidence of the expected 3 : 1 ratio, given the chance deviations also to be expected. From the statistical critic's point of view, the evidence was too good. Mendel got similar ratios for all the traits he studied. The tally for yellow to green peas, for example, was almost perfect – 6,022 yellow : 2,001 green! The probability of so many close fits is miniscule. Fisher could not avoid the conclusion that Mendel's data had been "cooked" (Fisher to D.

McKie, January 3, 1939, in Bennett, 1965, p. vii), perhaps by an overly helpful assistant who precisely "adjusted" the data to the expected results (Fisher, 1936, p. 132). Suffice it to say that Mendelism has not suffered for this revelation.

It is perhaps worth pointing out, before concluding this section, that while Darwin did not bring any statistical tools of the management of chance to bear on variation, and while the biometricians and Mendelians clearly did, the terminology "chance variation" still carries the connotation that Darwin attached to it. As one evolutionary biologist explains the notion in a current textbook, "Mutation is random in that *the chance that a specific mutation will occur is not affected by how useful that mutation would be*" (Futuyma, 1979, p. 240). This is not to say that the biometricians' or the Mendelians' special interests in chance aspects of variation have proved fruitless programs of research. Quite the opposite is the case. But the notion of chance variation, as originally conceived by Darwin, continues to play a conceptually very important role in discussions of evolutionary change.

4.5 SAMPLING AND SELECTION: CHANCE IN EVOLUTIONARY BIOLOGY

As Darwin unhappily reported the opinion of the philosopher-scientist, John Herschel, "I have heard, by a round about channel, that Herschel says my book 'is the law of higgledy-piddledy.' What exactly this means I do not know, but it is evidently very contemptuous" (Darwin to C. Lyell, December 12, 1859, in F. Darwin, 1887, vol. 2, p. 37). In time, though, Darwin was praised rather than scorned for his appeal to chance. For instance, looking back at the turn of the century, another philosopher-scientist, Charles Peirce, assessed Darwin's contributions in this regard more favorably:

The Origin of Species was published toward the end of the year 1859. The preceding years since 1846 had been one of the most productive seasons – or if extended so as to cover the great book we are considering, *the* most productive period of equal length in the entire history of science from its beginnings until now. [For] the idea that chance begets order, which is one of the cornerstones of modern physics . . . was at that time put into its clearest light (Peirce, 1893, p. 183).

The developments to which Peirce referred were those connecting the social physics of Quetelet with the statistical mechanics of Maxwell and finally with the evolutionary thought of Darwin (Peirce, 1893, pp. 183–4). The tradition of comparing and contrasting Maxwell and Darwin has been continued by historians of ideas (e.g. Merz, 1904–12, vol. 2, p. 624; Schweber, 1982). Just as Maxwell understood orderly properties of gases in part in terms of statistically distributed differences between their component molecules (velocity distributions), Darwin understood the orderly evolution of species in part in terms of chance variations among species members. It is a point of contrast between Maxwell and Darwin, though, that is most interesting for present purposes. Maxwell acknowledged not only chance differences in molecular velocities, but also the consequent possibility of chance fluctuations in the behavior of gases made up of those molecules. Maxwell believed that the second law of thermodynamics could be violated in an invisibly small volume of gas, a number of molecules of greater velocity just by chance coming to occupy one area of the gas, a number of molecules of less velocity by chance coming to occupy another area (e.g. Maxwell, 1875a, pp. 328–9; see also chapter 5).

Darwin worried little if at all about the effects of small population size on chance fluctuations in the course of evolution. Since the turn of the century, however, and especially since the 1930s evolutionary biologists have, and have accordingly formulated stochastic versions of evolutionary theory that Darwin himself might have regarded as higgledy-piggledy. Indeed, proponents of one such position have been labeled "non-Darwinian" on account of the distance of their views from his.

Recall that, according to Darwin, the *origin* of variation is a matter of chance, while the *evolutionary fate* of variation once arisen (its changes in frequency from generation to generation) is not, being due instead to natural selection. It was not far into the twentieth century before evolutionary biologists set to work to formalize the conditions under which the evolutionary fate of variation might also be a matter of chance. The Russian geneticists Nicolai Dubinin and D. D. Romaschoff elaborated this possibility in terms of the classic means of illustrating chance processes, namely, the blind drawing of beads from an urn (Dubinin and Romaschoff, 1932; discussed in Dobzhansky, 1937, p. 129). Theirs has become, in turn, the classic means of illustrating this form of evolution.

The beads in this case are genes for alternative traits (e.g. for different pigmentations, or different blood types, etc.). The alternative gene-beads are different colors, but they are otherwise indistinguishable by a blindfolded sampling agent. One urn of beads represents one generation of alternative genes – a finite number, characterized by particular gene frequencies. The frequencies of the next generation of genes are determined by a blind drawing of beads from the urn. This second generation of genes fills a new urn, blind drawings from which determine the frequencies of genes in the third generation, and so on. The frequencies of genes will inevitably differ from urn to urn – generation to generation – as a result of the fact that frequencies of otherwise indistinguishable beads sampled by blind drawings will inevitably not be representative of the frequencies in the urns from which the samples were drawn. The probability of drawing a representative sample from a population of given finite size is easy to calculate – the smaller the population, the smaller that probability. Gene frequency changes that occur in this way are referred to as "random drifts" in gene frequency.

Imagine now that we start with two urns, representing two separate populations, each with the same initial gene frequencies. For each of the two urns, there is a second-generation urn, a third-generation urn, and so on. If the genes are again indistinguishable by the blindfolded sampling agent, then not only will the frequencies of genes differ from generation to generation in each set of urns, as a result of random drift, but also the frequencies of genes in the *same* generation of the two sets will inevitably differ – e.g. the frequencies of genes in the two tenth-generation urns will inevitably differ, as will the frequencies of genes in the two eleventh-generation urns, the two twelfth-generation urns, etc.

Dubinin and Romaschoff thus pictured one form of evolution in terms of sampling error. But what biological circumstances could give rise to this sort of sampling error? It could have at least two sources (Beatty, 1984). In the first place, it might be the case that the alternative genes confer the same overall survival and reproductive capabilities on their possessors. Thus nature would be like the blindfolded sampling agent, in charge of deciding which genes get passed on, but unable to distinguish one gene from another (or unable to distinguish possessors of one gene from possessors of another). And just as blindfolded sampling from a finite population leads to a certain degree of sampling error, so too when nature has no way of discriminating as to which genes get passed on, and when the population sampled is finite, then a certain amount of sampling error takes place. Gene frequencies drift randomly.

Another source of random drift is Mendelian heredity. Given that heterozygous (*Aa*) organisms produce 50% *A* gametes and 50% *a* gametes only in the long run, or when a very large number of heterozygotes is considered, and given that in a particular generation the number of heterozygotes may be quite limited, then *Aa* organisms may, just by chance, contribute more *A*'s than *a*'s to their offspring. The frequencies of *A* and *a* may thus change from generation to generation – a real evolutionary change – as a result of chance alone. Again, there is an "error" in sampling the gene frequencies of the parents. And again, gene frequencies are said to drift randomly in this case.

The ever-present Mendelian source of random drift means that, even when there are slight selective differences between possessors of the different genotypes of a population, its gene frequencies can still drift randomly to some extent. The larger the population in question, and the larger the selective differences between the different genotypes of the population, the less will its gene frequency changes be a matter of random drift.

It was clear to evolutionary theorists like R. A. Fisher and Sewall Wright that evolutionary theory would have to be formulated stochastically in order to take random drift into account. Differences of opinion concerning the exact formulation of the theory were ultimately worked out. What is especially interesting, though, is that while evolutionary biologists were in agreement that a stochastic theory of evolution was required, and also in agreement as to the formulation of that theory, they still disagreed vehemently about the general extent to which evolutionary changes are due to random drift (Provine, 1986, pp. 207 ff.).

The possibility of this disagreement arose (and the disagreement is still with us) because although biologists may agree as to the formulation of evolutionary theory, they may disagree considerably with regard to the values that the theoretical variables will generally take (Beatty, 1984). As Wright acknowledged in his review of Fisher's landmark *The Genetical Theory of Natural Selection* (Fisher, 1930a), "our mathematical results on the distribution of gene frequencies are now in complete agreement, as far as comparable" (Wright, 1930, p. 352). But as Wright also made clear, agreement with regard to mathematical theory still left room for considerable disagreement. And the most important source of disagreement was Fisher's assumption of large population sizes in nature – which effectively ruled out the actual importance of evolution by random drift – and Wright's assumption that actual conditions were much more conducive to drift. Again, this issue was to some extent detachable from the mathematical theory. As for the real disagreement, as Wright later put it, "It is a question of the relative values of certain coefficients" (1948, p. 291).

There has been considerable waxing and waning of positions concerning the extent of random drift in nature (i.e. as opposed to "in theory"). During the 1930s and 1940s, drift was very often invoked to account for differences between populations with respect to variations that had no apparent selective significance. Dobzhansky invoked drift to explain why the frequencies of different chromosome shapes should vary so much from population to population within species of the fruitfly *Drosophila* (e.g. Dobzhansky and Queal, 1938). Charles Diver invoked drift to explain why frequencies of different banding and color patterns should vary so much between populations of species of the snail *Cepaea* (Diver, 1940). Wright himself suggested that blood group frequencies within human populations were governed mainly by drift. Differences between alternative blood groups were, Wright claimed at the time, of no adaptive significance "as far as known" (Wright, 1940, p. 179). The same was true of the adaptive significance of differences between chromosome shapes in *Drosophila*, and banding and color patterns in *Cepaea*.

But the tide turned against these, and other, early drifters. Dobzhansky himself, in a rather dramatic turn around, found that the frequencies of the various chromosome shapes studied by him changed regularly with the seasons, suggesting some sort of selective control (e.g. Dobzhansky, 1943). He went on to show that possessors of different chromosome shapes survive better or worse in different temperatures (Wright and Dobzhansky, 1946).

Diver's and similarly minded views on *Cepaea* were criticized severely by the respected English evolutionary biologists Arthur Cain and Phillip Sheppard in the early 1950s (Cain and Sheppard, 1950, 1954; Sheppard, 1951, 1952). They found that the seemingly innocuous differences in color (yellow vs. brown) and banding pattern (0 to 5 bands) of these snails were correlated with differences among the environments in which populations of the snails lived. In particular, they found that the color and banding patterns most frequent in an environment were those that provided more camouflage in that environment, thus better protecting the snails from their bird predators.

Apparently in contradiction to Wright's views, investigators found that possessors of different blood groups were susceptible in different degrees to different diseases. For instance, O-group individuals were shown to be more susceptible to peptic ulcers than were either A- or B-group individuals, while A-group individuals were shown to be more susceptible to stomach cancer (Clarke, 1961). No straightforward correlations between blood group frequencies and environments were established in the time period in question, but findings that different blood groups had different effects on survival led many investigators to expect that such correlations would be found.

Combined with Dobzhansky's success in accounting for frequencies of chromosome shapes in *Drosophila* in terms of selection, the apparent successes of selectionists in accounting for color patterns in *Cepaea* and blood groups in humans seemed to many of them to constitute over-whelming support for their efforts. It was particularly important to proponents of the all-importance of evolution by natural selection in the 1950s and 1960s to trot out these successes as evidence of the shortsightedness of proponents of the importance of drift (e.g. Mayr, 1963, pp. 203–14; see also Gould, 1983; Provine, 1986, pp. 207 ff.; Beatty, 1987; Turner, 1987).

Selectionists of this period began to wonder whether any purported case of drift would stand up to rigorous investigation. Invocations of drift seemed to them to be just admissions of ignorance regarding the subtle selective mechanisms actually at work in the cases at issue. Cain, perhaps the most vocal of these selectionists, derided the logic of the proponents of the importance of drift: "This is the real basis for every postulate of . . . genetical drift. The investigator finds that he, personally, cannot see any [evidence of selection], and concludes that, therefore, there is none" (Cain 1951a, p. 424). It is unfortunate, he added, that drift explanations owe their only success to the "failure of the investigator" to find evidence of selection (Cain, 1951b, p. 1049).

According to the selectionists of the 1950s and 1960s and according to some still, the worst thing a biologist could do would be to pursue a drift hypothesis without having first exhausted all selectionist alternatives. And even then the invocation of drift would be at best a stopgap measure. As Mayr recently argued, "[The evolutionary biologist] must first attempt to explain biological phenomena and processes as the product of natural selection. Only after all attempts to do so have failed, is he justified in designating the unexplained residue tentatively as a product of chance" (Mayr, 1983, p. 326).

But in the meantime, the selectionist program ran into probems of its own. For instance, while Dobzhansky's selectionist account of chromosome shapes in *Drosophila* has pretty well stood the test of time, the selectionist accounts of banding and color pattern in *Cepaea*, and of blood groups in humans have not. The French population geneticist Maxine Lamotte has argued forcefully that selection alone is not responsible for *Cepaea* color patterns – that drift is also largely responsible (Lamotte, 1959). And the Italian-American population geneticist, Luigi Cavalli-Sforza, has successfully accounted for differences in blood group frequencies among different populations in northern Italy in terms of drift alone (Cavalli-Sforza, 1969).

Other biological considerations have also contributed to the rise in recent years of interest in drift and even to the founding of a "neutralist" (in the sense of selectively indistinguishable) or "non-Darwinian" school of evolution. Molecular biological findings played a large role. Beginning in the 1950s and 1960s it became clear how different permutations of the "bases" that make up the DNA code for different amino acids. But it also became clear that the sequence of bases that codes for a particular amino acid can mutate in such a way that the same amino acid is produced. Finally, it was realized that these so-called "synonymous" genetic variations are prime candidates for the sorts of selectively neutral variations whose frequencies would be expected to be entirely a matter of random drift. Theoretical considerations also suggested to molecular biologists of the 1960s that proteins could differ in some of their constituent amino acids – the result of non-synonymous genetic variations – and still be functionally equivalent, and hence selectively neutral. Again, the frequencies of such variations in a population would be a matter of drift, not natural selection. As the American geneticists, Jack King and Thomas Jukes, expressed these basic ideas in their classic position paper, "Natural selection is the editor, rather than the composer, of the genetic message. One thing the editor does *not* do is to remove changes which it is unable to perceive" (King and Jukes, 1969, p. 788).

Another line of reasoning that played a large role in the rise of neutralist thought in the late 1960s and 1970s concerned findings of constant evolutionary rates across different taxa. Evidence was gathered suggesting that the evolution of even a functionally very important protein like hemoglobin proceeded at the same rate (where rate is measured in terms of amino acid changes per unit time) in very diverse groups of mammals. If the evolution of hemoglobin in each group of mammals were mainly a matter of natural selection in favor of appropriate hemoglobin forms for each taxon under the changing environmental conditions faced by that taxon, then it would be very unlikely for the rate of hemoglobin evolution to be so similar from group to group. If most of the amino acid changes in question were selectively neutral, on the other hand, there would be no reason to expect them to proceed faster in one group of mammals than another. The Japanese population geneticist, Motoo Kimura, played a large role in bringing rate-of-evolution evidence to bear on the neutralist position (e.g. Kimura, 1968). He has since been among the most important spokespersons for the neutralist position (Kimura, 1983).

So far we have discussed selection/drift controversies mostly as either/or disputes: either selection is responsible for the evolutionary changes in question, or those changes are a matter of drift. But for many evolutionary biologists, the interesting question concerning the changes in frequency of any partiuclar set of variations is: to what extent are the changes a matter of selection, and to what extent a matter of drift? No one has objected more to the either/or construal of the issues than Wright. Consider, for instance, his criticism of Fisher and Fisher's collaborator, E. B. Ford:

They hold that fluctuations of gene frequencies . . . must be supposed to be due either wholly to variations in selection (which they accept) or to accidents of sampling. The antithesis is to be rejected. The fluctuations of some genes are un-doubtedly governed largely by violently shifting conditions of selection. But for others in the same populations, accidents of sampling should be much more im-portant and for still others both may play significant roles. It is a question of the relative values of certain coefficients (Wright, 1948, p. 291).

To summarize this section up to this point, we see in the development of evolutionary biology what we see as well in the development of other scientific disciplines like thermodynamics and quantum mechanics, namely, the rise of stochastic theories. But just to say that evolutionary theory has become stochastic, and that is that, is to overlook an important aspect in which stochasticity continues to be an issue in evolutionary biology. That is not to say that the issue has been transformed into the sort of stochasticity vs. *in-principle* stochasticity issue characteristic of quantum mechanics (see chapter 5). Rather, there is another respect in which the stochasticity issue in evolutionary biology is far from being settled. The actual relative magnitudes of population size and selection pressure in the various populations being studied are still at issue, and it is for this reason that stochasticity is still an issue in evolutionary biology.

Nineteenth-century thermodynamics provides a better comparison in this regard. Fisher's commitment to a stochastic theory of evolution, in spite of his confidence that evolutionary changes are not actually due to any great extent to random drift, is reminiscent of Maxwell's and Boltzmann's commitment to a stochastic theory of gases, in spite of their confidence that physicists would rarely if ever come across systems whose behaviors were visibly stochastic. They both supposed that any system big enough to be studied by a physicist would also be big enough – i.e. would contain enough randomly moving molecules – that local stochastic effects would cancel out. As Boltzmann confidently asserted, "Even in the smallest neighborhood of the tiniest particles suspended in a gas, the number of molecules is already so large that it seems futile to hope for any observable deviation, even in a very small time, from the limits that the phenomena would approach in the case of an infinite number of mol-ecules" ([1896–98] 1964, p. 318).

Similarly, Fisher believed that biological populations were in general big enough that local sampling errors of the sort discussed above would also cancel out. This comparison is not mere philosophical fabrication. Fisher himself conceived of evolutionary theory on analogy with statistical mechanics. The analysis of evolution by natural selection, he suggested, "may be compared to the analytic treatment of the theory of gases, in which it is possible to make the most varied assumptions as to the nature of the individual molecules, and yet to develop the general laws as to the behavior of gases . . ." (1922a, p. 324). If Wright had continued the analogy (this *is* mere philosophical fabrication), he might have pointed out that just as the erratic Brownian motion of an observable, suspended particle was a manifestation of invisible, randomly moving particles colliding with it, so too had random drift manifested itself in many particular cases.

By way of concluding this section and this chapter, let us return briefly to indeterminism, the subject with which the chapter began. What about indeterminism in evolutionary biology? Wright was indeed an indeterminist. He argued that the evidence – for example, the successes of statistical mechanics and the stochastic version of evolutionary theory –. simply pointed that way. Wright claims to have begun his scientific career as a Laplacian determinist. It is interesting in connection with section 4.2 that at one stage in the development of his indeterministic perspective Wright "looked with sympathy on Jenning's position in his famous controversy with Jacques Loeb on the interpretation of animal behavior: trial and error vs. tropism, but felt that the overtones of vitalism in his position were unsatisfactory" (Wright, 1964, p. 281). Wright listed some of his articles on the importance of drift to show how much he had changed over time.

But one need not look to the most avid proponents of random drift in order to find indeterminists. Fisher was also an avowed indeterminist; he invoked the same evidence for his indeterminism as had Wright, namely evolutionary theory plus the kinetic theory of gases. Again of interest in connection with section 4.2, Fisher noted that the evidence for indeterminism comes in large part from the physical sciences, as a result of which he supposed that biologists of his time must "wonder what the controversy between 'mechanism' and 'vitalism' can have been all about" (Fisher, 1934, p. 194).

Unfortunately, neither Wright nor Fisher discussed their views on determinism and indeterminism in connection with their dispute concerning the importance of random drift. Fisher's indeterminism clearly does not help us to understand his doubts about the importance of drift;

and for that reason, Wright's self-proclaimed indeterminism can hardly be used to explain his advocacy of the importance of drift.

Wright actually had a more ambivalent attitude toward indeterminism than Fisher. The main problem with indeterminism, according to Wright, is that it so often discourages deeper analysis. Whereas the determinist so unflaggingly seeks the causes of phenomena, trying to control the conditions of the phenomena to the point of getting precisely the same outcomes from the same circumstances, the indeterminist is prone to giving up, resting satisfied with average outcomes and correlations. Of interest in connection with section 4.4, Wright picked out Pearson for special criticism in this regard – Pearson, who had been satisfied with a "merely statistical" account of heredity. Pearson had failed to see the promise of Mendelism, which, of course, also "runs at once into mere probabilities in the Mendelian ratios but it carries analysis of the basis of the probabilities to deeper levels and gives more insight than a mere regression equation" (Wright, 1964, p. 288). His concerns about the possible laziness of indeterminists aside, Wright believed that biological generalizations must ultimately be cast in terms of probabilities. However, acceptance of this point of view should not, he advised, deter determinists from their goal of attaining as deep a level of understanding as possible.

For most evolutionary biologists, determinism vs. indeterminism has not been a particularly pressing issue. What has been important is simply whether evolutionary theory can be made to account for more phenomena by incorporating more probabilistic features, and whether the tools of probability and statistics can be brought to bear on the testing of evolutionary hypotheses. For all their concern to make their indeterministic positions explicit, both Fisher and Wright acknowledged that the indeterministic turn makes no difference to the practice of biology. As, for instance, Wright noted, "Acceptance of this point of view requires little change in the actual practice of science, especially as determinism has never been more than an ideal admittedly unrealizable in full because of the invariable errors of observation and, in many cases, practically irreducible probabilities like those in the fall of dice (or segregation and assortment of genes). The deterministic expressions do not lose their usefulness as approximations" (Wright, 1964, p. 288; see also Fisher, 1930a, pp. 102–4).

A quotation from a standard text on statistical methods and statistical inference reveals the generally accepted attitude of biologists in this regard:

Whether biological phenomena are in fact fundamentally deterministic and only the variety of causal variables and our inability to control these make the phenomena appear probabilistic, or whether biological processes are truly probabilistic, as postulated in quantum mechanics for elementary particles, is a deep philosophical question beyond the scope of this book and the competence of the authors. The fact remains that, as recorded by the observer, biological phenomena can only be discussed within a probabilistic framework (Sokal and Rohlf, 1969, pp. 5–6).

This is probabilism in practice rather than in principle. In the next chapter we will look at the lower levels of the hierarchy of nature studied by physics. Here indeterminism is both more pervasive and deep-rooted, as a matter of principle as well as of practice.

The problems of statistical physics are of greatest interest in our time, since they lead to a revolutionary change in our whole conception of the universe.

Richard von Mises (1928)

5

◁ == ▷

The probabilistic revolution in physics

5.1 THE BACKGROUND: CLASSICAL PHYSICS

The first unified program of modern physics was created by Isaac Newton. He showed how the motion of diverse objects, including the planets, the tides, falling bodies and projectiles, could be derived from a single force ruling them all: universal gravitation. Newton's successes were generalized into a mechanical world view based on the assumption that, in principle, *all* phenomena could be explained in a similar fashion, though perhaps requiring other forces besides gravitation. Some of those additional forces were evident, such as the force that accounts for the elasticity in the collisions of billiard balls. Whatever the range of qualitatively different forces still to be discovered, they were all conceived to operate within a general formal framework, originally set up by Newton and further developed and perfected by d'Alembert, Euler, Lagrange, Laplace, and others, so that by 1800 a well-established scheme for the explanation of natural phenomena was available. Special assumptions about the forces proved in the end to be less crucial for this scheme than a certain mathematical structure. The basic physical properties of a system were explained using differential equations of second order in time, and later also mathematically equivalent tools such as variation principles.

The decisive feature of this scheme for our purposes is that it permits the skilled mathematician or scientist to infer all properties of a system for future and past times uniquely and precisely, once certain key properties are known at a given time. The most notable successes were predictions and retrodictions of the positions of the planets, given their present configuration. This is how astronomy became a major support for philosophical determinism. Laplace, whose writings on probability we encountered in chapter 1, is equally celebrated for his epochal work on the planetary system, the *Treatise of Celestial Mechanics* (1799–1805). His uncompromising and vastly influential pronouncements of the metaphysical creed of determinism were conditioned by the methods and results of astronomy: "All events, even those which, by their insignificance, seem not to follow from the great laws of nature, follow from them just as necessarily as the revolutions of the sun" (*Philosophical Essay on Probabilities*, [1814] 1951, p. vi).

It was, of course, clear to the adherents of the mechanical world view that their philosophy was more a beginning and a program than an achievement. But the successes during the century after Newton in conceptual clarification and empirical application were so striking that there seemed to be no reason to question the general validity of the view, the more so since it epitomized the highest aim of science: full knowledge of nature and thereby complete predictability, if not domination, of its course.

Kant, whose background in natural science is reflected in his (and Laplace's) theory of the emergence of the planetary system out of rotating gaseous masses, went even further. He promoted the universal lawful determination of phenomena to the status of a necessary condition of all experience, in particular of all scientific knowledge. The impact of this philosophico-scientific view has survived to our day. But this determinism began to be undermined almost simultaneously with its full articulation in the early nineteenth century. The reasons for this gradual "erosion of determinism" (Hacking, 1987, p. 53), so far as they belong to the history of physics and its interpretations, are the theme of this chapter.

One condition of the viability of the mechanical program should be stressed at once. For any given system or phenomenon, the physicist must identify and measure precisely those properties that can be put into the machinery of the differential equations in order to be calculated for some other time. But it is not enough that they be suitable for the calculation. They should also be sufficient to determine uniquely all other phenomenological properties of the system we are, or might become, interested in. Only research can determine whether in a given case involving perhaps a wealth of observable phenomena, a well-defined and manageable set of mechanical properties can be found that determine the entire system completely. This question became a critical issue once it was seen that not only space and time, but also their content, are a continuum. A finite number of ideally rigid bodies can be characterized by a finite set of positional variables and their rates of change; a continuous phenomenon demands an extension of the mechanical scheme from discrete particles in a void to continuous matter and fields. The pertinent differential equations then require not only a finite but an infinite number of parameters for the description of the state of a system at a given time. To satisfy this requirement would seem impossible at first glance; but it can be approximated to a sufficient degree in practical cases, so that it looked as if it might be no more serious an idealization than the unverifiable assumption of unlimited precision in general that is involved in determinism.

It was one of the greatest triumphs of the Newtonian program that macroscopic treatments of continuous-material media could be developed within its framework. Moreover, between 1855 and 1864 Maxwell succeeded in applying this formalism of differential equations also to electromagnetic fields, including the whole of optics. True, all attempts to devise a mechanical model of the ether, supposed to be the medium carrying electromagnetic waves, failed; but the theory fit the general mechanical ideal of complete lawfulness of the phenomena over time no less because of that. Hence classical physics, the stronghold of modern scientific determinism, can be defined as the domain of particle mechanics, continuum mechanics, and electrodynamics.

This definition neglects the fact that around the middle of the nineteenth century problems of electricity theory and the continuum stimulated diverse attempts to modify the classical program – by introducing velocity-dependent forces, for example. Indeed, the continuum was even suspected by some physicists, such as George Gabriel Stokes and William Thomson (Lord Kelvin), to entail dynamical instabilities, hence indeterministic motions – a speculation that was not without influence on Maxwell's cautious and unpublished anticipation of a new kind of physics described at the end of section 5.6. Although these developments themselves were only briefly successful, it was increasingly recognized that a serious threat to the unity and validity of the classical program arose from the incompatiblity between the mechanical theory of matter and its twin theory of electromagnetic fields. The problem was well known by 1900 and became a matter of great concern in the mechanics of the electron. To the great benefit of classical physics, Einstein solved it in 1905 by revising mechanics in his special theory of relativity so that it fit electromagnetic theory. His discovery may well be called revolutionary, yet from our perspective its conservative character is more striking: by reconciling these two fundamental physical theories, it supported determinism. It even removed some difficulties inherent in the deterministic reading of classical physics, if only difficulties that were unknown then and are still largely ignored today (Earman, 1986). Moreover, the great experimental success of Einstein's theory could only strengthen the classical conception of physics. It would undoubtedly have done so, had it not been for the challenge presented by other new discoveries. Indeed, the label "classical" for the established part of physics was usually intended to include relativity (for typical statements see Planck, [1929] 1936, part III; von Mises, [1921] 1964, §1, and [1928] 1957, pp. 208ff.). Physicists even used the term to describe themselves as the theory of quanta grew and gradually assumed the role of *the* alternative to the traditional program. This theory, called the "new physics," was the one with which the expression "classical" was contrasted (Planck, [1929] 1936, title and pp. 22f.).

In terms of this distinction the place of thermodynamics – the third great and independent theory of physics around 1900 – is unclear. There is a widespread tendency to include it indiscriminately with classical physics. It will become clear, however, that this is a mistake. Probability made its appearance in thermodynamics as soon as the connection with the rest of classical physics was taken into account, and that concept has no place whatsoever in other classical theories. If this is so, one may well ask if classical physicists ignored probability altogether, even after it had become a pervasive tool elsewhere in science and everyday life. The answer to this question is a clear "no." But what role could they possibly assign to it, having committed themselves to a thoroughly deterministic theoretical scheme?

5.2   PROBABILITY IN CLASSICAL PHYSICS: THE EPISTEMIC INTERPRETATION

If the nature of things admits a fully determinate description at any given time and over time, probability obviously cannot have any place in the theory of objects. It can only serve either to characterize our relationship to that theory or to fill preliminary gaps left in the implementation of the ideal program. Since our actual knowledge is always preliminary and incomplete, a lesser degree of belief than certainty calls for as controlled and as precise a characterization as possible. Similarly, since the adaptation of available theory to a particular complex case in all its details is often too cumbersome, alternative possible specifications of an object may need to be considered. Therefore probability could have great importance in everyday and scientific practice, the more so because the theoretical standards of full and genuine knowledge were set so high in classical physics. Laplace, once again, is exemplary. His other major work, besides his book on the planetary system, was the *Analytical Theory of Probabilities* (1812), which was to become the standard source for much of nineteenth-century probability theory and for probabilistic applications to all kinds of problems.

The heart of Laplace's interpretation was the mandate to reduce all probabilities to a number of equally possible cases and to determine how many of them are favorable to a given event or state of affairs. He meant the phrase "equally possible" to define cases with respect to which we are ignorant in the same way (Laplace, [1814] 1951, p. viii). This is the epistemic interpretation of probability. It seems to be the only one that is left open by classical physics. Conversely, determinism was thought to be an indispensable presupposition of any mathematical description of nature, including the application of probability theory to reality, as may be illustrated by Jakob Bernoulli's *Ars conjectandi* of 1713. Laplace was the most prominent heir of this eighteenth-century legacy of determinism and epistemic probabilism. What he did was to codify this tradition and to surround it with an impressive belt of mathematical refinements in its application, which made him the outstanding authority for the nineteenth century in this field.

The most successful and systematic use of probability in classical physics was the theory of errors. It became particularly important in astronomy but gradually spread over all observational and experimental disciplines. To deal scientifically with errors of measurement meant to derive the "best" value for the measured magnitude or to estimate the likelihood of a certain deviation of the true value from the best estimate. For this one needs to know the law of the distribution of errors. In 1798, Carl Friedrich Gauss discovered how to derive, from relatively unrestrictive qualitative assumptions, what is now known as the normal curve or the Gaussian distribution, but was usually called "the law of errors" in the nineteenth century (Sheynin, 1979, p. 29). Gauss' distribution of errors provided a mathematical justification for the method of least squares, which was to become a standard technique for reducing discrepant measurements to one value for each parameter (see 3.3). Gauss had begun using this method even before 1798, and some years before he published it (in1809), it was independently developed by Legendre. Gauss' derivation, however, first established the connection between the proper method of evaluating measurements and the foundations of this method in probability theory. Laplace clarified the probabilistic character of the error curve further by showing that a sum of many independent errors will be normally distributed (Laplace, 1810). This result was applied by Hagen in 1837 and Bessel in 1838, who explained the normal error distribution by arguing that each single observable error is itself a composite of many independent invisible elementary errors – an idea that had been first suggested in 1819 by Thomas Young, best known in connection with the wave theory of light.

Within the context of error theory, probability is strictly confined to the methodological level. Moreover, since the assessment of an error amounts to a statement about the precision and the reliability of a piece of knowledge without implying anything about the structure of the object of that knowledge, it is natural to interpret those probabilities as epistemic. On the other hand, probability served implicitly in Laplace and explicitly in Hagen and Bessel as an explanation of observable phenomena – the bell-shaped distribution of actual errors – in much the same way as the probability distribution of a fair die serves to explain the observable distribution of a sample of actual results in rolling the die. In this latter case, of course, one may invoke the symmetry and homogeneity of the die as a reason – be it sufficient or not – for assuming a particular distribution. But provided that the errors of observation were not systematic, as they are for instance in the so-called "personal equation" for the individual observer, they were not taken seriously as natural phenomena. In actuality, and contrary to first appearances, the law of errors constituted not just a statement about our knowledge but also a statement about the world. The ambivalence between a subjective and an objective meaning of probability that emerged from chapter 1 carries over almost inevitably into the domain of physics.

Such implicit problems were not recognized until much later. Physicists were content to have a law of error that was plausible and in sufficient agreement with most experimental findings. Its purpose was to help ascertain the true value of the magnitude in question, which was the only thing that mattered for physical theory. This reaction was natural enough in a time when rapid progress in the technology of precision measurements supported the belief that the error of measurement could be reduced indefinitely, at least in principle. Even if that should prove impossible in some cases, one could reasonably hope to eliminate remaining errors – arising inevitably in the measurement apparatus – with the help of theoretical analysis. For physics was fortunate in comparison with most other disciplines. In contrast to the so-called Baconian sciences – including the early investigations of chemical reactions, electricity and magnetism, of life, and of the earth – the Newtonian tradition of mechanics, astronomy, optics, and, later, theories of heat, electricity and magnetism did not rely predominantly on an extended qualitative study of the phenomena, but rather on mathematical theory and experiment or observation that was informed by that theory. In this tradition it was natural for physicists to assume that their theories would always be strong enough to tell them what structure they might expect in their objects. They saw no need to assemble statistical data as a basis for inferences to underlying laws, as social scientists not infrequently are forced to do. These two characteristic features of modern physics, its highly theoretical character and its geometrical method, have saved it the long and arduous path through natural history that might have required descriptive and inferential statistics and probabilistic methodology in the search for the hidden lawlike order of nature.

The lawful pattern of errors, however, belongs to a different level, that of an auxiliary clarification of the tools of research. Given the impressive successes that proved possible even before such clarification was achieved, it is not surprising that a conscious examination of the collection and evaluation of data came late. In this respect, the situation in physics is just the opposite of that encountered in some recent developments of psychology, where methodological tools preceded, and then also influenced, theories about the subject matter (see chapter 6). The connection between theories of observation and theories of the observed in physics (though a concern in the nineteenth century, e.g. for Helmholtz) became a serious problem only in the twentieth century, when doubt arose concerning the unlimited possibility of improving the precision of measurement, and then even more when measurement became a research problem in theoretical quantum mechanics. Apart from that, the normal distribution did not call for an explanation as long as it figured as a distribution of errors. This changed only when error as the subject matter of the distribution was replaced by something else and more substantial. That occurred in 1860 when Maxwell announced that the velocities of the molecules in a gas were also distributed according to the law of error (see 5.6 below).

5.3   THREE LIMITATIONS OF CLASSICAL PHYSICS: SOURCES OF PROBABILISM

The increasing importance of probabilistic concepts and statistical methods, in physics no less than in other fields, had many sources inside and outside the sciences. But physicists had, in addition, specific internal reasons for adopting or inventing probabilistic ideas. Three serious limitations of classical physics can be identified as such reasons: (1) the requirement of the complete description of the state of a physical system; (2) the reversibility of all mechanical processes in time; and (3) the requirement of a complete description of all phenomena across space and time.

(1) As has already been remarked in section 5.1, classical physics requires a complete specification of a certain set of properties of a system at a given time in order to define the state of that system in such a way that it can be calculated for any other time from the dynamical equations. Given the formal structure of Newton's equations, the most natural set of such properties consists of local positions and velocities (or momenta). The system can be most concretely visualized when these properties are ascribed to basic and indivisible particles composing it. Moreover, an atomistic conception of this kind carries the promise of explaining the wealth of observable qualities in a parsimonious and unified fashion. Variants of this picture are, of course, possible, such as the assumption of dynamical centers of force rather than massive particles by Boscovich and Kant. But in any case, a drastically simplified scheme of the basic constitutents and their properties was indispensable for a generalization of the mechancial theory into a mechanical world view. The application of the formal theoretical framework of mechanics of this scheme requires, then, the specification of all positions and all momenta of the basic constituents.

It is obvious that this requirement raises practically insuperable difficulties for complex systems, such as a macroscopic volume of a gas consisting of about 10^{23} molecules. So long as we are concerned only with macroscopic properties – say, volume, pressure, temperature and the like – the apparatus of classical physics may be applied to them, provided suitable phenomenological laws for these magnitudes are known. But as soon as the dynamics of the system are located at the level of the minute constituent parts, the classical scheme becomes unworkable. And that would be true, even if the macroscopic properties could be calculated for each microscopic state. For a given macrostate there must be enormously many different microstates all having some claim to being the actual one, so that they must somehow be dealt with simultaneously. Now, a typical tool for treating many possible alternatives together in an exact and quantitative way is the calculus of probabilities. Its use, however, requires additional principles about the statistical distribution of the possible microstates, principles that follow neither from the classical laws nor from observation. The adequacy of the principles can only be tested by experimental results that are derivable from them. Hence, as soon as a macroscopic theory (which, as far as this point is concerned, may be entirely classical) is brought into contact with the microscopic dynamics, the resulting theory necessarily includes independent probabilistic assumptions.

This feature of the theory might, of course, prove to be eliminable if the additional principles could, in their turn, be shown to follow from the microdynamical laws. As long as this last point is an open question, one is free to assert classical determinism in principle, while admitting the pragmatic usefulness, indeed the inevitability, of additional probabilistic assumptions. The concession to probabilism need then only amount to the traditional view about probability described in section 5.2: probability rationalizes the gaps left by our ignorance, an ignorance that may be assumed to be reducible without limit as research progresses.

(2) The basic dynamical laws of classical physics can be expressed as differential equations that contain only the second derivative with respect to time. Hence, for any movement admitted by the laws, the movements obtained by reversing all motions in time is equally admissible under those laws. In the actual reality of our daily experience, however, there are very few processes that display this reversibility, be they ordinary motions subject to friction, chemical reactions, or the equalization of temperature, to mention only a few. The same is true for a grander scale of phenomena, comprising human history and its natural conditions, the evolution of life, or even that of the entire cosmos.

All these phenomena received growing attention during the eighteenth and nineteenth centuries. Darwin's theory of evolution and the discovery of the second law of thermodynamics made irreversible processes central to the theories of two of the most prestigious sciences. Thus, even apart from the increased sense of history among intellectuals generally, there were good reasons for calling the universal validity of the mechanical world view into question. Philosophers as different as Friedrich Engels and Charles Sanders Peirce could agree that the age of Newton had come to an end and that an evolutionary or dialectical world view must replace the mechanical one. At the beginning of the nineteenth century, G. W. F.

Hegel had adopted the ambitious philosophical project of formulating a world view that transcended history in its basic tenets and yet conceived all being as inherently historical. Though Engels and Peirce, each in his own way, disagreed with Hegel, they saw themselves confronted with a similar task.

The mere complexity of systems only limited the effective execution of the classical mechanical world view. The discovery of an all-embracing historicity of human life and non-human nature was seen as a substantial and massive counterexample to that view by some of the more perceptive minds of the age. Evolutionism, historicism, and similar philosophical views conquered the intellectual world rapidly and almost completely. The situation inside physics, however, was far less clear. The most fundamental and powerful theories were characterized by the features that are here called "classical," so that there could be no question of simply replacing the traditional theoretical perspective with a new one. Physicists could only try to enlarge the compass of their theories and to relate the new parts dealing with irreversible phenomena to the core of their reversible theories, or, better still, to accommodate irreversibility within the classical framework. This program was taken up by Ludwig Boltzmann around 1870. Its guiding idea, that of reconciling the basic mechanical constitution of nature under reversible laws with the wealth of observable irreversibilities, still remains alive today. Certainly, however, it was never able to score as clear a success as did special relativity for the analogous program of integrating electromagnetism into the classical framework. On the contrary, it undercut the harmonious edifice of classical physics at its foundation by securing a fundamental theoretical role for probability, a role that proved to be beyond reinterpretation in mere pragmatic terms, quite independently of further complications due to quantum phenomena.

(3) The use of differential equations typical for classical physics implies the ability to pursue change continuously through space and time. It would accord ill with the requirement of full specification discussed above if a natural process that connects two states separated by a finite spatial and temporal interval could not be conceived as being an uninterrupted chain of events without gaps and jumps. It should be possible to examine experimentally any given intermediate stage between the initial and the final states, and to show that it, too, is fully specified in all relevant respects.

If we ignore continuous fields for a moment and consider only particles, we find ourselves confronted with the contrast between their discreteness and discontinuity on the one hand and, on the other, the continuous gradation of those of their properties, most notably their spatial location, whose change is the subject matter of the theory. The rest of their properties – such as size and shape, or at least mass – must be assumed to be invariant and to characterize the discrete nature of the particle in question. In fact, the structure of the theory entails that some assumptions about the underlying carriers of change cannot be included in the domain of explanada. In other words, the theory recognizes motion or, more generally, change as the basic explanandum and, for that very reason, neglects another kind of explanandum: the possibility and actual existence of stable (or quasi-stable) things, kinds of things, and equilibrium states of matter. The only explanation of such things and states that is open within the framework of particle mechanics is in terms of dynamical systems that consist of particles of a lesser magnitude; but this only iterates the problem.

Hermann von Helmholtz's *On the Conservation of Force* (1847) illustrates how the initial successes of the mechanical program made it easy to overlook this explanandum. That famous memoir was the first comprehensive and definitive statement of energy conservation, and thus a central piece of physics interconnecting all its theories. In its introduction, Helmholtz sketched his conception of the tasks of physics, indeed of science in general. He wrote: " . . . we distinguish in it [matter] spatial distribution and quantity (mass) that is supposed to be eternally unchangeable. We must not ascribe qualitative differences to matter as such. . . Matter as such cannot be subject to change other than motion" (Helmholtz, [1847] 1889, pp. 4–5). From this reduction of the physical picture to uniform matter in motion Helmholtz concluded that the diversity of properties presented, for example, by the chemical elements, is to be explained in terms of qualitatively different and temporally invariant forces regulating all temporal change, which is to say all motion. This thought then led him to the idea of the "analysis of the universe into elements with unchangeable qualities" (p. 5) – a presupposition of all theoretical explanation. The lack of any further discussion of this presupposition by Helmholtz is somewhat disappointing, because the aim of his entire reduction to matter, motion and forces was precisely the quest for "complete intelligibility of nature" (p. 6, cp. p. 4); but it was natural for him, because he thought in terms of pointlike particles.

About twenty-five years later, the characteristic line patterns of light spectra had been correctly interpreted by Kirchhoff as being due to the specific structure of the atoms emitting the light. Several physicists, such as Stokes and William Thomson, had by then begun to think about atomic structure. Thus James Clerk Maxwell became puzzled by the very fact Helmholtz had taken for granted as an ultimate foundation of all explanation. On several occasions he stressed how remarkable it is that any molecule of, say, oxygen is completely like any other, regardless of how it was formed and under what circumstances it is encountered (Maxwell, [1873b] 1890). Not only did he clearly recognize this fact as an explanandum, he also stressed its novelty and asserted that the formation of molecules is "an event not belonging to that order of nature under which we live" ([1875b] 1890, p. 482), and hence that "we are therefore unable to ascribe either the existence of the molecules or the identity of their properties to the operation of any of the causes which we call natural" ([1873b] 1890, p. 376). Apart from the religious implications Maxwell had in mind, it is clear from these remarks that he identified "natural causes" with the determining factors of a process, in this case of the formation of the molecules. Once having done so, he recognized that the theoretical explanation of this process could not possibly fit into the scheme of traditional, or classical, physics.

In contemporary physics, the theory of stable kinds of elementary entities or of equilibrium states requires the use of probability concepts. Furthermore, any useful characterization of stable or quasi-stable systems does not employ descriptions of their internal motions so much as the ascription of tendencies or propensities to behave in certain ways under certain conditions.

Maxwell's new explanandum became inescapable for physics when, thanks to Einstein's theory of Brownian motion (1905a) and Jean Perrin's experiments (1909), the existence of discrete atoms and molecules at last became generally accepted. Discontinuity also entered physics in another, equally important, way: the interpretation of the interaction of radiation with matter. Several phenomena, notably black body radiation, radioactive decay, the photoelectric effect, and atomic and molecular spectra, led physicists not only to seek explanations for the discontinuous structure of matter but also to recognize a similar structure of radiation fields. Energy, too, was found to be quantized. The transition from a discrete state of a system of matter and radiation to another such state proved more or less intractable in terms of a continuous motion of the system through space and time. By the early 1920s Niels Bohr and a few other physicists suspected that elementary processes in a world of discontinuous entities and states might, as a matter of principle, not allow for a continuous description in space and time (e.g. Bohr, [1923/24] 1976, p. 492; Bohr,

1925, p. 156). Such descriptions were typically replaced by transition probabilities between the discrete states; these were introduced by Einstein in 1916 and finally adopted as the basis of discontinuity physics in Heisenberg's matrix machanics of 1925.

The three problems discussed in this section – the impossibility of a complete specification of complex systems, the irreversibility of many physical processes, and the discontinuity of matter and energy – mark three distinct limitations of the program of classical physics. At the same time, all three alike called for the introduction of probability into the fundamental theories of physics. They thereby provided decisive reasons for the emergence of probabilistic post-classical physics. Before analyzing the effect of these reasons in more detail, it will be useful to address the following two questions: (a) What connections, historical as well as conceptual, are there among those reasons? (b) Do they lead to distinguishable uses or interpretations of probability, or do they instead cooperate in reinforcing a unique conception of the role of probability in the new physics of our century? Question (a) is taken up in the next section, question (b) in section 5.5.

5.4 COMMENTS ON THE THREE LIMITATIONS

The first two limitations – that classical physics relies on the possibility of a full specification of physical states, and that it implies the reversibility of all processes in time – came to be analyzed within the same theoretical context in spite of their conceptual differences. That context was the kinetic theory of matter, which coincides with the kinetic theory of heat if heat is motion of the invisible constituents of bodies. The kinetic theory is also relevant to chemical transformations, so that it covers the most important classes of irreversible phenomena. The third limitation, however, was finally treated in another theory, quantum mechanics. As we briefly indicated in the last section, this theory solved two problems simultaneously: how (quasi-stable) units of matter are possible, and why matter and energy are discontinuous.

It is widely believed that only the second theory made probability irreducible and uneliminable in principle, so that classical determinism was finally overthrown. This view implies that irreversibility can be accommodated in the classical framework, and that, in this context, probability can be shown once again to admit an epistemic interpretation – to arise for us as crude observers only. Boltzmann's impressive work was the cornerstone of the defense of such implications, nowadays reinforced by the mathematical refinements of ergodic theory and recent chaos theory. The overall goal of this line of thought is to demonstrate that a quasi-stable equilibrium state for systems that fall under the entropy law (hence virtually all real systems) is obtained from the time-reversible laws of classical theory. This reductionistic aim involves in particular the reduction of thermodynamics to mechanics. The reduction, if successful, would render thermodynamics an integral part of classical physics in the sense of section 5.1. Yet, the 'if' is a big one, and later developments have strongly supported an independent position for thermodynamics, or at least have pointed to a much more general significance for its statistical versions. Since these comprise quantum mechanical as well as classical systems, a reduction to classical mechanics would seem to be unattainable.

A few early critics did argue that irreversibility is incompatible with all known classical theories, so that revisions of principle might be required (Poincaré, 1893; cp. also Zermelo, 1896). Doubts as to the reducibility of thermodynamics were shared by a few physicists, among them some leading figures. Einstein, for instance, relates in his autobiography (see Schilpp, 1949, pp. 30–3) that, as early as about 1900, he felt that while Newton's great achievement would always stay with us, it would need modifications, whereas the very abstract and general principles of thermodynamics conferred upon that theory a more fundamental status that was unlikely ever to require revision. In a similar vein, Max Planck admitted in 1920 that the quantum inevitably would cut pieces out of classical physics, whereas all signs were in favor of the persistence, indeed the expansion, of the role of "the great principles of thermodynamics" (Planck, [1920] 1958, p. 131; cp. also [1913] 1958, pp. 67–8). Even Boltzmann, the protagonist of the reductionist mechanical program, had already given in halfway when he spoke of the "for ever incontestable importance" of thermodynamics (Boltzmann, 1896–98, § 89).

Utterances such as these underline the problem, already raised at the end of section 5.1, of whether thermodynamics should be reckoned a part of classical physics, or rather the beginning of a revolutionary transformation of physics. The latter view, which emphasizes temporal irreversibility and the pervasive importance of non-equilibrium systems in our world, is forcefully advocated nowadays by Ilya Prigogine (1962) and others. It was already clearly stated by some scientists around 1915, among them the mathematicians Emile Borel and Richard von Mises, the physicist Marian von Smoluchowski and the philosopher Hans Reichenbach. Quantum problems played no role in the arguments of these thinkers. Some quantum theorists, most prominent among them Niels Bohr, confessed later in their careers that statistical mechanics had already taken the revolutionary step they had at first connected to quantum theory (e.g. Bohr, 1932, pp. 376–7; Bohr, [1957] 1958, p. 97). Moreover, one may note that ergodic theory, the stronghold of the mechanistic reductionist program, proved to contain irreducible probabilistic components (for a recent account see von Plato, 1987). Furthermore, its assumptions, like those of later chaos theory, could only be proved for a very few mechanical systems, and these still somewhat unrealistic. The first circumstance limits the conceptual strength of modern determinism, the second its practical importance for the working theoretician. If thermodynamics is subsumed under classical physics at all, then it is undoubtedly its problem child.

There are important conceptual and historical reasons for grouping thermodynamics with the new physics rather than classical physics. The conceptual bridge is the notion of entropy that is at the heart of irreversibility in physics. The second law of thermodynamics, formulated by Rudolf Clausius in 1850, asserts that the entropy of any isolated system will always increase until it reaches a maximum. Ludwig Boltzmann's great achievement was his attempt to explain this law in terms of molecular statistics. He argued that the entropy (a magnitude that is a function of certain observable properties of the system) is nothing but a macroscopic measure for the probability of finding the system in the state characterized by those properties. Now, if each system moves from less probable to more probable states, it will ultimately reach the most probable one, that of the highest entropy compatible with the specific nature of the system at hand. Hence the entropy law should hold, at least with a certain probability. For sufficiently large systems this probability is equal to unity for all practical intents and purposes.

A fundamental problem for the determination of entropy values from probabilities inevitably arose for systems of an infinite number of degrees of freedom, hence for all applications involving radiation. The problem has been recognized to be solvable only by introducing suitable discrete partitions of the continuous magnitudes involved, or by mathematically equivalent devices (e.g. Ehrenfest, 1906a; Borel, 1914).

This connection between irreversibility and discontinuity became decisive in the actual historical development. The probabilistic methods developed by Boltzmann in order to deal with irreversibility were essential to the discovery of the quantum by Max Planck. The latter announced his famous law of black body radiation, later called "Planck's radiation law" in October 1900. This law contained a new constant of nature, the elementary quantum of action or, as it is called nowadays, Planck's constant. This constant was to become the mark of all quantum physics. In Planck's original use it determined the elements of energy ("*Energieelemente*") hv for any frequency contained in a radiation field. Planck introduced these energy elements to provide an explanation of his radiation law. That law was surprisingly good empirically, but since it contained this new constant whose meaning and legitimacy were obscure, Planck viewed it (at least retrospectively) as no more than "an interpolation formula guessed with luck" (Planck, [1920] 1958, vol. 3, p. 125).

Given the nature of the case, an explanation could only be sought within the framework of thermodynamics and, via thermodynamics, in statistical mechanics. Therefore, in his famous paper of December, 1900, in which he announced the quantum (Planck, 1900b and 1901), Planck invoked a technique Boltzmann had used in 1877 for determining the entropy of a complex system by relating it to the probability of its state (see Kuhn, 1978). To calculate the probability required that he consider all possible distributions of the energy of the radiation field over the different frequencies; but the number of such distributions is, as he remarked, infinite. In an attempt to circumvent this difficulty, Planck was led to partition the energy into elements of the finite size hv. He called this "the most essential point of the whole computation" ([1900b] 1958, vol. 1, p. 700). Thus the statistical theory of heat gave birth to the idea of the discontinuous quantum of energy whereas, classically, energy had intimately been tied to the continuous character of motion and, thereby, to the continuity of space and time. Planck's reasoning was to become the first instance in a flurry of similar arguments employed by the early quantum theoreticians. Among them was Einstein, whose arguments in favor of the existence of light quanta were all based on considerations from statistical mechanics (for a more detailed account see 5.8 below).

Thus the transition from the statistical mechanics of atoms of the quantum theory of radiation displays an important element of continuity. Some later accounts stressed this aspect. For example, von Mises spoke of "the revolutionary upheaval created by some . . . ideas of modern physics" whose role he described in the following sentence: "Using the tools of probability and statistics, these new concepts have led us from the kinetic theory of gases to quantum theory and wave mechanics" ([1928] 1957, p. 210). We should, however, be wary of exaggerating the unity of statistical physics, as an examination of the second question posed at the end of the preceding section will make clear. Does probability admit of a unified interpretation in the new physics?

5.5   MASS PHENOMENA AND PROPENSITIES

With the replacement of reasonable man by average man, described in the first two chapters, probability came to refer paradigmatically to a complex object, society, consisting of many partly independent, though interacting, individuals. As pointed out in chapter 2, the existence of statistical regularities in this collective object encouraged physicists in their turn to use statistical reasoning, which for them meant to apply probability to their objects. In accordance with the pattern of social science, those concepts were used to characterize not elementary parts of physical systems, such as molecules, but a collective object, here a macroscopic entity consisting of very many interacting molecules. In short, probability was applied to mass phenomena; the minute component parts were conceived to be fully determinable in principle, so that they did not need, or even admit, probabilistic characterization. For instance, a molecule in a gas was assumed, at any given time, to possess a uniquely defined velocity, even though that velocity changed rapidly and frequently due to collisions with other molecules or the walls of the container.

This picture does not leave room for ascribing to the molecule a tendency or propensity to assume a certain velocity. The probability of a specified velocity can only be understood in the following two ways: (i) as the average number of times one encounters the molecule with that velocity in a long series of trials (more precisely: as the number of times in which the velocity lies within a specified interval around the given value), or (ii) as the average number of molecules in a gas that move with the specified velocity at a fixed time. In the second case, probability clearly must be measured in terms of a relative frequency of a property occurring randomly in a large collective of distinguishable objects. In the first case, however, one might want to say that the molecule "tends" to show a given velocity more frequently than another; but this "tendency" is entirely due to the fact that it belongs to a given collective of molecules. If that collective changes, the values of that tendency change as well. A single ideally elastic molecule in a container with ideally elastic walls will keep its initial velocity forever. A large number of such molecules in the same container will rapidly redistribute their velocities through collisions in such a way that a stable distribution is reached and probabilistic concepts become applicable. For this consequence it is essential that we are dealing with a mass phenomenon. Hence we are led to conclude that probabilities characterize the collective object rather than the individual constituents of it.

In order to illustrate this result, one may refer to the mechanical explanation of temperature. Statistical mechanics establishes a proportionality between the mean of the squared velocities (or equivalently, the average kinetic energy) of the molecules and the temperature of the gas. Temperature, however, characterizes a body that is in equilibrium – at least locally within macroscopically observable volumes. It is a concept that does not have any significance for the elementary parts of the body taken in isolation.

It is worth emphasizing that the two interpretations of probability occurring in statistical mechanics did not prevail because physicists had a predilection for empirical notions like countable frequencies and disliked the *a priori* or epistemic arguments based on equally possible cases that were typical under the classical interpretation of probability. Physicists may or may not have had such inclinations. But they used frequencies because they believed the existence of stable averages and distributions of values to be a result of physical interactions within their collective objects. For that reason alone, the probabilities could only be directly related to those collectives, and at best in an as-if fashion to single parts. In this way, physics confirmed a conception of probability, the frequency interpretation, that had become dominant in all disciplines during the nineteenth century, be it social science or population-oriented evolutionary biology. The older conception of the eighteenth century, according to which probabilities characterize states of mind, or degrees of reasonable belief – and in that sense something like an intensive magnitude – seemed to have been finally driven out of the scientific domain.

But this state of affairs was not to last for long. In 1896 Henri Becquerel discovered that uranium compounds emit radiation without being previously irradiated or excited in any way from outside. After several years of pioneering studies, especially by Marie and Pierre Curie and Ernest Rutherford, it became clear that this sort of radiation was due to the disintegration of single atoms belonging to certain elements at the upper end of the periodic table, among them uranium. Furthermore, all attempts at influencing the intensity of the radiation failed. In particular, Rutherford succeeded in demonstrating that a mutual interaction of neighbouring atoms had no effect on the speed or kind of radioactive decay. Nevertheless, the disintegration processes occurring in different atoms of a macroscopic sample of radioactive material seemed to be somehow correlated with each other. The sample as a whole obeys a well-defined decay law: after a characteristic time (the half-life of the substance) half of the atoms of the radioactive element present at the beginning of the time interval will have decayed. To be precise, this is true for sufficiently large samples. For small samples (or alternatively, small selections from the total number of occurring decays) certain chance fluctuations around the number one-half are observed.

This pattern is most easily explained by assuming that each radioactive atom, independently of all others, has an inherent probability of disintegration in each unit of time. That explanation was first offered by Rutherford and Frederick Soddy (1903; Rutherford, 1904, p. 319). It was soon realized (von Schweidler, 1905) that certain consequences follow from this hypothesis: the total decay rate in successive time intervals as well as the time intervals between two successive decay processes – for example, the appearances of emitted alpha-particles – should show certain statistical distributions. For sufficiently low total intensities, these distributions ought to be observable. Thanks to skilled experimentation, beginning in 1906 (Kohlrausch, 1906) and soon refined by techniques of counting single decays separately – developed by Erich Regener, Hans Geiger, and Ernest Rutherford – it was established beyond doubt that the results were in "agreement with the laws of probability" (Rutherford and Geiger, 1910, p. 704).

The similarity to the long familiar case of statistical mechanics was striking. Rutherford and Geiger, for instance, remarked that the distribution of time intervals between two successive decays "is similar in general shape to the probability curve of distribution of the velocity of molecules in a gas" (Rutherford and Geiger, 1908, p. 599). As a matter of historical fact, Kohlrausch's results on decay distributions appeared just when Perrin published his experiments, confirming the theory developed by Einstein and Smoluchowski (see Nye, 1972), and vindicating strikingly the atomic structure of matter presupposed by statistical mechanics. This work focused on Brownian motion, which presented fluctation phenomena similar to those encountered in radioactive decay. A natural result of this coincidence was a unified conception of probability distributions as characteristic of aggregates of many similar physical systems, a conception that one finds summarized in a book by Reinhold Fürth (1920), entitled *Fluctuation Phenomena in Physics*.

This book contains a very brief and tentative last chapter dealing with black body radiation and citing Einstein's work on fluctuations of radiation, which was the main argument then available for interpreting Planck's energy elements in a realistic way as light quanta (Einstein, 1905b, 1909, 1916). In sum then there is prima-facie evidence of an unbroken continuity between the statistical mechanics of molecules, radioactive decay, and quantum phenomena of radiation. They could all be seen as mass phenomena that, taken as wholes, obey probabilistic laws, while leaving room for a determinstic, though unknown, history of each of their parts. Yet, there was some occasional and vague anticipation of fundamental differences. Thus, Rutherford and Geiger called radioactive decay "a spontaneous process" and stated that "the particles are emitted at random" (Rutherford and Geiger, 1910, p. 704). Indeed, given both the probabilistic decay law and the complete independence of each single disintegration process from any other, both well-established experimental facts by 1910, it must have seemed puzzling that the aggregate of noninteracting radioactive atoms could obey a common law at all. In gas theory, it had always been argued that the probability distributions resulted from innumerable collisions between the molecules. In striking contrast to this situation, Rutherford and Soddy saw no interaction between radioactive atoms, and assumed an inherent instability of each single radio-atom. This was a revival, now at the heart of physics rather than the human sciences, of probability as an intensive magnitude – one characterizing basic constituents of matter, not the human mind. In a similar way, Einstein realized that in his treatment of radiation in terms of probability laws the single elementary process was left to chance, though he expressed misgivings about that ([1916], 1917, p. 128). To restore the mutual correlation of apparently disconnected elementary processes provoked unusual theoretical efforts (Bohr, Kramers, and Slater, 1924), but failed nevertheless in the end, as quantum mechanics has taught us.

The upshot of this section then is a negative answer to question (b) posed at the end of section 5.3. In spite of historical and systematic connections among the various reasons for introducing probability into fundamental physical theories, no unique conception of it emerged. Something like the old duality that was already a birthmark of probability (Hacking, 1975, esp. chapters 1 and 2) has intruded into modern physics as well. In physics, probability may refer to frequency distributions produced by interactions in large aggregates of similar systems or to a quantified tendency or propensity inherent in elementary constituents composing such aggregates.

We shall now pursue the discovery of the three limitations of classical physics in more detail.

5.6 EXPLANATIONS FROM PROBABILISTIC ASSUMPTIONS

As we pointed out in section 5.3, an atomistic picture of matter was a central idea in the universalization of classical mechanics into a comprehensive mechanical world view. Apart from that, this picture is as old as the European philosophy of nature. Its concrete specification and usefulness, however, did not match its promise until the nineteenth century when the advance of the mechanical explanatory program disclosed the first bits of evidence concerning the number, size, and further properties of the minute constituents of matter. Ironically, this development not only advanced and articulated, but simultaneously also undermined the program by contaminating its theoretical expression with probabilistic conceptions.

As early as 1736 Daniel Bernoulli had succeeded in explaining the relation between pressure and volume of gases (the so-called Boyle–Mariotte–Charles law) in terms of an atomistic model. A number of authors followed him on this path during the next 125 years. Some mentioned that the magnitudes to be related to macroscopic observables, such as temperature, are averages of microscopic qualities, such as molecular velocities. None of them probed deeper into this problem of incomplete description before 1860. To the contrary, many statements suggested a fully determinate physical state description. Thus the German chemist Krönig, in an 1856 paper on the kinetic theory of gases, based his calculations on a simplifying model according to which all molecules move with the same velocity. This strictly mechanical approach still characterized the work of Rudolf Clausius, the discoverer of the second law of thermodynamics. It was James Clerk Maxwell, and a few years later Ludwig Boltzmann, who replaced the formulation in terms of unique values for microscopic magnitudes by a probabilistic treatment of value distributions (Brush, 1976, vol. 1, p. 170).

Maxwell recognized the importance of the fact that the molecules of a gas cannot possibly move with constant velocity, nor all with the same velocity, because they collide with each other. Only a statistical approach is viable for dealing with the innumerable collisions. Yet, since the molecules are unobservable, their statistics can only be based on probabilistic assumptions. Maxwell was the first to introduce such assumptions into the description of objective physical systems (as opposed to the evaluation of hypotheses or the like). The most important of these assumptions, in his first paper on the kinetic theory of matter (1860), was the hypothesis that the velocity components along three orthogonal directions in space are mutually independent. From this *non-mechanical* premise and further purely mechanical assumptions he could derive the famous velocity distribution of the molecules that is formally identical with the law of errors and bears his and Boltzmann's names. Maxwell's probabilistic theory marks the birth of statistical physics. It is to be noted that in physics the label "statistical" does not refer to the evaluation of data, a familiar theme, but to the probabilistic ingredients of theoretical explanation.

Quetelet had interpreted the normal distribution as expressing a deep law of nature that united the various individuals of a population into a "type" or natural kind (see 2.5). Maxwell confirmed the status of this distribution as a law of nature that governs objective features of nature rather than describing a state of knowledge. But, deviating from Quetelet – Maxwell's understanding was more like Galton's view of biological variation (see 2.5 and 4.4) – he did not imply any commitment to an ideal type characterized by the mean value of the distributed magnitude. The law simply asserted the stability of the velocity distribution that characterized the mass of particles as a whole. It implied nothing about its single constituents, or a norm to which Quetelet's interpretation would seem to subject them. This reading of the distribution law was biased towards philosophical realism, especially since the probabilistic approach is obviously a reaction to the merely practical impossibility of tracing the paths of single molecules. But even if this detailed knowledge were available, it would be uninformative and without any scientific interest. For the explanandum is an overall structure of the entire system, a stable pressure or temperature of a gas, not the innumerable motions of its components.

In this respect, we should note an analogy to social statistics. In social science, as opposed to molecular physics, it is possible to trace individual life histories and, as we may (counterfactually) grant for the sake of the argument, explain them in terms of determining causal chains. But for the sociological purpose of explaining the overall structure of a society and its changes, this "historical" or "dynamical" treatment (these are Maxwell's terms) would have to give way to a structural treatment, one form of which is statistics. In order for a statistical treatment to make sense, the overall structures must be invariant with respect to changes in the many detailed histories (of molecules or of people). That such invariance is possible seemed to be demonstrated by the existence of stable social averages, as borne out by social statistics. Seen in this light, it is less surprising that Maxwell and Boltzmann referred to social science in order to recommend their novel statistical approach in physics (see chapter 2).

Maxwell's main problabistic assumption of 1860 was soon attacked on the simple grounds that the conservation of energy is incompatible with the statistical independence of the three components of velocity.

Maxwell had to admit that this derivation was faulty (1866, pp. 30, 43); he therefore introduced a new probabilistic assumption. Appealing to the stationary and stable condition of a gas in thermal equilibrium, he assumed that, on the average, the number of collisions per unit of time that lead from the initial velocities v_1 and v_2 to the velocities v_1' and v_2' of the two interacting molecules must be equal to the number of collisions that lead from v_1' and v_2' to v_1 and v_2. From this hypothesis he once again obtained his velocity distribution. This derivation, no less than the first, appealed to a non-mechanical principle, the reciprocity of collisions. But the new derivation was a more credible one, and it became the most favored argument for the Maxwell distribution. It was adopted, for example, by Kirchhoff and Planck, and even by Boltzmann (1896–98, vol. 2, § 92), who had at first attempted to dispense with it for reasons to be discussed in the next section.

The need for an additional principle is brought to our attention even more distinctly in Maxwell's third great paper on the kinetic theory published in 1878, shortly before his death. Here he set out from a principle that Boltzmann had already used ten years earlier but only as a mathematical shortcut and without assigning it any physical reality. It says that a system in equilibrium, in the course of time, takes on every microscopic mechanical state that is compatible with its total energy. Later, systems with this (or a modified, but similar) property were called "ergodic." Maxwell knew that no isolated system could satisfy this condition if mechanics were to be true. He therefore assumed that contact with the environment, such as the collisions of the gas molecules with the container, would somehow produce the ergodic property (1878, pp. 714–15). Thus, it became clearer than even before that the mechanical character of a physical system, at least so far as it is governed by the known deterministic theory, does not secure the observed thermodynamical behavior of the system, but that suitable instabilities or "disturbances" (Maxwell's term), plus a certain regular pattern of their effects, were needed in addition to the mechanics of the system. In an unpublished paper (1873a) he recommended "the study of the singularities and instabilities, rather than the continuities and stabilities of things," an investigation that, he thought, might "tend to remove that prejudice in favour of determinism which seems to arise from assuming that the physical science of the future is a mere magnified image of that of the past" (p. 444).

Since the ergodic assumption was lacking any independent support, almost all physicists distrusted it and tried to dispense with it. Most of them finally turned to an alternative interpretation of this assumption that was inaugurated by Maxwell in the same paper, the conception of the ensemble. Maxwell, after introducing ergodicity, remarked at once (1878, p. 715) that it is "convenient" to consider a large set of systems that are similar to each other in that they agree in their observable properties but differ in their microscopic mechanical specifications. This set or ensemble was intended to mirror the temporal sequence of states of the actual system at hand. Since all experimentally relevant assertions refer to averages over many microstates, he expected that they would not be affected by this transition from the real system to the purely conceptual construction of the ensemble. For investigations based on this conception Maxwell proposed the term "statistical method" (1878, p. 721), in contrast to the dynamical method that had generally been used so far.

Now, the new method suggested a new interpretation. Since we do not, and cannot, know the detailed dynamical specifications of a given physical system, we must somehow simultaneously deal with the entire range of such specifications, so far as they are compatible with the observed macrostate (see e.g. Jeans, [1904] 1925, § 58). The description in terms of ensembles would, therefore, seem to reflect our incomplete knowledge rather than any objective feature of reality. If so, the adequacy of a particular ensemble employed by the theoretician does not require explanation in terms of an underlying objective structure or process, but only a justification in terms of the observable conclusions derived from it. Since Willard Gibbs' pioneering work of 1902, *Elementary Principles in Statistical Mechanics*, the method of ensembles has remained a standard device of statistical physics. Frequently, though not always, it has been interpreted in epistemic terms (Gibbs, 1902, p. viii; Tolman, 1938, §§1, 23, 25; Jaynes, 1967).

Whether one interprets statistical mechanics in a dynamical fashion on the basis of the ergodic assumption, or epistemically, in terms of ensembles, the implications for the classical world picture are similar. Both possibilities involve abandoning the complete description of physical states. But classical mechanics is not (at least not explicitly) violated. It is only complemented by additional assumptions, be they dynamical or epistemological. Hence the step from pre-statistical to statistical theories does not appear to lead outside the classical world picture as described in section 5.1. Nor does the probabilistic outlook implied by the additional principles appear to be at variance with the epistemic character of probabilistic notions discussed in section 5.2. Nevertheless, a certain divergence between the statistical theory and the mechanical world view can hardly be denied. The concrete articulation of the mechanical view must be incomplete when the dynamical theory that is effectively available appeals to basic probabilistic premises in order to fit the phenomena. In contrast to the mutual support of Laplacian mechanics and philosophical determinism depicted in section 5.1, statistical mechanics cannot be taken by itself to support this general philosophical view. At best, it can be considered as compatible with determinism and classical mechanism. And, to be sure, it was so considered by most physicists, yet not by all. As mentioned above, as early as 1873 Maxwell sensed a "new kind of knowledge" (1873a, p. 444) in physics. That he was right in this became much clearer when attention turned to the second limitation of classical physics, the restriction to theories that are symmetric with respect to past and future.

5.7 THE PUZZLE OF IRREVERSIBILITY IN TIME

Maxwell's statistical physics, though it broke new ground, still suffered from a serious restriction: it only dealt with equilibrium states. For that very reason he was unable to show that the structure he had ascribed to those states was the only possible one, in the sense that every non-equilibrium process necessarily leads to it. It was Boltzmann's great achievement to recognize the problem and offer a solution for it. This was his mechanical theory of the second law of thermodynamics, also known as his H-theorem (1872). On the basis of an ingenious statistical treatment of molecular collisions he defined a magnitude H – a function of the velocity distribution of the molecules – that can only decrease with time until it reaches a minimum. Its negative, therefore, can only grow until it reaches a maximum, so that Boltzmann was able to identify it with the thermodynamical function of macroscopic observables known as entropy. The equation for the time development of H, later called "the Boltzmann equation," is still an essential tool for dealing with irreversible processes, such as diffusion.

Boltzmann knew as well as Maxwell that the mechanical treatment of heat phenomena requires the calculus of probabilities (1871, p. 295; 1872, p. 317). Nevertheless, he believed he had given "a strict proof" of the entropy law, a proof that was "free from all hypotheses" (1872, p. 345). In other words, he believed he had reduced thermodynamics to mechanics, at least for certain types of mechanical systems for which plausible models allowed the treatment of the collision processes. Four years later his Viennese colleague Loschmidt raised the following objection, known as the reversibility paradox. Assume we have a system that obeys Boltzmann's

H-theorem, and hence exhibits "normal" thermodynamic behavior. At some time stop the motions of all its molecules and precisely reverse their directions. Thanks to the time-symmetric character of mechanics, the result of this operation will again be a possible mechanical system. Yet such a system will evolve, as it were, "backwards" in time, from larger to smaller values of entropy, hence in an "abnormal" and empirically unknown way.

The only possible conclusion is that Boltzmann's proof was not "strict" but contained hidden premises that limited the range of possible mechanical systems to those that behave normally. Closer inspection reveals that the decisive premise is again probabilistic in nature: Boltzmann had assumed that the number of collisions can be found from the *average* density of the molecules in the gas. But this is a new hypothesis about the overall distribution of the paths of the molecules, regardless of their previous mechanical history. When confronted by Loschmidt with this objection, Boltzmann saw at once that this hypothesis could not be universally true. But, as he argued (1877), it is true in the overwhelming majority of cases, hence with a very high probability.

This remarkable statement implied for the first time that a law of nature may not hold with necessity but only with probability, and hence allow for exceptions. True, Boltzmann at first thought that those exceptions would never be discovered because they are too rare in systems of observable dimensions. But an exception had already been recognized. In 1828, the British botanist Robert Brown observed the erratic movement of small particles suspended in a liquid under the microscope. During the last decades of the nineteenth century some physicists attempted to understand this phenomenon in terms of the kinetic theory of matter. By 1896, Boltzmann was among them (1896–98, vol. 1, p. 778; English trans. p. 223; for a brief survey see von Smoluchowski, 1906, parts I–II). The final confirmation of this idea was achieved by the theoretical analysis of Einstein (1905a) and von Smoluchowski (1906), in connection with Perrin's experiments (1909; cp. 5.3). Thereafter the study of fluctuation phenomena of diverse kinds rapidly grew to a major trade among physical scientists. In the eyes of some less traditional minds they became a visualizable demonstration of the probabilistic constitution of things (see 5.8, Radioactivity).

It lay in the nature of Boltzmann's argument that it barred dynamical considerations, because they would inevitably have led back to the time-reversible and deterministic processes of mechanics. Instead Boltzmann calculated the inherent probabilities of observable macrostates from the number of different microstates that were compatible with each macrostate. The method of counting such numbers depended, of course, on the mechanical properties and laws of the microstates, but the transition from one microstate – or for that matter from one macrostate – to another was not, and could not be, treated mechanically. The defense against Loschmidt's objection rested entirely on the intuitive plausibility of the claim that any system will pass from an improbable initial state through ever more probable states until it finally reaches the most probable state (Boltzmann, 1877, p. 165). Had not Loschmidt just shown that this was not necessarily so? Indeed, later investigations by Boltzmann himself revealed that his magnitude H, or equivalently the entropy, had to be symmetric with respect to the exchange of past and future (1895) – at least as far as this argument goes. So long as probability is only employed to characterize the state of an object at a fixed time, but does not enter into the dynamical laws, there is no less reason to think that the object has been in a more probable state in the past than that it will be in a more probable state in the future. At this point, we are up against an inevitable competition between deterministic mechanics and probabilistic laws of change.

The problem of irreversibility became clearer still thanks to a second objection that was put forward against Boltzmann's mechanical theory of the second law by Ernst Zermelo in 1896, the recurrence paradox. The French mathematician Henri Poincaré had proved that every isolated mechanical system returns arbitrarily closely to any given state of its development after a sufficiently long time. Boltzmann could show that these recurrence times will be exceedingly long in all cases of interest, but he could not ultimately clarify why we do not find many systems that are about to approach an improbable state of their career. Concerning this question, he fell back once again onto his arguments of 1877 (Boltzmann, 1896, appendix, esp. footnote 1). He finally came to think that the reason for irreversibility "lies uniquely and solely in the initial conditions" (1896–98, vol. 2, § 87); hence he engaged in cosmological speculations about special conditions of improbability that obtain in our spatio-temporal region of the universe. This move provided a defense of the mechanical world picture, but it offered no positive account of the nature of irreversible processes. All such accounts that have since been given are essentially probabilistic, from simple stochastic models like that of Ehrenfest (1906b) to Ilya Prigogine's great program of non-equilibrium statistical mechanics, in which the typical elements of the classical mechanical descriptions, positions and momenta, are replaced by a statis-

tical distribution function (1962, p. 6) and the second law of thermodynamics is taken to be a sufficient reason to develop a completely new
conception of dynamics (1984, sections VII.1, X.1). Within this conception the competition mentioned above reappears as a "new complementarity" of the dynamical (i.e. mechanical) and the thermodynamical
descriptions (1984, VII.6).

The situation with respect to the irreversibility problem can briefly be
summarized as follows. To accommodate irreversible processes, the full
specification of the mechanical system has to be dropped. This is true not
only because it is beyond our actual epistemic capacities or interests, so
that physicists must resort to additional principles without any known
connection with the laws of mechanics – the case of the last section. A
fully specified mechanical description necessarily implies reversibility,
that is, the wrong, temporal behavior of complex physical systems. Boltzmann's defense of 1877 only brought to light what was already involved
in his H-theorem of 1872, the restriction of the dynamical theory to
statistical distributions as its proper new subject matter. Current irreversible dynamics are a generalization of this fundamental innovation.

5.8   THE DISCONTINUITY UNDERLYING ALL
CHANGE

The Problem

Irreversible dynamics, though it offers a novel framework for analyzing
physical processes, does not itself call into question the traditional picture
of the ultimate constituents of matter or the basic carriers of motion. It
can accommodate classical and quantum mechanical systems alike (see e.g.
Prigogine, 1962, p. 9 and chapter 13; 1984, chapters VII and VIII). The
basic entity of statistical mechanics, the distribution function, may still be
taken to represent the distribution of "classical" unchangeable atoms.
Problems like the one raised by Maxwell (see 5.3) remain open: What
makes each atom or molecule of a chemical element exactly like every
other? Why do certain kinds of atoms exist, but not others? What makes
the basic constituents of matter stable, or at least quasi-stable?
The classical theory of motions in continuous space and time does not
address these questions. It does not even suggest where to look for a
solution. Only quantum mechanics gave answers. At the same time, it
finally and, as it appears, irrevocably blew up the mechanical world view.
The full articulation of classical determinism required presuppositions
which in the end undermined its basic tenets.

Studies of the emergence of quantum mechanics usually emphasize the following features: the discovery of the quantum structure of radiation and, conversely, the wave structure of matter, hence, also, the discovery of a unified theory of both that overcame the particle–wave duality. Of course, probability makes its appearance here and there in such accounts, but it usually remains on the margins. This section is a deliberate attempt to select those aspects of the story that gradually persuaded even reluctant physicists to consider probability as a basic feature of their theories. It is intended also to show how probabilistic ideas relate to the need to account for the nature of the carriers of motion, in particular of atoms and photons. Not surprisingly, we find once again that a full spatio-temporal specification of the objects of physical theory had to give way to a characterization in terms of probabilities.

Our account has two natural starting points whose relationship was not at first clear: radioactivity, and the interaction of light and matter (the radiation problem). From the probabilistic point of view, the history of radioactivity is comparatively neat and straightforward. In contrast, the history of the radiation problem is extremely involved, though it finally proved more successful and absorbed radioactivity into its domain. Exaggerating somewhat, Pascual Jordan once wrote: "The law of radio-active decay indicates a non-causal process so obviously and so unmistakably that nobody has ever tried to reduce it to a causal mechanism" (1928, p. 166). The radiation problem, on the other hand, inspired Max Jammer, in the opening pages of his history of quantum mechanics, to speculate that "much intellectual effort could have been saved on the part of the early quantum theorists . . . if a conceptually less involved issue than that of black body radiation had initiated the development of the theory" (1966, p. 1). We shall devote the first subsection to the simpler story in order to exhibit some probabilistic ideas that are less easily perceived in the second.

Radioactivity

In section 5.5 we have already described two major insights concerning radioactivity: (1) The observed exponential law of radioactive decay can most easily be explained by assuming a characteristic propensity of disintegration inherent in each radioactive atom, or, more precisely, nucleus, independently of its history or environment. For the first time in the development of modern physics the elementary nature of an object was characterized not by manifest properties but by dispositional properties or potentialities. (2) This explanation of a phenomenological law implies the existence of observable chancelike fluctuations of the decay rate or, equivalently, of the time intervals between two successive disintegration processes. These implications were fully confirmed by experiment. The experimental findings could be read as a direct proof of the existence of chance mechanisms in nature that obey probabilistic laws. This immediate "visibility" of probabilistic structures may have inspired Jordan's confident statement quoted above.

But, of course, the experimental results in themselves no more show that probability is an irreducible feature of reality than does a macroscopic phenomenon of a similar kind, say, the random series of throws of a die. Irreducible randomness can only be made convincing by embedding the experimental results in a much broader probabilistic context. The context of about 1910, however, pointed in another direction. As we mentioned in section 5.4, fluctuations due to mass phenomena, as in Brownian motion, and fluctuations due to propensities, as in radioactive decay, were not initially seen as different in nature. On the contrary, reasonable attempts were made to explain radioactive instability as a mass phenomenon, in strict analogy to Brownian motion. In the latter an accidental alignment of many molecules pushes the Brownian particle in a particular direction. Similarly, an accidental correlation of the fairly large number of nuclear particles was thought to lead to the expulsion of an alpha-particle from the nucleus. This conception seemed to accord well with a surprising experimental fact that was discovered by Geiger and Nuttall (1911–12): the decay rate L varies with a stupendously high power of the energy E of the emitted particles, $L = c\,E^{80}$. Lindemann (1915) offered an explanation that started from the following assumptions: (1) The energy of a typical nuclear particle is proportional to the frequency of its return to a certain "critical" region of its orbit. (2) The instability leading to disintegration occurs whenever all relevant particles happen to reach their critical regions at the same time. (3) (The most interesting assumption from our point of view:) The particles move independently from each other, much as the colliding molecules of a gas were believed to do. (4) The number of electric charges of a nucleus indicates the number of independently moving particles that are relevant for disintegration. On the basis of these hypotheses Lindemann argued as follows: Since all radioactive atoms (known at the time) carried roughly eighty nuclear charges, the disintegration, in view of (2)–(4), can be understood as an eighty-fold chance coincidence of their reaching the critical part of the orbits simultaneously. The probability of this event should be proportional to v^{80}, where v is the orbital frequency, or alternatively, due to assumption (1), proportional to T^{80}, where T is the energy of a particle within the nucleus.

If, in addition, one grants (5) that T is proportional to the visible energy E of an emitted particle, at least a qualitative agreement with the Geiger–Nuttall relation is reached.

According to this "classical" line of argument, radioactivity appears to be just another statistical mass phenomenon. At first sight, therefore, it seemed to be no less, and no more, possible to assume an underlying deterministic motion of each single nuclear constituent than of each molecule in a gas. A closer look, however, directs us back to an important difference between gases and radioactive samples that was mentioned at the end of section 5.5. Disregarding all problems of irreversibility, the interaction of the molecules in the gas with each other and with the container can be taken to produce the observed probabilities, at least if the motion is ergodic. On the other hand, in order to establish a similar situation for the radioactive sample, according to Lindemann's assumption (3), the initial configurations of the nuclear particles of all (or very many) atoms in the sample would have to belong to one unified dynamical system that, taken as a whole, could be assumed to satisfy an ergodic property. But according to the available experimental evidence there is no physical connection between different radioactive atoms that has any influence on the decay rate. In other words, the statistical distribution of the nuclear particles over their orbits as required by Lindemann's argument cannot be accounted for in terms of an underlying deterministic mechanics; it is to be viewed as a basic feature of reality, at least as far as this theory goes. Is Jordan's dictum vindicated? It was no more than plausible, until a broader theoretical context was established. That context only emerged in the development of new ideas concerning the nature of radiation in general and of its interaction with matter.

Light and matter

As mentioned in section 5.4, the version of statistical mechanics best suited to enter quantum theories was Boltzmann's purely probabilistic treatment of entropy of 1877. Its central result was the relation: $S = k \log P + c$ (where S is the entropy, P the probability of a state, and k and c are constants). Using it, Planck could explain his experimentally correct law of thermal radiation, but only by introducing discrete "energy elements" $h\nu$ of the electromagnetic field (where ν is the frequency of the radiation and h Planck's constant). An important feature of Planck's revolutionary step was that he took thermodynamics as well as Boltzmann's principle for granted, but reversed the direction of the argument. Boltzmann had

calculated the probability P on the basis of purely mechanical considerations in order to defend what he viewed as his purely mechanical derivation of the entropy law. Planck could not follow this scheme, because
there was no empirically acceptable theory of the emission and absorption
of light. After he had ingeniously guessed a suitable S from the experimental data, he inferred the correct method of calculating P from it,
using luckily chosen bits of Maxwell's electrodynamics that later proved
to be unaffected by the necessary revisions due to quantum theory. In
this way he not only discovered a new constant of nature but also tied its
appearance to one of the deepest probabilistic principles of physics
(Planck, 1900b).

Einstein pursued this line of argument more uncompromisingly than
anyone else; for about two decades he remained almost alone in his belief
in the reality of light quanta. In his first quantum paper (1905b), for
which he recieved the Nobel prize (but, significantly, not until 1921), he
asked how much the entropy of a black body – a cavity filled with radiation
in thermal equilibrium – would change if all radiation of a given small
range of frequencies around v were condensed to a subvolume V' of the
original volume V of the cavity. From Planck's law and Boltzmann's principle he obtained an expression for the probability of this spatial fluctuation of the radiation which is a formal analog of the probability that is
obtained for a similar chancelike condensation of the molecules of a gas
from volume V to the subvolume V'. Where the second probability contains simply the number of molecules, the first features (an equivalent of)
the expression E/hv, where E is the total energy of the radiation in the
relevant frequency range around v. Hence Einstein inferred that "mono-
chromatic radiation of low density . . . behaves as if it consisted of independent energy quanta" of magnitude hv (1905b, p. 143). The as-if
rendering sounds noncommittal; but Einstein concluded his paper by
suggesting that the actual occurrence of the quanta could explain several
experimental phenomena that were at variance with the wave theory of
light – most notably the photoelectric effect, the emission of electrons
from material surfaces under the impact of light.

In 1909, Einstein further generalized and confirmed his treatment of
the fluctuations of radiation. This paper connected the statistical
approach with the search for a carrier of the effects that are transmitted
by light from the source to the absorbing body. Einstein first reviewed
the attempts to account for such transmission in terms of the ether,
which he deemed hopeless because incompatible with his special theory
of relativity. He therefore concluded that light cannot consist in a series

of modifications of some medium (the ether) but must be "something independently existing like matter" (1909, p. 820). According to the wave theory, he argued, an elementary emission process produces an expanding spherical wave. Correspondingly, an elementary process of absorption would require a contracting spherical wave; but such a creature does not exist in nature because it would require an enormous mass of coordinated elementary emitters. Hence, as far as emission and absorption is concerned, Newton's corpuscular theory of light seemed to him closer to the truth than the wave theory. For radiation to remain available for absorption processes the emission must be spatially directed.

In 1911, Rutherford inferred from the scattering of alpha-particles in matter that atoms consist of a very small and condensed nucleus carrying a positive electric charge and a cloud of surrounding electrons. Niels Bohr took this picture as his starting point in developing his famous model of the atom (1913). As we emphasized in section 5.3, the stability of basic particles, and hence of Rutherford's atom in particular, could not be understood within the classical mechanical framework. Worse, according to Maxwell's electrodynamics the electrical charges orbiting around the nucleus should rapidly lose their energy, while emitting a continuous spectrum of radiation, until they crash down into the nucleus. But atoms are stable, and their spectra consist of discrete lines. After 1900, physicists saw hope of explaining these facts only in Planck's and Einstein's idea of energy quanta. Niels Bohr achieved the great breakthrough; he sensed that not only the light emitted by atoms but also the motion of the electrons in the atom must be subject to quantum rules involving Planck's constant. The simplest, if not the earliest, form of such a rule holds that the angular momentum of an electronic orbit must be an integral multiple of Planck's h divided by 2π. This principle was mechanically arbitrary, and electrodynamically it was even forbidden; otherwise, Bohr's model of the stationary state of an atom was still classical. Yet Bohr saw well what price he had to pay for his bold violation of classical physics. One of the main conclusions of his memoir reads thus: "the dynamical equilibrium of the systems in the stationary states is governed by the ordinary laws of mechanics, while these laws do not hold for the passing of the systems between the different stationary states" (1913, p. 874). What laws do hold for these transitions Bohr could not tell. Today we know that they cannot be phrased in terms of a continuous space-time description. Here the need for a completely new dynamics first became evident.

Einstein ([1916]1917) first recognized that the available information about the stable states of matter and the transitions between them could neatly be captured in terms of probabilities inherent in a molecule or atom. Once again he rested his case on the validity of thermodynamics. Bohr's work enabled him to make a few more specific assumptions. The constituents of a gas can take on a number of discrete states Z_m, Z_n, etc. with total energies E_m, E_n, etc. A transition between those states can only occur in connection with the emission or absorption of an amount $E_m - E_n$ of radiation energy. The decisive further idea was this: Any pair of states Z_m and Z_n can be characterized by three probabilities per unit of time: (1) the probability A_{mn} for a spontaneous transition from Z_m to Z_n and the simultaneous emission of the energy quantum $E_m - E_n$ ($E_m > E_n$ is presupposed) without any interference from outside; (2) the probability $B_{mn}d$ for a similar process but now induced by the surrounding radiation, where d is the radiation density for quanta of the appropriate energy $E_m - E_n$; and finally (3) the probability $B_{nm}d$ for the transition from Z_n to Z_m and a simultaneous absorption of the energy $E_m - E_n$ from the radiation field. From this schematic picture of possible processes and the validity of Boltzmann's thermodynamics Einstein could derive Planck's radiation law and Bohr's frequency condition for the light quanta, $v = (E_m - E_n) / h$ in a very simple manner.

Still more important for Einstein was the following further argument. The thermal equilibrium between matter and radiation implies not only that the energy of the radiation is quantized (Planck's law) but also that each quantum has a spatially well-defined momentum E/c (where E is the energy of the quantum and c the speed of light). In other words, the picture of the discrete states with their inherent transition probabilities leads again to the particle picture of light that Einstein had already advocated in 1909. Most phycisists then had hesitated to accept the reality of light quanta, but Einstein was fully convinced of their existence, since it was the inevitable consequence of the combination of thermodynamics with all known features of radiation. This new theoretical unity embraced radioactivity as well. Einstein noted: ". . . the assumed statistical law [that of spontaneous emission probabilities A_{mn}] corresponds to that of a radioactive process" ([1916]1917, p. 123).

Moreover, Einstein was fully aware of the philosophical significance of his theory. Probability governed every emission and absorption. Concerning emission without external excitation he concluded that, since the spherical waves of a classical electromagnetic emission had been replaced by a directed process, the direction of the light quantum or, equivalently, of the recoil of the emitting molecule was "only determined by 'chance'," at least "according to the present state of the theory" (p. 127). Although fully convinced by this theory he was profoundly uneasy about its probabilistic structure. Thus he wrote: "The weakness of the theory lies on the one hand in the fact that it does not get us any closer to making the connection with wave theory; on the other, that it leaves the time and direction of the elementary processes to 'chance'. Nevertheless I am fully confident that the approach chosen here is a reliable one." ([1916]1917, pp. 127–8; English trans. p. 76; I have replaced the word "duration" with "time," because Einstein was obviously referring to the impossibility of predicting the moment of an emission, not to the duration of such a process.) Einstein's dilemma is evident. Coherent physical theorizing drags him in one direction, deep-rooted philosophical habits of thinking in another. In comparison with the isolated phenomenon of radioactivity, the evidence for probabilism had become much stronger. Yet it was far from being consolidated, let alone intellectually acceptable. Einstein, at least, put the term "chance" between inverted commas.

Philosophically less conservative minds, like Niels Bohr, also struggled with the paradoxes entailed by Einstein's results. In his papers on the quantum theory of line spectra and the structure of the atom (1918–24), he expressed his uneasiness with the quantum on the grounds that the wave theory of light remained indispensable as well. Indeed, Bohr argued, even a definition of the frequency v characterizing the energy and momentum of quanta was excluded by the particle conception of radiation. Hence the success of the quantum hypothesis could not be taken as a confirmation of the particle picture with its strict retention of general laws such as the conservation of energy and momentum, even in individual processes. To him it suggested a different conclusion: ". . . in contrast to the description of natural phenomena in classical physics in which it is always a question only of statistical results of a great number of individual processes, a description of atomic processes in terms of space and time cannot be carried through in a manner free from contradiction by the use of conceptions borrowed from classical electrodynamics" (1923/24, III.1). His emphasis on the need for statistics was combined with a tendency to hold back from a complete description of individual processes.

This strategy was applied in the highly remarkable attempt by Bohr, Kramers, and Slater (1924) to reconcile the existence of elementary processes of emission and absorption with the continuous wave structure of radiation. On the one hand, the existence of interference phenomena required the idea of a macroscopic correlation between distant emission and absorption processes. Although Einstein's quantum picture of light suggested that interference phenomena should disappear for low intensities or light beams travelling in different directions, all experiments strictly reconfirmed the wave theory. On the other hand, only a "formal theory" (pp. 785, 788, 790) – a theory that does not describe the spatio-temporal process, but is restricted to considerations of probability – seemed possible for individual emissions and absorptions. Hence Bohr, Kramers, and Slater abandoned the causal connection between distant atoms, and declared untenable the conservation of energy and momentum in individual radiation processes. They argued that basic conservation principles hold only on the macroscopic average. What had been said about the law of entropy long ago was now claimed for the law of energy, that it is "a statistical law" (p. 793).

When this bold paper by Bohr, Kramers, and Slater was written, Compton had already published his results concerning the scattering of X-rays by matter (1923), in which he proved that the variation of the frequency of the scattered X-rays with the angle of deflection agrees fully with Einstein's particle picture of radiation, including the strict conservation of momentum and energy in each single encounter of a light quantum and an electron. A specific refutation of the Bohr–Kramers–Slater view, however, was only provided by experiments in which the coincidence of the scattered X-rays with the recoil electron was directly measured (Bothe and Geiger, 1925; Compton and Simon, 1925). In reaction to these results, Bohr surmised that the still unknown correct theory would deviate equally far from the "ordinary spatio-temporal pictures" of particle mechanics as from the wave representation of optical phenomena (1925, p. 156). In this he was right.

Both particle mechanics and the wave representation were conceived in strict analogy to a classical physics characterized by the complete determination of its objects in terms of manifest and visualizable properties. It was only the rejection of both pictures, therefore, that finally provided room for an alternative description of individual micro-objects and microprocesses, a description that essentially involves probabilistic properties.

Quantum mechanics

During the first twenty-five years of this century a mass of experimental and theoretical evidence accumulated that to some physicists suggested the impossibility of an ordinary spatio-temporal-causal picture of the microworld, be it in terms of waves or of particles. What was still missing until the summer of 1925 was a coherent alternative account. Werner Heisenberg made the last decisive step toward it. One of his motives was a radical belief in Bohr's conjecture referred to above. In a letter accompanying the manuscript of his first revolutionary paper on matrix mechanics (1925), he wrote to his friend Wolfgang Pauli on July 9, 1925: "I am really convinced that an interpretation of the Rydberg formula [i.e. the formula describing the line spectra of atoms] in terms of the circular and elliptic orbits of classical geometry does not have the least physical significance, and all my poor efforts aim at completely killing the concept of orbits that cannot be observed anyhow, and at finding a suitable replacement" (see van der Waerden, 1967, p. 27). As the title of this paper indicates, Heisenberg's point was not only to introduce new dynamical principles – perhaps of a statistical rather than deterministic kind – or to favor a wave representation over the particle picture, but to establish new kinematic concepts – an altogether new way of relating physical objects to our space–time framework (cf. van der Waerden, 1967, pp. 28, 29; Jordan, 1928, pp. 187–8). This is what is formally expressed by the replacement of simple numbers that represent, say, a position of an object at a certain time by a "matrix," or array of numbers, possibly even an infinite one.

As a consequence of the matrix representation of physical magnitudes, such as position and momentum or velocity, the character of their mutual relationships changed fundamentally. As Heisenberg (1927) proved, it is impossible to ascribe precise values simultaneously to, say, position and momentum – which possibility had been essential for the scientific articulation of determinism (see 5.1). At least one of the two so-called conjugate properties could no longer be rendered by a precise numerical value, but only by a probability distribution of such values. This is the content of Heisenberg's famous "uncertainty relations." They were extremely important for the attempt at understanding how classical physics could possibly be compatible with quantum mechanics. A more direct way of exhibiting the probabilistic content of the new theory is indicated by Heisenberg's original intention to include none but observable magnitudes in his theory. The individual numbers making up the matrix, and hence replacing a classical magnitude, turned out to characterize a set of probabilities, either of a transition between different states of a system or of the value distribution of a classical magnitude in one of the states. These probabilities are observable, but they are not manifest properties. Instead they resemble ordinary dispositional properties, such as the property of being a reliable person, that are ascertained by observing an entire spectrum of reactions under varying circumstances. At any rate, the matrices do not give a spatio-temporal description of an event or a chain of events, let alone a continuous process. They characterize a stable or long-lived structure, such as a hydrogen atom. In this way quantum mechanics avoids the arbitrary and ad-hoc assumptions that are typical of the earlier quantum theoretical accounts of stable structures.

For a brief time it seemed as if the same result might be obtained without sacrificing the completeness and the nonprobabilistic character of the classical spatio-temporal pictures. Pursuing the pioneering ideas of Louis de Broglie (e.g. 1924) on wavelike properties of matter, Erwin Schrödinger (1926a) discovered the famous wave equation that was soon named after him. It was to become the most convenient and most widely used mathematical tool for doing all sorts of microphysical problems. Significantly, this equation described not only waves that spread out through space indefinitely – like light or water waves that are not enclosed in a vessel with reflecting walls – but also waves that, though undisturbed from outside, nevertheless remain forever confined to a finite region. Such waves then might well represent a stable micro-structure. Schrödinger showed that his equation could indeed be used to derive the properties of Bohr's atom – again without the ad-hoc assumption of the older quantum theory. Schrödinger's waves appeared more attractive than Heisenberg's abstract notion of a new kinematics, however, because they were much in keeping with traditional pictures familiar from optics. The hope of preserving the continuity of classical physics was reinforced by experiments (e.g. Davisson and Germer, 1927) which showed that electrons indeed behaved like waves, no less than light or X-rays, when deflected by a crystal.

Schrödinger therefore thought at first that the absolute square of the amplitude of his wave function (the amplitude itself, being a complex number, could not possibly have an immediate physical meaning) represented the density distribution of the electric charge that more conventionally had been supposed to be concentrated on a well-localizable particle, such as an the electron. He tried to explain the particle-like appearances of the waves by constructing so-called wave packets. But in almost all cases the theory entails that the wave packets dissipate over ever-expanding regions of space. In contrast to this behavior of the theoretical waves, experiments with particles, such as the scattering of electrons by matter, always produce particles again in the final stage of the interaction process. Moreover, as was recognized by Max Born, the problems Einstein had encountered when dealing with light arise for matter waves as well. In the case of the scattering of a beam of electrons by matter the theory predicts that the emerging electrons will flow outward in an expanding spherical wave, whereas each particular electron is found to travel in a well-defined direction. It remains available for further scattering processes no less than Einstein's light quanta remain available for absorption.

From this situation Born (1926a, b) concluded that the waves could not themselves be taken to describe the structure of matter. Instead, he found himself driven towards the conclusion that we ought to recognize two different realities: particles *and* waves. What then could be the meaning of the waves? Presumably under the influence of Heisenberg's interpretation of his matrices as arrays of transition probabilities, Born answered that "only one interpretation is possible": the wave function (more precisely, its asbolute square) "defines the probability that the electron coming [from a particular direction] will be projected into [the new] direction" (1926a, p. 865). According to this interpretation Schrödinger's equation shows that the forces determine directly only the probability waves. These in turn reflect the motion of the particles, if only statistically. For Born, probabilities were real in a special way (Cartwright, 1987). Whether or not one accepts this realism, Born had certainly shown that Schrödinger's version of the new mechanics was no less probabilistic than Heisenberg's. Born's interpretation of the Schrödinger function was accepted at once. This function is now generally understood to define the probability of finding a given value (or range of values) of a magnitude characterizing a particle. This means that Schrödinger's waves themselves are indeed continuous and exactly determined by given physical conditions, the forces and the initial state of the waves at a given time. But they do not directly represent any of the measurable physical properties, such as position, momentum, and angular momentum, which characterize material processes or states. The full determination of those characterizations, as required in the classical pictures, is at variance with Schrödinger's description. The appearance of spatio-temporal completeness and full determination of physical reality, under Schrödinger's approach, proved to be an illusion. Quite in accordance with this result, it was soon recognized, first by Schrödinger himself (1926b), that his and Heisenberg's approaches to quantum dynamics are strictly equivalent, however much they differ in mathematical form. Hence, as far as quantum theory is correct, probability is irreducible. Both approaches alike solve the problems of microphysics by incorporating dispositional properties, measured by probabilities, among the basic conceptual tools of physics.

In particular, they answer, or at least provide a perspective for answering, the question as to how stable structures of well-distinguished kinds can exist. Maxwell's puzzle (cp. 5.3) was finally resolved; the existence of atoms of different sorts whose exemplars exactly resemble each other was explained. It is significant that this was not done in terms of another supertheory of change and motion, such as a theory of the production of atoms and molecules (as Maxwell had envisaged), but in terms of possible structures and transitions between them. The very combination of stable structures and motions, however, appears to be the deeper reason why probability has conquered a central position in physics since Bohr's and Einstein's pioneering work on matter and radiation, and certainly since the consolidation of this work by quantum mechanics. Statistical physics thus became, as it were, a bridgehead of the empire of chance. In spite of all intricate historical and systematic relations between thermodynamics and quantum theory this reason is different from, and just as deep as, the problem of the irreversibility of change. It is hard to see that either of these two reasons will soon lose its impact. We may therefore expect probability to stay with us. The empire of chance seems to be rooted not only in the human mind, but also in the constitution of the universe.

[Statisticians] have already overrun every branch of science with a rapidity of conquest rivalled only by Attila, Mohammed, and the Colarado beetle.

Maurice Kendall (1942)

6

◁ ═══ ▷

Statistics of the mind

6.1 INTRODUCTION

Probabilistic and statistical ideas have transformed experimental psychology not once but twice in the past fifty years: first at the level of method, and then at the level of theory. The two transformations are in fact intimately connected, and in a way perhaps peculiar to psychology. Because psychologists observe and theorize about their subjects just as their subjects observe and theorize about the world, the methods of the psychologists are prone to become models for the mental processes they study. Once psychologists came to view statistics as an indispensable method, it was not long before they began to conceive of the mind itself as an intuitive statistician.

Around 1960, our understanding of cognitive processes such as perception and thinking was radically transformed by a new metaphor: the mind as statistician. Questions such as how does the mind discriminate between two sounds, recognize an object as a person, attribute a cause to an event, or solve a problem, were approached from this new point of view. Brain functions are today described in terms of calculating probabilities and likelihood ratios, taking random samples, setting a decision criterion and estimating prior probabilities. This metaphor emerged at about the same time as another, similarly powerful one: the mind as computer. These two gave the new science of mind its novelty and conceptual vocabulary. And they accelerated the rise of the new cognitive psychology in the 1960s over the then dominant school of behaviorism. Both revolutionary metaphors stem from tools: statistics and computers were originally tools of the behavioral scientist. In the recent science of mind, tools that are considered both as indispensable and prestigious lend themselves to transformation into metaphors of mind.

What follows is a necessarily abbreviated account of the checkered career of statistics in psychology. First, inferential statistics entered psychology as a tool for analyzing experimental results, and was rapidly institutionalized: textbooks taught it, and journals required it. Second, the tool inspired an impressive and varied range of cognitive theories, which cast new light on perception, memory, and reasoning. Third, one of these new theoretical developments, the psychology of thinking that makes judgment under uncertainty its focus, in effect revived the reasonable man of classical probability, and with him, a host of problems concerning the descriptive and normative implications of probability theory and statistics. In the hands of the new psychologists of thinking, probability theory once again became synonymous with rationality, and psychology concerned itself with how people should think as well as how they in fact do.

6.2   THE PRE-STATISTICAL PERIOD

Before 1940, statistical ideas played only a minor role as tools of experimental psychologists, and before 1950, they played almost no role in theory construction. Psychologists were, however, not ignorant of statistics. The "father of psychophysics," Gustav Theodor Fechner, wrote a volume on statistics, posthumously published as *Kollektivmasslehre* (Fechner, 1897), and percentages, means, and coefficients of variation were used from the very start of the new discipline to measure the elements of mental experience, such as sensory thresholds. What we call the pre-statistical period is a time where statistical ideas were known and used, but not considered as of the first importance. Statistics was not yet the foremost topic in psychological method, and it was not yet an indispensable element in theory construction.

The ideal and self-image of experimental psychology as a deterministic Newtonian science was widespread. Pioneers of experimental psychology like Helmholtz had no doubts about the deterministic nature of psychological processes. Kurt Lewin argued that there is no place for statistics in a strictly systematic discipline, and he and Clark Hull, a major theoretician of American behaviorism, considered Galileo's study of falling bodies as the prototype of research and the law of falling bodies as the prototype of psychological laws (Lewin, 1935; Hull, 1943). As late as 1955, David

Krech, a leading experimentalist, voiced the determinist's confession of faith: the belief that we eventually will discover deterministic laws, describing one-to-one correlations between cause and effect or stimulus and response. Examples could be multiplied. Contemporary statistical physics was not the ideal – neither the indeterminism of nineteenth-century statistical mechanics nor that of twentieth-century quantum mechanics.

There were voices in the desert. In 1927, L. L. Thurstone proposed a model for measuring perceived loudness, brightness, and other sensory qualities, which assumed a normal distribution of sensory processes. A decade later, Egon Brunswik proclaimed his probabilistic functionalism, assuming that perceptual cues are always uncertain and, as a consequence, that the perceptual system operates like an intuitive statistician. Brunswik found almost no followers at the time; Thurstone's measurement model was more successful, but soon replaced by the simpler scaling methods of S. S. Stevens, which did not need probabilistic assumptions (Gigerenzer, 1987b). None of these voices established probability as an indispensable part of method or theory.

The dream of the psyche as a universe without chance was of course not peculiar to experimental psychology. Sigmund Freud, the Sherlock Holmes of the unconscious, considered every slip of the tongue, all deviant behavior and every detail of a dream as psychically determined, if not overdetermined – to use the technical term. Edwin G. Boring, the dean of the history of psychology, even organized the history of psychology around the deterministic forces of the Zeitgeist, as opposed to the incalculable Great Man (e.g. Boring, 1963).

6.3 THE NEW TOOLS

Statistical methods may serve three functions as tools: measurement, data description, and inference. Already before 1940, experimental psychologists used statistics in all three ways. The great breakthrough came between 1940 and 1955, with statistical tools for inference from data to hypothesis. The institutionalization of inferential statistics as the *sine qua non* of scientific method during that time has been called the "inference revolution" (Gigerenzer and Murray, 1987).

How did psychologists draw inferences from their data before that time? A heterogeneous spectrum of informal and formal approaches was used, but the issue was incidental rather than essential to the experimenter. For instance, the volumes of the *Journal of Experimental Psychology* in the 1920s contain articles in which results are summarized

and described in detail, but no inference is drawn, articles in which inferences on hypotheses are drawn by eyeballing the curves, by personal
judgment, by bargaining with the reader, or by comparing mean differences with the variances without specifying a rule of comparison. More
formal criteria such as the probable error, the critical ratio, or Karl
Pearson's chi-square method were also used, but in other articles the
issues of data description and inference were not even distinguished. The
overall picture is a piecemeal report of descriptive results and details of
experimental procedures, and a non-standardized approach toward the
issue of inference, including everything from ignorance to eyeballing to
some formal criteria. Experimental psychology did not yet need inferential statistics. Wolfgang Köhler derived his Gestalt laws, Jean Piaget his
theory of intellectual development, B. F. Skinner his principles of operant
conditioning, and Sir Frederic Bartlett his theory of memory, all without
a statistical method of inference.

The change occurred in the English speaking countries. In 1934, R. A.
Fisher's analysis of variance appeared for the first time in psychological
journals, but the interest was still small. Rucci and Tweney (1980)
counted only seventeen applications between 1934 and 1939, about half
of them in education and parapsychology. However, from 1940 on, an
institutionalization of statistical methods occurred that was unprecedented
in psychology. A flood of textbooks on statistics was published, university
curricula started to teach statistics, and editors of the major journals made
statistical significance a main criterion for the acceptability of manuscripts.
But this was only the beginning. By 1955, more than 80% of the articles in
four leading journals from different areas of psychology used significance
tests to justify conclusions from the data (Sterling, 1959). (Today, the
figure is between 90 and 100%.) In 1962, A. W. Melton stated his criteria
for the acceptance of manuscripts in the *Journal of Experimental
Psychology*, criteria which had guided his editorial policy for the last twelve
years. Melton's message was, in short, that manuscripts that did not reject
the null hypothesis were almost never published, and that results significant only at the 0.05 level were barely acceptable, whereas those significant at the 0.01 level deserved a place in the journal. Psychology students
could no longer avoid statistics, and the experimenter who hoped to publish could no longer avoid a test of significance.

What kind of statistics had been made the indispensable instrument?
Psychologists first encountered Fisher's theory of null hypothesis testing.
Fisher had published on analysis of variance using agricultural examples
during the 1920s, and his message came to psychology from agriculture.

By the mid-1930s, books were available which presented the theory cleansed of the smell of agricultural examples such as the weight of pigs, soil fertility, and the effect of manure on the growth of potatoes. Of special influence was Fisher's *Design of Experiments* (1935). It took psychologists only a few years to grasp the Fisherian message and to make it the basis for a general methodological doctrine that could unify psychologists in all fields. From the late 1930s on, a steady stream of statistical textbooks deluged the largely mathematically unsophisticated psychologists, and from 1940 on, various educational journals, *Psychometrika*, and later the *Psychological Bulletin*, began to publish articles on Fisher's statistical ideas (for details see Rucci and Tweney, 1980). G. W. Snedecor at Iowa State College, Harold Hotelling at Columbia University, and Palmer Johnson at the University of Minnesota pushed Fisher's ideas in the United States. All three were taught by Fisher himself, the latter two when they visited Fisher in England, Snedecor when Fisher was at Iowa State as a visiting professor. Influenced by the agricultural statistician Snedecor and his two books (Snedecor, 1934, 1937), E. F. Lindquist from the University of Iowa wrote his influential statistical textbook for educational researchers. Psychologists became involved in the statistical development of Fisher's ideas mainly through Hotelling. Quinn McNemar, at Stanford University, for instance, received his statistical training from Hotelling, when the latter was an associate professor at Stanford. Through McNemar, Fisher's ideas became the field of research for L. G. Humphreys, Allen Edwards, David Grant, and many others.

Graduate students in psychology received training in analysis of variance in 1934 at Iowa State College, and in 1935 at Stanford, where it became a graduate program requirement in the same year. By 1950, half of the psychology departments in leading American universities had offered courses on Fisherian methods, and had made statistics a graduate program requirement between 1951 and 1954 (Rucci and Tweney, 1980).

However, the triumph of the Fisherian statisticians soon became complicated, as the theory of Jerzy Neyman and Egon S. Pearson became known, in particular after the Second World War. As shown in section 3.4, Neyman and Pearson had engaged in a heated controversy with Fisher. Neyman had rejected Fisher's program of disproving null hypotheses as a method of inductive inference and set forth his idea of inductive behavior, in which hypothesis testing was understood as a decision between two hypotheses, and where power was introduced as the fundamental concept.

How could the textbook writers and the teachers of the new curricula

cope with the subtlety of the controversial issues, the fundamental disagreement, and the bitter personal and polemical tone? J. P. Guilford,
who in 1942 published the first edition of his *Fundamental Statistics in Psychology and Education* (probably the most widely read text) simply declared
the concept of power (even as late as the third edition in 1956) too complicated to discuss (p. 217). The more sophisticated textbooks, however,
started to teach Neyman and Pearson's ideas of specifying significance
levels and sample sizes in advance to achieve the desired power, of random sampling, of avoiding probability statements about particular intervals and outcomes, and so on. However, almost no text presented
Neyman and Pearson's theory as an alternative to Fisher's, still less as a
competing theory. The great mass of texts tried to fuse the controversial
ideas into some *hybrid* statistical theory, as described in section 3.4. Of
course, this meant doing the impossible. But it was not the time for alternatives: statisticians were eager to sell and psychologists were eager to
buy *the* method of inductive inference. The statistical texts now taught
hybrid statistics, of which neither Fisher nor, to be sure, Neyman and
Pearson would have approved. The type-II error became added to null
hypothesis testing (although it could not be determined in this context),
Neyman and Pearson's interpretation of the level of significance
as the proportion of type-I errors in the long run became mishmashed
with Fisher's, and so on.

Whatever the textbooks taught, it was *not* indicated that some of the
ideas stemmed from Fisher, others from Neyman and Pearson. The
hybrid statistics was presented anonymously, as if it were the only truth,
and as if there existed *only one type of statistics*. There was no mention of
the existence of a deep controversy, much less of the controversial issues,
nor of the existence of alternative statistical theories. If the originators of
the ideas were mentioned at all in a textbook, as in the exceptional case of
Hays (1963), then the reader was told a story of cumulative progress:
Fisher's theory "was carried to a high state of development in the work of
J. Neyman and E. S. Pearson" (p. 287). But, the "high state" was and is
not practiced in psychology; Neyman and Pearson's concepts were merely
tacked onto the earlier Fisherian skeleton.

Fisher has linked significance testing to experimental design (3.3), and
the "inference revolution" was consequently a revolution in experimental
design. This revolution has been so successful that it is often difficult for
today's experimenters to imagine that "experiment" could mean something different from what Fisher had taught (see 3.2). Wilhelm Wundt,
who is credited with founding the first experimental psychological labor-

atory in 1879 in Leipzig, combined the philosophical method of introspection with recent experimental practice in physiology (Danziger, 1987b). Wundt's conception of experiment as systematic introspection had nothing to do with the key elements of Fisher's: repetition, randomization, and blocking. There were still other ideas of experiment, among them the demonstrative experiment, as practiced by Gestalt psychologists; the Galtonian comparative experiment, in which individual differences were analyzed; Egon Brunswik's representative design, in which judgment was studied in the natural environment; and B. F. Skinner's method of single-case operant conditioning. Although Fisher's design could have been used without his statistics, his statistics did not mesh well with different designs. Thus, many alternative ideas of experiment did not survive the inference revolution, and Fisher's model won a monopoly. In psychology, of course, no monopoly could exclude deviant behavior. The Skinnerians, for example, succeeded in ignoring Fisher's statistical program of design and analysis, and Skinner himself (1984, p. 111) thought of dedicating one of his books "to the statisticians and scientific methodologists with whose help this book would never have been completed."

How could this institutionalization of the anonymous hybrid statistics happen? As we have argued above, the techniques of institutionalization were the neglect of controversial issues and alternative theories, and the anonymous presentation of an apparently monolithic body of statistical techniques. This in itself is a strange event in psychology, where controversies and alternative theories had always been the rule rather than the exception, and where the citation of authors, and more authors, had been common practice. The attractive illusions with which the notion of a "significant result" was fraught played an important function in the institutionalization. Well-known textbook authors and editors of journals put forward numerous erroneous beliefs, such as that the level of significance by itself determines (1) the magnitude of the effect, (2) the probability that the null hypotheses is true or false, (3) the probability that the alternative hypothesis is true or false, and (4) the degree of confidence that the experimental result is repeatable (see Bredenkamp, 1972; Carver, 1978; Hogben, 1957; Morrison and Henkel, 1970). Wishful thinking did its part in making the level of significance seem an answer to all these questions. And, interestingly, wishful thinking seems to be facilitated by similar commonsense errors in inductive reasoning of both experimenters and laymen (Eddy, 1982; Oakes, 1986; Tversky and Kahneman, 1971).

This does not mean that the institutionalization of an apparently uncontroversial hybrid statistics as the *sine qua non* of scientific inference went without protest. Both Fisherian elements of the hybrid, such as null hypothesis testing and the neglect of power calculations, and Neyman–Pearsonian elements, such as reject/accept decisions (instead of degrees of belief) and cost considerations, were targets of sharp criticism (e.g. Edwards, Lindman, and Savage, 1963; Meehl, 1978; Morrison and Henkel, 1970). One damaging criticism was that in typical applications the null hypothesis is always wrong. For instance, Bakan (1966) divided a large sample of 60,000 subjects by such arbitrary criteria as east versus west of the Mississippi River, and Maine versus the rest of the United States, and obtained in all cases significant differences (although the actual differences in the measurements, the effect sizes, were minimal). As Nunnally (1960, p. 643) put it: "If the null hypothesis is not rejected, it usually is because the N [sample size] is too small. If enough data is gathered, the hypothesis will generally be rejected. If rejection of the null hypothesis were the real intention in psychological experiments, there usually would be no need to gather data."

Two factors seem to have been crucial for the institutionalization of statistics in American psychology: first, the drive to demonstrate psychology's practical relevance, and second, the dream of the mechanization of knowledge. Significance tests were early applied to educational questions, and inferential statistics made its way from the applied fields into the laboratory of the experimenter. Experimenters were not the prime target (Lovie, 1979), and it was rather the *Journal of Educational Psychology* that evidenced the largest increase in Fisherian techniques through 1942 (Rucci and Tweney, 1980). Education provided the main area of application for psychological knowledge and methods in America, and group comparisons using analysis of variance seemed to fit the needs of educational administrators exactly: an objective criterion for their decisions. Danziger (1987a) provides evidence that the new methods were used by psychologists to prove the practical relevance of their knowledge, and fresh from that success in the classroom, the new methods conquered the laboratories of the experimenters. Two observations support this view. Emphasis on practical relevance was more characteristic for American than for German psychology. In Germany, where experimental psychology traditionally set itself philosophical rather than practical problems, and where the educational system was oriented to authority rather than to experimentation, statistics could not then enter the laboratory as easily. The second observation is that the strongest resistance against the institutionalization of inferential statistics came not from the applied fields, but from the experimental laboratory. B. F. Skinner and Sir Frederic Bartlett accused their less famous contemporaries of only teaching "statistics in lieu of scientific method" (Skinner, 1963, p. 328) and of designing their experiments to yield data to which the methods of statistics could be applied. Despite their otherwise great influence, those psychologists could not stop the onslaught of inferential statistics.

The second factor that supported the institutionalization was the dream of mechanization of knowledge. The idea that by means of statistics one could mechanically derive a degree of certainty for a hypothesis is an old dream. Many a solution has been proposed, and all of them failed in a scientific context. Physics, which many social scientists took as a model, in fact rarely if ever uses null hypothesis testing. Whether light is composed of particles or of waves – physicists never seriously believed they could assign numerical probabilities to such theories or discover the "true" theory by significance testing. Social scientists, in contrast, seemed to be strongly susceptible to the idea that statistics is indispensable for deciding between hypotheses. And Fisher (1935), who claimed that "every experiment may be said to exist only in order to give the facts a chance of disproving the null hypothesis" (p. 16), could easily be understood as having said that scientific knowledge comes only through inferential statistics. Fisher claimed that statistical science gives a formal solution to the problem of scientific inference "as satisfying and complete, at least, as that given traditionally of deductive processes" (Fisher, 1955, p. 74). The dream of the scientist who arrives at new knowledge by a completely mechanized procedure seemed to have become a reality. As a mere tool, statistics could now be used in experimental psychology in the service of a traditional ideal, namely *objectivity*. Significance testing seemed to allow for an application of probability theory that eliminated personal judgment and promised objectivity in inductive inferences without threatening the prevailing determinism (Gigerenzer, 1987a). Last, and not least, the institutionalization unified psychology at the methodological level in the absence of a consensus on the level of theory.

6.4 FROM TOOLS TO THEORIES OF MIND

After four decades' reign over American psychology, behaviorism was unseated around 1960 by the cognitive revolution. American psychologists reverted to the topic of the earlier German programs, the mind, but not to the old vocabulary with vague terms such as apperception, restructuring, and insight. The rising cognitive revolution was on the outlook for a new conceptual language to understand the nature of mental processes. The indispensable and prestigious tools of the behavioral scientists were reconsidered as the processes of the mind. Computers and statistics were the main sources of the new theoretical vocabulary that made the cognitive revolution. We are concerned here only with the view of the mind as an intuitive statistician, an analogy that changed our understanding of a broad range of cognitive functions – from elementary sensory discrimination to social judgment (Gigerenzer and Murray, 1987). The mind thus came to be understood, *inter alia*, to draw random samples from the incoming information, to calculate probabilities, to set decision criteria, and to perform hypothesis testing: this (according to the modern view) is what happens when we say that we perceive an object, memorize an event, or find an explanation. The mind is an intuitive statistician. We will present as examples two influential theories, from different fields of experimental psychology.

Detection and discrimination

To detect an object, and to discriminate between two objects (detecting a difference) are two elementary cognitive processes that have been studied since the beginning of psychophysics. Examples are detecting whether two coins have the same weight, whether sugar has been added to wine, and whether two stars have different brightnesses. Such detection processes have long been explained using a metaphor derived from Herbart (1816): detection occurs only if the effect the object has on our nervous system exceeds an *absolute threshold*, and discrimination between two objects occurs if the excitation from one exceeds that of another by an amount greater than a *differential threshold*.

Around 1955, the psychophysics of absolute and differential thresholds was revolutionized by a point of view called "the theory of signal detectability" (or "signal detection theory"). In essence, this theory postulates that the mind "decides" whether there is an object (now called a "signal") or only noise, just like a statistician of the Neyman–Pearson–Wald school decides between two hypotheses (Tanner and Swets, 1954; Green and Swets, 1966). That is, the mind first calculates the two sampling distributions for "signal plus noise" and "noise," respectively. Then a decision criterion is set after weighting the costs of the two possible errors, i.e. false alarms and misses of signals, which correspond to the type-I and type-II error, respectively (as well as other considerations, such as the prior probability of signals). Finally, if the value of the inner representation of a signal (noise) is greater than the decision criterion, the answer "yes, there is a signal" is given; otherwise "no, there is no signal."

The mind was called a "Neyman–Pearson detector" (Tanner, 1965), or "Neyman–Pearson observer," if it adopts the decision goal of maximizing the hit rate (i.e. the correct detection of a signal) for a given false alarm rate (i.e. the erroneous "detection" of a signal). This view of perceptual processing was in analogy to Neyman and Pearson's concept of "optimal tests," where the power (hit rate) of a test is maximized for a given type-I error (false alarm rate).

The new metaphor of the mind as a statistician went far beyond a mere change in language, it generated new questions, a new kind of data, a revision of the threshold concept, and a new conception of the mind. The analogy between the Neyman–Pearson–Wald theory and detection processes separated non-sensory processes (the setting of the decision criterion) from sensory processes (the sensitivity, measured by the difference between the means of the two sampling distributions). The subjective part in Neyman and Pearson's theory became the subjective, non-sensory processes in signal detection theory, depending on attitudes and cost-benefit considerations of the observer. Thus, a new question emerged that gave rise to an avalanche of experiments: How can the mind's decision criterion be experimentally manipulated?

To answer this question (as well as the question concerning the sensitivity and the criterion setting of an individual), two types of error were generated in the experiments, false alarm and misses. These correspond to the type-I and type-II errors in Neyman and Pearson's theory. In contrast, the traditional methods, such as the method of average error in psychophysics or in recall tasks in memory research, had generated only one kind of error. Thus, a new kind of data emerged. Finally, the concept of a single, fixed threshold was revised and replaced by statistical concepts, and the processes of "inference," "decision," and "hypothesis testing" were freed from their conscious connotations, and seen as the unconscious mechanisms of the brain.

Causal reasoning

The perception of causal relations had been studied before 1960 under the influence of Gestalt psychology. Psychologists analyzed the temporal-spatial relationships between events that produced phenomenal causality

(Michotte, [1946] 1963, 1952; Heider, 1958). Interest in the issue sky-rocketed when Harold H. Kelley in 1967 proposed a completely new account of causal attribution. In essence, he postulated that the mind attributes a cause to an effect in the same way as behavioral scientists do, namely by performing an analysis of variance and testing null hypotheses. For illustration, consider the following information presented to the subjects in a typical experiment: "Paul is enthralled by a painting he sees at the art museum. Hardly anyone who sees the painting is enthralled by it. Paul is also enthralled by almost every other painting. In the past, Paul has almost always been enthralled by the same painting." (McArthur, 1972, quoted in Kelley, 1973, p. 110). The subjects were asked what probably caused the observed behavior (being enthralled by the painting): Has the cause to do with Paul (person), the painting (entity), or the circumstances (time)? The problem is constructed to provide the intuitive Fisherian mind information about the covariation of the three independent variables, person, entity, and circumstances, with the observed behavior. Kelley assumed that the mind tests a null hypothesis for each of the possible causes. In the above example, variability is high for "person" and low for "entity" and "time"; therefore the mind should calculate a high F-value for person, and attribute the cause to Paul.

Kelley's analysis of variance (ANOVA) model of causal attribution became the fastest expanding research area in experimental social psychology, and the dinosaurian proportions of empirical research on the ANOVA-mind in the 1970s and 1980s are well documented (Fisch and Daniel, 1982).

6.5 A CASE STUDY: FROM THINKING TO JUDGMENTS UNDER UNCERTAINTY

Thinking without probabilities

The experimental study of human thinking that started in 1900 with the Würzburg school in Germany neither used nor mentioned probability theory. The same must be said of the Gestalt school, the immediate successors of the Würzburgers in the 1920s. They saw thinking as a successive restructuring or reorganization of the functional relations between parts. The classical examples are found in Köhler's experiments, in which a chimpanzee had to perceive new functional relations to solve a problem – e.g. to perceive the stick lying around as an instrument to reach the fruit hanging high above, and the table as a platform upon which to climb, stick in hand.

Karl Duncker, who developed the most elaborate application of Gestalt theory to thinking, considered restructuring in thinking in analogy to the phenomenon of reversible figures, where one structuring "tips over" into the next structuring. These successive restructurings continue until "the organization is completed," i.e. the system-under-stress settles into an equilibrium. The following two problems are typical examples: (A) "Prove that there is an infinite number of prime numbers." (B) "Given a human being with an inoperable stomach tumor, by what procedure can one free him of the tumor by these rays and at the same time avoid destroying healthy tissue which surrounds it?" (Duncker, [1935] 1945, pp. 1, 9).

To solve such a problem means, according to Duncker, to successively reformulate or restructure the original problem until a solution is attained. For the prime number problem such reformulations might be: "I must prove that for any prime number p there exists a greater one," followed by "To prove the existence of such a prime number, I must try to construct it," followed by "One must therefore construct a number greater than p which cannot be represented as a product," and finally arriving at the solution "Take the product of all prime numbers from 1 to p and add 1."

Just as the Gestalt laws tell us that the particular layout of objects in the visual field – in other words, their relations – is decisive for which "whole" we see, the "layout" or context of the problem is decisive for the direction of the restructurings. Duncker concluded from his experiments that a change in the phrasing of the problem (although it preserved its meaning), a change in the specific example given, and other contextual factors all had an impact on the flow of thought. For instance, Duncker presented the Tumor Problem in two different versions, which differed only in a change from the active to the passive case in the last two sentences. The active version was: "The rays would thus destroy healthy tissue, too. How could one prevent the rays from injuring the healthy tissue?" The passive version read: "Healthy tissue, too, would thus be destroyed. How could one protect the healthy tissue from being injured by the rays?" The active phrasing emphasizes the rays, the passive one the tissue. A comparison between the two groups which had received the active and passive versions showed that three times as many subjects given the active one dealt with the intensity of the rays.

The major historical point to be made is that none of the

experimenters in these two major schools thought that human thinking should be understood in terms of statistical calculation. Consequently, the nature of thought was not yet studied with problems that could be solved by mere calculation or application of the laws of probability theory. Even when mathematical problems were posed, such as the Prime Number Problem, calculation was neither necessary nor sufficient to obtain a solution.

This psychology of thinking declined in the 1940s and 1950s as a consequence of several forces. In America, J. B. Watson's behaviorism abandoned the study of mental concepts, and reduced thinking to "subvocal speech" or "competition of response tendencies." In Germany, where psychology had already lost track of foreign movements just as its international preeminence was waning during the 1920s and 1930s, most of the key figures of the Würzburg and Gestalt schools ran afoul of the Nazi regime, either because they or their wives were Jews, or for political reasons. Some were forced to retire early or to emigrate (Max Wertheimer, Wolfgang Köhler), others lost their lives in Auschwitz (Otto Selz) or committed suicide after emigration (Karl Duncker). Not until the 1960s, when behaviorism was eroded by the cognitive revolution, did the study of human thinking reappear as a major topic in psychology. But it reappeared with a completely new vocabulary, that of tools, namely statistics and computers. We shall deal here with the former, ignoring various other approaches, such as deductive reasoning or problem solving.

Thinking as intuitive statistics

The view that the nature of human thought might be statistical calculation, or at least, should be, arose at the same time as the view that sensory detection and discrimination, perception, recognition from memory, and other cognitive processes might involve statistical calculation (Gigerenzer and Murray, 1987). All these statistical perspectives emerged around 1960, shortly after statistics had been institutionalized as the indispensable tool of the experimenter.

The group around Ward Edwards at the University of Michigan seems to have been the first to study thought processes, which they called in more fashionable lingo "human information processing," using Bayesian-type urn-and-balls problems. In Edwards' work, the double role of statistics as both the experimenter's tool and the subject's mental program is obvious. Together with Harold Lindman and Leonard J. Savage, in 1963, he proposed that experimenters use Bayesian statistics, and he at the same time investigated whether subjects learn from experience in the same way as probabilities are revised by Bayes' theroem. The first part of that program, Bayesian statistics for experimenters, was a complete flop, since the experimenters already had their statistics. Experimenters have never been very interested in the raging debates between various statistical schools. For the mass of researchers, statistics was statistics was statistics. But the metaphor that the reasoning mind works like a Bayesian statistician became a most influential research program, similar to that stimulated by the computer analogy of thinking.

Bayesian-type problems of probability revision were prominent at the beginning of the psychology of statistical thinking and are still a central issue in the present day research on judgment under uncertainty (e.g. Kahneman, Slovic, and Tversky, 1982). Therefore, we shall focus in the following analysis on these. We shall work out how the new metaphor transformed the research questions, the problems constructed, the kind of explanations looked for, and the kind of data generated.

New questions, new problems, and new phenomena

Edwards' question was whether the mind is a Bayesian. Reporting on his original hypothesis, he declared that William L. Hays, Lawrence D. Phillips and he suggested that the mind processes information like a Bayesian, and that they believed they would need a fairly complex situation in order to find the limits of Bayesian behavior (Edwards, 1968; Edwards, Lindman, and Phillips, 1965). The original fairly complex situation was a computerized radar system with four possible hypotheses, such as "enemy attack" and "meteor shower," and twelve possible observations (dot patterns on the radar screen). The subjects had to revise their prior probabilities for the four hypotheses on the basis of new observations. The subjects generally revised their probability to a lesser extent than Bayes' theorem would dictate, a phenomenon which was dubbed "conservatism." Furthermore, the sums of the probability estimates for the four hypotheses in general added up to more than 1; for this and other reasons, the complex situation seemed to be too complex and was soon replaced by a simpler type of problem, which became a standard for the following years, the tried-and-true urns-and-balls problems. These were now often updated as bookbag-and-pokerchips problems. Here is a prototypical example:

"Two urns are filled with a large number of poker chips. The first urn contains 70% red chips and 30% blue. The second contains 70% blue chips and 30% red. The experimenter flips a fair coin to select one of the two urns, so the prior probability for each urn is .50. He then draws a succession of chips from the selected urn. Suppose the sample contains eight red and four blue chips. What is your revised probability that the selected urn is the predominantly red one?" (Peterson and Beach, 1967, p. 32)

This type of problem is simpler than the radar-screen problems because (a) only two hypotheses are considered, (b) only two events (red or blue) are considered as data, and (c) the compositions of the urns are symmetrical. If $p(H_R)$ is the prior probability that the selected urn is the predominantly red one, $p(H_R \mid D)$ is the posterior probability of H_R after the data D (eight red and four blue) has been observed, and $p(D \mid H_R)$ is the probability that D will be observed if H_R is true, then Bayes' theorem states

$$p(H_R \mid D) = p(H_R)p(D \mid H_R)/p(D) \qquad (6.1)$$

The unconditional probability $p(D)$ can be calculated as follows:

$$p(D) = p(D \mid H_R)p(H_R) + p(D \mid H_B)p(H_B) \qquad (6.2)$$

If you think that the data raises the probability that the urn is the predominantly red one from 0.50 to about 0.75, then you agree with the majority of subjects tested. Bayes' theorem, however, revises the probability from 0.50 to 0.97. This conservative revision was the major finding of Edwards and his colleagues.

Interest in this new kind of mental testing quickened when around 1970 Daniel Kahneman and Amos Tversky posed the same probability revision problems as "real-world" problems rather than as urn-and-ball problems. A famous example is the Cab Problem (Tversky and Kahneman, 1980, p. 62):

A cab was involved in a hit and run accident at night. Two cab companies, the Green and the Blue, operate in the city. You are given the following data:

(i) 85% of the cabs in the city are Green and 15% are Blue. (ii) A witness identified the cab as a Blue cab. The court tested his ability to identify cabs under the appropriate visibility conditions. When presented with a sample of cabs (half of which were Blue and half of which were Green) the witness made correct identifications in 80% of the cases and erred in 20% of the cases.

Question: What is the probability that the cab involved in the accident was Blue rather than Green?

The structure of the Cab Problem is the same as in the bookbag-and-pokerchip problems. Two kinds of information are presented, the prior probabilities $p(H)$, also called "base rates," and the probabilities $p(D \mid H)$, also called "diagnostic information." The subject is then asked for the posterior probability. The median posterior probability (that the cab involved in the hit and run accident was Blue) estimated by their subjects was 0.80. Kahneman and Tversky, however, calculate 0.41 as the "correct" Bayesian answer. Since the median answer is numerically equivalent to the diagnostic information (80% correct identifications), the authors concluded that their subjects ignore the other kind of information, the prior probability or base rate (15% Blue cabs). The same conclusion was drawn from other problems posed.

In the 1970s, base-rate neglect was considered a well-established fact, and was presented together with other "biases" and "errors" as evidence for the fallibility of human reasoning. Recall that during the 1960s conservatism has been considered as the well-established fact. Conservatism, however, means *overweighting* base rates and largely ignoring the diagnostic information. The question of why people seemed to be conservative during the 1960s and anti-conservative after 1970 has not yet been answered, if only because it was almost never posed. It should be very disturbing that established facts suddenly do an about face. But the new facts were instead enthusiastically received as revelatory of underlying mental heuristics, and the opposite facts largely ignored as too old to be true.

Discontinuity

The metaphor of the mind as an intuitive statistician radically changed the research questions rather than merely producing a new fashionable language to talk about old things. To show this, we shall compare the expected future of the psychology of thinking, as it appeared around 1950, with that part of the field most influenced by the new metaphor. The major statements of these two positions can be found in George Humphrey's *Thinking* (1951) and in D. Kahneman, S. Slovic, and A. Tversky's *Judgment Under Uncertainty: Heuristics and Biases* (1982).

Humphrey concludes that "Fifty years' experiment on the psychology of thinking or reasoning have not brought us very far, but they have at least shown the kind of road which must be traversed" (p. 308). After this honest statement, he gives his precise summary of the main questions posed in these fifty years that await an answer, and of the main facts found that await a theory. Humphrey starts with three persistent problems. The first is the question about the "motor" or motivation of the thought flow. For instance, Gestalt theorists rejected the idea that habit or association is the motor of thinking, and proposed instead their hypothesis of the unitary system-under-stress. The second main question is how conscious processes interact with unconscious processes (such as determining tendencies). The third question is about the relationship between motor processes and inner processes, e.g. the idea that animals deal with a problem mainly by "acting out," as opposed to "thinking out" by humans. None of these is important for the question whether the mind is a Bayesian, or the more general question whether the mind performs good descriptive and inferential statistics. None has been addressed in the attempts to explain so-called conservatism and base-rate neglect.

Humphrey continues with a sixteen-point statement of the state of the art in 1951. Almost all these points are either irrelevant or incidental for the new psychology of thinking based on the statistical metaphor. A few points are given here for illustration. Humphrey defined thinking as "what occurs in experience when an organism, human or animal, meets, recognizes, and solves a problem." In contrast, thinking is now analyzed in terms of whether the mind performs the "correct" calculations, and if not, what "short-hand strategy" might explain the biases, i.e. the deviations from probability theory. What the subject experiences during thinking is irrelevant or incidental. Other points include facts such as trial-and-error behavior, the existence of muscular tone even if the thinker is still, language as an obstacle to thinking, the distinction between reproductive and productive thinking, the question whether thought is free of sensory content, and so on. The majority of these issues, which provided both the factual basis and the foundation of disputes, are absent in the new research on the mind as an intuitive statistician. In the present-day literature references to concepts and authors from the pre-statistical period are few and far between, and those few appear mainly in historical introductions.

This discontinuity in theoretical perspective, of course, went hand-in-hand with a change in the type of problem constructed. The new problems posed could be solved by statistical calculation, as in the Cab Problem, or, more generally, by the application of fundamental principles of probability theory. The problems constructed in the Würzburg school or Gestalt school, such as the "Tumor" problem above, could not be solved by calculation. Linked to this is another important change. Problems posed in the pre-statistical period had typically more than one reasonable answer. The new problems, in contrast, were designed to have a single correct answer. As we shall soon show, this is often an illusion (see also Cohen, 1981). However, this illusion is not an incidental one. If one holds that the nature of thought is the association of ideas or the restructuring of functional relationships, then the existence of a single answer would indeed be an incidental issue. However, if one believes in the metaphor of the intuitive statistician, then one correct, or at least, one best answer must exist, for the statistician calculates only one best estimate. Of course, this latter view is based on a certain God-like picture of the statistician. First, it is based on the belief that there are no rival statisticians who might offer different answers to the same problems. Second, it is believed that even real-world problems – as opposed to urns-and-balls – can unambiguously be answered by statistics without considerations of the content and context of the problem.

The judgment-under-uncertainty research program is centered around two main questions. First, where do people violate the laws of probability theory and second, how can we derive the laws of human thinking from these violations? Like the Gestalt psychologists, these psychologists of statistical thinking liken their investigations to perceptual research, and like the Gestalt psychologists, see illusions – either in perception or in thinking – as the key to the underlying psychological laws (e.g. Tversky and Kahneman, 1974, p.1124). For the Gestalt psychologists, the illusion was a discrepancy between physical reality and perception; for example, between two points flashed sequentially and the perceived motion of a single moving point, as in Wertheimer's famous phi-phenomenon. But in the new research program, probability theory has replaced physical reality, and the new illusions are discrepancies between the results of probability theory and human thinking.

New explanations

This section shows how the new metaphor transformed not only the research questions and problems constructed, but also the idea of what an explanation is. All three changes are interdependent. Gestalt theorists such as Duncker had offered as an explanation an interaction between inner processes and the layout or context of the problem. Inner processes were restructurings or reformulations that were in turn initiated by "heuristic methods," such as "looking around" and "inspecting the problem." Whether a subject found a reasonable solution or not, and how long it took, depended also on the context, e.g. the kind of phrasing of the problem or the kind of example given to illustrate it. For instance, Duncker was one of the first to show that a problem is approached in different ways depending on which problems the subject worked immediately before. The temporal layout of problems induces a "set" of problem-solving strategies that may facilitate or hinder the solution of a subsequent one. Such findings made clear that any explanation of thinking exclusively in terms of inner processes such as context-independent general rules would be insufficient.

Beginning with Edwards' research on conservatism, a quite different type of explanation emerges. What needs explaining now is the *discrepancy* between human judgment and Bayes' theorem. From the range of explanations offered for conservatism, two major ones serve to illustrate the new type of explanation. In an article entitled "Man as Intuitive Statistician" (1967), C. R. Peterson and L. R. Beach proposed as an explanation that the mind systematically miscalculates the probabilities $p(D \mid H)$, e.g. the probability that eight red and four blue pokerchips are drawn from an urn that contains 70% red chips and 30% blue chips. They assumed that the mind intuitively uses Bayes' theorem in a correct way, but with the wrong probabilities inserted. Edwards, in contrast, proposed that the mind correctly calculates the probabilities, but systematically miscalculates Bayes' theorem, e.g. by overweighting the base rates. Just as statistical calculation is the general metaphor for thinking, miscalculation is the new explanation for the subjects' actual reasoning. This new type of explanation stems from the vocabulary of probability theory, just as the research questions and the problems do. How does Kahneman and Tversky's explanation of their phenomenon, base-rate neglect, compare?

The representativeness heuristic

Kahneman and Tversky offer two major explanations, each for a different type of problem: first a "heuristic" called "representativeness," and second, the distinction between "causal" and "incidental" base rates. The latter is proposed for the Cab Problem. We shall deal here only with the representativeness heuristic. Representativeness has been offered as an explanation for a class of problems, the Engineer–Lawyer Problem being one of the most prominent. A group of students was given the following cover story (Kahneman and Tversky, 1973, p. 241):

A panel of psychologists has interviewed and administered personality tests to 30 engineers and 70 lawyers, all successful in their respective fields. On the basis of this information, thumbnail descriptions of the 30 engineers and 70 lawyers have been written. You will find on your forms five descriptions, chosen at random from the 100 available descriptions. For each description, please indicate your probability that the person described is an engineer, on a scale from 1 to 100.

The same task has been performed by a panel of experts, who were highly accurate in assigning probabilities to the various descriptions. You will be paid a bonus to the extent that your estimates come close to those of the expert panel.

A second group of students received the same instructions with inverted base rates, i.e. prior probabilities, namely 70 engineers and 30 lawyers. All subjects were given the same five personality descriptions such as the following:

Jack is a 45-year-old man. He is married and has four children. He is generally conservative, careful, and ambitious. He shows no interest in political and social issues and spends most of his free time on his many hobbies which include home carpentry, sailing, and mathematical puzzles. The probability that Jack is one of the 30 engineers in the sample of 100 is __ %.

Kahneman and Tversky found that the mean responses in the two groups were for the most part the same, and concluded that the base rates were ignored. The explanation was that the subjects solve the problem by judging only the similarity between the description and their stereotype of an engineer, i.e. the degree to which a description is *representative* of the stereotype: hence the "representativeness heuristic." Together with a few other heuristics, representativeness was proposed as a law of human thinking.

Let us examine the nature of this explanatory concept more closely. It is presented as an informal shorthand strategy, and Tversky and Kahneman (1982a, p. 88) explicitly claim that this heuristic "has a logic of its own, which departs systematically from the logic of probability" and is not "based on impressions of probability or frequency." Another way to view the situation is as follows: Bayes' theorem has not only provided the kind of questions and problems posed, including the vocabulary in which the phenomenon is described, but also the explanation. In order to make the point, we refer to Tversky and Kahneman's (1982a) own recent attempt to clarify the various meanings which they have previously given the term "representativeness" and to define the explanatory concept of a "representativeness heuristic" more precisely. They explain that a judgment by a representativeness relation falls in one of four categories. In the first case, representativeness is defined as a relation between a class *H* and the value *D* of a variable defined in this class. For illustration, Kahneman and Tversky speak of (more or less) representative values of the income of college professors. A value *D* will be most representative if it is close to the mean of the frequency distribution of incomes; the distribution itself is determined by what a subject knows or assumes about these incomes. It is easy to see that in this first case the meaning of representativeness is assessment of frequency and probability. (Under certain conditions, such as equal symmetric frequency distribution, this meaning of representativeness can be reduced to the probability $p\,(D\mid H)$ as it occurs in Bayes' theorem.)

In the second case, representativeness is defined as a relation between a class and an element. An example is the above Engineer–Lawyer Problem, where the relation is between the class of engineers and a particular personality sketch. The third case is a relation between a class and a subset, such as in the question whether students of astronomy are less representative of the entire student body than are students of psychology. Tversky and Kahneman (1982a, p. 87) themselves state that the second case can be derived from the first by generalizing the one-dimensional attribute (e.g. income) to more than one attribute (as in the personality sketch), and the third case follows from the second by generalizing from one element to a subset of elements. Therefore, we conjecture, all three meanings refer to the assessment of frequency and probability.

In the fourth and last case, representativeness is defined as a relation between a causal system and a possible consequence. Kahneman and Tversky consider both "frequently associated" variables and causal connections to fall under this heading, making no distinction between the two. Frequent associations are at least formally equivalent to the first case, except that the relation between the system H and the value or event D is now given a causal interpretation. Such an interpretation, however, does not change the formal identity.

All these four meanings of representativeness are shaped by the language of probability. This analysis has two important consequences. First, just as for conservatism, we see that the conceptual vocabulary for explaining why people's judgments deviate from Bayes' theorem (base-rate neglect) is itself derived from the language of probability. Probability theory has now replaced earlier explanatory concepts such as association of images, restructuring and insight. Second, it is now obvious that the "explanation" is hardly more than a redescription of the phenomenon. The phenomenon is called base-rate neglect because people's judgments vary with $p(D\mid H)$ but not with $p(H)$, and this is explained by saying that people use a representativeness heuristic, which means that they use information of the type $p(D\mid H)$ and not $p(H)$. That is, neglect of base rates is explained by neglect of base rates. Probability theory has encompassed all. And the two concepts $p(H)$ and $p(D\mid H)$, from which the posterior probability is calculated, now serve as the vocabulary for both the phenomena and the explanations.

New data

We have shown that the metaphor has changed the research questions, the problems posed, the phenomena observed, *and* the explanations looked for. But did it also influence the data? What kinds of data were generated to study the nature of thinking? For instance, Gestalt theorists such as Duncker instructed their subjects to think aloud during problem solving, and used these verbal reports to infer reformulations and restructuring processes. In addition, the time between stimulus (problem) and answer (solution) was usually measured. None of these earlier experimenters, however, used ratings of probabilities. Nobody thought about asking subjects for probabilities, and basing a theory on this kind of data, either for studying thought or for other psychological topics.

The idea of asking subjects to translate uncertainty into a number between 0 and 1 did not occur until the experimenters themselves learned to express their confidence in experimental results in terms of levels of significance and likelihoods. The idea of generating data by asking subjects for numbers (but not for probabilities) is a little bit older, owing particularly to the work of Stanley S. Stevens from the late 1930s on.

But are there probabilities in our heads, and for all events? Numerical judgments of probability are not the only way subjects express uncertainty. Recall that even experimenters have learned to do this only recently, since the inference revolution. Their subjects, however, may still express uncertainty by other modes. As an illustration, consider a woman anxious about whether she is pregnant. Does it make sense to assume that her uncertainty is represented numerically, say by a subjective probability of 35% that she is indeed pregnant? Her feeling of uncertainty may not be represented as a fixed numerical probability. Rather she may shift between states of certainty, where only the transition phases contain uncertainty. At one time she may believe she is definitely pregnant, then she may shift to the belief she definitely is not, and some more shifts may follow. Such uncertainty might be represented by transition probabilities, such as relative frequencies of switching from one certain state to the other, rather than by a numerical subjective value between 0 and 1. However, whether numerical estimates of probability or transition probabilities between states of *certainty* or other modes are the appropriate data for a theory of judgment under uncertainty is a question almost never posed.

6.6 THE RETURN OF THE REASONABLE MAN

In the eighteenth century, probability theory was intended as at once a formal description of the intuitions of a prototypical reasonable man, and as a prescription for the rest of us. This interpretation disappeared in the nineteenth century, when probability theory and statistics became the mathematical means of describing the irrationality of the masses, as opposed to the rationality of individuals (see chapters 1 and 2). But in the last decades, the reasonable man of the classical probabilists was revived in psychology, and along with him, the normative view of probability theory as a mathematical codification of rational belief and action in uncertain situations. Many twentieth-century psychologists, like the eighteenth-century mathematicians, assume that their problems have one and only one correct answer, and that this answer can (indeed, must) be calculated according to the rules of mathematical probability theory. Deviations from this answer reveal biases and irrationality in human thought. For instance, Kahneman and Tversky (1972) conclude that "for anyone who would wish to view man as a reasonable intuitive statistician, such results are discouraging." Nisbett, Krantz, Jepson, and Kunda (1983, pp. 339–40) conclude that "people commit serious errors of inference" and that "it is disturbing to learn that the heuristics people use in such tasks do not respect the required statistical principles." And others ring changes on the same theme: people "lack the correct programs for many important judgmental tasks" (Slovic, Fischhoff, and Lichtenstein, 1976) and finally, the experimental results have "bleak implications for human rationality" (Nisbett and Borgida, 1975).

The reasonable man was indeed back, but only in the shadow form of an ideal in the minds of these psychologists. Whereas eighteenth-century probabilists had assumed at least a small elite to be reasonable, the new psychologists of thinking discovered to their dismay that almost no one was reasonable – at least in their experiments. Even their colleagues in the Mathematical Division of the American Psychological Association performed dismally in a test of their statistical intuitions (Tversky and Kahneman, 1971). Faced with a comparable case in the solution to the St. Petersburg problem, the eighteenth-century probabilists had revised their mathematics to better fit the dictates of common reason. However, the twentieth-century psychologists had come so to revere the mathematical theory of probability and statistics that they instead insisted that common reason be reformed to fit the mathematics.

For the above conclusion about human irrationality, the existence of a single correct answer is a *necessary* assumption. This can be seen from the two major steps of the new research program: First, identify biases in judgment, and second, use these "biases in judgment to reveal some heuristic of thinking under uncertainty" (Tversky and Kahneman, 1974, p.1124). A bias is defined as the *deviation* from a normatively correct answer, and this makes the assumption of a single correct answer essential. For instance, the deviation of the group average of 0.80 from the supposed correct answer of 0.41 in the above Cab Problem is the bias to be explained by some heuristic of thinking. Thus, it is not the data itself, i.e. the group averages, that are to be explained, but its deviation from the normative answer. If there existed more than one solution, the deviation would be different, and if, for instance, a solution of 0.80 were chosen, the deviation would be zero and the supposed base-rate neglect would disappear. In contrast, whether a problem had several or only one solution was incidental to the Würzburg and the Gestalt school. For instance, the Tumor Problem has many reasonable solutions, and it was not necessary to have one single correct solution for the theoretical analysis of the restructuring process.

The normative view that statistics (1) speaks with one voice and (2) should replace personal judgment by formal rules emerged first with the institutionalization of the hybrid statistics. It is not the view usually associated with Bayesian statistics. Although the above studies of human probability revision look like a Bayesian program, they are not, in at least one important respect. The subjectivity which earned Bayes' theorem its classification under "subjective probabilities" has been eliminated. Subjectivity enters Bayes' theorem, since in most real-world applications there is no unique or objective way to determine the prior probabilities. For this reason, the application of the theorem beyond urn-and-balls problems has been criticized since its inception. Thomas Bayes himself seemed to have doubts about the application of his theorem to the real world, and it was not published during his lifetime. Proponents of the subjective interpretation of probability usually allow that different subjects have different subjective prior probabilities, and therefore respond to the same new information with different posterior probabilities. Thus the claim that a given problem has exactly one correct answer for all individuals seems not to come from this camp.

Neyman and Pearson's theory had more influence on the insti-

tutionalized hybrid statistics than Bayes'. What was their attitude towards
the issue of one correct answer? From their first joint paper in 1928 on,
Neyman and Pearson presented their approach as *one among alternatives*,
and they continued to emphasize that the competent reader has to make
judgments in every particular application. They clearly distinguished a
mathematical or formal part from the subjective or informal part of their
theory – both necessary and neither sufficient in itself:

Of necessity, as it seemed to us, we left in our mathematical model a gap for the
exercise of a more intuitive process of personal judgment in such matters – to
use our terminology – as the choice of the most likely class of admissible hypotheses, the appropriate significance level, the magnitude of worthwhile effects and
the balance of utilities (Pearson, 1962, p. 396).

Since personal judgments in these matters vary, the Neyman and
Pearson theory is also no candidate for the normative only-one-answer
view. Thus let us turn to Fisher, whose theory of null hypothesis testing
is the heart of the hybrid statistics. In his influential *Design of Experiments*,
first published in 1935, we find a quite different message. He presented
his statistics as if it were the formal solution of the problem of inductive
inference. Mediated by enthusiastic textbook writers, psychologists were
taught that the null hypothesis method is statistics and that thou shalt
have no other gods before this one. This only-one-answer view of statistics seems to be a main component in the normative view in the psychology
of judgment under uncertainty.

The normative "only-one-answer" view: an illustration of the exaggerated imperialism of statistics

The idea spread by the textbooks that "statistics" is an uncontroversial,
objective instrument for inductive inference is, of course, an illusion.
Statistical theories diverge not simply in the third decimal place, but in
the very questions they ask. Is the same true at the level of theory? Can
statistics give a single correct answer to the problems posed? In contrast
to the proponents of "judgment under uncertainty," we shall argue: No.
The more the urns and balls are filled with content, the more content-
dependent reasoning becomes important in addition to the formulae.
With that content, rationality is more than repetitive and mechanical calculation. We shall present examples of alternative but equally
rational solutions (for other examples see Jeffrey, 1987).

What happens if we apply Neyman and Pearson's theory to the Cab
Problem? The whole perspective changes, not just the third decimal. The

fundamental difference arises with the decision criterion, which is essential for Neyman and Pearson and non-existent in Bayes' theorem. (Here and in the following we refer to Bayes' theorem as stated in equation 6.1 and used in the judgment-under-uncertainty research. Today's Bayesian statistics and reasoning, of course, go beyond this.) Applying Neyman and Pearson's theory, or "signal detection theory" as it is known in psychology, the subjective representation of Blue and Green cabs are two overlapping distributions on a subjective continuum (Birnbaum, 1983). Recall that the criterion is a point on this continuum: if a subjective value falls to one side, the subject says "Green," if to the other, "Blue." The criterion may vary from one situation to another, depending on the cost-benefit analysis of the two types of "hits" and "errors" possible. Since the court tested the witness under the same visibility conditions as on the night of the hit-and-run accident, the sensitivity of the witness is in both cases the same, but his criterion may vary. We do not know where the criterion was on the night in question except that it was a point on the so-called receiver operator characteristic (ROC) curve. The Neyman and Pearson analysis shows us that we need in addition to the formal calculus a psychological theory of criterion shift in witnesses.

There exist several candidates from which we choose the *error minimizing hypothesis* for illustration. Let us assume that the witness has calibrated his criterion on the night of the accident in a way that minimizes incorrect testimony. Let us further assume that the witness knows the acutal base rates $p(B)$ and $p(G)$ of Blue and Green cabs in the city. Now we can calculate his criterion setting that minimizes the overall number of errors, i.e. the sum $p("B" \mid G)p(G) + p("G" \mid B)p(B)$. The probability $p("G" \mid B)$ is the error of saying "Green" although the cab was actually Blue. This gives us the numerical values for the two likelihoods searched (since the criterion is a likelihood ratio). Inserting them into Bayes' theorem we calculate 0.82(!) for the probability that the cab was actually Blue given the witness' testimony "Blue."

The moral of this is twofold: First, different statistical approaches can lead to different views on the same problem. The essential point in this example are the probabilities that specify the witness' errors. Seen from the perspective of Bayes' theorem (as it is used in the judgment-under-uncertainty research), the witness is characterized by a single pair thereof, but seen from that of Neyman and Pearson's theory, he is characterized by a continuum of such pairs (located on the ROC curve). From the latter point of view, the need for a psychological theory of criterion shift becomes obvious. This reflects the fundamental duality in Neyman and

Pearson's theory: the statistical part must be supplemented by a psychological part. Second, since there exist alternative solutions (and there exist many more; see Birnbaum, 1983), phenomena such as base-rate neglect which are defined relative to the allegedly single correct answer, dissolve into thin air. The alternative solution given above (0.82) is close to the median answer reported (0.80). Recall that this solution is derived from the assumption that base rates do indeed enter the calculation. We have chosen this example, because it shows that using base rates can give the same value, $c.$ 0.80, from which Kahneman and Tversky conclude that base rates are neglected.

If we leave textbook problems and enter the outside world, the only-one-answer view runs into a second type of problem: the issue of information search and judgment of relevance. Information is already prepackaged, often in numerical form, in textbook problems such as the above Cab Problem. What kind of information people search for, what they judge to be relevant, and what quantitative values they estimate for the relevant variables (if they do) – this was rarely considered a topic for research into judgment under uncertainty. Rationality and reasoning apparently did not begin with the subject's search for information and selection of variables to decide whether a person is an Engineer, or whether the cab was Blue. Even the term "heuristic," as in "representativeness heuristic," is now used (as shown above) for subjective calculation of frequencies and probabilities, rather than for general strategies of information search, as in Duncker's terminology.

Information search and judgments of relevancy are, however, an indispensable part of real-world application of statistical reasoning. Consider, for instance, the following real-world version of the Cab Problem. Assume there is a judge confronted with the hit-and-run accident described. Let us further assume that she belongs to the minority of judges who are Bayesians (she does not know about Neyman and Pearson; thus we ignore the issue discussed above). She knows the testimony of the witness and the likelihood that the witness errs. Now she needs the relevant base rate. What is it? Her concern is not only the exact numerical value, but, in the first place, the question of *which* base rate is relevant. Is it the base rate of Blue cabs in the city? This base rate may not be very informative, since we are dealing with hit-and-run accidents at night. Or the base rate of Blue cabs involved in accidents? (Kahneman and Tversky suggest this second base rate in a later publication on the grounds that only it is "causally" linked to the event, whereas the first base rate is called "incidental.") However, the judge may see that there is little ground to bet on a "causal" link between driving incompetence and the dishonesty involved in hit-and-run crime. Thus she might look at the base rate for hit-and-run accidents, but she may realize that the part of the town, the time of night, etc. could also be relevant, since one company might prefer one part of town or time over others. She must sift the information for potentially relevant variables and decide to what variable(s) the base rate should refer. There is no single correct or mechanical solution to this question; it is a matter of informed judgment. And, since informed judgment does not guarantee consensus, various Bayesian judges will calculate different posterior probabilities.

All these critical remarks are concerned not with statistical models, but rather with their application. Again, there are some parallels between their application to the study of the mind and as tools of the behavioral scientists. The tendency to neglect the processes of information search has its parallel in the tendency to pay much less attention to the question of data generation (measurement) than to that of statistical inference. The tendency to neglect crucial assumptions is mirrored in many cookbook-like presentations of the statistical tools in the textbooks. Consider the above Engineer–Lawyer Problem, where the subject estimates the probability that the person described is an Engineer. The claim that the subjects should take account of the base rate specified (via Bayes' theorem) hinges on the crucial assumption that the descriptions were *randomly* drawn out of the population to which these base rates refer. In fact, there exist studies in which this crucial information is not even mentioned to the subjects (e.g. the "Tom W." study and the "medical" problem; Kahneman, Slovic, and Tversky, 1982, pp. 50, 154). In the Engineer–Lawyer Problem, random sampling is asserted, but falsely: the descriptions were deliberately constructed to match the American stereotypes of an engineer or lawyer, or to be completely uninformative. Smart subjects might notice, and others may simply skip over the word "randomly" in the instructions. In fact, if care is taken that subjects *know* that the descriptions were randomly drawn, e.g. by letting the subjects themselves draw each description from an urn, then they no longer ignore base rates (Gigerenzer, Hell, and Blank, 1988). Base-rate neglect disappears if the crucial information is made explicit.

Such results indicate that the "quality" of probabilistic reasoning found in studies depends on how the information is presented to the subject. If textbook problems are distributed in booklets in classrooms, as in most of the Kahneman–Tversky research, then subjects are likely to ignore base rates. But when individual subjects are put into an experimental setting where they can see, feel, or manipulate crucial information, they are less likely to ignore base rates. This consideration also may help reconcile the apparent contradiction between the "cognitive illusions" reported in the research on judgment under uncertainty and the research of Jean Piaget and Bärbel Inhelder ([1951]1975) on probabilistic reasoning. According to Piaget and Inhelder, children's probabilistic reasoning is much better developed than the research on judgment under uncertainty would imply. Piaget uses a single-case approach, where care is taken that every child understands completely the problem posed, even at the cost of non-standardized instructions and casual conversations with the child. Probabilistic reasoning, at least in naive subjects, seems to be strongly determined by the way in which crucial information is presented. The bulk of experimental evidence available today, both on probabilistic and on deductive reasoning, suggests that the judgment of children and adults is not so much conditioned by the structure of a problem – as the various normative views would have it – but rather by the content, context, and presentation of information – which should be irrelevant according to most normative models. The history of probability theory, with all its changes in the interpretation of probability, in the meaning of "descriptive" and "normative," however, should warn us to be cautious in using one formal method as *the* norm, against which such judgments are denigrated as irrational, independent of their content and context. A rational mind may be more than the kind of intuitive statistician who mechanically applies the same formula (be it expected utility, Bayes' theorem, or some other) to all contents and in all contexts. But such a rational mind is much harder to define.

We have seen that statistics was first institutionalized in experimental psychology as an indispensable tool, and that afterwards experimenters began to conceive the mind itself as an intuitive statistician. Given the diversity of psychological approaches and theories in the decades considered, and the abundance of research, the present account is by necessity selective and incomplete. Let us round out a few of the main issues here.

The institutionalization of a hybrid of Fisher's and Neyman and Pearson's ideas as the *sine qua non* of scientific inference was by no means restricted to psychology and education. Most empirical social sciences, if not all, have been conquered by the hybrid approach, as documented for archeology by Cowgill (1977) and for sociology and other fields by Morrison and Henkel (1970). A characteristic double standard came to govern the application of statistics to hypothesis testing and inference. Experimenters considered their subjects to be "rational" if they used

Bayes' theorem to test hypotheses (e.g. whether the person described was an engineer), but they themselves used Fisherian and Neyman–Pearsonian statistics to test their own hypotheses. The reasons for this double standard seem to be mainly rhetorical and institutional rather than logical. In general, behavioral scientists still rarely use Bayesian methods to evaluate their own hypotheses, although since the 1970s some textbooks have included chapters on Bayesian statistics. Bayesian reasoning, however, has re-entered some of its traditional territories outside the experimenter's laboratory, such as judicial decisions (see chapter 7). And in recent years effect size and power of studies are increasingly emphasized (e.g. Cohen, 1977), rather than mere significance. More progressive editorials such as that of the *Zeitschrift für Sozialpsychologie* (Bredenkamp and Feger, 1970) state explicitly that acceptance of articles is independent of the level of significance achieved, and that they welcome non-significant results to correct for the inflation of type-I errors due to earlier editorial policies (Melton, 1962).

If we put some of the various cognitive functions that have been seen as intuitive statistics together, we get the picture of an eclectic brain where different homunculi statisticians control different functions. Elementary functions such as sensory detection, discrimination, and recognition in memory are controlled by a statistician of the Neyman–Pearson–Wald school, causal reasoning by a Fisherian statistician, perceptual estimation and judgment by a statistician of the Karl Pearson school, and induction and opinion revision by a Bayesian statistician. To read the current psychological literature on cognitive functioning, it would seem as if each of the homunculi operated in ignorance of the others, and by dogmatic adherence to a single statistical school.

6.7 CONCLUSION

Probability has transformed our view of cognitive processes, as it has our understanding of physical and biological processes. The theories discussed in this chapter, however, originated in a different way from those in physics and biology. They stem from tools. This history, and the peculiar attitude of psychologists towards their statistical tools, accounts for the problematical normative view and the blind spots we have discussed. However much interpretations of probability have changed since Pascal and Fermat, one thing has been constant and almost universal: the identification of number with objectivity. Natural science has long been a model for public knowledge, which means knowledge that does not depend on seasoned judgment, but is, in a sense, mathematical, and hence "objective." Probability theory has become a model for personal knowledge in psychology, which means that the processes by which the individual arrives at knowledge are, in the same sense, mechanical, and in essence numerical. Current theories in cognitive psychology reflect a deep commitment to the view that our brains represent the outside world numerically, that there exist subjective probabilities in our heads for everything under the sun, and that the very nature of cognition *is* computation (Pylyshyn, 1980). This "objective" characteristic of both public and personal knowledge, though partly an illusion, accounts for much of the authority of science. Statistics is a powerful mechanism for generating objective knowledge, and psychologists, like insurance companies, have valued it as a way to escape the idiosyncracies of personal decision. In terms of our imperial metaphor, the sovereignty of statistical law cannot be compromised by the arbitrary and capricious decisions of its administrators.

"You can't fight the law of averages."
— Grover Snood in Thomas Pynchon (1984, p. 142)

7

◁ ══ ▷

Numbers rule the world

7.1 INTRODUCTION

In our century, the empire of chance has greatly expanded. R. A. Fisher called statistics "the peculiar aspect of human progress" that has given "to the twentieth century, its special character" (Fisher, 1954, p. 276), which is an exaggeration, but not an untruth. Descriptive statistics are featured in every issue of every newspaper, and mathematical statistics has become indispensable to public health and medical research, to marketing and quality control in business, to accounting, to economic and meteorological forecasting, to polling and surveys, to sports, to weapons research and development, and to insurance. For practitioners in many areas of the biological, social, and applied sciences, standardized procedures from inferential statistics virtually define the process of forming hypotheses, conducting experiments, and analyzing results that is taken to be "the scientific method." Statistical tools fortified by assumptions of underlying probability distributions measure or, some would say, call into being entities such as IQ, economic indices, and attitude and opinion ratings. Business executives, nuclear safety experts, and weather forecasters are instructed in Bayesian probabilities to sharpen their intuitions. From the Earned Run Average to the probability of today's precipitation to the certification of a new drug for sale, statistics and probability are all-pervasive.

The authority of experts has been enhanced by this boom in probability and statistics. Indeed, the explosion of numbers has created a new kind of expert, one whose claims rest more on information and formal techniques than on concrete experience and personal judgment. Not since

Pythagoras has the prestige of numbers been so great, and this has been both a boon and a temptation to the new-style experts. If it is now said that statistics can prove anything, that is because they are so often (mis)used to *prove* things, not merely to provide reasoned support for a position. If experts often claim too much, however, it is the political and social system that permits, even encourages their pretensions. The objectivity and techniques of the modern expert parallel the impartiality and rules of the modern bureaucrat. Both exclude personal discretion and emphasize the consistent and even mechanical application of established procedures across the board to avoid bias, the one aiming at truth to fact, and the other at fairness. Both seek the high ground, above the political fray. Echoes of the exclusion of opinion by the nineteenth-century London Statistical Society are still heard.

Leadership in the development of statistical methods, and even more in their application to practical problems, has in this century passed decisively to the United States. Clearly there are institutional and economic reasons for this; the size and wealth of American universities have facilitated the attainment by that nation of leadership in a wide range of fields. But the extraordinary public influence of statistics is not entirely a matter of professional scientists and mathematicians in universities. Its role is perhaps even more impressive in government, business, and other bureaucratic institutions with responsibility to a wider public. This prominence of statistical tools reflects not so much an implicit faith in experts as the weakness of alternative authorities, the absence of strong traditional elites. Statistics, in the form of standardized mental tests, even plays a large role in the selection of elites in the United States – much more than in most of Europe, where, at least until quite recently, education has generally been highly stratified from early childhood on. Technocratic elites have thus found a multitude of opportunities in the modern United States. The relative openness of American institutions to public scrutiny has also encouraged at least the pretense of formal, objective processes of decision – believed to exclude arbitrariness. Milton Russell and Michael Gruber, writing on quantitative risk analysis, have argued that an "absence of guidelines may lead to idiosyncratic decisions that cannot easily be explained or defended and that are subject both to accusations of capriciousness and to real or perceived manipulation in the service of political expediency" (1987, p. 287). The leadership of the United States in practical quantification is a matter of degree rather than of kind. The appeal of statistics is wide, especially in pluralistic democracies. Where values clash and consensus is elusive, numbers and the techniques that manipulate them are esteemed for their ostensible neutrality. With statistics, hotly debated issues can seemingly be turned into problems to be solved.

Today's applications of statistics and probability theory to matters of daily concern to ordinary citizens draw upon the full complement of techniques and interpretations accumulated by the mathematics of chance in its three-hundred-year history. Bayesian methods with an eighteenth-century lineage and an eighteenth-century interpretation as mechanized rationality have made a comeback in contemporary courtrooms, while the descriptive statistics of sociological studies and opinion polling continue to reflect the disdain for the countable that in the nineteenth century was attached to the "mass" of workers and peasants. Quetelet's beloved normal distribution is still fundamental to the measurement of intelligence, and indeed to much of mathematical statistics. Twentieth-century developments in inference statistics have made randomized trials central to testing new medical therapies, industrial quality control, agricultural experiments, and a host of other experimental studies. Subjective and objective probabilities coexist peacefully in applications like weather forecasting, where both the past frequency of precipitation and the individual forecaster's personal conviction about tomorrow's possible downpour come into play.

This formidable array of techniques and interpretations, all familiarly known as "statistics," helps explain the extraordinary flexibility of that multifarious rubric in application. Statistics is now used in a variety of ways – description, inference, measurement, and modeling. Our examples of mundane applications do not exhaust the field, but rather emphasize the ways in which statistics in all its guises has remade the world of daily experience in its own image. It has redefined old notions like intelligence and public opinion and thereby made them more important than ever before; it has transformed traditional values of individualism, particularly in law and medicine; it has replaced judgments with rules. New objects, new values, new rules – all reflect the fascination with the numerical and the longing for certainty that the numerical symbolizes, preconditions for the remarkable success of the mathematics of uncertainty.

7.2   NEW OBJECTS

Baseball

Baseball is among the most impressive – because seemingly most incongruous – objects of statistical mathematics. The sport grew up from sandlots and city streets, supported by a culture of working men and farm boys, informed by the notoriously ungrammatical wisdom of generations of managers. Yet statistics have been part of baseball from its beginnings, and can even be traced back to its ancestry in cricket (see Thorn and Palmer, 1986, pp. 9 ff.). These sports have been said to be amenable to statistical analysis in ways that many others, such as American football, are not (McKean, 1982). Fans of these other sports complain that the statistics of their favorites have simply been neglected. At any rate, venerable traditions have developed around the statistics of baseball and cricket, and both have annual abstracts – e.g. the *Wisdon* and the *Bill James Baseball Abstract*. Both developments are worth recounting, but the baseball story is rich enough for our purposes.

One of the most influential early promoters of baseball was also a great champion of its statistics. In his *The Game of Base Ball: How to Learn It, How to Play It, and How to Teach It*, published in 1868, Henry Chadwick explained how baseball statistics were integral to his attempt to establish a national game for the U.S., on the model of cricket in England. A former cricket reporter, he directed his baseball interests to devising "a systematized plan of recording the details of a game." In connection with this pursuit, he began to have some influence on changing the game "from the almost simple field exercise it was some twenty years ago up to the manly, scientific game of ball it is now" (Chadwick, 1868, p. 11).

As Chadwick perceived, the identity of the game would be partly formed by the way in which games were recorded, i.e. the statistics used to represent them. He was very concerned that statistics be used that would promote the virtues (literally) of the game. Above all, he wanted the national game to be a "moral recreation" (p. 12). Certain statistics reflected real virtues , while others did not, and Chadwick wanted to expunge, or at least deemphasize, the latter. He deprecated home run hitters, and hence the home run category, as overly "showy" (pp. 62–8). He lobbied hard to stop the practice of counting bases reached on fielding errors toward batters' averages, since these clearly did not demonstrate batting skill (e.g. p. 66).

Statistics could promote moral baseball in other ways as well. One instance involved the loss of a team with a better record to a team with a worse record. The loss prompted accusations from some members of the press that the better team had "thrown" the game for the purpose of winning big bets on the second matchup between the two teams. The press had been hasty, Chadwick charged: "Knowing nothing of the uncertainties of base ball, and ignorant of the fact that the strongest clubs sometimes play the poorest of games when least expected," those naive journalists had overlooked the possibility that the loss was simply a matter of chance (p. 104). The individual statistics also supported the integrity of the implicated team. For instance, they had no more errors in the game in question than they had had on average throughout the year (see pp. 103–7).

Quite in contrast to Chadwick, the early twentieth-century baseball statistician, Ernie Lanigan, author of the fact-filled *Baseball Cyclopedia* (1922), cared mainly about the statistics themselves. Lanigan was blunt about his real interests: "I don't really care much about baseball, or looking at ball games, major or minor. All my interest in baseball is in its statistics" (see Lieb, 1973, p. 30). His regard for the figures was especially well expressed by his contempt for Chadwick, who, presumably for reasons of the sort we have already discussed, neglected to include some previously recognized statistical categories in his box scores. Lanigan referred to Chadwick as the "demon eliminator" of numerical information (Lanigan, 1922, p. 45). In fairness, he referred to himself as the "demon compiler" (p. 63). Lanigan's goal was completeness in the recording of baseball. Every conceivable statistic seemed to interest him. He is said to have passed up a number of well-paying jobs in order to maintain the independence necessary for this magnificent enterprise (see the introductory remarks to Lanigan, 1922).

According to John Thorn and Pete Palmer, authors of the detailed statistical analysis, *The Hidden Game of Baseball* (1985), the first revolutionary development in baseball statistics did not occur until halfway through this century. The recording of this event marks one of those seemingly great incongruities that characterize the tradition of baseball statistics. In1954, *Life* magazine posed a man at a calculator (Alan Roth, the Brooklyn Dodgers' statistical specialist), and behind him the burly figure of the great baseball manager Branch Rickey, pointing to a long equation on a blackboard:

$$G = \left(\frac{H + BB + HP}{AB + BB + HP} + \frac{3(TB-H)}{4AB} + \frac{R}{H + BB + HP} \right)$$

$$- \left(\frac{H}{AB} + \frac{BB + HB}{AB + BB + HB} + \frac{ER}{H + BB + HB} - \frac{SO}{8(AB + BB + HB)} - F \right)$$

The formula is less recondite than it appears. *G* (for games) is a measure of winning efficiency, expressed in terms of hits (*H*), bases on balls (*BB*), bases when hit by pitcher (*HP*), total bases (*TB*), at bats (*AB*), runs (*R*), hit batters (*HB*), earned runs (*ER*), strikeouts (*SO*), and fielding (*F*). The equation can be more simply written as $G = O - D$; winning efficiency equals an offense component (top line) minus a defense component (bottom line). The three subcomponents of offense are "on base average," "extra base power," and "clutch" or percentage of men on base who later score. Defense reduces to "average hits allowed," "pitcher control," "earned run average," "strikeout average," and "fielding." This equation and its descendants represent a bid by IBM and its clones to capture baseball from its Casey Stengels and Earl Weavers, to replace the intuition of the managers with calculation. By weighting the subcomponents of offense and defense optimally, the formula could be made 96.2% accurate in predicting major league standings over a twenty-year period.

Rickey used the formula to reveal the relative values of the elements of the game in contributing to the final standings. For instance, the fact that the formula worked so well to predict final standings when strikeout average was weighted so low (⅛) suggested to Rickey that a pitcher's strikeout ability is not really crucial. This was one of several surprises resulting from the statistical approach. Branch Rickey (described by *Life* as baseball's "brainiest leader") claimed that it transformed his understanding of the game:

Baseball people are generally allergic to new ideas. We are slow to change. For 51 years I have judged baseball by personal observation, by considered opinions and by accepted statistical methods. But recently I have come upon a device for measuring baseball which has compelled me to put different values on some of my oldest and most cherished theories. It reveals some new and startling truths about the game. . . It is the most disconcerting and at the same time the most constructive thing to come into baseball in my memory.

Such was the importance of mathematical statistics in the judgment of the man best known to history for opening up the major leagues to black players. He inaugurated the scientific, or perhaps scientistic, phase of baseball statistics. Granted, Chadwick had already conceived of something like a science of baseball – he forecast a time when "the game will be brought down almost to a mathematical calculation of results from given causes" (Chadwick, 1868, p. 69) – but this program only began to be worked out in the literature of baseball statistics after Rickey.

Subsequent developments have been published in rather more scholarly outlets than *Life*. The journal *Operations Research* has published regularly on baseball science. One article explored in depth the purported advantage enjoyed by batters of handedness opposite to that of the pitcher (Lindsey, 1959). Another employed Monte Carlo simulations to test the effect of batting order on game outcome, and determined that the effect is remarkably small (Freeze, 1974). Yet another invoked sophisticated statistical results to justify the seemingly obvious conclusion that "the runs adding most to the probability of winning are the one tying the score and the one that puts the batting team ahead" (Lindsey, 1963). In 1966, MIT Press took over publication of *Percentage Baseball* written by the metallurgist Earnshaw Cook. Cook combines statistical analysis with physical considerations – such as the resiliency of the baseball – in analyzing baseball strategy.

By the 1970s, baseball science had become well established. It received a considerable boost in 1971 from the founding of the Society for American Baseball Research, and the creation of SABR's yearly *Baseball Research Journal*. The acronym of the organization is now the root of the name of an almost professional statistical pursuit, "sabermetrics," which baseball statistics guru Bill James defines as "the search for objective knowledge about baseball" (James, 1986, p. 702).

Is the science of baseball transforming the game of baseball? Inevitably, statistics has been represented by some of its champions as a simple extension of what players and managers have always done. Thorn and Palmer follow psychologists in suggesting that every ballplayer is an "intuitive statistician" (see chapter 6), forever calculating the probabilities of success for alternative plays and strategies:

While he is racing to the hole, the shortstop is figuring: Based on the speed of the runners and how hard the ball is hit, he probably has no chance of a double play; he may have little chance of a play at second; and he almost certainly has no play at first. He throws to third because the distance from the hole to the bag is short, and his calculation of the various probabilities led him to conclude that this was his "percentage play."

Now not so much as a glimmer of any number entered the shortstop's head in this time, yet he *was* thinking statistically (Thorn and Palmer, 1985, p. 5).

Similarly, the manager who positions the shortstop, and who himself thus helps to erase the leading runner, is "playing the percentages," even if he does not consciously calculate them. The question that Thorn and Palmer rhetorically ask is, why stop here?

Computers in the dugouts are, according to some, the next natural extension. Some think they will even add to the drama of the game. Says Steve Mann, baseball consultant in Philadelphia: "When a manager needs a designated hitter, he'll punch the buttons and get four alternative batters, along with each one's record against particular types of pitches. But the other manager can punch the same buttons and get the same answers. Now we're playing poker." (McKean, 1982, p.31). Baseball computer systems such as the "Edge 1.000" have already been sold to a number of professional teams (McKean, 1982).

Statistics does not just measure baseball. Purists have every reason to condemn it, along with artificial turf and designated hitters, for transforming the game. We find this same effect in a variety of statistical applications. Statistical methods of description, inference, and measurement have made matters heretofore inaccessible the objects of scientific study. New mathematics and a heightened brazenness have made possible quantitative study of the most subtle, private, and elusive phenomena. Francis Galton published in 1872 a notorious inquiry into the efficacy of prayer, using mortality tables and insurance rates to suggest that prayer was without power in this world. R. A. Fisher began his *Design of Experiments* by showing how to investigate taste with inference statistics – can a certain lady really discriminate whether the milk was added to her cup before or after the tea? (Fisher, 1935, pp. 13 ff.). Raymond Pearl claimed to be the first to give tables of frequency of coitus, in 1925; such studies are now a cottage industry, though a century ago they would have seemed impossible as well as improper (see Pearl, 1939, p. 67; also Boorstin, 1974, part 3). But the more powerful and refined mathematical statistics did not simply make it possible for social and biological scientists to answer old questions more precisely, or with less inconvenience. As is so often the case in science, the availability of a new tool inspired researchers to address new issues and to look at old ones from a new standpoint. When phenomena hitherto elusive from the standpoint of science are brought into the laboratory, they take on an altered character.

ESP

This new character bears the stamp of the methods used to make the phenomenon scientifically visible. Consider the remarkable case of the scientific study of the supernatural, in which the application of inference statistics replaced messages from the dear departed and clairvoyant insights into the future with card guessing as the key phenomenon. It is a striking irony that in response to the oppressive scientific determinism that seemed to follow from Helmholtz, Du Bois-Reymond, Darwin, and Buckle, science should be turned to the task of demonstrating the limitations of naturalism. Prominent among the instruments chosen was the most flexible of these scientific methods, statistics. The Society for Psychical Research, in Britain, pioneered the use of statistical methods to investigate telepathy and clairvoyance, and enlisted Francis Edgeworth to assist in the analysis. J. B. Rhine, the Duke parapsychologist who during the 1930s made extrasensory perception (ESP) famous, also gave his purported demonstration of its reality in the language of statistics. To accomplish such a feat he was obliged to deal with the extrasensory world in the most mundane possible terms. The miraculous inspiration that seems to arrive in a crucial moment may be real, but is not replicable, and hence cannot be part of the public knowledge that is science. Instead Rhine set up experiments involving card guessing. His subjects were never perfect guessers, so Rhine built his proofs on long series of repetitions involving six or eight or ten correct guesses out of twenty-five, when only five would be expected by chance. In *Extra-Sensory Perception*, he rejected the non-existence of ESP with probabilities as low as 10^{-320}.

There were, it later appeared, a number of problems with Rhine's experimental techniques, such as the use of cards that, under certain lighting conditions, could be read from the back. But the initial attacks on these implausible results were directed at his statistics – the mathematical field of statistics was still none too secure in the 1930s. R. R. Willoughby of Clark, alluding to one of the classic probability calculations, wondered if any probability could be as small as 10^{-50}, even that of the sun not rising tomorrow. Chester Kellogg questioned the independence of successive trials. E. G. Boring suggested that the idea of a chance distribution was meaningless, and insisted that here, as in all of experimental psychology, real controls were indispensable (see Mauskopf and McVaugh, 1979). The ensuing controversy involved a number of statistical luminaries, including even R. A. Fisher, and inspired several of the leaders of American statistics to sign a proclamation announcing that, whatever might be the validity of Rhine's conclusions, at least his statistics was sound. But there was a deeper objection to his relatively straightforward statistical procedure: it offered nothing like an explanation of ESP, or even a clear indication of what circumstances elicited ESP phenomena. Statistical demonstrations of ESP continue to issue forth in a steady stream, but as Seymour Mauskopf and Michael McVaugh observe, parapsychology has remained an elusive science, on the margins of academic respectability (Mauskopf and McVaugh, 1979, 1980).

Mental testing

As the example of ESP shows, the power of statistics to isolate and measure elusive phenomena is not always easily distinguished from the scientific construction of facts and entities which, in a sense, had not previously existed. IQ, perhaps the most controversial product of statistical reasoning, seeks to measure something whose very existence is largely defined by statistics. Although intelligence as a character trait, possessed in greater or smaller degree by various persons, seems to have emerged in the mid-nineteenth century, what Charles Spearman first called *g*, the general factor underlying all manifestations of intelligence, was a statistical construct defined by the method of factor analysis. Spearman, in fact, invented factor analysis in the context of his studies of intelligence, and Bernard Norton has shown why it was no accident that he ended with a unitary factor, the "monarchical" theory of intelligence, supporting a view of the mind as active, in contrast to the passive associationism that he despised (Norton, 1979; also Spearman, 1930).

Spearman's theory held that general intellectual ability was primary, the result of some underlying factor, probably physiological, such as energy or power of the brain. People of equal general ability would of course exhibit different special abilities, but these were like perturbations – in the standard astronomical analogy of statistics – the results of particular features of training or social convention. The general factor, he wrote, can be found "simply by measuring promiscuously any large number of different abilities, and pooling the results together. In such a hotch-potch of multitudinous measurements the specific factors must necessarily – since they vary randomly from one measurement to another – tend in the average or mean to neutralize one another. Whereas the general factor, being in every measurement just the same, must in the average more or less completely dominate" (quoted in Tuddenham, 1964). Spearman was unperturbed by the need for indirect measurement: "It is no new thing thus elaborately to deal with and precisely measure things whose real nature is concealed from view; of this nature, for instance, is obviously the study of electricity, or biology, and indeed of all physical science whatever" (Spearman, 1904). But his was not the only possible interpretation of the results. Godfrey Thomson proposed a rival "anarchic" or "sampling" theory of intelligence which reduced Spearman's general factor to a sum of a host of independent abilities. Thomson was the founder of Moray House, the first important producer of intelligence tests in Britain, and by no means an enemy of mental measurement. But he thought the factors of intelligence, and particularly Spearman's g, should be regarded as no more than "statistical coefficients, possibly without any more 'reality' than an average, or an index of the cost of living, or a standard deviation, or a correlation coefficient" (Thomson, 1939, p. 42).

The American champion of unitary intelligence was the Stanford psychologist Lewis Terman, pioneer of intelligence testing in the United States. Terman looked to the Frenchman Alfred Binet rather than to Spearman as his mentor, and he did not use Spearman's factor analysis, but rather a more descriptive procedure based on adding up correct answers to heterogeneous questions. It was Binet who had first brought psychology out of the clouds and made it useful, Terman thought, by recognizing that intelligence is properly assessed relative to age. This made possible the definition of an intelligence quotient, initially proposed – and later renounced – by Wilhelm Stern, but championed most effectively by Terman. Wechsler later replaced this quotient form with a purely statistical definition of IQ, according to which the mean for each age was 100, and the standard deviation defined in advance as 15 (Wechsler, 1939).

Terman did not worry much about issues of metaphysical realism. He acknowledged that intelligence has many aspects, and is not strictly homogeneous. But some of these aspects are more important than others, since they represent the highest stages of evolutionary progress, and the most useful abilities in an advanced society. We must recognize that abstract, conceptual thinking stands atop the "hierarchy of intelligences," and not condemn a test "because it yields low correlations with success as a mill hand or street car motorman" (Terman, 1921, pp. 129, 131). Although he opposed Spearman's g, he routinely spoke of children as having a given mental age, different from their chronological age, and insisted that the former rather than the latter should determine grade level in school. Wechsler's replacement of the intelligence "quotient" by a standardized distribution undercut this concept of mental age.

Already in 1921 there were many psychologists prepared to challenge this stress on a single measure of intelligence. In a symposium that year on intelligence, F. N. Freeman, S. S. Colvin, V. A. C. Henmon, and L. L. Thurstone all called for increased attention to particular character traits, or tests of various types of intelligence, and B. Ruml insisted that "in any test which yields a single quantitative result or score, the content should be as homogeneous as possible" (Ruml, 1921, p. 143). Edward Thorndike was willing to use a broad average of diverse traits, but firmly denied that the measure of someone's intelligence is "some general power which resides in him and determines his ability in every capacity of intellectual task" (Thorndike, 1921, p. 126). Thurstone became the most influential critic of the unitary IQ, though not because he thought it merely a statistical convention. Rather it was a mistake. Thurstone preferred to perform the factor analysis differently, so that it gave not a single intelligence measure and a range of deviations for various special abilities, but a set of perhaps seven "primary mental abilities." These, and not IQ, were real. Unfortunately, it proved impossible to limit the PMAs to seven, for the same analysis was capable of giving – and, according to the scheme proposed by J. P. Guilford, did in fact give – more than one hundred of them. Moreover, since Thurstone's PMAs were not generally orthogonal (or independent), a second-order g could be inferred from the correlations among them. As Stephen Jay Gould points out in his elegant treatment of this issue, it is in practice often impossible to decide between Thurstone and Spearman on statistical grounds (Gould, 1981, chapter 5). But both believed in the reality of their statistical constructs. Read Tuddenham writes: "To the statistician's dictum that whatever exists can be measured, the factorist has added that whatever can be 'measured' must exist" (Tuddenham, 1964, p. 516).

Whatever the difficulties of interpretation, mental testing has become enormously influential. IQ tests have quasi-legal standing in commitment for mental deficiency, and are widely used in education, especially in the United States. An enthusiastic president of the Educational Testing Service once called standardized testing America's "secret weapon" in its contest with the Russians (Wigdor and Garner, 1982, vol. 1, p. 95), and ETS tests are required for admission to selective colleges and graduate and professional schools in the United States. Ability testing has been the target of much criticism, for its alleged association with eugenics and racism, or its baleful influence in serving and legitimating an inegalitarian capitalist order.

There are, perhaps, good reasons for such criticism. IQ enthusiasts from Terman to Arthur Jensen have tended to favour a hereditarian interpretation with more fervor than the evidence would seem to require. Terman often suggested that people with low IQ could never achieve much, and it was foolish sentimentality for parents or teachers to hold out any ambition for them. IQ testing was closely linked to eugenics, and in some American states evidence of "feeble-mindedness" in three generations provided legal grounds for sterilization. The massive testing of American recruits in the First World War (Kevles, 1968–69), using tests that clearly required English language skills as well as a considerable measure of acculturation, produced dubious results which became part of nativist propaganda and may have contributed to the new immigration laws that discriminated against south and east Europeans.

But the nefarious aims and achievements of the intelligence testers have surely been exaggerated. Even Terman, despite his anti-egalitarian rhetoric, counseled teachers in a 1923 book *not* to tell students their IQ scores under ordinary circumstances, for fear of discouraging them (Terman, 1923, pp. 24–5), and he held women and Asians to be intellectually equal to white men – hardly a reactionary move in interwar California. Gould points out that mental testing can be and often is used to help students. With the introduction of universal schooling at the end of the nineteenth century, some way of identifying children with learning problems was needed. In regard to selective admissions, ability tests have rarely discriminated against lower-class children even as much as alternative forms of discrimination. Gillian Sutherland notes that British educational authorities did not interpret low mental test scores as evidence that students were ineducable. The thoroughly class-bound system of secondary education that prevailed there until after the Second World War existed for reasons quite independent of mental test results. In fact, testing exerted by far its greatest influence in the United States, perhaps because admission to advanced education there was much less class-bound than in England or Germany. Those educational districts in Great Britain that used intelligence tests in the 11+ examinations to award scholarships to grammar schools seem to have provided somewhat better opportunities for working-class children than did those that tested for "attainment." It was even argued against reliance on intelligence tests that too many working-class students would be admitted, and that they would ruin the "tone" of the school, or do more poorly than their tests predicted because of their backgrounds (Sutherland, 1984; also Evans and Waites, 1981, pp. 106–8).

The use of testing in the United States has been less closely studied. There was, of course, nothing equivalent to the 11+ examination in Britain that channeled most children from outside the upper classes to technical schools. Intelligence and aptitude testing in schools has been extremely widespread, almost universal, but it is difficult to generalize about how the results have been used. Columbia was inspired by the results of the army tests to impose an intelligence test in 1918, in hopes of screening out Jews, but elite colleges were soon forced to find other ways to accomplish this. The multiple-choice Scholastic Aptitude Test, for college admissions, appeared in 1926, and given the extraordinary diversity and decentralization of the United States school system, standardized testing is probably inevitable (Resnick, 1982). Perhaps it "legitimates" a hierarchical system, but it evidently does not much change the character of the classes entering selective universities.

The difficulty of defining the heterogeneous aggregate "intelligence," or even "aptitude," that their respective tests are designed to measure, has evidently not interfered too much with their practical use for advising and admissions. It does, however, give debates about intelligence a certain elusiveness, which is only partly overcome when the more firmly grounded context of quantitative genetics is brought in. Certainly the statistical method of measuring intelligence has not, as some of its founders hoped, rendered psychology an exact science, for it has proven impossible, at least within the Galtonian tradition of statistical measurement, to frame a convincing theory of intelligence.

This is the weakness that annoyed E. B. Wilson about certain medical studies, inspiring him to assert that critical analysis is better than "statistical legerdemain," except for propaganda purposes (Wilson, 1932). Because statistical measurement is often indirect, it is possible to produce a flood of numbers without ever defining clearly just what is being measured. Economic index numbers, whose influence rivals that of IQ, have less of this looseness. As Otis Dudley Duncan remarks, the components that go together to make up index numbers have at least a common unit of measurement, money (Duncan, 1984, p. 229). Although index numbers plainly derive from the collection and manipulation of statistics, abstract probabilistic considerations have in this century become less prominent in the discussion of them. In the 1880s, Francis Edgeworth analyzed the ways in which the proper measure of the value of the currency might depend on precisely how one conceives it. One might see the value of gold as a real entity, underlying all commodity prices and imperfectly indicated by them, but not reducible to some function of these prices. In that case the best measure of the value of gold would weight these other commodities according to the stability of their prices rather than according to their volume. If, on the other hand, the value of gold is conceived as identical by definition to what it can buy, measured by some average over all commodities, then the price of grain should be weighted more highly than that of pineapples precisely in proportion to the quantity consumed (Edgeworth, 1888–90). Irving Fisher, writing in the early 1920s, made the calculation of index numbers almost entirely pragmatic; he required of the ideal index number merely that it be stable, unbiased, reversible, and the like, not that it measure some long-hidden entity (Fisher, 1911,

1927). In contrast to IQ, the reality of the phenomena measured by index numbers – in particular, inflation and deflation of the currency – has never really been at issue. Like polling results, this is a case in which the measurement acts back on the process measured; routine reports of consumer and wholesale price indices affect interest rates, stock and bond prices, investment decisions, and so on. Nor are index numbers unique in this respect. Most economic statistics involve sampling; many are calculated in more than one way, so that techniques akin to least squares are used to reconcile divergent results, and all are watched attentively by managers, investors, and government officials. Without these numbers, the economic process would be something quite different.

Public opinion

Public opinion polling displays even more clearly the tendency of statistical results to shape phenomena as much as they measure them. Respondents to polls are often asked for opinions on issues about which they may never have thought much, and almost always are obliged to choose an answer with which they will only partly agree. In addition, polling results are broadcast widely, and help to set the terms of public debate. If IQ may be said to be invented, or socially constructed, public opinion comes close to being manufactured.

Since at least the French Revolution, public opinion has been a political force to be reckoned with, and with the advent of polling based on statistical sampling in our century, it also became one that could be reckoned. This was not obvious to the pioneers. Edward L. Bernays was a champion of public relations in the first generation of that enterprise, which drew much of its inspiration from the apparent success of propaganda during the First World War (see Lippmann, 1922). He saw medical tact as a better model for the new professional public relations consultant than actuarial computations. He did not deny the usefulness of surveys and samples. But "the ability to estimate group reactions on a large scale over a wide geographic and psychological area is a specialized ability which must be developed with the same painstaking self-criticism and with the same dependence on experience that are required for the development of the clinical sense in the doctor or surgeon" (Bernays, 1923, pp. 53–4). As in the case of IQ, statistics – here the study of sampling probabilities – both enhanced the importance and changed the nature of the opinion it quantified. The pioneers of scientific sampling, like George Gallup and Elmo Roper, would have seconded the former and denied the latter, for they insisted that theirs was the way to give the average citizen an opportunity to make his or her voice heard. Probabilistic sampling, carefully designed to represent all groups, permitted the pollster to find out what people were thinking by contacting just several hundred of them, which could thus be done for an extraordinary variety of issues. Polling would provide the key to vigorous democracy in a mass society, they thought, and this was surely a good thing. Gallup and Roper agreed with Hadley Cantril that the average individual, though not intellectually distinguished, possessed a "hard-headed common sense," whose soundness, happily, is attested by its accordance with "the more objective opinions of realistic experts" (Cantril, 1944, p. 230; also Roper, 1940, p. 334).

The methods of sampling that made public opinion possible were largely worked out in the twentieth century. The probability mathematics needed to estimate error had been available since the time of Laplace, but nineteenth-century statisticians eschewed what they saw as the conjectures and speculations of the old political arithmetic, insisting that theirs was a science of facts. The Norwegian statistical director A. N. Kiaer began in the 1890s to use sampling, though he was unable to convince the International Statistical Institute of its viability. More influential, perhaps, was the economist Arthur Bowley, a student of Alfred Marshall and admirer of Francis Edgeworth, who wrote on the theory of sampling and used it extensively (see Kruskal and Mosteller, 1980; also Bowley, 1901). Roper, Gallup, and Archibald Crossley, however, had their roots in a different use of sampling, market research, which had become important to large corporations by 1930. Roper took this as a model for political polling: "Business long ago learned that it could no longer expect success while dictating to the public the color or size or shape or price of those things which the public purchased. The public now makes those important decisions, and unless a manufacturer can find some way of learning what the public wants, he soon goes out of business. I should like to see the application of the principles of market research and public opinion research to government. . ." (Roper, 1940, pp. 332–3). The analogy is even better than Roper could anticipate, for opinion polls, like marketing studies, have come to be used as much to manipulate the public as to understand it.

Gallup, Roper, and Crossley got their start in the 1930s, and were vaulted into the limelight in 1936 as a result of the *Literary Digest* fiasco. The *Digest* had begun conducting presidential straw polls in 1916, using lists of potential subscribers for its sampling population. Its polls had worked out reasonably well in the first five attempts, and at least got the winner right, and by 1936 the *Digest* displayed no small measure of smugness. Just before the election it quoted this piece of cautionary advice from an earlier year: "We make no claims to infallibility. We did not coin the phrase 'uncanny accuracy' which has been so freely applied to our polls" (*Literary Digest*, October 31, 1936, p. 6). The *Digest*, notoriously, predicted a sweeping victory for Landon, and the editors were befuddled by the actual result. They called their critics second guessers, beneficiaries of the wisdom of hindsight: "Hosts of people who feel they have learned more about polling in a few months than we have learned in more than a score of years have told us just where we were off" (*Literary Digest*, November 14, 1936, p. 7). But in fact Gallup and Roper knew well in advance that the *Digest*'s method, polling millions of people, most of them relatively affluent, was likely to fail in 1936. Gallup did not just poll a random population, but a stratified one, divided according to age, sex, financial status, and so on. Hence he knew that in 1936, for the first time in forty years, a wide gap separated the political preferences of the comfortable from the poor. He was able both to forecast that Roosevelt would win by a wide margin and to predict how far off the *Literary Digest* poll would be (Gallup and Rae, 1940, pp. 34–55). Gallup's air of invincibility lasted only until 1948, when his American Institute of Public Opinion predicted that Dewey would defeat Truman. He decided after that to be more careful about late shifts of opinion, and to avoid forecasting the outcome, but only to make available his numbers. Most charmingly, his press release acknowledging the error and announcing these changes included also the most compelling vindication of his profession that Gallup could conceive: he announced that 54% of the American people still affirm that polls "have value to the people," while only 28% deny it (Gallup, 1948, p. 6).

7.3   NEW VALUES

Attitudes

Intelligence and the vitality of an economy are common if vague notions that IQ and the GNP, in effect, redefine through measurement. By dint of being numerical, these indices acquire apparent precision and a kind of solidity that their originals never had. They also acquire new meanings implied by the measure used: IQ defined as mental age and IQ defined as deviation from the mean of a normal distribution are quite different entities, and neither corresponds to the everyday sense of the word "intelligence." Moreover, the use of IQ and aptitude measures to decide the educational paths open to a student inevitably implies that students will be evaluated statistically rather than as individuals – though this is doubtless mainly an effect rather than cause of a decentralized mass educational system designed to maximize opportunity and at the same time to select out elites. The attempts to measure ESP or intelligence thus carry with them a certain vision of the nature and uses of these things.

The intellectual and ethical problems of statistical study are especially pronounced in the social and behavioral sciences. In a sense, to be classified and counted is to have one's individuality denied, to be insulted. Marie-Noëlle Bourguet shows that in the Napoleonic census of France there were considerable doubts as to whether it made sense to count bourgeois citizens, since they (unlike the people) are distinctive individuals (Bourguet, 1987). "It is noticeable," remarked P. Sargant Florence in 1929, "that while the poor are continually subjected to statistical enquiries into their family budget, wages, hours of work, the behaviour of the rich is described and accounted for by common sense" (Florence, 1929, p. 218). Indeed, statistical inquiry was closely associated with studies of poverty, labor, nutrition, and crime until well into the twentieth century. Statistics were needed where rationality could be assumed not to operate. Statistical prediction, for example, was first used for two purposes: study of voting behavior, which in the new political science of Graham Wallas and others was assumed to be determined largely by stereotypes and prejudices, and likelihood of violation of parole by released criminals, whose basis in irrationality is even more obvious (see Bulmer, 1984, pp. 162–80; Gough, 1964; Kelley, 1923, pp. 182–5).

The most problematical area of all, from the standpoint of individuality, is the statistical study of opinions, attitudes, ideas, and intellectual achievements. Here statistical classification displays most strikingly its disdain for individuality, and indeed for the individual, since polls and surveys almost always probe for gut feelings rather than rational judgments. It is interesting that the form of intellectual quantification to which there has been the most serious resistance in the academic community is one that directly concerns the scholars themselves, "scientometrics," which uses indices such as number of publications or of researchers as a measure of the vitality of a field, or university, or age cohort. The objects counted, it is argued, are too inhomogeneous for their number to mean much – not all papers, or books, or scientists, are equal. To suppose they are is to reduce the scholar to an assembly-line worker, to ignore the spark of originality that makes for great science.

The point, of course, has some validity, but it is curious that scholars rarely apply it except to themselves.

The values underlying opinion measurement are perhaps clearest in the academic form of this enterprise, which had already become prominent by 1930. American social scientists insisted on a different terminology from that of the pollsters. Although the Round Table on Political Science in 1924 resolved that "opinion need not be the result of a rational process," most, like Stuart Rice, preferred to speak of "attitudes" as implying still less of rationality (Rice, 1928, p. 51). Donald Fleming has located the source of this concern with attitudes in the classic work of the Chicago school of sociology, William Thomas and Florian Znanieckie's book of 1920 on *The Polish Peasant in Europe and America.* The attitudes of Polish peasants, they held, had become rigid – which was fully appropriate for an old-world peasant, but made adaptation to a new life in America very hard. Mere amelioration of their material condition would be inadequate to bring them into the modern world; the social psychologist must instead learn how to elicit more flexible attitudes through suitable reforms (Fleming, 1967, pp. 322–30).

These subrational attitudes underlying social behavior became the object of measurement as a result of L. L. Thurstone's work. Thurstone, who also spent most of his career at Chicago, decided around 1927 that psychophysics could be made a lot more useful and a lot less boring if he took attitudes and prejudices rather than lengths and weights as the object of research. He would measure the attitudes that underlay both words and deeds concerning such topics as prohibition, militarism, or liking for other races and nationalities, by presenting his subjects with a set of statements on the topic in question. He used the first set of subjects to place the statements in order – for example, with those most hostile to blacks on top and those most favorable at the bottom. From the discrepancies in these rankings he was able also to assign distances between each, the unit of measurement being the "standard discriminal error of a single statement of opinion." Using this scale, he could measure the attitudes of a second set of experimental subjects, based on the statements with which they expressed agreement.

Thurstone's statistical procedure virtually presupposed an absence of individuality, or indeed of rationality, in his experimental subjects. What he sought was not ideas, or nuances of opinion, but statements of feeling, more visceral than cognitive, by which the subject could be located along a single axis. This was a technique for dealing with workers, women, immigrants, the poor, and minorities, the usual subjects of sociological investigation, not with people like us (Fleming, 1967, p. 360). "When a man says that we made a mistake in entering the war with Germany, the thing that interests us is not really the string of words as such or even the immediate meaning of the sentence as it stands, but rather the attitude of the speaker." We "shall be dealing with opinions," he went on, "not primarily because of their cognitive content but rather because they serve as the carriers or symbols of the people who express or endorse these opinions" (Thurstone, 1927–28, pp. 531–2, 537).

Attitude measurement received its big stimulus during the Second World War, just as intelligence testing had during the First. The purpose of the army IQ tests had been to help place recruits and select potential officers; here the aim was to check and preserve morale, and to assess adaptation to army life and, later, back to civilian life. Both wars gave practitioners of a nascent social science the opportunity to test and sharpen their tools on a virtually unlimited number of subjects whose participation was enjoined by the army. The analogies of their situation were not lost on the students of attitude, though their services seem to have been rather more highly valued by the army than were the IQ tests of the previous war. This, as Peter Buck (1985) argues, was because the army encountered increasing cynicism towards the end of the war, and was pleased to have personnel policies certified to be favored by the soldiers themselves. Attitude measurement had also in common with IQ testing the use of factor analysis. The sociologists were particularly indebted to Thurstone, not just for his work on attitude, but also for his statistical methods. Samuel Stouffer, Louis Guttman, and Paul Lazarsfeld sought the primary factors of attitudes, just as Thurstone had identified primary mental abilities (Stouffer *et al.*, 1949, pp. 34–7).

Not content with surface opinions, Lazarsfeld used statistics to identify traits that lay below consciousness. He posited, for example, a latent character – favorable attitude toward the army. The soldiers were asked a variety of questions to ascertain if the character was present: Did the soldier like the army? Did he think the army was looking out for his interest? After discharge, would he speak favorably of the army? None of these is decisive with respect to the presence or absence of the latent trait. Even if the soldier's answers are all favorable to the army, that only gives him a high probability of possessing the trait in question. That he may give good reasons for responding sometimes one way and sometimes the other is of no interest. What matters is the inference of attitudes from responses, and the variation in answers is only probabilistic. The subjects, in effect, make mistakes in articulating these attitudes. As with

Thurstone, the researcher is not concerned with conscious, rational thought, but with the unarticulated non-rational attitudes that lie behind these responses (Stouffer, 1950; Lazarsfeld, 1950; also Fleming, 1967).

This approach, we may note, was well suited to the authoritarian structure of the military. The respect of the sociologists for the opinions of these enlisted men was comparable to that of their officers. It is questionable, however, whether their approach implied any less consideration for the views of their subjects than did that of the effusively democratic pollsters, Gallup and Roper. Perhaps the esteem in which the average man was held by these social researchers is less decisive than their obligation to have recourse to statistics in order to acquire concise and reliable information about the attitudes, or thoughts, of large numbers of individuals.

Insurance

The quality of thinking displayed by *l'homme moyen* has also been at issue in debates over the rationality of gambling. These turn on the notion of expectation, either in its simple or modified forms. Twentieth-century economists and psychologists (see 6.6) are caught in much the same contradiction between prescription and description that trapped the eighteenth-century probabilists (see 1.5). On the one hand, they profess to be interested in an empirical account of how people in fact do reason; but on the other, they pronounce their subjects rational or irrational by the standards of probability theory. Of course, unlike their eighteenth-century predecessors, today's upholders of expectation are unwilling to amend probability theory in the face of evidence that most people do not honor its axioms and theorems in practice. Probability theory has become the arbiter of practical rationality, not merely its mathematical codification. When asked to defend this equation of probability with practical rationality, economists often point to the spectacular financial success of the insurance industry: here, they claim, reasoning by expectation coupled with the use of descriptive statistics has proved its worth in the marketplace.

However, the realities of applying probability and statistics to the pricing of insurance premiums are considerably more complicated than this claim suggests. It is true that insurance was the first great practical success in the application of statistical and probabilistic models, and it is still the most pervasive. Daniel Defoe's dream of insurance against "all the Disasters of the World" has almost come true in today's enormous and diverse insurance market. The post of the actuary has evolved from that of a lowly clerk to one of great prestige and power within the insurance firm, a development already obvious in the last century. It is also true that the insurance actuary is the prototype of the new-style expert who owes his authority to the arcane information and techniques he wields, an impression fostered by the amount and sophistication of the mathematics required on accreditation exams. Indeed, such is the reputation of actuaries that some economists have complained of the myth of "actuarial perfection," as if the statistics and the calculations performed on them eliminated all uncertainty from the business (Pfeffer, 1956, p. 5).

Yet in fact not all branches of insurance make great use of such methods, and even those that do must inject a fair amount of educated guesswork and hunches to price their premiums. Life insurance is the oldest form of mathematically based insurance (see 1.6), and the one best fortified with data and techniques. But even that warhorse of the trade, the mortality table, cannot be constructed from the data without a modicum of judgment and a good eye. Graphing the mortality figures yields an irregular scatter of points, not a smooth curve, from which the actuary extracts a mortality curve by "graduation techniques" – i.e. by drawing a curve freehand through the cloud of points. This is a tricky business, for the curve must strike a balance between the regularity expected and the "indications" that new trends have emerged, and the only qualification for making such nice distinctions is long experience in the business (Spoerl, 1951, p. 335). Other even older forms of insurance such as fire and maritime are almost as innocent of statistics as they were three hundred years ago, with a consequently heavier reliance on what is known in the trade as "underwriting judgment" (Pfeffer, 1956, p. 67).

This conservatism is not simply due to Luddism on the part of the underwriters but also to well-founded doubts about whether phenomena like fires and shipwrecks really satisfy the conditions of the statistical model. The policyholders should constitute a well-defined class, large enough to profit from the law of large numbers, and each equally likely to be struck down by misfortune, independent one from the other. Automobile and life insurance meet the criteria of large numbers, but the homogeneity of the risk class is doubtful; fire and workman's compensation insurance (and *a fortiori* insurance against catastrophes like floods) must often pay for disasters that destroy the assumption of independence. Faced with these disparities between model and reality, underwriters are understandably reluctant to trust the enormous sums they insure entirely to statistics. They sometimes use a form of subjective probability to find a compromise between the dictates of the statistical model and those of judgment: when individuals are suspected of deviating from the risk experience of the class, actuaries assign them a "credibility" factor ranging from 0 to 100% as a rough adjustment to the class average.

This assumes that the class is large, and statistics are available for it. But some forms of insurance cover rare or singular events for which no base rates are available: this applies not just to Lloyds of London's policies on the hands of a celebrated concert pianist, but also bizarre or unprecedented disasters – for example, blizzards in Florida or nuclear power plant explosions. Here statistics are no help to the underwriter, who instead fixes upon the proportion between possible claims and the company's assets, and, where human performance is a factor, on his own personal opinion of the competence of those involved. Like his predecessor in sixteenth-century Venice, today's maritime underwriter gauges "the integrity of the shipowner, the skill of the ship's officers, the quality of the crew" (Pfeffer, 1956, p. 68).

Medical diagnosis

As the practice of insurance actuaries shows, it is not necessarily irrational to modify or set aside the canons of probability theory and the tables of statistics when they do not match the phenomena in question. The dream of reducing ineffable judgments to clearcut rules cannot escape the initial judgment of whether the rules – here statistical and probabilistic models – apply to the particular case. Even when the statistics are at hand and the model is a reasonable approximation of the situation, judgments about how to apply the rules are not straightforward. Such judgments are sometimes of considerable subtlety and proportionate importance, as in the use of mammography to diagnose breast cancer. Mammography works on the principle that malignant cells absorb X-rays differently from benign cells, and is used by physicians to help decide whether a patient should have a biopsy operation, an expensive procedure usually done under general anesthesia that often results in scars and sometimes in infection. Like all such tests, mammography is not 100% accurate. The clinician's problem is how to weight the evidence from the mammography with that from family and personal history, symptoms, and other particulars in deciding whether to perform a biopsy or not.

Here the difficulty lies not in the availability of statistics – the predictive accuracy of mammography has been extensively studied, as have base rates for breast cancer in various populations – nor in the existence of a probabilistic model for such decisions – Bayes' theorem fits such situations quite well. Nor does it lie in the clinician's mistrust of statistics in diagnosing the individual case, for here physicians themselves also talk the language of probabilities, both qualitative and quantitative. Rather, it lies in the conceptualization of the problem. A survey of the medical literature on mammography reveals that physicians regularly confuse the predictive accuracy of the test (the probability the patient has cancer given a positive mammography) with its retrospective accuracy (the probability of a positive mammography given that the patient has cancer) (Eddy, 1982, pp. 254–6). These probabilities are by no means interchangeable, any more than the probability that someone is a man given that he or she is President of the United States is with the probability that someone is President of the United States given that he is a man. Studies of mammography report a predictive accuracy of 79 to 90%, but it is the retrospective accuracy that is at issue in the clinical decision to go ahead with a biopsy. Equating the two can result in errors of an order of magnitude or more.

Even when physicians are able to distinguish correctly the predictive and retrospective accuracies, they must still deal with the impact of this evidence on the patient's prior probability of having breast cancer. Imagine the patient consults her doctor because she has discovered a lump in her breast. Her prior probability of having cancer is signficiantly different from that for an asymptomatic patient examined in a screening clinic. If both patients have positive mammograms, Bayes' theorem shows that, even assuming the same predictive accuracies in both cases, the probabilities of each having cancer diverge sharply. Yet practicing physicians, following the medical texts and journals that instruct them, usually ignore or drastically underweight these prior probabilities in evaluating the import of a positive mammogram, greatly increasing the number of biopsies performed. Physicians do reason probabilistically in such cases, but here a little probability, like a little learning, can be a dangerous thing.

Probability and the law

The attempts to apply statistical and probabilistic models to an ever-widening circle of phenomena, from life expectancies to traffic snarls, carry with them a certain vision of the nature of these things. Other recent applications in medicine and the law sometimes bespeak a vision of how the world ought to be, as well as how it is. Methods originally introduced to test new drugs or to detect discrimination more objectively have an ethical as well as a technical component, since they require that individuals be classified and averaged. The application of statistics to medicine or law commits its users willy-nilly to new values, just as statistical measurement committed them to new objects. In this context statistics becomes the vehicle of utilitariansim, championing the greatest good for the greatest number, even at the expense of occasional injustice (or worse) to this or that individual.

The conflict between this utilitarian perspective and the traditional right to be treated as an individual before the law lies at the heart of current controversies over whether statistics belongs in the courtroom. Statisticians have taken the stand as expert witnesses for almost a century now: their testimony was used in the Dreyfus case to establish the authorship of letters by a comparison of handwriting quirks; and more recently in cases like *People v. Collins* in California, where the prosecution based its case on the improbability of a random match between the defendants and the culprits, both answering to the description of an interracial couple with a yellow car. (Convictions in both cases were ultimately reversed and the statistical arguments discredited.) However, the anti-discrimination legislation of the past three decades has considerably widened and deepened the legal role of statistics as an instrument of proof. Rather than arguing in the traditional fashion of intent to discriminate against this or that individual, lawyers now pore over the long-term pattern of hiring and firing to make their case that minorities or one or the other sex were victims of discrimination.

Sometimes the situation is intrinsically statistical, as in the suit brought against the Los Angeles Department of Water and Power by its female employees. They charged that the pension plan was discriminatory because it required larger contributions from female employees on the actuarial grounds that they live longer on average and therefore (again, on average) benefited more than their male colleagues. The Supreme Court agreed, upholding the principle of "fairness to individuals rather than fairness to classes." However, the court trod gingerly, adding that this decision was not intended to revolutionize the insurance industry, and there were dissenting voices that insisted on the inevitability of the statistical approach where large groups are concerned. Chief Justice Burger in effect put restrictions on the right of individuals to be treated as such: "This is in no sense a failure to treat women as 'individuals'. . . It is to treat them as individually as it is possible to do in the face of the unknowable length of each individual life. Individually, every woman has the same statistical possibility of outliving men. This is the essence of basing decisions on reliable statistics when individual determinations are infeasible or, as here, impossible" (quoted in Player, 1980, p. 369). But an English judge commenting on another case involving mortality tables drew precisely the opposite conclusion from the irreducible uncertainty of applying statistical generalizations to the particular case, contending that "nobody can say whether an individual plaintiff is an average man, or that he will live for the expectation of an average man his age" (Downton, 1982, p. 397).

In general, the courts in the United States and Great Britain have taken a jaundiced view of any innovation that threatens to undermine the particularity of the judicial perspective. They have not only resisted the statistical aggregation of individuals, but also the introduction of "summary statistics" that purport to be better and more consistent measures of important legal notions. Their proponents aim to streamline judicial decisions by applying a single criterion to all cases. For example, "voting power," defined as the probability that an individual will cast the tie-breaking vote in an election, might be applied to reapportionment cases (Finkelstein, 1978). But both the courts and many legal scholars have balked at such suggestions, holding that mathematical simplifications filter out particulars that might be essential to a fair decision in any given trial. Indeed, the courts have hinted that statistical justice is a contradiction in terms, for it replaces the individual with an average, the case at hand with a generality, and the exercise of judgment with the application of rules.

Despite this judicial attitude toward statistics of suspicion verging on hostility, statistics and probability have modified key legal concepts like negligence, liability, and intent. In the late nineteenth century the startling regularities in the annual number of workplace accidents led to workman's compensation legislation that all but eliminated the ancient idea of the responsibility of both employer and employee for the safety of the workplace. The dismal predictability of accidents made them also appear inevitable, severing the old legal equation of forseeability and responsibility (Defort *et al.*, 1977). In the past decade a rash of damage suits concerning environmental and occupational carcinogens – the so-called "toxic torts" – have similarly altered legal concepts of causation and intention. Courts have traditionally required that plaintiffs prove cause in order to claim liability, and causation understood in necessary and sufficient terms. However, the epidemiological evidence linking, say, smoking and lung cancer does not meet these standards, being mostly assertions of correlations. For example, the central epidemiological concept of "attributable risk," or the proportion of all new cases of a disease due to a given toxic substance, is reckoned probabilistically: How likely is the observed correlation of disease and exposure to have occurred by chance? This is difficult to square with the legal "but for" criterion – "but for this act, that damage would not have come to pass" – with its orientation toward particular events rather than the larger samples of epidemiological studies (Brennan and Carter, 1985, pp. 51–2). However, regulatory legislation specifically couched in epidemiological terms has forced the courts to revise older notions in the statistical direction.

As in the case of workman's compensation and discrimination legislation, the rise of statistical views of causation has edged out the personal elements of intent and responsibility: paradoxically, the chains of causation are both too tangled and uncertain in the individual case, and too unambiguous and certain in the mass for these traditional values to make sense. Statistics tends toward ethical behaviorism, in which the simple fact of the matter – a record of fewer women hired, of birth defects associated with a drug – suffices for conviction without further probing of motives.

Medical therapeutics

The ethical clash between traditional professional values centered on the individual and the statistical necessity of taking averages is even sharper in medicine, where matters of life and death often hang in the balance. The ethical and epistemological issues implicit in this are as consequential as any presented by modern science. Not all of the pertinent disciplines have given much attention to these issues, but in medicine they are well known and have been sharply formulated. Statistics contributed enormously to the public health measures, effected mainly since the 1830s, that constitute by much the most important medical contribution to longevity and general health in the world. Perhaps the greatest pioneers in this area were William Farr and Louis-René Villermé, who studied death rates by district, especially during cholera years, to resolve the conditions of housing and sanitation that were responsible for the differential mortality (see Eyler, 1979; Coleman, 1982). Studies of puerperal fever, by Semmelweiss, and of scurvy, are legendary, as is the reluctance of the relevant authorities to enact the measures that the statistics seemed so obviously to dictate. That reluctance was bolstered by the persistence of variation in the statistics that the advocates of the new remedies or procedures could not explain.

Ironically, the new standards of experimental statistical demonstration enunciated by R. A. Fisher after he worked them out in the context of agricultural research have not made the problems of medical research any easier. Fisher who had, notoriously, accepted money as a consultant to the tobacco industry, refused to accept the findings of public health studies linking smoking with cancer, for the very simple reason that his experimental protocol had not been followed. There was, of course, no question that those who smoked were found to have much higher rates of lung cancer than those who did not, and indeed that the risk increased monotonically with number of cigarettes smoked per day. But the world is full of spurious correlations, and this one might be caused by a genetic factor that tends both to promote smoking and to cause cancer (see Box, 1978, pp. 473–6). An experiment, Fisher believed, could settle the issue; we need only assign individuals to two groups, smokers and non-smokers, in advance and at random, and take care that they maintain their smoking habits throughout the experiment. We can then analyze the resulting cancer rates in the various treatments to determine the actual effect of smoking on cancer. But such an experiment would be at once impossible and unethical.

Tests of therapies involve closer medical supervision and greater physician control than do public health studies. Hence experimentation often is possible – but the problem of ethics is scarcely less pressing on that account. Any therapy whose mechanism is not understood in complete detail – and that includes virtually all therapies – can only be shown to be safe and effective when adequate experimental controls are used. But if there is reason to suppose the experimental therapy superior to its alternatives, it is difficult to justify withholding it, even if the solidity of the knowledge thereby attained will result in the saving of far more lives in the long run. The new double-blind procedures, in which neither patient nor physician knows who is in the control group and who in the experimental, heightens the dilemma. There is, believes at least one unnamed researcher, "no justification for adding to the anguish of a cancer patient by introducing the irrational element of 'flipping a coin' " (see Miké and Good, 1977, p. 678).

Sinclair Lewis portrayed the moral delicacy of medical testing with controls in his novel *Arrowsmith*, first published in 1925. Martin Arrowsmith journeys to a Caribbean island infested with plague with the dual mission of ending it and of testing his new bacteriophage inoculation. He is confident the phage will be effective, but he plans to administer it to only half the population, at least in some areas, and to leave the rest as controls. The public health enthusiast who accompanies him, Sondelius, refuses to accept the inoculation until Arrowsmith agrees to renounce his cruel experiment and administer the phage universally, and later dies of the plague, his dying words an appeal to give the phage to everyone. The governor of the island, when told of Arrowsmith's plan, announces that "as far as possible I shall certainly prevent you Yankee vivisectionists from coming in and using us as a lot of sanguinary corpses" (Lewis, 1925, p. 376). Arrowsmith nonetheless commences his experiment, confident that in the long run a conclusive result will save more lives in Asia than will be lost now on this little island. But the death of his wife destroys his icy resolve, and he wrecks the experiment by permitting the control population to receive the treatment after all.

Arrowsmith's fictional experiment is certainly unethical by modern standards, and the ingenuity of medical researchers is sometimes greatly taxed to justify double-blind, controlled studies in cases of serious illness. (We should add, however, that most of the truly bizarre and cruel medical experiments carried out in modern times predated (or ignored) the rigid experimental procedures that came with contemporary statistical methods.) Something like Laplace's equidistribution of ignorance is often posited: since we have no real knowledge of the efficacy of the experimental treatment, we assume provisionally that it is just as likely to be an improvement as not. But ignorance is rarely total. Perhaps the first large-scale randomized, double-blind clinical trial, in 1946, was a study of streptomycin in tuberculosis, and was justified by the convenient shortage of foreign currency in postwar Britain, which made it impossible to secure enough streptomycin to treat everyone. For that reason it was ethically legitimate, perhaps even obligatory, to use what streptomycin was available in a careful test that would secure sound knowledge for the benefit of future patients (Tukey, 1977b, p. 682). Current policy in the United States takes advantage of a different contingency. Federal law generally permits the use of new drugs only after, or in, approved clinical trials. That lifts the burden from experimenters of justifying the deprivation of a highly promising treatment from the control population. The law is more lenient on the use of old drugs for new purposes, and the problem of justifying experimental study correspondingly aggravated.

7.4 NEW RULES

The Bayesian juror

Counting patients, victims, or expressions of opinion implies that, for the purpose of the census, all of the units are identical. By its very nature, counting erases the distinctions that matter so crucially to the individual

– the motives for suicide, the arguments for a political stance, the originality of a monograph – in order to make global patterns visible. Descriptive statistics thus mask whatever individual circumstances or reasons created the act, attitude, or article counted; hence its longstanding associations with sociological condescension and irrationality. However, another kind of statistics now much in vogue harkens back to the reasonable calculus of the eighteenth century. Using the same tools as the classical probabilists – Bayes' theorem, expectation, subjective probabilities – the new generation of probabilists seeks to translate expert judgments into numbers and rules. The motives are the old ones: to provide an ersatz rationality for the perplexed, to mechanize inductive inference, and to forge consensus by standardizing the methods of decision-making. Some of the problems are equally old – for example, mathematizing the evaluation of legal evidence.

Since 1970, the issue of whether jurors should be instructed in how to draw inferences from evidence using Bayes' theorem (or, should they prove to be ineducable, replaced by expert statisticians) has excited a buzz of controversy among judges, lawyers, and scholars. Since there is obviously no way to test empirically whether Bayesian inference leads to more correct verdicts than does intuition, the debate turns on the question of whether Bayes' theorem captures the essentials of sound legal reasoning. The pro-Bayes faction argues that Bayes' theorem is simply a formal version of such reasoning, and that if jurors do not already conform to its dictates, then they should be taught to do so. They also proclaim the advantages of rendering inferences explicit, uniform, and consistent, and cite recent psychological studies to the effect that lay intuitions are hopelessly muddled according to the canons of probability theory (Finkelstein and Fairley, 1970). The opposition counters that Bayes' theorem is a flawed model of legal reasoning, for although it does measure the strength of inference given a certain body of evidence, it does not attend to the weight of the evidence per se. Moreover, evidence adduced to impeach other evidence may violate the axiom of additivity in probability theory (Brilmayer and Kornhauser, 1978, p. 145).

Introducing Bayesian inference into the courtroom would dramatically alter the trial process. Since a zero prior probability of guilt would make it impossible to apply Bayes' theorem, time-honored principles like "innocent until proven guilty" would have to be abandoned. Any application of Bayes' theorem must supply prior probabilities, and the difficulties of fixing these in a state of ignorance are notorious among probabilists (Keynes, 1921). For this reason, most of the examples to date treat identification problems using quasi-scientific evidence: for example, given the results of blood-type tests, what is the probability that the accused is the father of a given child? In Poland, some 1500 paternity cases were submitted to probabilistic analysis of this sort (Fairley, 1975). But since it is the exception rather than the rule for even forensic evidence to be presented in quantitative form – an expert is more likely to describe an accidental match of handprints as "rare" than to state precisely how rare – jurors must somehow combine mathematical with non-mathematical evidence. The pro-Bayesians conclude that this is reason enough to translate as much evidence as possible into numbers, even if they are only rough approximations; the anti-Bayesians warn against the dangers of specious quantification and of overweighting "hard" evidence *vis-à-vis* "soft." Once again, statistical and probabilistic methods tend to push considerations of individual motive and intent into the background: "One consequence of mathematical proof, then, may be to shift the focus away from such elements as volition, knowledge, and intent, and towards such elements as identity and occurrence – for the same reasons that the hard variables tend to swamp the soft" (Tribe, 1971, p. 1366).

Probability and risk

The controversy over Bayesian jurors is at root a controversy over expertise: what is it, and who has it? Those who would give lay jurors a crash course in probability theory believe that Bayes' theorem is a model, in both senses of the word, of how inferences derive from evidence. Just as for the eighteenth-century probabilists, it is a description, albeit a schematic one, of how the best legal minds reason, and a prescription for the rest of us (see 1.8). To teach jurors Bayes' theorem is thus to make instant experts of them – and to suggest politely that their untutored reasoning about such matters is deficient. Expertise becomes a technique to be mastered, rather than experience to be amassed, a leitmotiv of the applied literature on statistical inference since R. A. Fisher's enormously influential *Design of Experiments* (1935). In principle, this could democratize expertise, for experience is the hardest of all schools, but in fact the character of the techniques, set forth in intimidating mathematics, has widened the gap between experts and laymen. Those who oppose the techniques as bad likenesses of what they allegedly portray retort that right reasoning lies with the laymen, and the battle is joined.

These themes repeat like a refrain in the fledgling discipline of risk perception. Indeed, its *raison d'être* is the stubborn disagreement between experts and laymen over what we should fear most. The experts define risk in terms of expectation, as the product of the probability of the event and its outcome value. Numerous psychological studies show that laymen use different criteria – for example, the potential for irrevocable disaster – to assess their risks, fearing power plant accidents more than the far more frequent automobile accidents. In the cases of automobile accidents, trustworthy statistics exist, but that is more the exception than the rule in risk assessment. In practice, the experts' expectation rule proves singularly difficult to apply, for neither probability nor outcome value is easy to come by. In some cases, the probabilities can be derived from statistics, as for automobile accidents. But the most hotly discussed disasters are too rare and/or too novel for such data to have been collected, and the risk assessors must resort to guesswork and the subjective probabilities mentioned above. Some have simply thrown up their hands in dismay: "We want to do things rationally. We want to quantify, so we can compare. And we see that as 'good.' At today's level of information (and knowledge) I see substantial difficulties in quantifying risks. . . I remember reading that Pythagoras said 'All is number.' I think he was wrong" (Schneiderman, 1980, p. 37). Those that persevere must tackle the even more formidable problems of quantifying outcome values. Here, even the units are debated: traditionally, outcome values have been expressed in monetary terms – for example, so many dollars' worth of damage from a hurricane – but the risk assessors must also deal in the currency of lives, and somehow make the two commensurable. Current discussion centers not on the question of whether life can be quantified, but only on how: in terms of earning capacity lost? of what would be spent in medical services to save the life? of what individuals say they would pay to reduce the risk of death by a certain amount? of the damages actually awarded in court? (Moore, 1983, p. 180). Comparing risks to permit rational choices among them is the chief objective of risk assessment, and comparability poses even more delicate problems of constructing units. For example, inspectors of occupational hazards argue whether they should keep track of the number of deaths per year per million employees in a given industry, or the number of fatal accidents in a working lifetime (about 100,000 hours).

In cases where objective statistics are impossible to come by, because the risk is either too rare or too new or a unique case, risk assessors often resort to subjective probabilities. Once ridiculed by John Stuart Mill as the quantification of ignorance, the enterprise has regained its respectability with the rigorous revival of a personalist interpretation of probability by B. de Finetti and L. Savage in the 1950s. Probabilities have once more become subjective degrees of belief, but they are no longer anchored in objective experience, as they were for the classical probabilists. Still, there is more than an echo of the classical program in the use of such subjective probabilities to rationalize decision-making and to mechanize judgment.

Corporate executives, weather forecasters, and nuclear safety experts are all being schooled in the art of quantifying their hunches using subjective probabilities. These probabilities are "correct" insofar as they are internally consistent and mirror the assessor's true state of mind, rather than any state of the world. Usually the assessor is asked to choose between a bet on the event in question – will it rain tomorrow? shall we drill for oil at this site? – and a ticket for a lottery with given odds until a point of indifference is located, fixing the 50% probability level. The same process is then repeated to divide up the continuum more finely. It will not do simply to ask the assessor straight out for a subjective probability, for most naive responses tend to crystallize around values like 0, 50%, 75%, 100%, rather than taking full advantage of the continuum, and to confuse small probabilities that are nonetheless orders of magnitude apart (e.g. 0.001 and 0.0001), a particular difficulty for those estimating rare events. Considerable training is required, including persuading the scrupulous assessor "that he or she knows *something* about the amount of uncertainty" in cases where personal experience is nil – for example, with nuclear power plant disasters or speciality insurance of the Lloyds variety (Selvidge, 1975, pp. 204–5) – and that the exercise makes sense.

Why put numbers to judgments, particularly those upon matters where little or no information of any kind is forthcoming? Not only are such subjective probability judgments empty of any new empirical content; the mistakes most people habitually make despite arduous training strongly suggest that probabilistic thinking in the formal sense does not come naturally. This does not imply that people are bad at practical judgments in uncertain situations – a recent study of racetrack betting suggests they are very good indeed, especially when the stakes are high (Hoerl and Fallin, 1974) – only that they fumble with numbers when suspending judgment would be the better part of valor, a professional hazard for risk analysts who are hardest pressed for answers when the uncertainty is greatest (Levi, 1980, p. 441). The vogue for subjective probabilities is a vogue for numbers, and for all that numbers symbolize in our quantifrenic culture: precision, objectivity, truth to fact. It is indeed ironic that subjective probabilities live up to these virtues only to the extent that they are derived from the ineffable personal experience they are intended to supplant.

To the disappointment of the risk assessors, even when they were able to agree among themselves on the magnitude of various risks using such techniques, no amount of education could persuade the general public to follow suit. The rapidly expanding discipline of risk perception was born out of psychological studies that revealed systematic disparities between expert and lay views (referred to as "objective" and "subjective" risks, respectively, by the risk analysts) on the relative dangers of automobile accidents, floods, pregnancies, nuclear power plant explosions, etc. (Slovic, Fischhoff, and Lichtenstein, 1982). No psychological study was required to discover the widespread and vehement opposition among laymen to nuclear power plants, even though the experts estimated astronomically small probabilities for devastating accidents, and puzzled over public indifference to what they calculated to be the far greater risk of fatal automobile accidents. The public for their part dismissed the experts as "insensitive, and, sometimes, dangerous" (Kaspar, 1980, p. 78). Massive education campaigns, like that conducted on behalf of the nuclear industry in Sweden, failed to budge public opposition.

The experts shook their heads over what they perceived as mass hysteria and irrationality, and explained it by historical associations between nuclear power and nuclear weapons. They turned to psychologists and sociologists for help in understanding what sorts of irrational but nonetheless systematic factors – a preference for voluntary over involuntary risk, an innate tendency to overweight the outcome value and to underweight the probability in intuitive reckonings of expectation when the "disaster potential" is large, an unwarranted proportioning of risk to the vividness with which the event is depicted – that might distort lay risk perceptions. They created a new discipline to study the subject. Governments in Europe and the United States were also disappointed when large numbers of their citizens rejected the expert opinion they had commissioned. They had sought a solution to a technical problem about the relative risk-benefits of various forms of energy, in the hopes of shifting the decision from the realm of values and politics to that of calculations and consensus. But the experts' solution fanned rather than dampened controversy. Far from bowing to the much vaunted objectivity of the experts, laymen resented the intrusion of objectivity into an area where they believed values should count. "It is a travesty of rational thought to pretend that it is best to take value-free decisions in matters of life and death" (quoted in Douglas and Wildavsky, 1982, p. 73). Above all, they refused to accept the issue as a problem to be solved, insisting that it was rather a question to be debated. Here the ideals of technical expertise collided head-on with those of participatory democracy (Nelkin and Pollak, 1980).

Gambling

The very oldest divergence of expert probabilistic and lay opinion concerns gambling, and three-odd centuries have not brought them any closer together. Probabilists continue to condemn gambling as a losing proposition by calculations of expectation or utility; gamblers continue to ignore them. Since Girolamo Cardano, very few probabilists have had much firsthand experience at the gaming tables, although Karl Pearson once made a study of the roulette wheels at Monte Carlo. The averages were fair: out of 16,019 spins, red came up 8,053 times, deviating from the calculated expected value by only 0.25%. The standard deviations, on the other hand, suggested too many switches from red to black to be explained by chance (Pearson, [1894] 1897, p. 57; also Moore, 1983, p. 134). Probabilists have been almost unanimous in distrusting gambling systems, most of which are based on the principle of doubling bets on even chances. For example, with the Martingale, you begin with a bet of one unit on an even chance, doubling the bet every time you lose until you win, so that your net gain is one unit. The problem is that the stake mounts very quickly, either exhausting your capital or going over the casino maximum. With the advent of large-scale racetrack betting in the late nineteenth century, probability calculations became in any case less relevant than knowledge of the horses and the total amount bet on a given horse up to race time, since bookmakers change odds constantly to minimize their potential losses.

Economists, however, are still haunted by contradictions between widespread gambling and what they compute to be rational self-interest. This is in part due to the impact of the neo-(Daniel)Bernoullian theory of rational choice advanced by John von Neumann and O. Morgenstern's *Theory Of Games* (1944), which revived maximization of expected value as a prime criterion of economic rationality and forced economists literally to rationalize away the phenomenon of gambling (Ignatin and Smith, 1976; Lopes, 1986). Their predicament was further complicated by the need to distinguish irrational gambling from rational investments, particularly highly speculative investments like commodity future trading or even some forms of insurance. Economists generally admit the structural similarity of betting at a casino and betting on the stock market from the perspective of expectation, and fall back on the moral rather than mathematical distinction between investments that serve a "useful economic function" and those that do not. However, the distinction is hard to maintain for syndicates like the Coral Index, a scheme permitting investors to buy and sell units of the Financial Times Index in London (or the Dow Jones Industrial Index in New York) – i.e. outright betting on the market (Moore, 1983, p. 143).

7.5 CONCLUSION

Probability and statistics have indeed become the very guide of life. Their impact on daily life, as well as the sciences, is enormous and still growing. In this chapter, we have focused on those areas where the application of these tools has made for changes, stunning and subtle, in facts and in values; in reasons and unreason. Just because these applications cut so deep into traditional ways of thinking, they are bound to be the most controversial. This is not to say that statisticians are everywhere embattled. On the contrary, there are a great many less ambitious applications of statistics, broadly construed, that are almost universally accepted, like the census and the registration of traffic fatalities. However, there is no application so innocuous as to be neutral, in the sense of simply mirroring the bare facts of the matter. As we have seen, even the simple act of counting involves assumptions that can color attitudes and interpretations. It is part of our Pythagorean creed to believe that quantification is merely description, but the reverberations of the applications of statistics show how far this claim strays from the mark. These applications have called new objects into being, coined new values, and established new standards of rationality and new claims to authority. It is also part of the Pythagorean creed to believe that with numbers comes certainty. Thus the seeming paradox that, as the empire of chance has steadily expanded, chance's twin uncertainty appears to have just as steadily retreated.

Il faut parier.
Blaise Pascal (1669)

8

◁ ══════════════════════════════════ ▷

The implications of chance

8.1 PROBABILISTIC IMPERIALISM

The empire of chance began with an unsteady foothold in gambling problems some three hundred years ago and now sprawls over whole conceptual continents. All of the natural and social sciences belong to its territories, and there have been conquests – cliometrics, statistical comparisons of literary style – even in the humanities. It also encompasses important parts of law, medicine, industry, and practical economics, and, in its descriptive statistical aspect, has breached almost every wall. Insofar as we listen to weather reports, ponder political polls, undergo medical tests, pursue the sciences, plot the standard of living index, buy insurance, or even read the newspaper, we are all its subjects.

In these pages we have followed the steady and occasionally explosive growth of this empire as probability theory and statistics evolved as mathematical disciplines and at the same time acquired ever more diverse applications. These developments of course went hand-in-hand, but the mere existence of a new mathematical technique was not sufficient in itself to win the theory new applications. Here interpretation and analogy played critical roles, as we have seen. Whether probability was interpreted as a degree of certainty, as a relative frequency, as a propensity, or in some other way, determined the plausibility of particular applications, be they to evaluations of legal evidence or to life insurance. A shift in interpretations could discredit applications that had once been the core of probabilistic practice, as the fate of classical probability theory in the early nineteenth century shows. However, in our century the tendency has been to accumulate rather than to exclude interpretations of probability, and with them, a lengthening list of applications. Almost every application ever attempted by a probabilist is alive and well today in some form, however dubious its reputation in the intervening years.

The empire of chance grew in three phases. First, techniques and often interpretations were borrowed across disciplinary lines via analogy. Second, as these techniques came to be applied in this manner to numerous different subjects, they became truly formal, shedding the interpretations that had originally guided their use. Finally, as a result of this expansion and formalization, probability theory and statistics became effectively ecumenical with respect to meaning and interpretation in particular applications. Whereas in the eighteenth and nineteenth centuries one or another view of what probability meant had dominated applications as well as more philosophical discussions, in the twentieth century these various meanings peacefully coexist, at least in the context of application. Probabilists of a philosophical bent still debate the relative merits of frequentist or personalist interpretations, but the practice is eclectic. For example, psychologists analyze the degree to which their subjects reason by Bayes' theorem using a combination of Fisherian and Neyman–Pearsonian methods (see 6.4, 6.5).

Analogy was the bridge along which particular probabilistic techniques migrated from one discipline to another. The wanderings of the normal distribution from astronomy to sociology to physics to psychology and beyond is a dramatic and instructive example of a pattern that repeats several times over in the history of probability and statistics. A technique transplanted from one domain to another retains the marks of the original context of application. For example, when Adolphe Quetelet applied the curve describing observational errors in astronomy to social statistics, he took over the substance as well as the form; the interpretation as well as the technique. If astronomers understood the normal distribution as a scattering of observations around the mean, true value for, say, the position of a comet, then social statisticians must understand the same distribution as a scattering of nature's "errors" around the mean "true" value for, say, the moral condition of a nation (see 2.5). James Clerk Maxwell and Ludwig Boltzmann added another link to the analogical chain when they applied the social statistical version of the normal distribution to the velocities of molecules in an ideal gas. Just as unpredictable individuals produced social regularities taken *en masse*, so individual molecules inaccessible to observation produced a uniform temperature taken *en masse* (see 5.5, 5.6). In the cases of Quetelet, Maxwell, and Boltzmann, the analogies are quite explicit, revealing how tightly (and suggestively) intertwined mathematical technique and applied content could be.

There are numerous other examples of such analogical chaining, usually across disciplinary boundaries. For example, the route Fisherian (and later, Neyman–Pearsonian) statistics took to psychology ran through agricultural treatments and educational administration. Applications in psychology still show traces of these practical origins: in agriculture and education, a significance test leads to a yes–no decision concerning some course of action – e.g. whether to use a certain fertilizer or to adopt a new curriculum (see 6.3). Similarly, the social scientist makes a decision to accept or reject a hypothesis after each experiment, although scientific experiments usually have no immediate practical consequences which demand a decision of that sort or permit the estimation of the cost of errors. Bayesian methods that successively revise probabilities of hypotheses in light of new evidence might be considered more in keeping with the ideals of the scientific method, but for historical reasons are not part of established psychological practice.

In such early cases of interdisciplinary migration, more than the techniques are imported. The techniques could be compared to the Trojan horse, packed with assumptions about content and interpretation that may or may not be made explicit, and that may or may not fit the new context of application. But these assumptions and their consequences come to light only once they are already within the gates of a discipline.

Eventually however the sheer number and variety of such applications wore away the marks of their particular origins. Since its debut in late eighteenth-century error theory, the normal distribution has acquired so many applications in so many disciplines that it has indeed become a "mere" technique. To be sure, certain conditions must hold in order for the distribution to be applicable, and something of Francis Galton's enthusiasm lingers in the conviction that practically everything is normally distributed. But neither these conditions nor enthusiasm commit today's user of the normal distribution to the very specific interpretations that were part and parcel of the early history of the technique. A similar story might be told about the techniques of correlation and factor analysis. For Galton, regression towards the mean described biological heredity, and Spearman's factor analysis was for him a theory of general intelligence (see 4.4, 7.2). Now both techniques are widespread, and are no longer tied to their original contexts of application.

The field of mathematical statistics owes its existence to the accumulation of such multipurpose tools. It has joined together what the descriptive statisticians of the nineteenth century pulled asunder in their fervor for facts; namely, mathematical probability theory and empirical statistics. Techniques for measurement, sampling, and inference have enormously expanded the domain of applications for probability and statistics in the twentieth century, to the point where specific consider-ations of context and content seem secondary. The same techniques apply to sampling the political opinions of an electorate, the quality of products turned out by an assembly line, and the genes of organisms in reproduction. The mathematical statistician is as flexible and ubiquitous as these techniques, and is as likely to be consulted by medical researchers testing a new therapy as by architects of an office building worried about elevator traffic. Statisticians are in a sense experts about everything and nothing. Although long experience with medical regimens and elevators can't hurt, their claim to expertise rests upon techniques that do not in-here in any concrete subject matter – and for that very reason are breathtakingly general in application. These experts are, as it were, the knights errant of the empire of chance (see 3.7).

8.2   WHAT DOES PROBABILITY MEAN?

The interpretations of probability that lie behind these myriad appli-cations are a multifarious lot. Since Siméon-Denis Poisson's celebrated distinction between "raison de croire" and "chance" in 1837, it has been the received wisdom among probabilists that probability is a Janus-faced concept, with objective and subjective sides. Rudolf Carnap (1945) identified these sides with degrees of belief and relative frequencies, re-spectively, and believed the dualism to be irreducible. Although there have been militants in both the frequentist and subjective camps in recent years, the consensus has favored Carnap's opinion. The dualism is the basis of Ian Hacking's recent stimulating exploration of the origins of probability (Hacking, 1975). However, a close study of the history of probability in the context of its applications reveals that the situation is considerably more complex than this simple binary opposition would suggest. Here, we can do little more than point to that complexity, in the hope that others will complete and bring order to the enumeration we begin here.

The first generation of probabilistic works, from Huygens through Jakob Bernoulli, already interpreted probability in a variety of distinct senses that pertained to different kinds of subjects. Degrees of certainty (or degrees of probative weight) were states of mind – or rather, states of minds, for they were intersubjective, if not objective (see 1.3). The probative weight of this witness' testimony or that piece of circumstantial

evidence was assumed to be the same for all competent judges, and therefore has closer affinities in the twentieth century to John Maynard
Keynes' logical probabilities than to Leonard Savage's personal
probabilities. These latter should also be distinguished from the psychological probabilities of real (as opposed to ideal) subjects, which may not
be internally consistent, or even numerically continuous.

The early probabilists also spoke of degrees of facility, predicated of
physical objects: physically symmetric gambling devices are the classic but
not the sole example; Jakob Bernoulli sometimes writes as if human
bodies had such facilities or propensities with respect to susceptibility to
various mortal diseases. Quetelet's "penchants" toward crime or marriage
resemble these physical facilities, but apply to averages of collectives,
"*l'homme moyen*", rather than to single physical objects. Karl Popper's propensity interpretation of the probability that an atomic nucleus will decay
comes quite close to the original facility notion. Probabilities were also
early and long understood as frequencies applied to individual objects insofar as they are members of collectives; the original instances were predictions of individual longevity on the basis of mortality statistics. During
the heyday of descriptive statistics in the nineteenth century, this
frequentist interpretation drove all others from the field, and is still
strongly represented in current philosophy and applications of probability,
such as in the theory of random genetic drift.

There are still other interpretations of probability so unremarked as to
have no convenient twentieth-century label like "frequentist" or "propensity." Consider, for example, John Arbuthnot's 1710 attempt to enlist
mathematical probability and empirical statistics in the service of the
argument from design, or Daniel Bernoulli's similar argument concerning
the origins of the solar system. Arbuthnot argued that the observed proportion of male to female human births in the ratio of 18 : 17 over many
years was extremely improbable if the process was governed by chance.
Just what Arbuthnot meant by "chance" cannot be comfortably reconciled with frequency or propensity interpretations of probability, despite
his analogy of a two-sided die marked "M" and "F." As Nicholas
Bernoulli pointed out at the time, the birth statistics were perfectly compatible with a chance mechanism – say, an urn filled with 35 identical
balls, 17 marked "F" and 18 marked "M." (D'Alembert made analogous
criticisms of Daniel Bernoulli's planetary argument.) Yet Arbuthnot (and
De Moivre) insisted that because the discrepancy served a purpose, namely
insuring an equal number of men and women of marriageable age, it
could not be ascribed to "mere chance". That is, an event cannot be

identified as a chance event independently of considerations of purpose or design (see 1.7). Here, probability pertained to the old Aristotelian sense of chance: absence of purpose, order, or cause. For later natural theologians like William Paley, chance still meant simply absence of design. This sense was preserved by the Darwinians, with their emphasis on "chance" variations – i.e. those not occasioned by their usefulness to the organism (4.3).

There were also "practical probabilities" in which the probabilities were in effect invisible, since the situation called for a combined judgment of probabilities and outcome value. These sorts of expectations, which concern the preferences of agents, were the backbone of the first formulations of mathematical probability (see 1.2), and are familiar to today's probabilists from de Finetti's and Savage's system of personal probabilities. True to their name, practical probabilities surface only in cases that call for concrete action, like betting. They are subjective in that they express an individual's conviction that an event will or will not come to pass, but unlike degrees of certainty, they are neither intersubjective, nor do they stand alone. They are an indissoluble part of the expectation in which they arise.

This short list of the things probability has been thought to measure is far from exhaustive, and it is a list, not a taxonomy. But it is still enough to cast doubt on the view that probability can mean two, and only two things. The historical relationships of probability theory and statistics with determinism and indeterminism also defy any simple generalization. Probability and statistics have served both masters at one or another point in their history, depending on which interpretation of probability was then in the ascendant. Probability understood as a measure of ignorance harmonized with the most uncompromising form of determinism; probability understood as a measure of real variability could admit randomness to the world, or even suggest a fundamental stochasticity. In order to follow the twists and turns in the relationships between probability theory and determinism, we must first survey the several possible brands of determinism.

8.3   DETERMINISM

It seems useful to us to distinguish at least five versions of determinism: (1) metaphysical determinsim, (2) epistemological determinism, (3) scientific determinism, (4) methodological determinism, and (5) effective determinism.

(1)   *Metaphysical determinism* is characterized by the claim that, given the antecedent history of the world, any event or state of affairs now under consideration was necessarily bound to come about. In other words: for a given past there is only a single and uniquely determined future. Sometimes the claim is made symmetrical with respect to time, i.e. understood to comprise an additional thesis to the effect that a given future has only one uniquely determined past. Metaphysical determinism is common among scientists; anti-probabilists like the physiologist Claude Bernard (see 4.2) share it with prominent probabilists like Jakob Bernoulli or Pierre Simon de Laplace (see 1.4). Others have opposed it, whether in view of probabilistic phenomena, as the evolutionist Sewall Wright did (see 4.5), or for less specific considerations about variation in nature, like those propounded by the physiologist Bichat (see 4.2).

(2)   Metaphysical determinism is independent of our ability to specify the future (or the past) on the basis of our actual or potential information. *Epistemological determinism* makes the claim that, at least in principle, we can predict the future. Again, this position can be extended to include the possibility of retrodiction. At first sight, it would seem that epistemological determinism makes stronger claims than metaphysical determinism, since it implies the latter. But it may well be that it is only of equal strength, provided, as some philosophers would argue, there is no meaningful explication of "determination" short of predictability (or retrodictability) in principle. The "in principle" escape clause leaves open whether we will ever be able to predict certain classes of phenomena in practice. In this sense, epistemological determinism is no more than an explication (possibly one among several) of metaphysical determinism, since we can hardly drop the qualification "in principle" without making epistemological determinism trivially false. Hence, it comes as no surprise that protagonists of metaphysical determinism, such as Laplace and Bernard, also support epistemological determinsm, and that opponents of the former also reject the latter, as does Bichat.

(3)   The lack of an effective distinction between metaphysical and epistemological determinism is, of course, unsatisfactory. This situation is somewhat mitigated by focusing on the potential means of prediction (or retrodiction): the general laws or rules governing the world of observable phenomena, laws which are usually embedded in scientific theories. Scientific theories are called deterministic if they specify (i) a set of basic features of their objects that determine uniquely all observable properties of these objects, and (ii) the necessary laws from which these basic features can be obtained for future (or future and past) times, once they

are known at a given time. The basic features must be such that they can be ascertained to any desirable degree of accuracy and completeness. *Scientific determinism*, then, is a philosophical view that is characterized by the claim that the description of the world in terms of deterministic theories can be made as complete as we wish. In point of historical fact, initial successes of this descriptive program plus the absence of clear obstacles to its further expansion have usually been sufficient to make this position credible or acceptable. Many followers of Newton, though not Newton himself, believed in scientific determinism; some physicists remained faithful to it, although their own work did not conform to their creed, such as Max Planck and Albert Einstein (see 5.8). They should be contrasted with those probabilists who were willing to adjust their philosophical beliefs to the changing outlook of scientific theories without much delay or even in anticipation of more changes to come, including the physicist James Clerk Maxwell (see 5.6) or the philosopher-scientist Charles Sanders Peirce (5.3).

(4) Even though, given the narrow compass of the actually available scientific account of our complex world, the cognitive backing of scientific determinism can only be called modest, its acceptability is greatly enhanced by combining it with *methodological determinism*. This position is characterized not by an assertion that could be true or false, but by a maxim of cognitive behaviour which reads: Whenever two situations that look completely alike develop in different ways, watch out for an as yet undiscovered circumstance that is responsible for the difference. The *belief* in methodological determinism may, of course, be viewed as one more version of theoretical determinism in that it relies on the ubiquitous existence of such differentiating circumstances; but the *acceptance* of it may primarily be motivated by practical considerations, e.g. that it is always better to ask further questions than to rest satisfied with incomplete knowledge where further knowledge might be attainable. Methodological (or pragmatic) determinism is an option, even when (theoretical) scientific determinism is only poorly supported. It gets into trouble only if scientific indeterminism – the denial of scientific determinism – is positively supported by the actual development of empirically confirmed indeterministic theories. Thus, the protagonist of random drift in biological evolution, Sewall Wright (see 4.5), saw no problem in subscribing to methodological determinism, since all mutations may be supposed to have causes, and drift to be determined by contingent but identifiable macroscropic circumstances. Others seem to have found methodological determinism rationally so compelling that they clung to it despite adverse

theoretical developments; Max Planck is an example. His attitude shows that it is sometimes difficult to decide whether methodological determinism inspires metaphysical determinism, or vice versa (compare Planck, [1926] 1958, vol. 3, pp. 165–6, and [1929] 1936, pp. 43ff., with 1938, pp. 12–14, and 18).

(5) To explicate *effective determinism*, we need a distinction between several levels of scientific theorizing, such as the level of living organisms versus that of molecules. It is, then, conceivable that we have a deterministic situation at the first level, but an indeterministic situation at the second level. For example, we may be able to predict or produce a well-defined genetic change by the help of certain alterations of the environment, whereas the mutations at the molecular level occur spontaneously and in an unpredictable way. Nevertheless, as long as our cognitive ambitions remain restricted by our practical goals, say, of breeding a plant with specific properties, we are free to adopt a deterministic stance, with no commitment to the truth of scientific determinism in general. Effective determinism may be local, referring to a specified level or area of the phenomena; or global, claiming that, in spite of certain violations of scientific determinism, all applications of scientific knowledge will remain deterministic for all practical intents and purposes. Thus, Charles Darwin believed in the strict causal determination of each mutation (see 4.3), whereas post-quantum mechanical evolutionists may no longer do so. Nevertheless they need not, for this reason, abandon determinism at the level of macroevolution. Conversely macroevolution may be random, regardless of the complete microdetermination of each mutation.

In general, it is clear from the preceding distinctions and examples that the expansion of the empire of chance need not necessarily subvert determinism in general. It may, and it has been taken to, shake one version of it, while leaving others intact. In general, the advance of probability has been primarily directed against scientific determinism. Methodological determinism has only been affected indirectly. The prospects for effective determinism will depend on the complete pattern of diverse scientific theories and techniques in various areas of application, and hence again be influenced only at one or two removes. The fate of metaphysical determinism, however, remains open, as long as we do not specify exactly what counts for and what against it. We must be prepared to observe a certain slack between philosophical world views and their articulations in terms of scientific theories. At any rate, discrepancies between them appear to structure the history of probabilistic thinking to a remarkable extent. Also epistemological determinism, as defined above, would seem to depend on the kind of such discrepancies, and whether they are perceived. Thus, within the metaphysical and epistemological framework of the seventeenth century, the early probabilists came to think that the complete determination of nature is the only explanation, hence also the presupposition, for the applicability of mathematics, and thus of probability, to the real world. Conversely, the discrepancy between probabilistic scientific practice and deterministic metaphysical opinions has stimulated the impressive development of ergodic theory and current chaos theory, whereas those who, like Peirce, believed in the unity of metaphysics and science as practiced, were inevitably turned toward a probabilistic world view.

The remarkable force and persistence of metaphysical and epistemological determinism in an era of probabilistic methods and theories owes much to the traditional philosophical concept of knowledge in a strict sense, as it is found, say, in Aristotle: someone can be said to possess knowledge only if it is established that the thing known could not possibly be otherwise. When, with the rise of modern science and philosophy, this conception was specialized to causal processes in time, it led to strong deterministic claims like those made by Kant: we could not have any knowledge of nature if the phenomena composing it were not each and every one of them necessitated by antecedent conditions in accordance with a rule or a law.

It is plausible to assume that this view would not have been convincing without the parellel support of deterministic mechanical theories, especially of their successful application to the planetary system. Conversely, given the neat coincidence of epistemological ideals and scientific achievements, it was bound to get deeply entrenched into the growing scientific view of the world – witness Laplace's famous demon with his unlimited predictive power. In this intellectual setting, metaphysical, epistemological and scientific determinism merged and stablized each other. The resulting version of determinism has remained a live issue and a serious philosophico-scientific option until today.

How do stable deterministic beliefs relate to the probabilistic thinking that emerged in the seventeenth century and was certainly flourishing around 1800? The short answer is that probability served as a kind of protective belt for the hard core of the deterministic scientific program. The higher the epistemological and theoretical standards for genuine knowledge, the more urgently some subsidiary standards are needed for making less perfect knowledge scientifically acceptable. Wherever certainty and completeness are lacking and perhaps even undesirable, a well-reasoned and quantitative method of formulating and securing *beliefs* becomes indispensable, as soon as a branch of investigation is turned into an exact science. Probability theory appeared to fit the bill, from the treatment of observational errors or statistical data to the assessment of causal relationships and degrees of certainty for scientific hypotheses.

In light of metaphysical, epistemological, or scientific determinism, probability is to be interpreted as strictly *epistemic* – as expressing nothing but a restriction of our knowledge that might be removed, or at least diminished *ad indefinitum*. Where probabilistic notions are applied to purely epistemic entities (e.g. the trustworthiness of hypotheses), this interpretation is unobjectionable. In other applications, however, it is questionable, even though epistemological aspects may be involved. The random distribution of observational errors is a case in point. Granted that the errors might be reduced indefinitely, they would seem to be something purely epistemic. Yet, their lawlike distribution, e.g. according to the normal curve, is an objective fact about the nature of a material object, the experimental setup (possibly including a human observer as a relevant part).

As a matter of fact, the law of errors eventually became one of the sources of indeterministic views. Quetelet's position is far from being unambiguous; it is clear, however, that he listed human free will as one of the accidental causes whose superposition produces a lawlike pattern only on the level of society, expressed in the regularities of moral statistics and the law of errors. Maxwell applied the law to the velocity distributions of molecules, distributions whose shape obviously has nothing to do with the description of our knowledge. Again, the regularity concerns probabilities and appears at a higher level only, while the events at a lower level remain undetermined, *as far as the theory goes*. Once variation had become an important object of study in evolutionary biology, it became clear that other distributions besides the error curve were needed. A new field of study thus emerged, mathematical statistics. This discipline deals with distributions in their own right, and tries to make inferences from them on the basis of probabilistic assumptions. It not only neglects further determinations of its objects; it is based on the presupposition that such determinations, whether they exist or not, will not affect its conclusions. In this sense the very nature of mathematical statistics can be said to undermine the universal validity of scientific determinism.

Some philosophers such as Charles S. Peirce and Hans Reichenbach, and also some scientists, including the physicists Franz Exner and Marian von Smoluchowski and the mathematician Richard von Mises, have even gone a step further. Since we discover variation wherever we force the precision of our observation, they argued that we should view determination as the result of the mutual cancellation of variations rather than variation as the result of the summation of many independent determinations.

The connection between indeterminism and uncontrollable variations in nature easily associates itself with the natural interest in securing a place for free will. Maxwell is no less a case in point than Peirce. William James, Peirce's follower and friend, presented human free action as a forceful argument against determinism (James, 1884). Conversely, some of those who had been under the spell of successful deterministic theories of physics, such as Pascual Jordan, praised indeterministic quantum physics because it seemed to save the possibility of human freedom after all. But, as is to be expected in a question as deep as that of free will, the connection with indeterminism, let alone the support it might possibly obtain from it, is controversial, to say the least. Decisions or actions that are arbitrary, accidental and completely inexplicable, as opposed to actions determined by identifiable motives or reasons, are hardly a convincing instantiation of human freedom. The role of free will in the history of determinism has, therefore, remained ambiguous to this day. One will perhaps accept or reject metaphysical determinism in accordance with one's conception of freedom, but as long as this metaphysical issue remains unresolved, the correlation with scientific determinism will presumably become ever more loose. At any rate, this is what we observe. True, there is an important strand of metaphysical thought about determinism and indeterminism that interferes with the development of scientific ideas. But the more effective erosion of determinism resulted from the emergence of fundamental indeterministic scientific theories, whatever their impact on our conceptions of human will and freedom.

The more recent fate of scientific determinism strongly influences the present prospects for all other forms of determinism. Whatever the truth about other theories of physics (see Earman, 1986, for a recent and careful assessment), quantum mechanics was the first theory that was universally *recognized* to be irreducibly probabilistic and therefore indeterministic with respect to many significant observable applications, including technological devices triggered by atomic or subatomic processes, and natural processes like mutations of genetic material. Since such devices can be built and such processes exist, effective determinism is violated, at least in suitable cases and on a small scale. We may, however, plausibly claim that it is still preserved on a larger scale. For, ordinarily, we do not kill cats by electric shocks triggered by single undetermined quantum events, though that is certainly possible, as Erwin Schrödinger made clear in order to draw our attention to the "paradoxical" character of the the new theory. Moreover, the development of randomly drifting gene pools can presumably be determined by contact with sufficiently selective environments. In sum, then, as far as scientific indeterminism is based on quantum theory, it affects the validity of effective determinism only marginally.

By implication, the adequacy of methodological determinism in general is hardly impaired – *except* in the very realm of single elementary processes. On that basic level, the prospects of methodological determinism are as good or as bad as those of replacing current quantum theories by some equally good or better theory that is in addition deterministic. Under these circumstances, the interest and the confidence in finding such a theory are more likely to depend on epistemological and metaphysical inclinations than on methodological insights or pragmatic needs. Indeed, as can be shown by comparing the reactions to quantum mechanics on the part of American and European physicists (cf. Cartwright, 1987), a true pragmatic spirit and workday methodology are hardly threatened by indeterminism and related ontological puzzles like the wave–particle duality.

Conversely, quantum mechanics strikes a blow mainly against metaphysical determinism. Of course, granted the truth of quantum theory, epistemological determinism was also clearly refuted. Yet, as in the case of effective indeterminism, the practical import of this violation is restricted to specially contrived or otherwise rare occasions. In other words: the *overall* epistemic situation has not changed dramatically, although from a metaphysical point of view the question is one of principle. At this point, therefore, metaphysical and epistemological determinism part, after they had become almost indistinguishable companions in the heyday of classical determinism.

That they are radically distinct is also revealed in another no less important way. Not only quantum mechanics, but also classical physical theories can undermine determinism, as has been made clear by recent developments of the mechanics of complex systems and chaos theory. Even systems of moderate complexity, such as the (classical!) three-body configuration, let alone more complex systems, can be unstable, that is, start from (practically) indistinguishable initial conditions and nevertheless diverge radically within limited time spans. The deterministic structure of the theory does not bar such cases; on the contrary, stable or quasi-stable systems, like our solar system, are now recognized for what they are, rare exceptions. Many phenomena, often phenomena of great practical significance, like the weather, prove to be chaotic, even on the assumption that they are adequately covered by a fully deterministic theory.

Thus we are led to conclude that scientific determinism does not imply epistemological determinism. Chaotic systems, as a matter of principle, do not permit precise and long-term predictions, yet are deterministic nevertheless. Despite the cliché, it is not primarily quantum mechanics that undermines all forms of determinism, with the exception of metaphysical determinism, but rather the wide range of important applications of classical physical theories to complex and unstable phenomena. If one is willing to count the additional assumptions and approximations required by those applications as parts of the theories themselves, then those theories are to be considered as indeterministic; as a matter of fact, they all contain probabilistic elements explicitly. This is no less true for evolutionary population biology, the theory of economic behavior, or psychology than for physics.

Metaphysical determinism, however, is more resistant, sometimes stubborn. If we are willing to adopt a realistic interpretation of scientific theories, the assessment of metaphysical determinism will depend on how that interpretation is carried out. It will depend also, as was just mentioned, on how much of the belt of additional assumptions we include in the *interpretandum*. After we have severed the ties between metaphysical and epistemological determinism, our maxims of interpretation remain the only criteria for judging metaphysical determinism. It is certainly somewhat Pickwickian to base determinism solely on the mathematical structure that a theory assigns to its objects, if that structure does not enable us to determine the observable properties of these objects in any conceivable application.

Conversely, the paradigm case for indeterminism, quantum mechanics, is not entirely unambiguous. It has often been remarked that the breakdown of determinism is less than complete. If the states of a microsystem are defined by a Schrödinger wave function of maximal specification, the time development of *those* states is certainly deterministic. Moreover, under a realistic interpretation, maximal specification may be interpreted to be an ontological feature of the state, so that it would be misguided to describe this state as indeterminate in view of the fact that it does not unite precise values of all macroscopically characteristics, like position and momentum of a particle. The micro-reality may simply be of a different nature. Hence a claim for or against determinism should be conditional upon a previous ontological clarification of the nature of the microworld.

What remains, however, is the undisputed fact that, according to quantum mechanics, no determinate correspondence can be found between microstates and macroscopically observable properties of quantum systems. In view of this situation, resolute metaphysical determinists may still adhere to their principles. They may, indeed, assimilate the case of quantum physics to that of unstable or chaotic classical systems, for which deterministic claims also have to be narrowed down to their more or less elusive ontological core. Due to the philosophical nature of the claim, and to the weight of its long and glorious history, this core is a hard one. Nevertheless, it has gradually lost its protective belt: non-epistemic interpretations of probability suggested themselves ever more convincingly, and the development of several scientific theories has dissolved the fusion of metaphysical, epistemological and scientific determinism that characterized the picture of knowledge two centuries ago.

The combination of the enormous expansion of the rule of numbers (see 8.1) with the erosion of determinism described in this section, suggests the following generalization: At the beginning of modern science complete determination of nature seemed to be the indispensable presupposition of the applicability of scientific method to nature (section 1.4). As mathematical arguments were the most powerful articulation of the method, correspondingly the characterization of natural objects by numbers seemed to be the perfect expression of such a determination. But during the eighteenth and nineteenth centuries, the mathematical sciences gradually detached themselves from the strongest version of this deterministic ideal – that scientific knowledge must be demonstrated in the form of propositions, just as in mathematics. Scientific laws, expressed mathematically, were still understood to be deterministic, but not necessary. The nineteenth-century confrontation with recalcitrant experiments and observations in both the moral and natural sciences weakened that ideal still further. In order to apply mathematics of some sort to the new phenomena, a retreat from determinism became necessary. A choice had to be made: either narrow limits had to be set to the rule of numbers, or the use of numbers had to be detached from the idea of determination. The rise of probability marks very clearly which choice was made – the rule of numbers was rendered more flexible in order to extend its borders. There is a trade-off between determinism, at least in scientific practice if not in philosophical theory, on the one hand, and the adaptation of scientific method and content to the conditions of progress on the other.

8.4 MECHANIZED INFERENCE

Throughout the history of probability theory, the opposition of certainty versus uncertainty has clung like a shadow to that of determinism versus indeterminism. A certain complementarity traditionally governed their relationships: those who refused to give up their belief in determinism in the face of variable and unpredictable phenomena used probability theory to measure uncertainty; those who admitted indeterminism made probability theory a certain measure of an uncertain world. However, certainty also makes an appearance in some applications of probability theory that take no stand on the determinism/indeterminism issue. These applications deal with inference and decision under uncertainty; it is irrelevant here whether that uncertainty stems from human frailty or the construction of the world. In effect, these applications accept such uncertainty as a given, and make the best of a bad business by providing rules for rational belief and conduct. Although these rules cannot eliminate the uncertainty intrinsic to the situation, they do eliminate the uncertainty of opinion about how to weigh what information one has, and therefore, about what course of action to pursue. They aim to mechanize inference and thereby to rationalize (and standardize) opinion. The kinds of situations to which such rules have been applied are as varied as the human condition itself, ranging from hypothesis testing in the sciences to investment decisions in business. The rules also vary, including Bayesian, Fisherian, and Neyman–Pearsonian methods. But since all of them draw inferences about the future from past experience, we shall designate them collectively as techniques of inductive inference.

Since Leibniz, probabilists have dreamed of making theirs a calculus of such inferences, a dream that has never been stronger than it is today. But whereas Leibniz was never able to realize his dream of a Universal Characteristic, his successors are now armed with a battery of techniques for drawing inferences under uncertainty. There are, to be sure, important differences between the classical and modern forms of mechanized inference. The classical probabilists from Jakob Bernoulli through Poisson sought to codify the intuitions of the right-thinking, in order to make them available to the muddle-headed masses (or even the enlightened themselves when confronted with a problem of surpassing complexity) as a mechanical aid. That is, they conceived of probability as a mathematical model of sound inference under uncertainty, a conception made plausible by the further belief that thinking itself was a form of implicit calculation. As we have seen in chapter 1, when the results of probability theory were at odds with the intuitions of reasonable men, the mathematicians at first tried to correct their model, not the intuitions. Probability theory was to native good sense what a telescope or spectacles were to the naked eye: a mechanical extension designed along the same basic principles as the original. Just because it was mechanical, it was at everyone's disposal, was immune to the distortions that imagination or emotion introduced into intuitive judgments, and always gave the same answer.

Although the modern forms of statistical inference presume to correct the intuitions of even the enlightened, their appeal still rests upon claims to universality, neutrality, and uniqueness. These techniques have been notably most successful in disciplines where consensus is most difficult to command: it is social scientists, not physicists, who embraced inference statistics. Physicists accepted probability in their theories, but not in their reasoning. Social scientists, however, could never attain the consensus about theories that physicists achieved, and instead settled for consensus about methods, those of inference statistics. As chapter 6 shows in the case of psychology, this is a consensus under false pretenses, since it rests on the erroneous assumption that statistical inference was monolithic, and that its answers were unique. In fact, statisticians are divided into warring camps over the relative merits of Bayesian, Fisherian, and Neyman–Pearsonian methods. But since the allure of statistical inference was precisely that it silenced strife, the psychologists closed their ears.

They were not alone. Experts bent on applying Bayesian statistics in the courtroom or the doctor's office are just as deaf to the blandishments of rival forms of statistical inference. In such momentous practical decisions where lives may hang in the balance, the illusion of rational consensus, neutrality, and unique answers is even more precious. For reasons that are more historical than substantive, the various schools of statistical inference have specialized by areas of application. Certainly, biologists encountered Fisherian statistics because Fisher himself was a geneticist. While social scientists prefer Fisherian statistics, with an occasional admixture of Neyman–Pearson, experts in more practical contexts lean toward Bayesian methods. (Curiously, most psychologists who argue that their subjects are irrational because they defy Bayesian precepts nonetheless use Fisherian statistics to interpret their own data.) It is by no means obvious why scientists should always choose a form of statistical inference that leads to yes–no decisions rather than one that revises the standing of hypotheses on the basis of new evidence. Conversely, utility-based decisions of the Neyman–Pearson sort often seem better suited to the problems of evaluating medical tests than Bayesian methods. Accident created the associations between field and method, and the will to believe in a single, unequivocal method for inference under uncertainty froze them in place.

The steady advance of statistical methods in areas where judgment once prevailed is a leitmotiv of the history of mathematical probability and statistics. Of course, the yearning for rules to guide us in perplexity can take nonstatistical forms, as in the case of Descartes' method. But the function of rules is to eliminate ambiguity, and mathematical rules are the least ambiguous of all. Uncertain situations called for probability theory and statistics, the mathematics of uncertainty. Since it was precisely in those areas where uncertainty was greatest that the burden of judgment was heaviest, statistical rules seemed ideally suited to the task of ridding first the sciences and then daily life of personal discretion, with its pejorative associations of the arbitrary, the idiosyncratic, and the subjective. Our contemporary notion of objectivity, defined largely by the absence of these elements, owes a great deal to the dream of mechanized inference. It is therefore not surprising that the statistical techniques that aspire to mechanize inference should have taken on a normative character. Whereas probability theory once aimed to describe judgment, statistical inference now aims to replace it, in the name of objectivity.

Of course, this escape from judgment is an illusion. All inference techniques depend on a modicum of good judgment to guide their application. Once applicability has been decided, judgment must intervene again to set the decision criterion, in the case of Neyman–Pearson theory, or the level of significance in Fisherian null hypothesis testing, or the prior probabilities in Bayesian inference. No amount of mathematical legerdemain can transform uncertainty into certainty, although much of the appeal of statistical inference techniques stems from just such great expectations. These expectations are fed by ignorance of the existence of alternative theories of statistical inference, by the conflation of calculated solutions with unique ones, by the reduction of objectivity to intersubjective consensus, and above all by the hope of avoiding the oppressive responsibilities that every exercise of personal judgment entails. It would be unjust to blame the mathematical statisticians for these false hopes, although some of their number have shared them. Rather, the fascination with mechanized inference stems from more widespread yearnings for unanimity in times of strife, and for certainty in uncertain circumstances.

8.5 STATISTICAL *LEBENSGEFÜHL*

These considerations show how difficult it is to distinguish the impact of statistics and probability theory on society from the impact of society on statistics and probability. Whether the mathematics bred new attitudes and ideas, or whether these ideas and attitudes were the preconditions for the mathematics is an ill-posed question. The causal arrow no doubt points in both directions. However tangled these interactions, their outcome is clear: we live in a statistical age. Probability and statistics have transformed explanation and reasoning in the sciences, and views of contingency and risk in the wide world beyond. These transformations are too varied and vast to sum into a coherent picture of the world; what they constitute is more a new *Lebensgefühl* than a new *Weltanschauung*. Yet we who have been born into the empire of chance hardly notice its dominion over us; over the way we parse our world, make up our minds, argue our points, and judge our fellows. Our statistical way of life is too much a way of life to catch the eye.

But if we contrast it with what could be and has been, its commitments and consequences spring into relief. Let us briefly return to the late seventeenth century, when probability theory was still young, and review the days of John Evelyn, Esq. (1620–1706). Evelyn was a progressive man; Fellow of the Royal Society, a devoté of scientific horticulture, an indefatigable tourist, and, fortunately for our purposes, a sharp-eyed diarist. In the pages of his diary we see life recorded through modern yet pre-statistical eyes. Evelyn was of a factual bent, and avid for numbers wherever they could be had: we learn, for example, that the great bell of the cathedral of Notre Dame "so much talk'd off " is 13 feet high, 32 feet around, and weighs 40,000 pounds; and that the Egyptian obelisk recently erected in St Peter's Square in Rome cost 37,975 crowns and the labor of 907 men and 75 horses. But the numbers *not* to be had are even more impressive. Nowhere in Evelyn's travelogue can he fix a number to the inhabitants of the numerous "populous" cities he visited, and although he is keenly interested in the prosperity of England's Dutch rivals, he must infer their industry and productivity from their innumerable canals. The dimensions of wondrous objects and feats have entered the realm of the numerical, but not the mundane subject matter of censuses and economic indices. People and products are not yet countable.

Evelyn could have purchased fire and even life insurance towards the end of his life in London, but neither of these enterprises had any statistical or probabilistic basis at the time. They were either based on flat rates, or

a meticulous examination of the circumstances surrounding each case insured. Passionate gardener that he was, Evelyn duly noted seasons of
frost, drought, and storm, but his meteorological baseline extended no
further than his own memory. He was loathe to grant chance a role in the
world, admitting that comets might indeed be due to natural causes, but
nonetheless divine signs of things to come: for how could their connection with the deaths of princes and other momentous events be mere
coincidence? During his tenure as Fellow, the Royal Society investigated
many elusive and subtle effects, but never attempted to filter out the
counterfeit effects of chance systematically. Evelyn and his colleagues
recognized the variability of phenomena – indeed, they probably paid it
more heed than any group of natural scientists before or since – but they
were as reluctant to attribute it to chance as they were to ignore it in the
study of constant, uniform causes.

Averages did not figure in Evelyn's world. His breeches and waistcoat
were fitted to his individual dimensions, rather than to the anthropometric averages that served to standardize clothing sizes some
centuries later. Although Evelyn regularly attended Royal Society
sessions and may even have been present when Edmund Halley presented
the first empirical life table, he had no notion of an average lifespan.
When he recorded the deaths of his baby grandson, the aged Charles II,
and numerous other contemporaries, his measure of natural longevity
was the biblical ideal of three-score-and-ten years, not life expectancies
computed from Graunt's or Halley's tables. Evelyn was typical in his disregard for such averages. Had he subscribed to the British government's
issue of annuities in 1694, he would have paid the same price (seven years'
purchase) at age 74 as a young man of 20.

Indeed, averages were foreign to Evelyn's brand of empiricism, which
dwelt upon the particular and the singular. His diary is crammed with
vivid descriptions of the novel, the rare, and the striking: the anatomical
theater of the University of Leyden; streets of shops set up on the frozen
Thames one unusually bitter winter; a gemstone that "emitted a luculent
flame as bright and large as a small wax candle"; the exquisite table manners of the Moroccan ambassador to London. Statistics can astonish and
amaze just as well as the isolated instance, but they speak to different factual sensibilities. The texture of Evelyn's world is granular, full of individual objects and events to be appreciated in their particulars. His
perspective corresponds more closely to what is probably the universal
human tendency to weight the individual event observed or reported in
all its specificity more heavily than the thousands of faceless cases

summed up in statistics. But whatever our psychological leanings, we have learned to think and argue in terms of averages, and to thus confer on them a reality greater than the sum of their parts – greater than the individuals they summarize. Evelyn was no less attentive to experience than we, but for him, the individual – and the singular individual at that – was the fundamental unit of reality.

In the three hundred years since Evelyn wrote we have learned to believe in and even test for coincidences, to honor averages, and to count the invisible and the ineffable. Even if our untutored intuitions are still closer to those of Evelyn, our public discourse is cast in the language of statistics and probability: however deep the impression the automobile accident of a close friend may leave, it is the annual accident statistics that are the stuff of argument and recommendations concerning traffic safety. It is a language that rationalizes our decisions, shapes our research, and probes the deepest parts of nature – even if it is not our native tongue.

Our statistical *Lebensgefühl* is that strange beast, a public emotion. In our private musings and observations we may and usually do cling to something like Evelyn's pointillist vision of things, but for certain public purposes we shift our gaze from individuals to averages, from deep-felt certainties to probabilities, from impressions to numbers. Since Dickens' bitter anti-statistical novel *Hard Times* (1854), the warm-hearted and the tender-minded have feared that this was a shift from all that was alive and human to a frigid absence of all emotions. They have, however, mistaken different and perhaps novel emotions for none at all. From the outset, probability and statistics were invoked to settle disputes and to forge a consensus when no one alternative carried absolute conviction. In the best of times, these functions were exercised irenically; in the worst, tyrannically. In all cases, their function was a public one: to meld many minds or opinions into one, stopping short of force or fiat. Probability and statistics are the most versatile tools for generating the impersonal knowledge that Karl Pearson thought indispensable for a truly social existence. This is not Rousseau's general will, for it is neither universal nor infallible, but it summons up the same civic passions. Because of the margin of uncertainty that edges all such decisions, at least when honestly reached, we must collectively shoulder the burden of hope and fear, just as we must collectively submerge personal experience into public statistics and collectively stomach the possibility of local injustice in the name of global justice.

These shared emotions and risks – and above all awareness that they *are* shared – transform individuals into citizens of a certain kind of polity. Of course, neither citizenship nor civic emotion bear any necessary relation to probability and statistics, but probability and statistics represent one solution to settling differences without mayhem, be it a matter of government policy or scientific research. The price of our life together is sometimes a willingness to forego one kind of fact – Evelyn's odd particulars – for another kind – the statistician's averages and macroscopic regularities. Particulars surprise us with unsuspected singularity; statistics surprise us with unsuspected regularity. Readers of Laplace and Quetelet, upon learning that the same number of letters went astray each year, no doubt experienced a *frisson* of pleasant astonishment just as intense as that Evelyn experienced upon viewing a petrified salamander in an Italian cabinet of curiosities. *Pace* Dickens' Gradgrind, the statistical *Lebensgefühl* is no enemy of wonder. Fortuna was traditionally the very personification of surprise, that boon companion of wonder; each unpredictable spin of her wheel turning the world upside down. The story of probability and statistics is one of the domestication of unpredictable Fortuna. But it has nonetheless been a story full of wonders, and the only prediction we can make with certainty is that it will continue to be so.

References

Entries are arranged in order of first date of publication (which often appears in brackets), or in a few cases the date of composition, not that of modern reprintings. Page numbers cited in the text are in every case from the edition or translation published in the year not in brackets.

Acree, M. C. 1978. *Theories of Statistical Inference in Psychological Research: A Historicocritical Study*. Dissertation. Ann Arbor, Mich.: University Microfilms International H790 H7000

Agassiz, Louis. [1857] 1962. *An Essay on Classification*. Cambridge: Harvard Univ. Press

Albury, W. R. 1977. Experiment and Explanation in the Physiology of Bichat and Magendie. *Studies in History of Biology*, 1: 47–131

Allen, G. E. 1975. *Life Science in the Twentieth Century*. Cambridge: Cambridge Univ. Press

1978. *Thomas Hunt Morgan: The Man and His Science*. Princeton: Princeton Univ. Press

Alonso, William and Paul Starr, eds. 1987. *The Politics of Numbers*. New York: Sage

Arbuthnot, John. 1710. An Argument for Divine Providence, taken from the Constant Regularity observ'd in the Births of Both Sexes. *Philosophical Transactions of the Royal Society*, 27: 186–90

Arnauld, Antoine and Pierre Nicole. [1662] 1965. *La Logique, ou l'Art de penser*. Pierre Clair and Françoise Girbal, eds. Paris: Presses Universitaires de France

Atkinson, Anthony C. and Stephen E. Fienberg, eds. 1985. *A Celebration of Statistics: The ISI Centenary Volume*. New York: Springer

Baer, Karl Ernst von. 1828–37. *Über Entwicklungsgeschichte der Thiere: Beobachtung und Reflexion* (On the Development of Animals: Observation and Reflection). Königsberg: Bornträger

[1873] 1973. The Controversy over Darwinism. Trans. in Hull, 1973

1876. *Reden gehalten in wissenschaftlichen Versammlungen und kleinere Aufsätze vermischten Inhalts* (Discourses). St Petersburg: Schmitzdorff

Baily, Francis. 1835. *An Account of the Reverend John Flamsteed*. London

Bakan, D. 1966. The Test of Significance in Psychological Research. *Psychological Bulletin*, **66**: 423–37

Baker, Keith M. 1975. *Condorcet: From Natural Philosophy to Social Mathematics*. Chicago: Univ. of Chicago Press

Balzac. [1841] 1901. *Le curé de village*. Paris: Societé d'Editions Littéraires et Artistiques

Barnard, G. A. 1947. The Meaning of a Significance Level. *Biometrika*, **34**: 179–82

1958. Thomas Bayes – a Biographical Note (together with a reprinting of Bayes, 1764). *Biometrika*, **45**: 293–315. Reprinted in Pearson and Kendall, 1970

1980. Pivotal Inference and the Bayesian Controversy. In Bernardo *et al.*, eds.,1980

Barnard, G. A. and D. R. Cox. 1962. *The Foundations of Statistical Inference: A Discussion*. London: Methuen

Barnard, G. A. and R. L. Plackett. 1985. Statistics in the United Kingdom, 1939–45. In Atkinson and Fienberg, eds., 1985

Barndorff-Nielsen, O. E. 1985. The Fascination of Sand. In Atkinson and Fienberg, eds., 1985

Barndorff-Nielsen, O. E. *et al.* 1974. *Proceedings of Conference on Foundational Questions in Statistical Inference, Aarhus, May 7–12, 1973*. Memoirs, No. 1. Department of Theoretical Statistics, Univ. of Aarhus

Bartholomew, D. J. 1967. *Stochastic Theory for Social Processes*. New York: John Wiley

Bartlett, M. S. 1959. The Impact of Stochastic Process Theory on Statistics. In U. Grenander, ed., *Probability and Statistics – The Harald Cramér Volume*. Stockholm: Almquist and Wiksell

Bateson, W. 1913. *Mendel's Principles of Heredity*. Cambridge: Cambridge Univ. Press

Bayes, Thomas. 1763. An Essay Towards Solving a Problem in the Doctrine of Chances. *Philosophical Transactions of the Royal Society*, **53**: 370–418. Reprinted in Barnard, 1958

Beatty, John. 1984. Chance and Natural Selection. *Philosophy of Science*, **51**: 183–211

1986. Speaking of Species: Darwin's Strategy. In Kohn, ed., 1986

1987. Dobzhansky and Drift: Facts, Values, and Chance in Evolutionary Biology. In Krüger, Gigerenzer, and Morgan, eds., 1987: 271–311

Behrens, W. V. 1929. Ein Beitrag zur Fehlerberechnung bei wenigen Beobachtungen. *Landwirtschaftliche Jahrbücher*, **68**: 807–37

Benecke, F. W. [1858] 1861. On the Importance and Value of Arithmetic Means. Trans. by F. T. Bond. In *On the Importance and Value of Arithmetic Means*. New Sydenham Society, London

Bennett, J. H., ed. 1965. *Experiments in Plant Hybridisation: Gregor Mendel*. Edinburgh: Oliver and Boyd

Berger, J. O. and T. Sellke, 1987. Testing a Point Null Hypothesis: the Irreconcilability of *P* Values and Evidence (with discussion). *Journal of the American Statistical Association*, 82: 112–39

Bernard, Claude. [1865] 1957. *An Introduction to the Study of Experimental Medicine*. Trans. by H. C. Greene. New York: Dover

Bernardo, J. M. *et al.*, eds. 1980. *Bayesian Statistics. Proceedings of the First International Meeting, Valencia (Spain) 1979*. Valencia: Valencia Univ. Press

Bernays, Edward L. 1923. *Crystallizing Public Opinion*. New York: Boni and Liveright

Bernoulli, Daniel. [1738] 1954. Specimen theoriae novae de mensura sortis. *Commentarii academiae scientarum imperialis Petropolitanae*, 5: 175–92 (English trans. by L. Sommer, Exposition of a New Theory on the Measurement of Risk. *Econometrica*, 22: 23–36)

——— 1752. Recherches physiques et astronomiques, sur le problème proposé. . . Quelle est la cause physique de l'inclinaison des plans des orbites des planètes par rapport au plan de l'équateur de la révolution du soleil autour de son axe; et d'où vient que les inclinaisons de ces orbites sont différentes entre elles? *Recueil des pièces qui ont remporté les prix de l'Académie royale des Sciences*, 3: 93–122 (French text); 123–45 (Latin original)

Bernoulli, Jakob. 1713. *Ars conjectandi*. Basel

Bernoulli, Nicholas. 1709. *De usu artis conjectandi in jure*. Basel

Bessel, Friedrich Wilhelm. 1823. Persönliche Gleichung bei Durchgangsbeobachtungen. *Königsberger Beobachtungen*, 8: 3–6

——— 1838. Untersuchungen über die Wahrscheinlichkeit der Beobachtungsfehler. *Astronomische Nachrichten*, 15: 369–404

Bichat, Xavier. [1801] 1822. *General Anatomy, Applied to Physiology and Medicine*. Trans. by G. Hayward. Boston: Richardson and Lord

——— [1809] 1829. *Physiological Researches upon Life and Death*. Trans. by T. Watkins. Philadelphia: Smith and Maxwell

Birnbaum, M. H. 1983. Base Rates in Bayesian Inference: Signal Detection Analysis of the Cab Problem. *American Journal of Psychology*, 96: 85–94

Block, N. J. and Gerald Dworkin, eds. 1976. *The IQ Controversy*. New York: Random House

Blyakher, L. [1955] 1982. *History of Embryology in Russia: From the Middle of the Eighteenth to the Middle of the Nineteenth Century*. Anonymously translated. Washington, D.C.: Smithsonian Institution

Bohr, Niels. 1913. On the Constitution of Atoms and Molecules. *Philosophical*

Magazine, **26**: 1–25, 476–502, 857–75. Repr. in Bohr 1972ff., vol. 2, 159–233

[1923/24] 1976. On the Application of the Quantum Theory to Atomic Structure I: The Fundamental Postulates. *Proceedings of the Cambridge Philosophical Society, Supplement*, Cambridge: Cambridge Univ. Press: 1–42. Repr. in Bohr 1972 ff., vol. 3, 455–500

1925. Über die Wirkung von Atomen bei Stössen. *Zeitschrift für Physik*, **34**: 142–57

1932. The Faraday Lecture: Chemistry and the Quantum Theory of Atomic Constitution. *Journal of the Chemical Society of London*, **135**: 349–84

[1957] 1958. Physical Science and the Problem of Life. In Bohr, Niels, *Atomic Physics and Human Knowledge*. New York: J. Wiley: 94–101

1972ff. *Collected Works*. Amsterdam: North Holland

Bohr, Niels, H. A. Kramers, and J. C. Slater. 1924. The Quantum Theory of Radiation. *Philosophical Magazine*, **47**: 785–802

Boltzmann, Ludwig. 1871. Analytischer Beweis des zweiten Hauptsatzes der mechanischen Wärmetheorie aus den Sätzen über das Gleichgewicht der lebendigen Kraft. In Boltzmann, [1909] 1968, vol. 1: 288–308

1872. Weitere Studien über das Wärmegleichgewicht unter Gasmolekülen. In Boltzmann, [1909] 1968, vol. 1: 316–402

1877. Über die Beziehung zwischen dem zweiten Hauptsatz der mechanischen Wärmetheorie und der Wahrscheinlichkeitsrechnung respektive den Sätzen über das Wärmegleichgewicht. In Boltzmann, [1909] 1968, vol. 2: 164–223

[1886] 1905. Der zweite Hauptsatz der mechanischen Wärmetheorie. In Boltzmann, 1905. Trans. as Boltzmann, [1886] 1974

[1886] 1974. The Second Law of the Mechanical Theory of Heat. In *Theoretical Physics and Philosophical Problems: Selected Writings*. B. McGuinness, ed., Dordrecht: Reidel

1895. On Certain Questions of the Theory of Gases. *Nature*, **51**; In Boltzmann, [1909] 1968, vol. 3: 535–44

1896. Entgegnung auf die wärmetheoretischen Betrachtungen des Hrn. E. Zermelo. *Annalen der Physik* **57**: 773–84. Trans. in S. Brush, ed., *Kinetic Theory*, vol. 2, Oxford: Pergamon, 1966

1896–98. *Vorlesungen über Gastheorie*, 2 vols., Leipzig. English trans. by S. G. Brush. Berkeley: Univ. of California Press, 1964

1905. *Populäre Schriften*. Leipzig: J. A. Barth

[1909] 1968. *Wissenschaftliche Abhandlungen*, Fritz Hasenöhrl, ed., 3 vols., Leipzig: Barth. Repr. New York: Chelsea

Boorstin, Daniel J. 1974. *The Americans: The Democratic Experience*. New York: Vintage

Borel, Emile. 1914. Sur certaines hypothèses continues équivalentes aux hypothèses discontinues. *Comptes rendus de l'Académie des Sciences*, **5**

Boring, E. G. 1963. Eponym as Placebo. In E. G. Boring, ed., *History, Psychology and Science: Selected Papers*. New York: Wiley

Born, Max. 1926a. Zur Quantenmechanik der Stossvorgänge. *Zeitschrift für Physik*, 37: 863–7

1926b. Quantenmechanik der Stossvorgänge. *Zeitschrift für Physik*, 38: 803–27. English trans. in G. Ludwig, *Wave Mechanics*. Oxford: Pergamon, 1968

Bothe, W. and H. Geiger. 1925. Über das Wesen des Comptoneffekts: ein experimenteller Beitrag zur Theorie der Strahlung. *Zeitschrift für Physik*, 32: 639–63

Bourguet, Marie-Noëlle. 1987. Décrire, Compter, Calculer: The Debate over Statistics during the Napoleonic Period. In Krüger, Daston, and Heidelberger, eds., 1987: 305–16

Bowley, Arthur L. 1901. *Elements of Statistics*. London: P. S. King

1915. *The Nature and Purpose of the Measurement of Social Phenomena*. London: P. S. King

Box, G. E. P. 1986. An Apology for Ecumenism in Statistics. In G. E. P. Box *et al.*, eds., *Scientific Inference, Data Analysis, and Robustness*. New York: Academic Press, 1986

Box, Joan Fisher. 1978. *R. A. Fisher: The Life of a Scientist*. New York: Wiley

1980. Fisher: the Early Years. In Fienberg and Hinkley, eds., 1980

Bradley, James V. 1968. *Distribution-free Statistical Tests*. Englewood Cliffs, N. J.: Prentice Hall

Bredenkamp, J. 1972. *Der Signifikanztest in der psychologischen Forschung*. Frankfurt/Main: Akademische Verlagsgesellschaft

Bredenkamp, J. and H. Feger. 1970. Kriterien für die Entscheidung über die Aufnahme empirischer Arbeiten in die Zeitschrift für Sozialpsychologie. *Zeitschrift für Sozialpsychologie*, 1: 43–7

Brennan, Troyer A. and Robert F. Carter. 1985. Legal and Scientific Probability of Causation of Cancer and other Environmental Disease in Individuals. *Journal of Health Politics, Policy and Law*, 10: 33–80

Brilmayer, Lea and Lewis Kornhauser. 1978. Review: Quantitative Methods and Legal Decisions. *University of Chicago Law Review*, 46: 116–53

Broglie, Louis de. 1924. A Tentative Theory of Light Quanta. *Philosophical Magazine*, 47: 446–58

Browne, Janet. 1983. *The Secular Ark: Studies in the History of Biogeography*. New Haven: Yale Univ. Press.

Brush, Stephen G. 1976. *The Kind of Motion We Call Heat*. 2 vols., Amsterdam: North Holland

Buck, Peter. 1985. Adjusting to Military Life: The Life Sciences Go to War, 1941–1950. In Merritt Roe Smith, ed., *Military Enterprise and Technological Change*. Cambridge: MIT Press

Buckle, Henry Thomas. 1857. *History of Civilization in England, vol. 1*. London: J. W. Parker.

Bull, J. P. 1959. The Historical Development of Clinical Therapeutic Trials. *Journal for Chronic Diseases*, 10: 218–48

Bulmer, Martin. 1984. *The Chicago School of Sociology: Institutionalization, Diversity,* and the Rise of Sociological Research. Chicago: Univ. of Chicago Press

Burke, Edmund. [1790] 1970. *Reflections on the Revolution in France*. New York: Penguin

Burns, R. M. 1981. *The Great Debate on Miracles*. Lewisburg: Bucknell Univ. Press

Butler, Joseph. 1736. *The Analogy of Religion, Natural and Revealed, to the Constitution and Course of Nature*. London

Byrne, Edmund F. 1968. *Probability and Opinion. A Study in the Medieval Presuppositions of Post-Medieval Theories of Probability*. The Hague: Martinus Nijhoff

Cain, A. J. 1951a. So-Called Non-Adaptive or Neutral Characters in Evolution. *Nature*, **168**: 424

    1951b. Non-Adaptive or Neutral Characters in Evolution. *Nature*, **168**: 1049

Cain, A. J. and P. M. Sheppard. 1950. Selection in the Polymorphic Land Snail *Cepaea nemoralis*. *Heredity*, 4: 275–94

    1954. Natural Selection in *Cepaea*. *Genetics*, **39**: 89–116

Campbell, D. T. and J. C. Stanley. 1966. *Experimental and Quasi-Experimental Designs for Research*. Chicago: Rand McNally

Campbell, Lewis and William Garnett. 1882. *The Life of James Clerk Maxwell*. London: Macmillan

Campbell, Robert. 1859. On a Test for Ascertaining whether an Observed Degree of Uniformity, or the Reverse, in Tables of Statistics is to be Looked upon as Remarkable. *Philosophical Magazine* [4], **18**: 359–68

Campbell, Sybil. 1928. Usury and Annuities of the Eighteenth Century. *Law Quarterly Review*, **44**: 473–91

Cantril, Hadley, 1944. *Gauging Public Opinion*. Princeton: Princeton Univ. Press

Cardano, Girolamo. [comp. *c*. 1525] 1966. *Liber de ludo aleae*. In *Opera Omnia*, *vol. 1*. Stuttgart – Bad Cannstatt: Friedrich Fromm. Reprint of 1663 Lyon edition

Carlson, E. A. 1966. *The Gene: A Critical History*. Philadelphia: W. B. Saunders

Carnap, Rudolf. 1945. The Two Concepts of Probability. *Philosophy and Phenomenological Research*, **5**: 513–32

    1950. *Logical Foundations of Probability*. Chicago: Univ. of Chicago Press

Cartwright, Nancy. 1987. Max Born and the Reality of Quantum Probabilities. In Krüger, Gigerenzer, and Morgan, eds., 1987: 409–16

Carver, R. P. 1978. The Case against Statistical Significance Testing. *Harvard Educational Review*, **48**: 378–99

Cassedy, James. 1969. *Demography in Early America: Beginnings of the Statistical Mind*. Cambridge: Harvard Univ. Press

    1984. *American Medicine and Statistical Thinking, 1800–1860* Cambridge: Harvard Univ. Press

Cavalli-Sforza, L. L. 1969. Genetic Drift in an Italian Population. *Scientific American*, **223** (2): 26–33

Chadwick, Henry. 1868. *The Game of Base Ball: How to Learn It, How to Play It, and How to Teach It*. New York: Munro

Church, Robert L. 1974. Economists as Experts: The Rise of an Academic

References 299

Profession in the United States, 1870–1920. In Lawrence Stone, ed., *The University in Society, vol. 2*. Princeton: Princeton Univ. Press

Cicero, Marcus Tullius. [85 B.C.] 1960. *De inventione*. Trans. H. M. Hubbel. Loeb Classical Library. Cambridge: Harvard Univ. Press

Clarke, Cyril A. 1961. Blood Groups and Diseases. *Progress in Medical Genetics*, 1: 81–119

Cochran, William G. 1967. Footnote. *Science*, 156: 1460–2

1976. Early Development of Techniques in Comparative Experimentation. In Owen, ed., 1976

Cohen, L. Jonathan 1981. Can Human Irrationality be Experimentally Demonstrated? *Behavioral and Brain Sciences*, 4: 317–31

Cohen, Jacob 1977. *Statistical Power Analysis for the Behavioral Sciences*. 2nd ed. New York: Academic Press

Cohen, Patricia Cline. 1982. *A Calculating People: The Spread of Numeracy in Early America*. Chicago: Univ. of Chicago Press

Coleman, William. 1982. *Death is a Social Disease: Public Health and Political Economy in Early Industrial France*. Madison: Univ. of Wisconsin Press

1983. Neither Empiricism nor Probability: The Experimental Approach. In Heidelberger et al., eds., 1983: 275–86

1987. Experimental Physiology and Statistical Inference: The Therapeutic Trial in Nineteenth Century Germany. In Krüger, Gigerenzer, and Morgan, eds., 1987: 201–26

Compton, A. H. 1923. A Quantum Theory of the Scattering of X-Rays by Light Elements. *Physical Review*, 21: 483–502

Compton, A. H. and A. W. Simon. 1925. Directed Quanta of Scattered X-Rays. *Physical Review*, 26: 289–99

Comte, Auguste. 1830–1842. *Cours de philosophie positive*. 6 vols., Paris: Bachelier

Condillac, Etienne. [1754] 1798. *Traité des sensations*. In *Oeuvres*, vol. 3. Paris

Condorcet, M.J.A.N. 1785. *Essai sur l'application de l'analyse à la probabilité des décisions rendues à la pluralité des voix*. Paris

Cook, Earnshaw. 1966. *Percentage Baseball*. Cambridge: MIT Press

Coumet, Ernest. 1970. La théorie du hasard est-elle née par hasard? *Annales: Economies, Sociétés, Civilisations*, mai–juin: 574–98

Cournot, A. A. 1843. *Exposition de la théorie des chances et des probabilités*. Paris

Cowan, Ruth S. 1972. Francis Galton's Statistical Ideas: The Influence of Eugenics. *Isis*, 63: 509–28

1974. Nature and Nurture: The Interplay of Biology and Politics in the Work of Francis Galton. *Studies in History of Biology*, 1: 133–208

Cowgill, George L. 1977. The Trouble With Significance Tests and What We Can Do About It. *American Antiquity*, 42: 350–68

Cox, D. R. 1958. *Planning of Experiments*. New York: Wiley

1977. The Role of Significance Testing. *Scandinavian Journal of Statistics*, 4: 49–70

Craig, John. 1699. *Theologiae christianae principia mathematica*. London

Cramér, H. 1946. *Mathematical Methods of Statistics.* Princeton: Princeton Univ. Press

Cullen, Michael. 1975. *The Statistical Movement in Early Victorian Britain: the Foundations of Empirical Social Research.* Hassocks: Harvester

Daboni, L., A. Montesano, and M. Lines. 1986. *Recent Developments in the Foundations of Utility and Risk Theory.* Dordrecht: Reidel

Danziger, K. 1987a. Statistical Method and the Historical Development of Research Practice in American Psychology. In Krüger, Gigerenzer, and Morgan, eds., 1987: 35–47

1987b Social Context and Investigative Practice in Early Twentieth-Century Psychology. In M. G. Ash and W. R. Woodward, eds., *Psychology in Twentieth-Century Thought and Society.* Cambridge: Cambridge Univ. Press

Darwin, Charles. [1839] 1974. N Notebook. In *Metaphysics, Materialism, and the Evolution of Mind: Early Writings of Charles Darwin.* Transcribed and annotated by P. H. Barrett. Chicago: Chicago Univ. Press

1859. *On the Origin of Species by Means of Natural Selection, or the Preservation of Favoured Races in the Struggle for Life.* London: Murray. Facsimile edition 1964. Introduction by E. Mayr. Cambridge: Harvard Univ. Press

1862. *On the Various Contrivances by which British and Foreign Orchids are Fertilised by Insects, and on the Good Effects of Intercrossing.* London: Murray

1868. *Variation of Animals and Plants under Domestication.* 2 vols., London: Murray

1871. *The Descent of Man, and Selection in Relation to Sex.* London: Murray. Facsimile edition 1981. Princeton: Princeton Univ. Press

1872. *On the Origin of Species by Means of Natural Selection.* 2 vols., 6th ed. London: Murray

[1876] 1969. *The Autobiography of Charles Darwin.* Barlow, ed. New York: Norton

1887. *The Variation of Animals and Plants Under Domestication.* 2 vols., 2nd ed. New York: Appleton

Darwin, Francis., ed. 1887. *The Life and Letters of Charles Darwin.* 3 vols., London: Murray

Daston, Lorraine J. 1979. D'Alembert's Critique of Probability Theory. *Historia Mathematica,* 6: 259–79

1980. Probabilistic Expectation and Rationality in Classical Probability Theory. *Historia Mathematica,* 7: 234–60

1981. Mathematics and the Moral Sciences: The Rise and Fall of the Probability of Judgments, 1785–1840. In H. N. Jahnke and M. Otte, eds., *Epistemological and Social Problems of the Sciences in the Early Nineteenth Century.* Dordrecht: Reidel

1987. The Domestication of Risk: Mathematical Probability and Insurance, 1650–1830. In Krüger, Daston, and Heidelberger, eds., 1987: 237–60

1988. *Classical Probability in the Enlightenment.* Princeton: Princeton Univ. Press

Davenport, C. B. 1914. A Discussion of the Methods and Results of Dr. Heron's Critique. *Eugenics Record Office Bulletin*, 11: 3–24

Davisson, C. J. and L. H. Germer. 1927. Diffraction of Electrons by a Crystal of Nickel. *Physical Review*, 30: 705–40

Dawid, A. P. 1983. Inference, Statistical: I. In Kotz and Johnson, eds., 1983 *et seq.*

Defoe, Daniel. 1697. *An Essay on Projects*. London

 1719. *The Gamester*. London

Defort, D., J. Donzelot, G. Maillet, and C. Mevel. 1977. *Socialisation du risque et pouvoir dans l'entreprise*. Typescript, Paris: Ministre du Travail

DeGroot, Morris H., S. E. Fienberg, and J. B. Kadane. 1986. *Statistics and the Law*. New York: Wiley

Delboeuf, Joseph. 1882. Déterminisme et liberté: la liberté demontrée par la mécanique. *Revue philosophique de la France et de l'étranger*, 13: 453–80, 608–38; 14: 156–89

Demain, Thomas. 1935. Probabilisme. In A. Vacant and E. Mangenot, eds., *Dictionnaire du théologie catholique*, vol. 13: 417–619. Paris: Letouzey et Ané

De Moivre, Abraham. [1718] 1756. *The Doctrine of Chances*. 3rd ed. London

 1725. *Treatise of Annuities*. London

De Morgan, Augustus. 1832. Quetelet on Probabilities. *Quarterly Journal of Education*, 4: 101–10

De Witt, Johann. 1671. *Waerdye van Lyf-Renten*. English trans. by F. Hendriks. In Robert G. Barnwell, 1856. *A Sketch of the Life and Times of John De Witt*. New York

Diamond, Marion and Mervyn Stone. 1981. Nightingale on Quetelet. *Journal of the Royal Statistical Society, A*, 144: 66–79, 176–213, 332–51

Diver, C. 1940. The Problem of Closely Related Snails Living in the Same Area. In J. S. Huxley, ed., *The New Systematics*. Oxford: Clarendon

Dobzhansky, Theodosius. 1937. *Genetics and the Origin of Species*. New York: Columbia Univ. Press

 1943. Genetics of Natural Populations. IX. Temporal Changes in the Composition of Populations of *Drosophila pseudoobscura*. *Genetics*, 28: 162–86

Dobzhansky, Theodosius and M. L. Queal. 1938. Genic Variation in Populations of *Drosophila pseudoobscura* Inhabiting Isolated Mountain Ranges. *Genetics*, 23: 463–84

Dodson, James. 1775. *The Mathematical Repository*. London

Douglas, Mary and Aaron Wildavsky. 1982. *Risk and Culture*. Berkeley: Univ. of California Press

Downton, F. 1982. Legal Probability and Statistics. *Journal of the Royal Statistical Society, A*, 145: 395–402

Drobisch, Moritz Wilhelm. 1867. *Die moralische Statistik und die menschliche Willensfreiheit: Eine Untersuchung*. Leipzig

Dubinin, N. P. and D. D. Romaschoff. 1932. The Genetic Structure of Species and their Evolution. In Russian. *Biologichesky Zhurnal*, 1: 52–95

Duncan, Otis Dudley. 1984. *Notes on Social Measurement: Historical and Critical.* New York: Russell Sage

Duncker, K. [1935] 1945. On Problem Solving. Trans. by L. S. Lees. 1945. *Psychological Monographs,* **58** (5, Whole No. 270)

Eadington, William R., ed. 1976. *Gambling and Society.* Springfield, Ill.: Charles C. Thomas

Earman, John. 1986. *A Primer on Determinism.* Dordrecht: Reidel

East, E. M. 1910. A Mendelian Interpretation of Variation that is Apparently Continuous. *American Naturalist,* 44: 65–82

Eddy, David M. 1982. Probabilistic Reasoning in Clinical Medicine: Problems and Opportunities. In Kahneman, Slovic, and Tversky, eds., 1982: 249–67

Edgeworth, Francis. 1888–90. Measurement of Change in Value of Money. *Reports of the British Association for the Advancement of Science.* 1888: 254–301; 1889: 188–219; 1890: 133–64

Edwards, A. W. F. 1972. *Likelihood.* Cambridge: Cambridge Univ. Press

Edwards, W. 1968. Conservatism in Human Information Processing. In B. Kleinmuntz, ed., *Formal Representation of Human Judgment.* New York: Wiley

Edwards, W., H. Lindman, and L. D. Phillips. 1965. Emerging Technologies for Making Decisions. *New Directions in Psychology. II.* New York: Holt, Rinehard and Winston

Edwards, W., H. Lindman, and L. J. Savage. 1963. Bayesian Statistical Inference for Psychological Research. *Psychological Review,* 70: 193–242

Eggleston, Richard. 1978. *Evidence, Proof and Probability.* London: Weidenfeld and Nicholson

Ehrenfest, Paul. 1959. *Collected Scientific Papers,* Martin J. Klein, ed. Amsterdam: North Holland

Ehrenfest, Paul and Tatjana. 1906a. Bemerkung zur Theorie der Entropiezunahme in der statistischen Mechanik von Gibbs. *Sitzungsberichte der kaiserlichen Akademie zu Wien, Mathematisch-Naturwissenschaftlichen Klasse, Abteilung IIa,* **115**: 89–98. Repr. in Ehrenfest 1959, 107–16

1906b. Über eine Aufgabe aus der Wahrscheinlichkeitsrechnung, die mit der kinetischen Deutung der Entropievermehrung zusammenhängt. *Mathematisch-Naturwissenschaftliche Blätter No. 11–12.* Repr. in Ehrenfest, 1959, 128–30

Einstein, Albert. 1905a. Über die von der molekularkinetischen Theorie der Wärme geforderte Bewegung von in ruhenden Flüssigkeiten suspendierten Teilchen. *Annalen der Physik,* 17: 549–60

1905b. Über einen die Erzeugung und Verwandlung des Lichtes betreffenden heuristischen Gesichtspunkt. *Annalen der Physik,* 17: 132–48

1909. Über die Entwicklung unserer Anschauungen über das Wesen und die Konstitution der Strahlung. *Verhandlungen der Deutschen Physikalischen Gesellschaft,* **11**: 482–500. Also in *Physikalische Zeitschrift,* **10**: 817–26

[1916] 1917. Zur Quantentheorie der Strahlung. *Physikalische Zeitschrift,* **18**:

121–8. English trans. in *Sources of Quantum Mechanics*, B. L. van der Waerden, ed., Amsterdam: North Holland, 1967: 63–77

Eisenhart, Churchill. 1964. The Meaning of "Least" in Least Squares. *Journal of the Washington Academy of Sciences*, **54**: 24–33

1971. The Development of the Concept of Best Mean of a Set of Measurements from Antiquity to the Present Day. Unpublished presidental address, American Statistical Association, 131st Annual Meeting, Fort Collins, Colorado

Eisenhart Churchill, A. T. Craig, E. G. Olds, L. E. Simon, and R. E. Wareham. 1940. Report of the War Preparedness Committee of the Institute of Mathematical Statistics. *Annals of Mathematical Statistics*, **11**: 479–84

Ellis, R. L. [read 1842] 1849. On the Foundations of the Theory of Probabilities. *Transactions of the Philosophical Society of Cambridge*, **8**: 1–6

Evans, Brian and Bernard Waites. 1981. *IQ and Mental Testing: An Unnatural Science and its Social History*. London: Macmillan

Evelyn, John. 1955. *The Diary of John Evelyn*. E. S. de Beer, ed., 6 vols., Oxford: Oxford Univ. Press

Eyler, John. 1979. *Victorian Social Medicine: The Ideas and Methods of William Farr*. Baltimore: Johns Hopkins Univ. Press

Fairley, William B. 1975. Probabilistic Analysis of Identification Evidence. In Wendt and Vlek, 1975: 233–56

Fancher, Raymond. 1985. *The Intelligence Men: Makers of the IQ Controversy*. New York: Norton

Fechner, G. T. 1860. *Elemente der Psychophysik*. Leipzig: Breitkopf and Härtel 1897. *Kollektivmasslehre*. G. F. Lipps, ed. Leipzig: W. Engelmann

Fienberg, S. E. 1985. Statistical Developments in World War II: An International Perspective. In Atkinson and Fienberg, 1985

Fienberg, S. E. and D. V. Hinkley, eds. 1980. *R. A. Fisher: An Appreciation*. New York: Springer

Finetti, Bruno de. 1970. *Teoria delle probabilita*. Turin: Giulio Einaudi. Trans. as *Theory of Probability*. New York: Wiley

Finkelstein, Michael O. 1978. *Quantitative Methods in Law*. New York: Free Press/Macmillan

Finkelstein, Michael O. and William B. Fairley. 1970. A Bayesian Approach to Identification and Evidence. *Harvard Law Review*, **83**: 489–517

Finney, D. 1964. Sir Ronald Fisher's Contributions to Biometric Statistics. *Biometrica*, **20**: 322–9

Fisch, R. and H. D. Daniel. 1982. Research and Publication Trends in Experimental Social Psychology: 1971–1980. A Thematic Analysis of the *Journal of Experimental Social Psychology*, and the *Zeitschrift für Sozialpsychologie*. *European Journal of Social Psychology*, **12**: 335–412

Fisher, Irving. 1911. *The Purchasing Power of Money: Its Determination and Relation to Credit, Interest and Crises*. New York: Macmillan

1927. *The Making of Index Numbers.* 3rd ed., Boston: Houghton-Mifflin

Fisher, Ronald Aylmer. 1918. The Correlation between Relatives on the Supposition of Mendelian Inheritance. *Transactions of the Royal Society of Edinburgh,* **52**: 399–433

1922a. On the Dominance Ratio. *Proceedings of the Royal Society of Edinburgh,* **42**: 321–41

1922b. On the Mathematical Foundations of Theoretical Statistics. *Philosophical Transactions of the Royal Society of London, A,* **222**: 309–68

1925. *Statistical Methods for Research Workers.* Edinburgh: Oliver and Boyd (5th ed., 1934)

1929. The Statistical Method in Psychical Research. *Proceedings of the Society for Psychical Research,* **39**: 185–9

1930a. *The Genetical Theory of Natural Selection.* Oxford: Clarendon

1930b. Inverse Probability. *Proceedings of the Cambridge Philosophical Society,* **26**: 528–35

1931. Letter of December 30, 1930 to Gosset. Letter no. 134 in *Letters from W. A. Gosset to R. A. Fisher, 1915–1936, with Summaries by R. A. Fisher.* Dublin: Guinness

1934. Indeterminism and Natural Selection. *Philosophy of Science,* **1**: 99–117

1935. *The Design of Experiments.* (7th ed., 1960; 8th ed., 1966) Edinburgh: Oliver and Boyd

1936. Has Mendel's Work Been Rediscovered? *Annals of Science,* **1**: 115–37

1939. "Student." *Annals of Eugenics,* **9**: 1–9

1953. Croonian Lecture: Population Genetics. *Proceedings of the Royal Society of London, B,* **141**: 510–53

1954. The Expansion of Statistics. *American Scientist,* **42**: 275–82

1955. Statistical Methods and Scientific Induction. *Journal of the Royal Statistical Society, B,* **17**: 69–78

1956. *Statistical Methods and Scientific Inference.* Edinburgh: Oliver and Boyd

1962. The Place of the Design of Experiments in the Logic of Scientific Inference. *Colloques Internationaux du Centre de la Recherche Scientifique (Paris), no.* **110**: 13–19

Fleming, Donald, ed. 1964. *The Mechanistic Conception of Life.* Cambridge: Harvard Univ. Press

1967. Attitude: The History of a Concept, *Perspectives in American History,* **1**: 287–365

Florence, P. Sargant. 1929. *The Statistical Method in Economics and Political Science.* New York: Harcourt, Brace, and Co.

Forster, E. M. [1910] 1921. *Howards End.* New York: Knopf

Freeze, R. Allen. 1974. An Analysis of Baseball Batting Order by Monte Carlo Simulation. *Operations Research,* **22**: 728–35

Fries, J. F. 1842. *Versuch einer Kritik der Principien der Wahrscheinlichkeitsrechnung.* Brunswick

Fürth, Reinhold. 1920. *Schwankungserscheinungen in der Physik*. Braunschweig: Vieweg

Futuyma, Douglas. 1979. *Evolutionary Biology*. Sunderland, Mass.: Sinauer Associates

Gaertner, C. F. 1849. *Versuche und Beobachtungen über die Bastarderzeugung im Pflanzenreich* (Experiments and Observations upon Hybridization in the Plant Kingdom). Stuttgart

Gallup, George. 1948. Report on the 1948 Election and Announcement of Change in Reporting Election Surveys. American Institute of Public Opinion Press Release, 12 Nov.

Gallup, George and Saul Forbes Rae. 1940. *The Pulse of Democracy: The Public Opinion Poll and How it Works*. New York: Simon and Schuster

Galton, Francis. 1869. *Hereditary Genius*. London: Macmillan

1872. Statistical Inquiries into the Efficacy of Prayer. *Fortnightly Review, n.s.* 12: 125–35

1889. *Natural Inheritance*. London: Macmillan

1890. Kinship and Correlation. *North American Review.* 150: 419–31

1897. The Average Contribution of Each Several Ancestor to the Total Heritage of the Offspring. *Proceedings of the Royal Society,* 61: 401–13

Gani, J., ed. 1982. *The Making of Statisticians*. New York: Springer

ed. 1986. *The Craft of Probabilistic Modelling*. New York: Springer

Garber, Daniel and Sandy Zabell. 1979. On the Emergence of Probability. *Archive for History of Exact Sciences,* 21: 33–53

Gauss, C. F. 1809. *Theoria motus corporum celestium*. Hamburg: Perthes et Besser

1827. Gauss an Olbers. Letter no. 613 in C. Schilling, ed., *Wilhelm Olbers, Sein Leben und seine Werke*. Berlin: J. Springer, 1894–1909. 2 vols., vol. 2: *Briefwechsel Gauss-Olbers*, p. 480

Geiger, Hans and J. M. Nuttall. 1911–12. The Ranges of the α-Particles from Various Radioactive Substances and a Relation Between Range and Period of Transformation. *Philosophical Magazine,* 22: 613–21; 23: 439–45

Ghiselin, M. J. 1969. *The Triumph of the Darwinian Method*. Berkeley: Univ. of California Press

Gibbs, J. Willard. 1902. *Elementary Principles in Statistical Mechanics*. Yale Univ. Press. Repr. New York: Dover, 1960

Giere, R. N. and R. S. Westfall, eds. 1973. *Foundations of Scientific Method: The Nineteenth Century*. Bloomington: Indiana Univ. Press

Gigerenzer, Gerd. 1987a. Probabilistic Thinking and the Fight against Subjectivity. In Krüger, Gigerenzer, and Morgan, eds., 1987: 11–33

1987b. Survival of the Fittest Probabilist: Brunswik, Thurstone, and the Two Disciplines of Psychology. In Krüger, Gigerenzer, and Morgan, eds., 1987: 49–72

Gigerenzer, Gerd, W. Hell and H. Blank. 1988. Presentation and Content: The Use of Base Rates as a Continuous Variable. *Journal of Experimental Psychology: Human Perception and Performance,* 14: 513–25

Gigerenzer, Gerd and D. J. Murray. 1987. *Cognition as Intuitive Statistics*. Hillsdale, NJ: Lawrence Erlbaum Associates

Gillispie, Charles C. 1963. Intellectual Factors in the Background of Analysis by Probabilities. *Scientific Change*, A. C. Crombie, ed. New York: Basic Books: 431–53

1972. Probability and Politics: Laplace, Condorcet, and Turgot. *Proceedings of the American Philosophical Society*, 116: 1–20

1980. Laplace, Pierre Simon de. In *Dictionary of Scientific Biography*, C. C. Gillispie, ed., New York: Scribner, vol. 15: 273–403

Gough, Harrison G. 1964. Clinical versus Statistical Prediction in Psychology. In Postman, 1964

Gould, Stephen Jay. 1981. *The Mismeasure of Man*. New York: Norton

1983. The Hardening of the Modern Synthesis. In M. Grene, ed., *Dimensions of Darwinism*. Cambridge: Cambridge Univ. Press

Gower, Barry. 1982. Astronomy and Probability: Forbes versus Michell on the Distribution of Stars. *Annals of Science*, 39: 145–60

Graunt, John. [1662] 1975. *Natural and Political Observations Mentioned in a Following Index and Made Upon the Bills of Mortality*. New York: Arno Press. Reprint of 1662 London edition

Gray, Asa. [1860] 1963. Natural Selection not Inconsistent with Natural Theology. In *Darwiniana: Essays and Reviews Pertaining to Darwinism*. A. Hunter Dupree, ed. Cambridge: Harvard Univ. Press: 72–145

Green, D. M. and J. A. Swets. 1966. *Signal Detection Theory and Psychophysics*. New York: Wiley

Grenander, U., ed. 1959. *Probability and Statistics: The Harald Cramér Volume*. Stockholm: Almquist and Wiksell

Guerry, André-Michel. 1833. *Essai sur la statistique morale de la France* Paris: Crochard

Guilford, J. P. 1942. *Fundamental Statistics in Psychology and Education*. 1st ed., 1942; 3rd ed., 1956, 6th ed., 1978, with B. Fruchter. New York: McGraw-Hill

Hacking, Ian. 1965. *Logic of Statistical Inference*. Cambridge: Cambridge Univ. Press

1975. *The Emergence of Probability*. Cambridge: Cambridge Univ. Press

1980. The Theory of Probable Inference: Neyman, Peirce and Braithwaite. In D. H. Mellor, ed., *Science, Belief and Behaviour*. Cambridge: Cambridge Univ. Press: 141–60

1983. Nineteenth-Century Cracks in the Concept of Determinism. *Journal of the History of Ideas*, 44: 455–75

1987. Was there a Probabilistic Revolution 1800–1930? In Krüger, Daston, and Heidelberger, eds., 1987: pp. 45–55

in press. Telepathy and the Beginnings of Randomization. *Isis*

forthcoming. *The Taming of Chance*. Cambridge: Cambridge Univ. Press

Haeckel, Ernst. 1866. *Generelle Morphologie der Organismen* (General Morphology of Organisms). 2 vols. Berlin: Reimer

[1899] 1900. *The Riddle of the Universe.* Trans. by J. McCabe. New York: Harper and Brothers

Hagen, G. H. L. 1837. *Grundzüge der Wahrscheinlichkeitsrechnung.* Berlin: Dümmler

Hall, Alfred D. 1917. *The Book of the Rothamsted Experiments.* 2nd ed. E. J. Russel, ed. London: John Murray

Halley, Edmund. 1693. An Estimate on the Degrees of Mortality of Mankind, drawn from the Curious Tables of the Births and Funerals at the City of Breslau; with an Attempt to Ascertain the Price of Annuities upon Lives. *Philosophical Transactions of the Royal Society.* 17: 596–610

Harris, J. A. 1912. A Simple Test of the Goodness of Fit of Mendelian Ratios. *American Naturalist*, 46: 741–5

Harter, H. Leon. 1974–76. The Method of Least Squares and some Alternatives. *International Statistical Review*, 42: 147–74, 235–64, 282; 43: 1–44, 125–90, 269–78; 44: 113–59

Hartley, David. 1749. *Observations on Man, His Frame, His Duty, and His Expectations.* London

Hays, W. L. 1963. *Statistics for Psychologists.* New York: Holt, Rinehart and Winston

Hearnshaw, L. S. 1979. *Cyril Burt: Psychologist.* Ithaca: Cornell Univ. Press.

Heidelberger, Michael, L. Krüger, and R. Rheinwald, eds. 1983. *Probability since 1800: Interdisciplinary Studies of Scientific Development.* Bielefeld: *Report Wissenschaftsforschung*, 25

Heider, F. 1958. *The Psychology of Interpersonal Relations.* New York: Wiley

Heisenberg, Werner. 1925. Über quantentheoretische Umdeutung kinematischer und mechanischer Beziehungen. *Zeitschrift für Physik*, 33: 879–93. English trans. in van der Waerden, 1967: 261–76

1927. Über den anschaulichen Inhalt der quantentheoretischen Kinematik und Mechanik. *Zeitschrift für Physik*, 43: 172–98

Helmholtz, Hermann von [1847] 1889. Über die Erhaltung der Kraft. *Ostwald's Klassiker der exacten Wissenschaften, No. 1*, Leipzig: Engelmann

Herbart, J. F. 1816. *Lehrbuch zur Psychologie.* Hamburg and Leipzig: G. Hartenstein. 2nd ed., 1834, trans. by M. K. Smith as *A Text-Book in Psychology.* New York: Appleton

Heron, D. 1913. Mendelism and the Problem of Mental Defect. *Questions of the Day and Fray*, 7: 1–62

Heyde, C. C. and E. Seneta. 1977. *I. J. Bienaymé: Statistical Theory Anticipated.* New York: Springer

Hilts, Victor L. 1973. Statistics and Social Science. In Giere and Westfall, eds., 1973: 206–33

1978. *Aliis Exterendum*, or, the Origins of the Statistical Society of London. *Isis*, 69: 21–43

Himsworth, H. P. *et. al.* 1944. Clinical Trial of Patulin in the Common Cold. *Lancet*, vol. 2: 373–5

Hodge, M. J. S. and D. Kohn. 1986. The Immediate Origins of Natural Selection. In Kohn, ed., 1986

Hoerl, Arthur E. and Herbert K. Fallin. 1974. Reliability of Subjective Evaluations in a High Incentive Situation. *Journal of the Royal Statistical Society*, A,137: 227–30

Hogben, Lancelot. 1957. *Statistical Theory: The Relationship of Probability, Credibility and Error.* London: Allen and Unwin and New York: Norton

Holmes, F. L. 1964. Introduction. In Justus von Liebig, *Animal Chemistry, or Organic Chemistry in its Application to Physiology and Pathology* [1842]. Facsimile edition. New York: Johnson Reprint Corporation

1985. *Lavoisier and the Chemistry of Life: An Exploration of Scientific Creativity.* Madison: Univ. of Wisconsin Press

Hooper, George. 1699. A Calculation of the Credibility of Human Testimony. *Philosophical Transactions of the Royal Society*, 21: 359–65

Hotelling, H. 1940. The Teaching of Statistics. *Annals of Mathematical Statistics*, 11: 457–72

1951. The Impact of R. A. Fisher on Statistics. *Journal of the American Statistical Association*, 46: 35–46

Hotelling, H. and H. Working. 1921. Applications of the Theory of Errors to the Interpretations of Trends. *Journal of the American Statistical Association*, 24: 73–85

Huber, P. J. 1981. *Robust Statistics.* New York: Wiley

Hull, C. L. 1943. The Problem of Intervening Variables in Molar Behavior Theory. *Psychological Review*, 50: 273–91

Hull, David L. 1973. *Darwin and his Critics.* Cambridge: Harvard Univ. Press

Hume, David. [1739] 1975. *A Treatise of Human Nature.* L. A. Selby-Bigges, ed. Oxford: Clarendon Press

[1758] 1955. *An Enquiry Concerning Human Understanding.* Charles W. Hendel, ed. Indianapolis: Bobbs-Merrill

Humphrey, G. 1951. *Thinking. An Introduction to its Experimental Psychology.* New York: Wiley

Huxley, Leonard. 1901. *Life and Letters of Thomas H. Huxley.* 2 vols., New York: D. Appleton and Co

Huxley, Thomas H. [1864] 1888. Criticisms on the Origin of Species. In *Lay Sermons, Essays, and Reviews.* New York: Appleton

Huygens, Christiaan. [1657] 1920. *De ratiociniis in ludo aleae.* In *Oeuvres complètes de Christiaan Huygens*, vol. XIV. The Hague: Martinus Nijhoff.

Ignatin, George and Robert Smith. 1976. The Economics of Gambling. In Eadington, 1976: 69–91

International Statistical Conferences. 1947. *Proceedings of the International Statistical Conferences, held in Washington, D.C. on September 6–18 of 1947.* 4 vols. Calcutta: EKA Press

International Statistics Institute. 1986. Declaration of Professional Ethics. *International Statistical Review*, **54**: 227–42

James, Bill. 1986. *The Bill James Historical Baseball Abstract*. New York: Doubleday

James, William. 1884. The Dilemma of Determinism. *Unitarian Review* (September). Many reprints

Jammer, Max. 1966. *The Conceptual Development of Quantum Mechanics*. New York: McGraw-Hill

Jaynes, Edwin T. 1967. Foundations of Probability Theory and Statistical Mechanics. Chapter 6 of *The Delaware Seminar in the Foundations of Physics, vol. 1*. M. Bunge, ed. Berlin: Springer: 77–101

Jeans, James H. [1904] 1925. *The Dynamical Theory of Gases I*. 4th ed., Cambridge: Cambridge Univ. Press

Jeffrey, R. 1987. Risk and Human Rationality. *The Monist*, **70**: 223–36

Jenkin, Fleeming. 1867. The Origin of Species. *The North British Review*, **46**: 277–318. Reprinted in Hull, 1973

Jennings, H. S. [1906] 1962. *Behavior of the Lower Organisms*. Bloomington: Indiana Univ. Press

Jensen, A. 1926. Report on the Representative Method of Statistics. *Proceedings of the International Statistical Institute*, **22** (1): 359–439

Jevons, William Stanley. [1874] 1877. *The Principles of Science*. 2nd ed., London: Macmillan

Johannsen, W. 1909. *Elemente der exakten Erblichkeitslehre* (Elements of a Quantitative Study of Heredity). Jena: Fischer

Johnston, J. F. W. 1849. *Experimental Agriculture, Being the Results of Past, and Suggestions for Future Experiments in Scientific and Practical Agriculture*. Edinburgh: William Blackwood and Sons

Jordan, Pascual. 1928. Die Lichtquantenhypothese. *Ergebnisse der exakten Naturwissenschaften* 1: 158–208

Jordan, W. 1895. *Handbuch der Vermessungskunde*. Stuttgart: Metzler

Jorland, Gérard. 1987. The St. Petersburg Paradox, 1713–1937. In Krüger, Daston, and Heidelberger, eds., 1987: 157–90

Kahneman, D. and A. Tversky. 1972. Subjective Probability: A Judgment of Representativeness. *Cognitive Psychology*, **3**: 430–54

1973. On the Psychology of Prediction. *Psychological Review*, **80**: 237–51

Kahneman, D., P. Slovic, and A. Tversky, eds. 1982. *Judgment under Uncertainty: Heuristics and Biases*. Cambridge: Cambridge Univ. Press

Kaspar, Raphael G. 1980. Perceptions of Risk and their Effects on Decision Making. In Schwing and Abers, 1980: 71–84

Kelley, H. H. 1967. Attribution Theory in Social Psychology. In D. Levine, ed., *Nebraska Symposium on Motivation. Vol. 15*. Lincoln: Univ. of Nebraska Press.

1973. The Process of Causal Attribution. *American Psychologist*, **28**: 107–28

Kelley, Truman Lee. 1923. *Statistical Method*. New York: Macmillan

Kempthorne, O. 1976. Of What Use are Tests of Significance and Tests of

Hypothesis? *Communications in Statistics – Theory and Methods*, **A5**: 763–77

Kendall, Maurice G. 1942. On the Future of Statistics. *Journal of the Royal Statistical Society*, **105**: 69–80

1949. On the Reconciliation of Theories of Probability. *Biometrika*, **36**: 101–16

1956. The Beginnings of a Probability Calculus. *Biometrika*, **43**: 1–14

Kendall, M. G. and R. L. Plackett. 1977. *Studies in the History of Statistics and Probability*, vol. 2. London: Griffin

Kevles, Daniel J. 1968–69. Testing the Army's Intelligence: Psychologists and the Military in World War I. *Journal of American History*, **55**: 565–81

1985. *In the Name of Eugenics: Genetics and the Uses of Human Heredity*. New York: Knopf

Keynes, John Maynard. 1921. *A Treatise on Probability*. London: Macmillan

Kiaer, A. N. 1898. Die Repräsentative Untersuchungsmethode. *Allgemeines Statistisches Archiv*, **5**: 1–37

Kimball, A. W. 1957. Errors of the Third Kind in Statistical Consulting. *Journal of the American Statistical Association*, **52**: 133–42

Kimura. M. 1968. Evolutionary Rate at the Molecular Level. *Nature*, **217**: 624–6

1983. *The Neutral Theory of Molecular Evolution*. Cambridge: Cambridge Univ. Press

King, J. L. and T. H. Jukes. 1969. Non-Darwinian Evolution. *Science*, **164**: 788–98

Kingsland, Sharon. 1985. *Modeling Nature: Episodes in the History of Population Ecology*. Chicago: Univ. of Chicago Press

Kirchhoff, G. R. 1862. Untersuchungen über das Sonnenspectrum und die Spectren der chemischen Elemente, *Abhandlungen der Königlichen Akademie der Wissenschaften zu Berlin aus dem Jahre 1861*: 63–95

Knapp, Georg Friedrich. 1871. Die neueren Ansichten über Moralstatistik. *Jahrbücher für Nationalökonomie und Statistik*, **16**: 237–50

1872. A. Quetelet als Theoretiker. *Jahrbücher für Nationalökonomie und Statistik*, **18**: 89–124

Kohlrausch, Friedrich. 1870. *Leitfaden der praktischen Physik*. Leipzig: Teubner

Kohlrausch, K. W. Fritz. 1906. Über Schwankungen der radioaktiven Umwandlung. *Sitzungsberichte der kaiserlichen Akademie der Wissenschaften in Wien, Mathematisch-Naturwissenschaftliche Klasse, Abteilung IIa*, **115**: 673–82

Kohn, David, ed. 1986. *The Darwinian Heritage*. Princeton: Princeton Univ. Press

Kölliker, A. 1864. *Über die Darwin'sche Schöpfungstheorie* (On the Darwinian Theory of Origins). Leipzig

Kolmogorov, A. N. 1933. Grundbegriffe der Washrscheinlichkeitsrechnung. *Ergebnisse der Mathematik*, **2**(3): 196–262

Koopman, B. O. 1940. The Axioms and Algebra of Intuitive Probability. *Annals of Mathematics*, **41**: 269–92

Kotz, S. and N. L. Johnson, eds. 1983 *et seq. Encyclopedia of Statistical Sciences*. New York: John Wiley

Krech, D. 1955. Discussion: Theory and Reductionism. *Psychological Review*, **62**: 229–31

Krohn, W. and W. Schäfer. 1976. The Origins and Structure of Agricultural Chemistry. In G. Lemaine *et al.*, eds., *Perspectives on the Emergence of Scientific Disciplines*. Mouton: The Hague

Krönig, August Karl. 1856. Grundzüge einer Theorie der Gase. *Annalen der Physik* [2], **99**: 315–22

Krüger, Lorenz, L. Daston, and M. Heidelberger, eds. 1987. *The Probabilistic Revolution, Vol. 1: Ideas in History*. Cambridge, Mass.: MIT Press

Krüger, Lorenz, G. Gigerenzer, and M. S. Morgan, eds. 1987. *The Probabilistic Revolution, vol. 2: Ideas in the Sciences*. Cambridge, Mass.: MIT Press

Kruskal, William, and Frederick Mosteller. 1980. Representative Sampling, IV: The History of the Concept in Statistics, 1895–1939. *International Statistical Review*, **48**: 169–95

Kuhn, Thomas S. 1978. *Black-Body Theory and the Quantum Discontinuity*. Oxford: Oxford Univ. Press

Labys, Walter C. and C. W. J. Granger. 1970. *Speculation, Hedging and Commodity Price Forecasts*. Lexington, Mass.: Heath

Lamarck, J. B. [1809] 1914. *Zoological Philosophy*. Translated by H. Elliot. Facsimile edition of translation, 1984. Introductions by D. L. Hull and R. W. Burkhardt. Chicago: Univ. of Chicago Press

Lamotte, M. 1959. Polymorphism of Natural Populations of *Cepaea nemoralis*. *Cold Spring Harbor Symposia on Quantitative Biology*, **24**: 65–84

Lancaster, H. O. 1972. Development of the Notion of Statistical Dependence. *Mathematical Chronicle* (New Zealand), **2**: 1–16

Lanigan, Ernest J. 1922. *Baseball Cyclopedia*. New York: Baseball Magazine Company

Laplace, Pierre Simon. 1774. Mémoire sur la probabilité des causes par les événements. *Mémoires présentées à l'Académie des Sciences*, **6**: 621–56

1799–1805. *Traité de mécanique celeste*. 4 vols., Paris

1810. Mémoire sur les approximations des formules qui sont fonctions de très grands nombres et sur leur application aux probabilités. Reprinted in Laplace, 1878–1912, vol. 12: 301–53

1812. Théorie analytique des probabilités. Troisième édition, revue et augmentée par l'auteur. Paris: Courcies, 1820. Reprinted in Laplace, 1878–1912, vol. 7

[1814] 1951. *A Philosophical Essay on Probabilities*. F. W. Truscott and F. L. Emory, trans. New York: Dover

1878–1912. *Oeuvres Complètes de Laplace*. Paris: Gauthier-Villars.

Lavoisier, A. L. and P. S. Laplace. 1780. Mémoire sur la Chaleur. *Mémoires de l'Académie des Sciences*

Lazarsfeld, Paul. 1950. The Logical and Mathematical Foundation of Latent Structure Analysis. In Stouffer *et al.*, 1950: 312–61

Lehmann, E. L. 1986. *Testing Statistical Hypotheses*. 2nd ed., New York: Academic Press

Leibniz, Gottfried Wilhelm. [1677] 1951. Preface to the Universal Science. In

Philip P. Wiener ed., *Selections*. New York: Charles Scribner's Sons

[1703] 1962. *G. W. Leibniz Mathematische Schriften*. C. I. Gerhardt, ed. Hildesheim: Georg Olms. Reprint of 1855 edition

[comp. *c.* 1705] 1962. *Nouveaux essais sur l'entendement humain*. In *Sämtliche Schriften und Briefe*. Sechste Reihe: Philosophische Schriften, vol. VI. Berlin: Akademie Verlag

Lenoir, T. 1982. *The Strategy of Life*. Dordrecht: Reidel.

Levi, Isaac. 1980. *The Enterprise of Knowledge: An Essay on Knowledge, Credal Probability, and Choice*. Cambridge, Mass.: MIT Press

Lewin, Kurt. 1935. *Dynamic Theory of Personality*. New York: McGraw-Hill

Lewis, Sinclair. 1925. *Arrowsmith*. New York: Harcourt Brace

Lewontin, R. S., J. A. Moore, W. B. Provine, and Bruce Wallace. 1981. *Dobzhansky's Genetics of Natural Populations, I-XLIII*. New York: Columbia Univ. Press

Lexis, Wilhelm. 1875. *Einleitung in die Theorie der Bevölkerungsstatistik*. Strasbourg: Trübner

   1877. *Zur Theorie der Massenerscheinungen in der menschlichen Gesellschaft*. Freiburg: Wagner

   1879. *Gewerkvereine und Unternehmerverbände in Frankreich*. Leipzig: Duncker und Humblot

   1903. *Abhandlungen zur Theorie der Bevölkerungs- und Moralstatistik*. Jena: Gustav Fischer

Lieb, Frederick. 1973. Ernie Lanigan: Patron Saint of SABR. *Baseball Research Journal*, 2: 29–33

Lindemann, F. A. 1915. Note on the Relation between the Life or Radio-active Substances and the Range of the Rays emitted. *Philosophical Magazine* [6], 30: 560–3

Lindley, D. V. 1980. L. J. Savage: His Work in Probability and Statistics. *Annals of Statistics*, 8: 1–24

Lindsey, George R. 1959. Statistical Data Useful for the Operation of a Baseball Team. *Operations Research*, 7: 197–207

   1963. An Investigation of Strategies in Baseball. *Operations Research*, 11: 477–501

Lippmann, Walter. 1922. *Public Opinion*. New York: Macmillan

Locke, John. [1690] 1959. *An Essay Concerning Human Understanding*. Alexander Campbell Fraser, ed. New York: Dover

Loeb, Jacques. [1899] 1964. *Comparative Physiology of the Brain and Comparative Psychology*. Selections in Fleming, ed., 1964

   1906. *The Dynamics of Living Matter*. New York: Columbia Univ. Press

   [1909a] 1964. The Significance of Tropisms for Psychology. In Fleming, ed., 1964

   [1909b] 1964. Experimental Study of the Influence of Environment on Animals. In Fleming, ed., 1964

   [1912] 1964. The Mechanistic Conception of Life. In Fleming, ed., 1964

Lopes, Lola. 1986. What Naive Decision Makers Can Tell Us about Risk. In

Daboni, Montesano, and Lines, 1986

Louis, P. C. A. 1836. *Researches on the Effects of Bloodletting in some Inflammatory Diseases, and on the Influence of Tartarized Antimony and Vesication in Pneumonitis* [1835]. Trans. by C. G. Putnam. Boston: Hilliard, Gray

Lovie, A. D. 1979. The Analysis of Variance in Experimental Psychology: 1934–1945. *British Journal of Mathematical and Statistical Psychology*, 32: 151–78

McArthur, L. A. 1972. The How and What of Why: Some Determinants and Consequences of Causal Attribution. *Journal of Personality and Social Psychology*, 22: 171–93

McCloskey, Donald N. 1985. *The Rhetoric of Economics*. Madison: Univ. of Wisconsin Press

McKean, Kevin. 1982. Turning Baseball into a Science. *Discover*, June

MacKenzie, Donald. 1981. *Statistics in Britain, 1865–1930: The Social Construction of Scientific Knowledge*. Edinburgh: Edinburgh Univ. Press

Maistrov, L. E. [1964] 1974. *Probability Theory. A Historical Sketch*. Samuel Kotz, trans. New York and London: Academic Press

Markov, A. A. 1906. Extension of the Law of Large Numbers to Dependent Variables. (in Russian) *Izvestiia Fiziko-Matematicheskovo Obshchestva pri Kazanskom Universitete* [2], 15, no. 4

Martin-Löf, P. 1974. The Notion of Redundancy and its Use as a Quantitative Measure of the Deviation between a Statistical Hypothesis and a Set of Observational Data. In Barndorff-Nielsen *et al.*, 1974: 1–42

Mauskopf, Seymour H. and Michael R. McVaugh. 1979. The Controversy over Statistics in Parapsychology 1934–1938. In S. Mauskopf, ed., *The Reception of Unconventional Science*. Boulder: Westview Press

   1980. *The Elusive Science: Origins of Experimental Psychical Research*. Baltimore: Johns Hopkins Univ. Press

Maxwell, James Clerk. 1860. Illustrations of the Dynamical Theory of Gases. In Maxwell, 1890, vol. 1: 377–409

   1866. On the Dynamical Theory of Gases. In Maxwell, 1890, vol. 2: 26–77

   1873a. Science and Free Will. In Campbell and Garnett, 1882: 434–44

   1873b. Molecules. In Maxwell, 1890, vol. 2: 361–77

   1875a. *Theory of Heat*. London: Longmans, Green

   [1875b] 1890. Atom. In Maxwell, 1890, vol. 2: 415–84

   1878. On Boltzmann's Theorem on the Average Distribution of Energy in a System of Material Points. In Maxwell, 1890, vol. 2: 713–41

   1890. *Scientific Papers*. W. D. Niven, ed. 2 vols., Cambridge: Cambridge Univ. Press

Mayr, Ernst. 1963. *Animal Species and Evolution*. Cambridge: Harvard Univ. Press

   1982. *The Growth of Biological Thought: Diversity, Evolution, and Inheritance*. Cambridge: Harvard Univ. Press

   1983. How to Carry Out the Adaptationist Program. *American Naturalist*, 121: 324–34

Mayr, Georg von. 1895. *Theoretische Statistik*. Freiburg: Mohr

Meehl, P. E. 1978. Theoretical Risks and Tabular Asterisks: Sir Karl, Sir Ronald, and the Slow Progress of Soft Psychology. *Journal of Consulting and Clinical Psychology*, **46**: 806–34

Meijer, Onno. 1984. Mendel and Statistics. Unpublished paper given at the Zentrum für inderdisziplinäre Forschung, Bielefeld, FRG

Melton, A. W. 1962. Editorial. *Journal of Experimental Psychology*, **64**: 553–7

Ménard, Claude. 1978. *La formation d'une rationalité économique: A. A. Cournot*. Paris: Flammarion

1980. Three Forms of Resistance to Statistics. Say, Cournot, Walras. *History of Political Economy*, **12**: 524–41

Mendel, Gregor. [1865] 1966. Experiments on Plant Hybridization. Trans. by E. R. Sherwood. In C. Stern and E. R. Sherwood, eds., *The Origin of Genetics: A Mendel Source Book*. San Francisco: Freeman

Mendelsohn, E. 1963. Cell Theory and the Development of General Physiology. *Archives Internationales d'Histoire des Sciences*, **16**: 419–29

Merz, J. T. 1904–1912. *A History of European Thought in the Nineteenth Century*. 4 vols. Facsimile edition 1976. Gloucester, Mass.: Peter Smith

Meuvret, Jean. 1971. Les données démographiques et statistiques en histoire moderne et contemporaine. *Cahiers des Annales*, **32**: 313–40

Michell, John. 1767. An Inquiry into the Probable Parallax and Magnitude of the Fixed Stars From the Quantity of Light Which they Afford Us, and the Particular Circumstances of Their Situation. *Philosophical Transactions of the Royal Society*, **57**: 234–64

Michotte, A. [1946] 1963. *The Perception of Causality*. New York: Basic Books

1952. Albert Michotte van den Berck (Autobiography). In E. G. Boring *et al*., eds., *A History of Psychology in Autobiography. Vol IV*. Worcester, Mass: Clark Univ. Press, 1952: 213–36

Miké, Valerie and Robert A. Good. 1977. Old Problems, New Challenges (Medical Research: Statistics and Ethics). *Science*, **198**: 677–8

Mill, John Stuart. [1843] 1881. *A System of Logic*. 8th ed. New York

Mises, Richard von. [1921] 1964. Über die gegenwärtige Krise der Mechanik. *Zeitschrift für angewandte Mathematik und Mechanik*, **1**: 425–31 Reprinted in: *Selected Papers of Richard von Mises, vol. 2: Probability and Statistics, General*. Ph. Frank *et al*., eds. Providence, RI: American Mathematical Society, 1964: 478–87

[1928] 1957. Wahrscheinlichkeit, Statistik und Wahrheit. 1st ed., Vienna, 1929. 3rd (1951) ed. trans. into English as *Probability, Statistics, and Truth* by Hilda Geiringer, trans. London: Allen and Unwin, 1957

Montmort, Pierre Reymond de. 1713. *Essai d'analyse sur les jeux de hasard*. 2nd ed., Paris

Moore, Peter G. 1983. *The Business of Risk*. Cambridge: Cambridge Univ. Press

Morgan, T. H., H. J. Muller, A. H. Sturtevant, and C. B. Bridges. 1915. *Mechanism of Mendelian Heredity*. New York: Holt

Morrison, D. E. and R. E. Henkel, eds. 1970. *The Signficance Test Controversy.* Chicago: Aldine

Nagel, Ernest. 1955. Principles of the Theory of Probability. In Otto Neurath, Charles Morris, and Rudolf Carnap, eds. *International Encyclopedia of United Science*, vol. I, part 2. Chicago: Univ. of Chicago Press

Nelkin, Dorothy and Michael Pollak. 1980. Problems and Procedures in the Regulation of Technological Risk. In Schwing and Abers, 1980: 233–53

Neumann, John von and O. Morgenstern. 1944. *The Theory of Games and Economic Behavior.* Princeton: Princeton Univ. Press

Neumann-Spallart, F. X. von. 1885. Résumé of the Results of the International Statistical Congresses and Sketch of Proposed Plan of an International Statistical Association. In Royal Statistical Society, 1885

Neyman, Jerzy. 1934. On the Two Different Aspects of the Representative Method: the Method of Stratified Sampling and the Method of Purposive Selection (with discussion). *Journal of the Royal Statistical Society*, 97: 558–625

1941. Fiducial Argument and the Theory of Confidence Intervals. *Biometrika*, 32: 128–50

1950. *Probability and Statistics.* New York: Holt

1956. Note on an Article by Sir Ronald Fisher. *Journal of the Royal Statistical Society, B*, 18: 288–94

1957. Inductive Behavior as a Basic Concept of Philosophy of Science. *International Statistical Review*, 25: 7–22

1967. R. A. Fisher (1890–1962): An Appreciation. *Science*, 156: 1456–60

1976a. The Emergence of Mathematical Statistics: A Historical Sketch with Particular Reference to the United States. In Owen, 1976: 147–93

1976b. Tests of Statistical Hypotheses and their Use in Studies of Natural Phenomena. *Communications in Statistics, A5 (Theory and Methods)*: 737–51

Nisbett, R. E. and E. Borgida. 1975. Attribution and the Psychology of Prediction. *Journal of Personality and Social Psychology*, 32: 932–43

Nisbett, R. E., D. H. Krantz, C. Jepson, and Z. Kunda. 1983. The Use of Statistical Heuristics in Everyday Inductive Reasoning. *Psychological Review*, 90: 339–63

Nixon, J. W. 1960. *A History of the International Statistical Institute, 1885–1960.* The Hague: International Statistical Institute

Noonan, John T. 1957. *The Scholastic Analysis of Usury.* Cambridge, Mass: Harvard Univ. Press

Norton, Bernard J. 1973. The Biometric Defense of Darwinism. *Journal of the History of Biology*, 6: 283–316

1979. Charles Spearman and the General Factor in Intelligence: Genesis and Interpretation in the Light of Sociopersonal Considerations. *Journal for the History of the Behavioral Sciences*, 15: 142–54

Nunnally, J. 1960. The Place of Statistics in Psychology. *Educational and Psychological Measurement*, 20: 641–50

Nye, Mary Jo. 1972. *Molecular Reality: A Perspective on the Scientific Work of Jean Perrin*. New York: American Elsevier

1976. The Moral Freedom of Man and the Determinism of Nature. *British Journal for the History of Science*, 9: 274–92

Oakes, Michael. 1986. *Statistical Inference: A Commentary for the Social and Behavioral Sciences*. New York: Wiley

Ogborn, Maurice E. 1962. *Equitable Assurances*. London: George Allen and Unwin

Olbers, W. 1827. Olbers an Gauss. Letter no. 612 in C. Schilling, ed. *Wilhelm Olbers, sein Leben und seine Werke*, 2 vols., Berlin: J. Springer, 1894–1909, *vol. 2. Briefwechsel Gauss-Olbers*, 477–8

Olby, R. C. 1966. *Origins of Mendelism*. New York: Shocken

Old, B. S. 1961. The Evolution of the Office of Naval Research. *Physics Today*, 14: 30–5

Ondar, K.O., ed. 1981. *The Correspondence between A. A. Markov and A. A. Chuprov on the Theory of Probability and Mathematical Statistics*. New York: Springer

Orel, V. 1985. *Mendel*. New York: Hill and Wang

Ospovat, D. 1981. *The Development of Darwin's Theory: Natural History, Natural Theology, and Natural Selection, 1838–1859*. Cambridge: Cambridge Univ. Press

Owen, D. B., ed. 1976. *On the History of Statistics and Probability*. New York: Marcel Dekker

Paley, William 1802. *Natural Theology, or Evidences of the Existence and Attributes of the Deity, Collected from the Appearances of Nature*. London: Fauldner

Parshall, Karen Hunger. 1982. Varieties as Incipient Species: Darwin's Numerical Analysis. *Journal of the History of Biology*, 15: 191–214

Pascal, Blaise. [1654] 1970. *Oeuvres complètes de Pascal*. Jean Mesnard, ed. Paris: Bibliothèque Européenne – Desclès de Brouwer

[1669] 1962. *Pensées*. Louis Lafuma, ed. Paris: Editions du Seuil

Pauly, P. J. 1981. The Loeb-Jennings Debate and the Science of Animal Behavior. *Journal of the History of the Behavioral Sciences*, 17: 504–15

1987. *Controlling Life*. Oxford: Oxford Univ. Press

Pearl, Raymond. 1923. *Introduction to Medical Biometry and Statistics*. Philadelphia: W. B. Saunders

1939. *The Natural History of Population*. New York: Oxford Univ. Press

Pearson, E. S. 1938. *Karl Pearson: An Appreciation of Some Aspects of His Life and Work*. Cambridge: Cambridge Univ. Press

1939. "Student" as Statistician. *Biometrika*, 30: 210–50. Reprinted in Pearson and Kendall, eds., 1970

1962. Some Thoughts on Statistical Inference. *Annals of Mathematical Statistics*, 33: 394–403

Pearson, E. S. and M. G. Kendall, eds. 1970. *Studies in the History of Statistics and Probability*. London: Charles Griffin

Pearson, Karl. 1892. *The Grammar of Science*. 1st ed., London: Walter Scott

[1894] 1897. The Scientific Aspect of Monte Carlo Roulette. In *The Chances of Death and Other Studies in Evolution*. Cambridge: Cambridge Univ. Press

1900. *The Grammar of Science*. 2nd ed. London: Black

1911. *The Grammar of Science*. 3rd ed. London: Walter Scott

1914–30. *The Life, Letters, and Labours of Francis Galton*. 3 vols. in 4. Cambridge: Cambridge Univ. Press

1948. *Early Statistical Papers*. Cambridge: Cambridge Univ. Press

1978. *The History of Statistics in the 17th and 18th Centuries, Against the Changing Background of Intellectual, Scientific and Religious Thought*. Egon S. Pearson, ed. High Wycombe: Charles Griffin and Company. Based on lectures delivered 1921–33

Peirce, Benjamin. 1852. Criterion for the Rejection of Doubtful Observations. *Astronomical Journal*, 2: 161–3

Peirce, Charles Sanders. 1893. Evolutionary Love. In Peirce, 1931–58, vol. 6: 190–215

1887. Science and Immortality. In Peirce, 1931–58, vol. 6: 370–4

1892. The Doctrine of Necessity Examined. In Peirce, 1931–58, vol. 6: 28–45

1931–58. *Collected Papers of Charles Sanders Peirce*. Charles Hartshorne and Paul Weiss, eds. 8 vols., Cambridge, Mass.: Harvard Univ. Press

Perrin, Jean. 1909. Mouvement brownien et réalité moléculaire. *Annales de chimie et de physique*, 18: 1–114

Perrot, Jean-Claude and Stuart J. Woolf. 1984. *State and Statistics in France, 1789–1815*. Chur: Harwood

Peterson, C. R. and L. R. Beach. 1967. Man as an Intuitive Statistician. *Psychological Bulletin*, 68: 29–46

Pfeffer, Irving. 1956. *Insurance and Economic Theory*. Homewood, Ill.: Richard D. Irwin

Pfungst, O. 1907. *Das Pferd des Herrn von Osten*. Leipzig: Barth

Piaget, Jean and B. Inhelder. [1951] 1975. *The Origin of the Idea of Chance in Children*. New York: Norton

Planck, Max. 1900a. Ueber eine Verbesserung der Wienschen Spectralgleichung. In Planck, 1958, vol. 1: 687–9

1900b. Zur Theorie des Gesetzes der Energieverteilung im Normalspectrum. In Planck, 1958, vol. 1: 698–706

1901. Ueber das Gesetz der Energieverteilung im Normalspectrum. In Planck, 1958, vol. 1: 717–27

1913. *Neue Bahnen der physikalischen Erkenntnis*. (Rede z. Antritt des Rektorats. Berlin 15.10.1913.) In Planck 1958, vol. 3, 65–76

1920. *Die Entstehung und bisherige Entwicklung der Quantentheorie*. (Nobel prize lecture, June 2, 1920). In Planck 1958, vol. 3, 121–36

1926. *Physikalische Gesetzlichkeit im Lichte neuerer Forschung*. Leipzig: Barth

[1929] 1936. *Das Weltbild der neuen Physik*. Vortrag zum Gedenken an H. A. Lorentz, gehalten in Leiden am 18.2.29. Reprinted, Leipzig: Barth, 1936

1938. *Determinismus oder Indeterminismus?* Leipzig: Barth

1958. *Physikalische Abhandlungen and Vorträge*. 3 vols. Braunschweig: Vieweg

Plato, Jan von. 1987. Probabilistic Physics the Classical Way. In Krüger, Gigerenzer, and Morgan, eds., 1987: 379–407

Player, Mark A. 1980. *Employment Discrimination Law*. St Paul: West Publishing Co.

Poincaré, Henri. 1893. Le mécanisme et l'expérience. *Revue de Métaphysique et Morale*, 1: 534–7. Reprinted in: S. G. Brush, ed., *Kinetic Theory, vol. 2*, Oxford: Pergamon, 1966

Poisson, Siméon-Denis. 1837. *Recherches sur la probabilité des jugements en matière criminelle et en matière civile*. Paris: Bachelier

Popkin, Richard. 1964. *The History of Scepticism from Erasmus to Descartes*. Assen, Netherlands: Van Gorcum. Revised and enlarged edition, Berkeley: Univ. of California Press, 1979

Popper, Karl R. [1935] 1968. *Logic of Scientific Discovery*. London: Hutchinson

Porter, Theodore M. 1981. A Statistical Survey of Gases: Maxwell's Social Physics. *Historical Studies in the Physical Sciences*, 12: 77–116

1985. The Mathematics of Society: Variation and Error in Quetelet's Statistics. *British Journal for the History of Science*, 18: 51–69

1986. *The Rise of Statistical Thinking, 1820–1900*. Princeton: Princeton Univ. Press

1987. Lawless Society: Social Science and the Reinterpretation of Statistics in Germany, 1850–1880. In Krüger, Daston, and Heidelberger, eds., 1987: 351–75

Postman, Leo, ed. 1964. *Psychology in the Making: Histories of Selected Research Problems*. New York: Knopf

Price, Richard. [1767] 1811. *Four Dissertations*. 5th ed. London

1769. *Observations on Reversionary Payments*. London

Prigogine, Ilya. 1962. *Non-Equilibrium Statistical Mechanics*. New York: Interscience Publishers

1984. *From Being to Becoming*. 2nd ed., San Francisco: Freeman

Provine, William B. 1971. *The Origins of Theoretical Population Genetics*. Chicago: Univ. of Chicago Press

1986. *Sewall Wright and Evolutionary Biology*. Chicago: Univ. of Chicago Press

Pylyshyn, Zenon W. 1980. Computation and Cognition: Issues in the Foundation of Cognitive Science. *The Behavioral and Brain Sciences*, 3: 111–32

Pynchon, Thomas. 1984. *Slow Learner*. Boston: Little, Brown

Quetelet, Lambert Adolphe Jacques. 1835. *Sur l'homme et le développement de ses facultés, ou essai de physique sociale*. Paris: Bachelier. Trans. as Quetelet, [1835] 1842

[1835] 1842. *A Treatise on Man and the Development of his Faculties*. Translated by

R. Knox. Facsimile edition of translation 1969. Introduction by S. Diamond. Gainesville, Florida: Scholars' Facsimiles and Reprints

1846. *Lettres sur la théorie des probabilités*. Brussels: Hayez. Trans. as Quetelet, [1846] 1849

[1846] 1849. *Letters Addressed to H.R.H. the Grand Duke of Saxe Coburg and Gotha, on the Theory of Probabilities, as Applied to the Moral and Political Sciences*. Translated by O. G. Downes. London: Charles and Edwin Layton

1847. De l'influence de libre arbitre de l'homme sur les faits sociaux. *Bulletin de la Commission Centrale de Statistique* (of Belgium), 3: 135–55

1848a. *Du système social et des lois qui le régissent*. Paris: Guillaumin

1848b. Sur la statistique morale et les principes qui doivent en former la base. *Nouveaux Mémoires de l'Académie Royale des Sciences et Belles-Lettres de Belgique*, 21

1869. *Physique sociale ou Essai sur le développement des facultés de l'homme*. Brussels: Muquardt

Rabinovitch, Nachum L. 1973. *Probability and Statistical Inference in Ancient and Medieval Jewish Literature*. Toronto: University of Toronto Press

Radau, R. 1866. Über die persönlichen Gleichungen bei Beobachtungen derselben Erscheinungen durch verschiedene Beobachter. *Repertorium für physikalische Technik, für mathematische und astronomische Instrumentenkunde*, 1: 202–18

Radicke, G. [1858] 1861. On the Importance and Value of Arithmetic Means. Trans. by F. T. Bond. In *On the Importance and Value of Arithmetic Means*. The New Sydenham Society, London

Ramsay, F. P. 1931. *The Foundations of Mathematics*. London: Kegan Paul, Trench, Trubner

Renouvier, Charles Bernard. 1854–1864. *Essais de critique générale*. 5 vols., 2nd ed., Paris: Félix Alcan, 1912

Resnick, Daniel. 1982. History of Educational Testing. In Wigdor and Garner, eds., 1982: 173–94

Resnikoff, George J. and G. J. Lieberman. 1957. *Tables of the Non-Central t-Distribution*. Stanford: Stanford Univ. Press

Rhine, J. B. 1934. *Extra-Sensory Perception*. Boston: Boston Society for Psychical Research

Rice, Stuart A. 1928. *Quantitative Methods in Politics*. New York: Knopf

1947. The Future Role of the International Statistical Institute. In International Statistical Conferences, 1947, vol. 1: 169–74

Rickey, Branch. 1954. Goodbye to Some Old Baseball Ideas. *Life*, Aug. 2: 78–87

Rider, P. R. 1933. Criteria for Rejection of Observations. *Washington University Studies – New Series, Science and Technology* – no. 8

Risueño d'Amador. 1836. Mémoire sur le calcul des probabilités appliqué à la médicine. *Bulletin de l'Académie Royale de Médicine*, 1: 622–80

Rodewald, H. 1909. Die Bedeutung der Fehlerausgleichung für die Lösung landwirtschaftlich wichtiger Fragen. *Fühling's Landwirtschaftliche Zeitung*, **58**: 12–21

Roget, P. M. 1834. *Animal and Vegetable Physiology Considered with Reference to Natural Theology.* 2 vols., London: Pickering

Roper, Elmo. 1940. Sampling Public Opinion. *Journal of the American Statistical Association*, **35**: 325–34

Rose, Nikolas. 1985. *The Psychological Complex: Psychology, Politics and Society in England, 1869–1939.* London: Routledge and Kegan Paul

Roux, Wilhelm. 1895. The Problems, Methods, and Scope of Developmental Mechanics. Trans. by W. M. Wheeler. In *The Biological Lectures Delivered at the Marine Biological Laboratory of Woods Hole in the Summer Session of 1895*

Royal Statistical Society. 1885. *Jubilee Volume of the Statistical Society (founded 1834).* London: Edward Stanford
   1984. *Journal*, vol. 147, part 2 (150th anniversary Issue).

Rubin, D. B. 1978. Bayesian Inference for Causal Effects: the Role of Randomization. *Annals of Statistics*, **6**: 340–58

Rucci, A. J. and R. D. Tweney. 1980. Analysis of Variance and the "Second Discipline" of Scientific Psychology: A Historical Account. *Psychological Bulletin*, **87**: 166–84

Rümelin, Gustav. [1863] 1875. Zur Theorie der Statistik, I. In Rümelin, *Reden und Aufsätze*. Freiburg: J. C. B. Mohr
   1881. Ueber Gesetze der Geschichte. In *Reden und Aufsätze. Neue Folge.* Freiburg and Tübingen: J. C. B. Mohr: 118–48

Ruml, B. 1921. Intelligence and its Measurement. *Journal of Educational Psychology*, **12**: 143–4

Russell, Milton and Michael Gruber. 1987. Risk Assessment in Environmental Policy Making. *Science*, **236**: 286–90

Rutherford, Ernest. 1904. *Radio-activity.* Cambridge: Cambridge Univ. Press
   1911. The Scattering of X and β Particles by Matter and the Structure of the Atom. *Philosophical Magazine*, **21**: 669–88

Rutherford, Ernest and Hans Geiger. 1908. A Method of Counting the Number of Particles from Radio-active Matter. *Nature*, **77**: 599
   1910. The Probability Variations in the Distribution of α-Particles. *Philosophical Magazine*, **20**: 698–707

Rutherford, Ernest, and Frederick Soddy. 1903. Radio-active Change. *Philosophical Magazine*, **5** (May)

Sachs, J. [1882] 1887. *Lectures on the Physiology of Plants.* Trans. by H. Marshall. Oxford: Clarendon

Savage, L. J. 1954. *The Foundations of Statistics.* New York: Wiley

Say, Jean-Baptiste. 1803. *Traité d'économie politique.* 2 vols., Paris: Deterville
   1827. De l'objet et de l'utilité des statistiques. *Revue encyclopédique*, **35**: 529–53

Schiller, J. 1973. The Genesis and Structure of Claude Bernard's Experimental Method. In Giere and Westfall, eds., 1973

Schilpp, Paul Arthur, ed. 1949. *Albert Einstein: Philosopher-Scientist*. 2 vols., New York: Tudor Publ. Co. 2nd ed., 1951

Schneider, Ivo. 1968. Der Mathematiker Abraham De Moivre (1667–1754). *Archive for History of Exact Sciences*, **5**: 177–317

1987. Laplace and Thereafter: The Status of Probability Calculus in the Nineteenth Century. In Krüger, Daston, and Heidelberger, eds., 1987: 191–214

Schneiderman, Marvin A. 1980. The Uncertain Risks We Run: Hazardous Materials. In Schwing and Abers, 1980: 19–37

Schrödinger, Erwin. 1926a. Quantisierung als Eigenwertproblem. *Annalen der Physik*, **79**: 361–76, 489–527; **80**: 437–90; **81**: 109–39

1926b. Über das Verhältnis der Heisenberg-Born-Jordanschen Quantenmechanik zu der meinen. *Annalen der Physik*, **79**: 734–56

Schwann. T. [1838] 1842. *Microscopical Researches*. Trans. by H. Smith. New Sydenham Society, London

Schweber, S. 1982. Aspects of Probabilistic Thought in Great Britain During the Nineteenth Century. In A. Shimony and H. Feshback, eds., *Physics and Natural Philosophy*. Cambridge: MIT Press

Schweidler, Egon von. [1905] 1907. Über Schwankungen der radioaktiven Umwandlung. *Premier Congrès international de Radiologie, Liège*. Published in *Beiblätter*, **31**: 356ff

Schwing, Richard C. and Walter A. Abers. 1980. *Societal Risk Assessment*. New York and London: Plenum Press

Seidenfeld, T. 1979. *Philosophical Problems of Statistical Inference: Learning from R. A. Fisher*. Dordrecht: Reidel

Selvidge, Judith. 1975. A Three-Step Procedure for Assigning Probabilities to Rare Events. In Wendt and Vlek, 1975: 199–216

Semmel, Bernard. 1968. *Imperialism and Social Reform: English Social-Imperial Thought, 1895–1914*. New York: Anchor

Shafer, Glen. 1978. Non-additive Probabilities in the Work of Bernoulli and Lambert. *Archive for History of Exact Sciences*, **19**: 309–70

Shapin, S. and S. Schaffer. 1985. *Leviathan and the Air Pump: Hobbes, Boyle, and the Experimental Life*. Princeton: Princeton Univ. Press

Shapiro, Barbara. 1983. *Probability and Certainty in Seventeenth-Century England*. Princeton: Princeton Univ. Press

Sheppard, P. M. 1951. Fluctuations in the Selective Value of Certain Phenotypes in the Polymorphic Land Snail *Cepaea nemoralis* (L). *Heredity*, **5**: 125–34

1952. Natural Selection in Two Colonies of the Polymorphic Land Snail *Cepaea nemoralis*. *Heredity*, **6**: 233–8

Sheynin, O. B. 1970. On the Early History of the Law of Large Numbers. In Pearson and Kendall, eds., 1970: 231–9

1972a. On the Mathematical Treatment of Observations by L. Euler. *Archives for History of Exact Sciences*, **9**: 45–56

1972b. Daniel Bernoulli's Work on Probability. *Rete*, **1**: 273–300

322 References

1973. Mathematical Treatment of Astronomical Observations. *Archive for History of Exact Sciences*, 11: 97–126

1974. On the Prehistory of the Theory of Probability. *Archive for History of Exact Sciences*, 12: 97–141

1976. P. S. Laplace's Work on Probability. *Archive for History of Exact Sciences*, 16: 137–87

1977. Laplace's Theory of Error. *Archive for History of Exact Sciences*, 17: 1–61

1979. C. F. Gauss and the Theory of Errors. *Archive for History of Exact Sciences*, 20: 21–69

1980. On the History of the Statistical Method of Biology. *Archive for the History of the Exact Sciences*, 22: 323–71

Skinner, B. F. 1963. The Flight from the Laboratory. In M. H. Marx, ed., *Theories in Contemporary Psychology*. New York: Macmillan

1984. *A Matter of Consequences*. New York: New York Univ. Press

Slovic, P., B. Fischhoff, and S. Lichtenstein. 1976. Cognitive Processes and Societal Risk Taking. In J. S. Carroll and J. W. Payne, eds., *Cognition and Social Behavior*. Hillsdale, NJ: Lawrence Erlbaum Associates

1982. Facts versus Fears: Understanding Perceived Risks. In Kahneman, Slovic, and Tversky, 1982: 463–89

Smoluchowski, Marian von. 1906. Zur kinetischen Theorie der Brownschen Molekularbewegung und der Suspensionen. *Annalen der Physik*, 21: 756–80. Reprinted in: *Abhandlungen über die Brownsche Bewegung und verwandte Erscheinungen* (Ostwalds Klassiker der Exakten Wissenschaften, No. 207) ed. R. Fürth-Prag, Leipzig: Akad. Verlagsgesellschaft, 1923: 1–24

Snedecor, G. W. 1934. *Calculation and Interpretation of the Analysis of Variance and Covariance*. Ames: Iowa State College Press

1937. *Statistical Methods*. 1st ed. Ames: Iowa State College Press

1946. *Statistical Methods*. 4th ed. Ames: Iowa State University Press

Sober, Elliott. 1980. Evolution, Population Thinking and Essentialism. *Philosophy of Science*, 47: 350–83

Société Générale Néerlandaise d'Assurances sur la Vie et de Rentes Viagères. 1898. *Mémoires pour servir à l'histoire des assurances sur la vie et des rentes viagères au Pays-Bas*. Amsterdam

Sokal, Michael M., ed. 1987. *Psychological Testing and American Society, 1890–1930*. New Brunswick: Rutgers Univ. Press

Sokal, R. R. and F. J. Rohlf. 1969. *Biometry*. San Francisco: Freeman.

Sorabji, Richard. 1980. *Necessity, Cause and Blame. Perspectives on Aristotle's Theory*. London: Duckworth

Spearman, Charles. 1904. 'General Intelligence' Objectively Determined and Measured. *American Journal of Psychology*, 15: 201–93

1930. Spearman. In Carl Murchison, ed., *The History of Psychology in Autobiography, vol. 1*. Worcester: Clark Univ. Press

Spoerl, Charles A. 1951. Actuarial Science – A Survey of Theoretical Developments. *Journal of the American Statistical Association*, **46**: 334–44

Spottiswoode, William. 1861. On Typical Mountain Ranges. An Application of the Calculus of Probabilities to Physical Geography. *Journal of the Royal Geographical Society*, **31**: 149–54

Stegmüller, W. 1973. *"Jenseits von Popper und Carnap": Die logischen Grundlagen des statistischen Schliessens*. Berlin: Springer

[Stephen, J. Fitzjames]. 1858. Buckle's History of Civilization in England. *Edinburgh Review*, **107**: 405–512

Sterling, T. D. 1959. Publication Decisions and their Possible Effects on Inferences Drawn from Tests of Significance – or Vice Versa. *Journal of the American Statistical Association*, **54**: 30–4

Stigler, Stephen M. 1976. Commentary on a Paper by L. J. Savage. *Annals of Statistics*, **4**: 498–500

1986. *The History of Statistics: The Measurement of Uncertainty before 1900*. Cambridge: Belknap Press of Harvard Univ. Press

Stouffer, Samuel. 1950. Overview. In Stouffer *et al.*, 1950

Stouffer, Samuel, E. A. Suchmann, L. C. Devinney, S. A. Star, and R. M. Williams Jr. 1949. *The American Soldier: Adjustment During Army Life*. Princeton: Princeton Univ. Press

Stouffer, Samuel, L. A. Guttman, E. A. Suchman, P. F. Lazarsfeld, S. A. Star, and J. A. Clausen. 1950. *Measurement and Prediction*. Princeton: Princeton Univ. Press

"Student" [W. S. Gosset]. 1908. The Probable Error of a Mean. *Biometrika*, **6**: 1–25

1937. Comparison between Random and Balanced Arrangements of Field Plots. *Biometrika*, **29**: 363–79

1958. *'Student's' Collected Papers*. E. S. Pearson and J. Wishart, eds. Cambridge: Cambridge Univ. Press

Süssmilch, Johann. [1741] 1775. *Die göttliche Ordnung in den Veränderungen des menschlichen Geschlechts, aus der Geburt, dem Tode und der Fortpflanzung desselben erwiesen*. 3rd ed. Berlin

Sutherland, Gillian. 1984. *Ability, Merit, and Measurement: Mental Testing and English Education, 1880–1940*. Oxford: Clarendon Press

Swijtink, Zeno G. 1982. A Bayesian Argument in Favor of Randomization. *Proceedings of the Philosophy of Science Association*, 1982, vol. 1: 159–68

1986. D'Alembert and the Maturity of Chances. *Studies in the History and Philosophy of Science*, **17**: 327–49

1987. The Objection of Observation: Measurement and Statistical Methods in the Nineteenth Century. In Krüger, Daston, and Heidelberger, eds., 1987: 261–85

Talleyrand-Périgord, Charles de. 1789. *Des loteries*. Paris

Tanner, W. P. Jr. 1965. *Statistical Decision Processes in Detection and Recognition*. Technical Report of the Sensory Intelligence Laboratory, Dept. of Psychology, Univ. of Michigan

Tanner, W. P. Jr., and J. A. Swets. 1954. A Decision-Making Theory of Visual Detection. *Psychological Review*, **61**: 401–9

Tanur, Judith M. *et al.*, eds. 1972. *Statistics: A Guide to the Unknown*. San Francisco: Holden and Day

Terman, Lewis. 1921. Intelligence and its Measurement. *Journal of Educational Psychology*, **12**: 127–33

1923. The Problem. In Terman *et al.*, *Intelligence Tests and School Reorganization*. New York: World Book Co.

Thaer, Albrecht. 1809–12. *Grundsätze der rationellen Landwirtschaft*. 4 vols. Berlin: Realschulbuchhandlung

Thomas, Lewis. 1977. Biostatistics in Medicine. *Science*, **198**: 675

Thomson, Godfrey. 1939. *The Factorial Analysis of Human Ability*. Boston: Houghton Mifflin

Thorn, John and Pete Palmer. 1985. *The Hidden Game of Baseball*. New York: Doubleday

Thorndike, Edward. 1921. Intelligence and its Measurement. *Journal of Educational Psychology*, **12**: 124–7

Thurstone, L. L. 1927. Psychophysical Analysis. *American Journal of Psychology*, **38**: 368–89

1927–28. Attitudes Can Be Measured. *American Journal of Sociology*, **33**: 529–54

Todhunter, Isaac. 1865. *A History of the Mathematical Theory of Probability from the Time of Pascal to that of Laplace*. Cambridge

Tolman, R. C. 1938. *The Principles of Statistical Mechanics*. Oxford: Oxford Univ. Press

Tribe, Laurence H. 1971. Trial by Mathematics: Precision and Ritual in the Legal Process. *Harvard Law Review*, **84**: 1329–93

Tuddenham, Read D. 1964. The Nature and Measurement of Intelligence. In Postman, 1964

Tukey, John W. 1977a. *Exploratory Data Analysis*. Reading, Mass: Addison-Wesley

1977b. Some Thoughts on Clinical Trials, Especially Problems of Multiplicity (Medical Research: Statistics and Ethics). *Science*, **198**: 679–84

Turner, J. R. G. 1987. Random Genetic Drift, R. A. Fisher, and the Oxford School of Ecological Genetics. In Krüger, Gigerenzer, and Morgan, eds., 1987: 313–54

Turner, Stephen P. 1986. *The Search for a Methodology of Social Science: Durkheim, Weber, and the Nineteenth-Century Problem of Cause, Probability, and Action*. Dordrecht: D. Reidel

Tversky, A. and D. Kahneman. 1971. Belief in the Law of Small Numbers. *Psychological Bulletin*, **76**: 105–10

1974. Judgment under Uncertainty: Heuristics and Biases. *Science*, **185**: 1124–31

1980. Causal Schemata in Judgments under Uncertainty. In M. Fishbein, ed., *Progress in Social Psychology*. Vol. I. Hillsdale, NJ: Lawrence Erlbaum Associates

1982a. Judgments of and by Representativeness. In Kahneman, Slovic, and Tversky, eds., 1982

1982b. Evidential Impact of Base Rates. In Kahneman, Slovic, and Tversky, eds., 1982

Van Leeuwen, Henry. 1963. *The Problem of Certainty in English Thought, 1640–1680.* The Hauge: Nijhoff

Venn, John. 1866. *The Logic of Chance.* London: Macmillan.

Vierordt, K. [1858] 1861. Notes on Medical Statistics. Translated by F. T. Bond. In *On the Importance and Value of Arithmetic Means.* New Sydenham Society, London

Waerden, B. L. van der. 1967, *Sources of Quantum Mechanics.* Amsterdam: North Holland

Wagner, Adolph. 1864. *Die Gesetzmässigkeit in den scheinbar willkührlichen menschlichen Handlungen vom Standpunkt der Statistik.* Hamburg: Boyes und Geister

Wagner, P. and W. Rohn. 1880. Beiträge zur Begründung und Ausbildung einer exacten Methode der Düngungsversuche. *Journal für Landwirtschaft,* **28**: 9–57

Wald, A. 1947. *Sequential Analysis.* New York: John Wiley and Sons
1950. *Statistical Decision Functions.* New York: John Wiley and Sons

Walker, Helen M. 1929. *Studies in the History of Statistical Method with Special Reference to Certain Educational Problems.* Baltimore: Williams and Wilkins

Wallis, W. A. 1980. The Statistical Research Group, 1942–1945 (with discussion). *Journal of the American Statistical Association,* **75**: 320–35

Warner, John Harley. 1986. *The Therapeutic Perspective: Medical Practice, Knowledge, and Identity in America, 1820–1885.* Cambridge: Harvard Univ. Press

Wechsler, David. 1939. *The Measurement of Adult Intelligence.* Baltimore: Williams and Wilkins

Weinstein, B. 1886. *Handbuch der physikalischen Maassbestimmungen.* Berlin: Julius Springer

Weldon, W. F. R. 1895. Attempt to Measure the Death-Rate Due to the Selective Destruction of *Carcinus moenan* with Respect to a Particular Dimension. *Proceedings of the Royal Society,* **58**: 360–79

Wendt, Dirk and Charles Vlek, eds. 1975. *Utility, Probability, and Human Decision Making.* Dordrecht: Reidel

Westergaard, Harald. 1932. *Contributions to the History of Statistics.* London: P. S. King

Wigdor, Alexandra K. and Wendell R. Garner, eds. 1982. *Ability Testing: Uses, Consequences, and Controversies.* 2 vols., Washington: National Academy Press

Wilkins, John. [1675] 1699. *Of the Principles and Duties of Natural Religion.* 4th ed. London

Wilson, Edwin Biddell. 1932. The Value of Statistical Studies of the Cancer Problem. *American Journal of Cancer,* **48**: 1230–7

Wise, M. Norton. 1983. Social Statistics in a *Gemeinschaft*: The Idea of Statistical Causality as Developed by Wilhelm Wundt and Karl Lamprecht. In Heidelberger *et al.*, eds., 1983: 97–129
1987. How Do Sums Count? On the Cultural Origins of Statistical Causality.

In Krüger, Daston, and Heidelberger, eds., 1987: 395–425

Wright, Sewall, 1930. Review of *The Genetical Theory of Natural Selection* by R. A. Fisher. *Journal of Heredity*, 21: 349–56

1940. The Statistical Consequences of Mendelian Heredity in Relation to Speciation. In J. S. Huxley, ed., *The New Systematics*. Oxford: Clarendon

1948. On the Roles of Directed and Random Changes in Gene Frequency in the Genetics of Populations. *Evolution*, 2: 279–94

1964. Biology and the Philosophy of Science. *Monist*, 48: 765–90

Wright, Sewall and T. Dobzhansky. 1946. Genetics of Natural Populations. XII. Experimental Reproduction of Some of the Changes Caused by Natural Selection in Certain Populations of *Drosophila pseudoobscura*. *Genetics*, 31: 125–50

Yates, F. 1951. The Influence of 'Statistical Methods for Research Workers' on the Development of the Science of Statistics. *Journal of the American Statistical Association*, 46: 19–34

Yeo, R. R. 1986. The Principle of Plenitude and Natural Theology in Nineteenth-Century Britain. *British Journal for the History of Science*, 19: 263–82

Youden, W. J. 1951. The Fisherian Revolution in Methods of Experimentation. *Journal of the American Statistical Association*, 46: 47–50

1972. Enduring Values. *Technometrics*, 14: 1–11

Young, Robert. 1985. *Darwin's Metaphor: Nature's Place in Victorian Culture*. Cambridge: Cambridge Univ. Press

Young, Thomas. 1819. Remarks on the Probability of Error in Physical Observations, and on the Density of the Earth – In a letter to Capt. Henry Kater. *Philosophical Transactions of the Royal Society of London*, 109, part I: 70–95

Zahn, F. 1934. *50 Années de l'Institut International de Statistique*. The Hague: ISI

Zermelo, Ernst. 1896. Über einen Satz der Dynamik und die mechanische Wärmetheorie. *Annalen der Physik*, 57: 485ff. English translation in S. G. Brush, ed., *Kinetic Theory*, vol. II. Oxford: Pergamon, 1966

Name index

Subject index